Christ Triumphant

Christ Triumphant

Universalism Asserted as the Hope of the Gospel

on the Authority of Reason, the Fathers, and Holy Scripture

Annotated Edition

by

THOMAS ALLIN

Edited and with an introductory essay and notes
by Robin A. Parry

With a foreword by
Thomas Talbott

WIPF & STOCK · Eugene, Oregon

Christ Triumphant:
Universalism Asserted as the Hope of the Gospel on the Authority of Reason, the Fathers, and Holy Scripture. Annotated Edition

Copyright © 2015 Thomas Allin and Robin A. Parry. All rights reserved. Except for brief quotations in critical publications or reviews, no part of this book may be reproduced in any manner without prior written permission from the publisher. Write: Permissions, Wipf and Stock Publishers, 199 W. 8th Ave., Suite 3, Eugene, OR 97401.

Reprinted from the 9th ed. London: Williams and Norgate, 1905. (First edition London: T. Fisher Unwin, 1885)

Wipf and Stock Publishers
199 W. 8th Ave., Suite 3
Eugene, OR 97401

www.wipfandstock.com

ISBN 13: 978-1-4982-2912-8

Cataloging-in-Publication data:

Allin, Thomas.

Christ triumphant : universalism asserted as the hope of the gospel on the authority of reason, the Fathers, and Holy Scripture. Annotated edition / Thomas Allin, edited, and with an introductory essay and notes by Robin A. Parry; foreword by Thomas Talbott

lx + 346 p. ; 23 cm. Includes bibliographical references.

ISBN 13: 978-1-4982-2912-8

1. Universalism. 2. Universalism—Controversial literature. 3. Hell—Christianity. I. Parry, Robin A. II. Talbott, Thomas B. III. Title.

BX9941 A44 2015

Manufactured in the U.S.A.

For Ilaria Ramelli
—outstanding Christian scholar

"If we said or thought that what concerns Gehenna is not in fact full of love and mixed with compassion, this would be an opinion full of blasphemy and abuse against God our Lord. . . . Among all his deeds, there is none that is not entirely dictated by mercy, love, and compassion. This is the beginning and the end of God's attitude toward us."

—Isaac of Nineveh[1]

Oh yet we trust that somehow good
Will be the final goal of ill,
To pangs of nature, sins of will,
Defects of doubt, and taints of blood;

That nothing walks with aimless feet,
That not one life shall be destroyed,
Or cast as rubble to the void,
When God has made the pile complete.

Behold, we know not anything,
I can but trust that good shall fall.
At last—far off—at last, to all,
And every winter change to spring

The wish, that of the living whole,
No life may fail beyond the grave,
Derives it not from what we have,
The likest God within the soul?

I stretch lame hands of faith, and grope
And gather dust and chaff, and call,
To what I feel is Lord of all,
And faintly trust the larger hope.

—Lord Alfred Tennyson, *In Memoriam* (1849)

---

1 *Second Part*, 39.22. Long-lost, but rediscovered in the Bodleian Library, Oxford, in 1983 and published in 1995. Thomas Allin would have approved.

Contents

Introduction to Thomas Allin—*Robin A. Parry*   ix

Foreword to the Annotated Edition—Thomas Talbott   xxxviii

Foreword to the Fourth Edition—Edna Lyall   xlii

Preface to the Annotated Edition—Robin A. Parry   xliv

Preface to the Second Edition   xlviii

Letter from Canon Wilberforce to the Author   l

List of Abbreviations   li

I. Universalism Asserted on the Authority of Reason

1. The Question Stated   3
2. The Popular Creed Wholly Untenable: part 1   15
3. The Popular Creed Wholly Untenable: part 2   54

II. Universalism Asserted on the Authority of Tradition

4. What the Church Teaches: from the second to the fourth century   83
5. "What the Church Teaches: from the fourth to the nineteenth century   137
6. Universalism and Doctrine   199

III. Universalism Asserted on the Authority of Scripture

7   What the Old Testament Teaches   232

8   What the New Testament Teaches: universal salvation   241

9   What the New Testament Teaches: eschatological punishment   269

IV. Conclusion: Universalism Asserted

10   Summary and Conclusions   305

Bibliography   337

Introduction to Thomas Allin (1838–1909)

ROBIN A. PARRY

Thomas Allin's *Universalism Asserted* was, in its day, a generally well-regarded defense of the hope for a universal restoration. The following are some of the press notices it received:

> "By all odds the ablest universalist book of English authorship."—*Christian Leader* (Boston, USA)

> "Its points are well and freshly put, and its matter admirably arranged."—*Dover Mercury*.

> "In *Universalism Asserted* Mr. Allin has written the most valuable book thus far produced on this side of the Atlantic in defence of the ancient faith of the Christian Church. . . . Several years ago the *Universalist* called attention to its remarkable array of evidence in favour of our faith, and its peculiar and unique value to all who would understand the faith of the early centuries. The last edition shows that the author has continued his studies with great advantage to the Church and the original work."—*The Universalist* (Chicago, USA)

Introduction to Thomas Allin (1838–1909)

"Mr. Allin's Book is the ablest and most convincing assertion of universalism we have yet met with, it is also valuable as furnishing a thorough digest of the teachings of the Fathers on this subject, . . . it is equally strong in the Scriptural argument. It bristles all through with pointed texts . . . and all that is necessary to give them weight is to assume that when the Bible says 'all' it means all."—*Words of Reconciliation.*

"A masterly compendium of facts and arguments a most valuable book."—*Eternal Punishment* (C. F. Aked.)

"Advocates of the larger hope must welcome this book, closely argued and written in a true Christian spirit."—*Nottingham Daily Express.*

"It is certainly a very full, interesting, and vigorous book. . . . [W]e commend it warmly to those who want to know the pith and marrow of what has been advanced by many writers; and also for the earnest and cogent words of one who has himself thought long and deeply about these great questions."—*Literary World.*

"In this author the doctrine of eternal hope has found no common champion."—*The Star* (London).

And yet, Thomas Allin is in many ways hidden from our view. Unlike some other universalist authors, we do not know a great deal about him.

THE LIFE OF THOMAS ALLIN

Allin was an Irishman, born in 1838 to Thomas and Isabella Allin[1] in Avoncore, an area in the small rural town of Midelton, County Cork, in

---

1 Thomas' grandparents on his father's side were called Samuel and Rebecca Allin. His mother was Isabella Dorina, daughter of Thomas Sealy, of Ballylough, Co. Cork. Thomas had a brother called Henry Faulker Allin (d. 1902), who married a Catherine

x

Introduction to Thomas Allin (1838–1909)

southern Ireland. His family was part of the country's Protestant minority—their parish church being St. John the Baptist, a church erected in 1825 on the site of Chore Abbey, a twelfth-century Cistercian monastery.

The Ireland in which Thomas Allin grew up was a rural country with a majority Catholic population ruled over by a small, English-speaking, Protestant elite. In 1801, not too many years before Thomas was born, Ireland was incorporated into the United Kingdom, ruled directly from London. With this political union came a union of the Church of Ireland and the Church of England (both Anglican), with some Irish bishops being given seats in the House of Lords in London.

Despite numerous social and economic advantages to joining the Church of Ireland, most people chose not to. Indeed, relations between Protestants and Catholics were never easy. As the official state church in Ireland, the Anglican church was partly funded by enforced tithes from the general population. This state of affairs was bitterly resented by the majority population, who understandably did not see why they had to hand over a tenth of their income to a church they were not members of. Resentment would boil over from time to time, and the tithes were slowly phased out, though did not disappear finally until 1871, following the Irish Church Act of 1869, in which the Church of Ireland ceased to be the state church in Ireland.

When Allin was a child Ireland experienced the great famine of 1845–50. About two fifths of the population at that time were solely reliant on potatoes and so the potato blight that ravaged potato crops across Europe in this period had especially devastating effects in Ireland. In the area Thomas lived 30 percent of the population were on rations in 1847, but one did not have to travel far east before that number rose to 60 percent, or even as high as 100 percent in places. A million Irish died in this disaster and a million more emigrated, causing a 20 to 25 percent decline in population from the 8.2 million recorded in the 1841 census. This instigated a sustained period of population decline in Ireland through the nineteenth century. The famine further strained relations between the Irish population and the British government, who were perceived to have

---

Barnstable on 16 Nov 1871. Henry lived down the road from Midleton in Youghal. He was a Lieutenant in the 21st Regiment. Online: https://www.yumpu.com/en/document/view/13388254/cloyne-castlemartyr-castletown-roche-the-union-is-/5.

Introduction to Thomas Allin (1838–1909)

done too little too late to help. This resentment further fueled the political cause of Republicanism.

While we know a lot about the famine and its impact, we know nothing about how it was experienced by the Allin family. They were certainly not a part of the most vulnerable part of the population, but they could not have avoided the harrowing scenes of starvation and death that were ubiquitous at that time.

Thomas studied at Trinity College, Dublin (Ireland's oldest university, founded in 1592)—a natural place for Irish Anglican[2] men[3] to study—and in 1859, aged twenty-one, he graduated with a Bachelor's degree.

Five years later, in 1864, perhaps after some time serving as a magistrate back home,[4] Allin was ordained an Anglican deacon in Cork, a

---

2 Non-Anglicans had been permitted to study there since 1793, but until 1873, long after Allin's time, one could not get a professorship, a fellowship, or a scholarship unless an Anglican.

3 Women were only allowed to attend as full members from 1904.

4 In 1862 a Thomas Allin is listed as a magistrate in Midleton, County Cork. *Thom's Irish Almanac and Official Directory for the Year 1862.* If this is not his father

Introduction to Thomas Allin (1838-1909)

short distance from where he'd grown up in Midleton, just as work was beginning on the new Saint Fin Barre Cathedral. He then served a series of curacies. (Curate is the term used for assistant clergy—deacons and priests—who work alongside the parish priest.[5]) His first curacy was as a deacon at Christ Church in Lickmolassy in County Galway (1864-65) and his second as a deacon at All Saints Church in Fenagh, County Carlow (1865-66), both very small rural locations. He was ordained as an Anglican priest in the Diocese of Ossory in 1866, presumably by Bishop James Thomas O'Brien (Bishop of Ossory, Ferns, and Leighlin from 1842-74) at St. Canice's Cathedral in Kilkenny.[6]

For the period of 1870-74 Thomas moved to serve as a curate in Castrachore, in his hometown of Midleton, County Cork. The Church of Ireland was disestablished in 1871, soon after Thomas began ministering at this church. We do not know what he thought about this significant change in the status of his church. Given his liberalism, it is possible that he supported the change.[7]

During this curacy Allin indulged his love of Botany and in the years 1871-74 he contributed a number of notes on plants to the *Journal of Botany*.

It was also during this curacy, on 20th February 1873, that he was married to Emily Mildred (1849-98), second daughter of Samuel Philip Townsend and his wife Frances Helena. Emily was from the classes of the landed gentry in County Cork, being a direct descendant of Richard Townsend, an officer in Oliver Cromwell's Irish Army. Emily's father, a great great grandson of Richard, owned the Garrycloyne estate. Records show no indication that Thomas and Emily ever had children (although

---

then we must suppose that Thomas returned home to work as a magistrate before moving into ordained ministry.

5 Though, strictly speaking, it refers to the one charged by the bishop with the "cure (*cura*) of souls," i.e., the parish priest. Thus, the 1662 Book of Common Prayer uses the term of the parish priest. But in Anglicanism it has since come to designate the *assistant* clergy.

6 I have been unable to discover what Allin did after his ordination as a priest in 1866 and his third curacy in Midleton in 1870.

7 The legislation was introduced by the Gladstone government. Gladstone, a giant in Victorian politics, was himself a devout Anglican, but disestablished the Anglican Church in Ireland and fought long and hard for home rule for Ireland. The "Irish Question" was one of the major problems in Victorian politics.

Introduction to Thomas Allin (1838–1909)

if they had children who were stillborn, those children would not appear in registers).

Allin served one final curacy—in Myross, Ross (1874–77): "The parish forms an obtuse peninsula between Castlehaven and the harbour of Glandore, having the main ocean to the south. . . . The church is a very handsome cruciform edifice, with a tower: it occupies a gentle, eminence, near the western termination of Glandore harbour, having been erected on that new site in 1827."[8] This was Thomas' last curacy before leaving Ireland for England in 1877, aged thirty-nine. One source describes this move as "retiring to England." I have found no evidence of his working in active church ministry after leaving Ireland. Over the thirteen years in which he was serving in ordained parish ministry he never took on the role of parish priest, always serving instead as a curate.

At some point Allin seems to have been awarded a D.D. (Doctorate in Divinity). His wide-ranging knowledge of early Christian texts and history, demonstrated in all three of his theological books, would suggest that his research was focused on patristics. Exactly when and where he received this prestigeous degree—historically awarded for achievements beyond the level of a PhD—is not yet clear to me. There are various points in his life when he could have done so, but it was likely later in his life.[9]

In 1877, Thomas and Emily moved to Weston-super-Mare, on the Somerset coast, and lived there for many years.[10] Weston had been a small seaside village of about a hundred inhabitants until the nineteenth century, when the opening of the railway in 1841 brought thousands of visitors, making it into a popular Victorian resort destination. From the late 1840s there was a lot of housing development and in 1867 Birnbeck

---

8 Online: http://www.melocki.org.uk/lewis/Ireland/i03112.txt.

9 Suggested by the fact that he is referred to as Thomas Allin D.D. only on the title page of his final two books, *Race and Religion* (1899) and *The Augustinian Revolution in Theology* (1911).

10. On the 1891 census they are listed as still living there. On the 1901 census he appears as a visitor (a widower, aged sixty-three) in the town of Donnington, Herefordshire, visiting a Rev. Thomas Dunscombe. So we cannot tell from this census where Allin was living at the time. However, in 1901 he remarried in Bristol, which suggests that he was still living in the area. But he next appears in Newton Abbot, Devon, where he died and where his widow was listed as still living in the 1911 census. So at some time after their marriage in 1901, quite possibly soon after it, the new couple moved to Devon, where Allin remained until he died.

Introduction to Thomas Allin (1838–1909)

Pier was opened as an important, typically Victorian, tourist attraction. During the 1880s, while Thomas and Emily were living there, the sea front was upgraded, creating sea walls and a two-mile promenade.

Birnbeck pier, Weston-super-Mare

The sea front at Weston-super-Mare

Thomas and Emily called their new home "Myross," after the last parish he had served in back in Ireland.[11] All we know of Allin's activity in this period is that he researched and wrote books. As a good Anglican, we may suppose that he attended his local parish church, Christ Church,[12] but he seems not to have served as an active priest in an official role. He is described on the 1891 census as a "Clerk in Holy Orders (clergy)," but

---

11 The 1891 census indicates that Thomas and Emily has two live-in domestic servants: a cook, Sarah Fear (aged twenty-eight), and a housemaid, Mary L. Croft (aged twenty-one). It was standard for middle-class households in the Victorian period to have live-in domestic servants.

12 A Gothic-style church, built in 1855.

Introduction to Thomas Allin (1838–1909)

this simply means that he was an ordained Anglican priest, not that he was the incumbent at a church. The 1901 census calls him a "clergyman in the Church of England" but, again, this means nothing more than that he was ordained.

Myross: the Somerset home of Thomas and Emily

It was when in England that his publications came into their own. His work had two foci: botany and theology. He began by writing up his years of botanical investigation in Ireland and in 1883 published *The Flowering Plants and Ferns of County Cork* (Weston-super-Mare: J. Marche, 1883). It identifies 700 species of flora native to County Cork. Thomas' research made a modest contribution to the appreciation of the botany of Ireland.[13] Thomas himself discovered some species previously unfound in the area: "Allin made a number of records for Co. Waterford in or before 1872, four of these being the first county records: Autumn Lady's-tresses, Broad-fruited Cornsalad (the only county record), Marsh Hawk's-beard and Round-leaved Mint."[14] Here is one of Allin's submission slips for a botanical sample. His signature can be seen at the bottom.

---

13 See C.J. [James Coleman], "A County Cork Botanical Author, Rev. Thomas Allin." *Journal of the Cork Historical and Archaeological Society*, series 2 XXII (1916), 91.

14 Paul Green, *Flora of County Waterford*, 23. Online: http://www.botanicgardens.

Introduction to Thomas Allin (1838–1909)

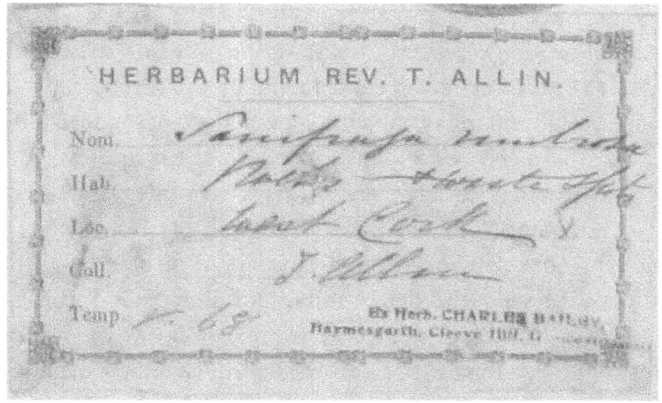

On the theological side, he boldly stepped straight into the nineteenth-century debates on hell with his *The Question of Questions: Is Christ Indeed the Saviour of the World?* (London: T. Fisher Unwin, 1885). This book was reprinted in an expanded second edition in 1887, retitled as *Universalism Asserted* (London: Elliot Stock, 1887). In total it went through nine editions (1885, 1887, 1888, 1891, 1892, 1895, ?,[15] ?,[16] 1905). The version that you hold in your hands is based on the ninth and final edition.[17]

We do not know what led Thomas to embrace what he called "the larger hope." According to John Wesley Hanson (1823–1901), Allin was in the British Museum in London (which then housed the British

---

ie/herb/floras/waterford/waterfd01.pdf

15 The seventh edition was available by 1899 (it is advertised at the back of *Race and Religion*). It was likely published around 1897. I have not been able to source a copy.

16 The eighth edition was published after 1899 and before 1905, perhaps around 1902. I have not been able to source a copy.

17 Allin, in an effort to spread the word, also published a series of eight "Larger Hope Leaflets" (Weston-super-Mare: Lawrence Bros.): 1. The Devil's Victory. 2. The Bible v. Endless Evil. 3. The Popular Heaven. 4. The Larger Hope and Sin. 5. The Unchanging God. 6. Causes of Unbelief. 7. The Popular Hell. 8. The Atonement and the Larger Hope. They cost 1s per 100 copies. I have not managed to locate any copies, but the first four were published by the time of *Race and Religion* (1899) and the final four were published after. According to an advert at the back of *Race and Religion*, Allin had also published a work called *Redemption: Its True Extent and Complete Success* (Weston-super-Mare: Lawrence Bros, n.d.). As yet, I have found no reference to this work anywhere else.

Library) and came across a work by the influential American universalist Hosea Ballou (1771–1852)—*Ancient History of Universalism* (Boston: 1828, 1842, 1872). "Incited by its contents he microscopically searched the fathers, and found many valuable statements that incontestably prove that the most and the best of the successors of the apostles inculcated the doctrine of universal salvation."[18] This is certainly possible, although we should note that Allin and Ballou were in other respects very different, Balou being a convinced unitarian and Allin being committed to the ecumenical creeds with their trinitarian vision of God. Perhaps more relevant is that Allin does not quote from Ballou or even allude to his book. Indeed, in his long list of universalists in chapter 5, he does not so much as mention Ballou. This is at very least surprising if Allin owed his own turn to universalism to Hosea Ballou.

His second major theological publication was entitled *Race and Religion: Hellenistic Theology: Its Place in Christian Thought* (London: James Clarke, 1899). It was the first part of a two-book project on the different theological schools and thinkers in the Christian East and West.[19] *Race and Religion* sketches out the basic thesis. In many ways this book can be seen as a development of an idea that underlies much of the historical-theological work in *Universalism Asserted*. In a nutshell,[20] Allin believes that we are mistaken to treat "the Fathers" as if they formed one undifferentiated whole. He argues that there are in fact *two quite distinct traditions of Christian theology and praxis* in the early church: the Hellenistic, rooted in ancient Greek culture, and the Latin, rooted in a hybrid of Roman and Carthaginian cultures. The Eastern church was, for the most part, Hellenistic, the West became mostly Latin, though the two ways are not so easy to pin down in geographic terms. Each is best thought of as "a type of thought."[21] Now these two traditions are not simply

18 Hanson, *Universalism: The Prevailing Doctrine of the Church*, 1.

19 Allin, *Race and Religion*, 7–8.

20 Allin is well aware that he is generalizing. He is happy to acknowledge that there is much that is bad in the Hellenistic Christian tradition and much that is good in the Latin (and he illustrates both claims). He further agrees that there was much interaction between the two traditions, with influences, good and bad, going both ways. Nevertheless, while acknowledging that his claims will need considerable nuancing, he thinks that the division between the two traditions is still very marked and of critical importance in understanding the development of Christianity and the state of the church today.

21 Ibid., 25.

Introduction to Thomas Allin (1838–1909)

neutral; the Hellenistic tradition is earlier, in terms of the dominance of its influence on Christianity, and in Allin's view it is vastly superior—ethically, theologically, and spiritually—to the Latin. Between them stands "a great divide." A considerable part of the book is given over to the attempt to identify and illustrate different features of the two kinds of early Christianity, and to trace their roots.[22] For instance, he sees Latin theology dominated by legal categories, a focus on human wretchedness, a God angry at humanity, purely retributive views of punishment, penal views of the cross, centralizing of power, bureaucracy, tendencies to elevate God's sovereignty at the expense of human freedom, and so on and so forth. Hellenistic Christian thought was more focused on the goodness and rationality of the created order, humanity in the divine image, human freedom, God's incarnation, resurrection, human destiny as deification, punishment as educative and remedial, and so on.

This is relevant to the debate about hell in that Allin sees universalism as widespread in the church when the Hellenistic mode of Christianity was in the ascendant, but that Carthaginian/Roman Latin theology introduced a doctrine of eternal torment that came to dominate the church in the centuries that followed.

The modern church in the West—both Catholic and Protestant (Lutheran, Reformed, Anglican, and Nonconformist)—is Latin to the core: "we are all Latins; we see with Latin eyes and hear with Latin ears. . . . We [Protestants] are Latin, even in our revolt against Rome."[23] In Allin's view, the church today needs to be liberated from its Latin inheritance. It needs to recover the early Hellenistic vision of God and the gospel, albeit in a contemporary manner. The good news, he thinks, is that this process is already underway—with the return to Hellenism led by the Germans and the English.[24]

The second volume in the project was entitles *The Augustinian Revolution in Theology*, and was published two years after Allin died (London: James Clark, 1911). As the title suggests, this book was intended to substantiate Allin's claim that Augustine brought about a massive

---

22 In a typical late-nineteenth-century manner, Allin seeks to locate a *part* of the reason for these differences between the two traditions in "national tendencies, in race instincts, and even in physical surroundings" (ibid., 84) of the ancient Greeks and Romans (and Semites), hence the focus on *race* in the title.

23 Ibid., 8–9. Cf. 104–5.

24 Ibid., 159–60.

and detrimental change within the theology of the Western church. The work is divided into two parts. The first is a brief exploration of some key figures associated with the school of Antioch. They provide a foil against which Augustine's theology is contrasted. While Allin appreciates Augustine's genius, zeal, sincerity, and personal devotion, he is *brutal* in his criticism of the directions Augustine's theology took in his later years. Augustine was always creedally orthodox, but his theology, while initially fairly typical (even seeming to affirm universalism to start with[25]), increasingly departed in major ways from previous church teaching:

> it stood alone in the close connection it established between original sin and sexual relations. . . . It further stood alone in maintaining an actual sinning on the part of mankind in Adam; alone in maintaining that only freedom to sin remained after the Fall; alone in teaching the endless damnation of all unbaptized infants. It stood alone in denying God's will to save all men and Christ's death for all men; alone in asserting an absolute and arbitrary predestination and double call. The gravity of these questions justifies the term "revolution" applied to the Augustinian movement.[26]

Other theological innovations, such as Augsutine's argument for the use of force against schismatics, further serve to reveal the problematic nature of his mature thought. The end result of Augustine's theological revisions—revisions made during years of polemical controversy—is a view of God that Allin might have described, had he been feeling cheeky, as "God in the hands of an angry sinner." These novel beliefs, which Allin sees as uncatholic and errant, war within Augustine's writings against his more healthy and classical ideas.

For various historical reasons, Western theology was, in Allin's view, permanently disfigured by the impact of Augustine and yet is still often blind to its own disfigurement. His aim is to reveal the problem as a first step towards what he sees as theological healing.

---

25 Allin, *Augustinian Revolution*, 112–14. Ilaria Ramelli has also noted Augustine's apparent early sympathy with universalism. *Christian Docrtine of Apokatastasis*, 659ff.

26 Ibid., 180–81.

Introduction to Thomas Allin (1838–1909)

Places in Ireland and England linked with Thomas Allin

Emily died on 12th February 1898. What Thomas did after her death is not clear. We know from an aside he makes in *Race and Religion* (1899) that he was writing at least a part of that book while in Italy.[27] It is very possible that he went to Italy after Emily's death to research and write and get away from things back home. Thomas next shows up in the 1901 census as a visitor at the Rectory of his friend Rev. Thomas Dunscombe in the town of Donnington, Herefordshire.[28] We do not know how long he stayed in Donnington.

Thomas remarried in October 1901, aged sixty-three. His new wife was forty-one-year-old Ellen Constance Slater. The couple married at St. Stephen's Church in Bristol and thereafter moved from Somerset to Chelston Mount in the parish of St. Matthew's, Torquay, Devon. It was here that Thomas worked on *The Augustinian Revolution in Theology* and made the final revisions to his *Universalism Asserted*.

Thomas Allin died in Torquay in the district of Newton Abbot on 4th March 1909, aged seventy-two.[29]

HELL IN NINETEENTH-CENTURY BRITAIN

It is helpful to be able to locate Allin's contribution within the context of his religious world.

The Forty-Two Articles of 1552/53, intended to summarize Anglican doctrine, included an article designed specifically to rule out universalism as a permissible Anglican view. Article 42 read as follows: *"All men shall not be saved at the last. They also are worthy of condemnation, who endeavor at this time to restore the dangerous opinion, that all men be they never so ungodly, shall at length be saved, when they have suffered pains for their sins a certain time appointed by God's*

---

27 Allin, *Race and Religion*, 113.

28 Rev. Dunscombe was from County Cork, so it is very possible that he and Allin had known each other back in Ireland, though Dunscombe, twenty years Allin's junior, would have only been nineteen when Allin left Ireland, aged thirty-nine.

29 His obituary is in *The Times* on Saturday 6 March 1909. The Calendar of Wills and Administration 1858–1922 in the National Archives of Ireland contains the following entry: "Allin (The Reverend) Thomas [299] 26 July. The Reverend Thomas Allin[,] late of Chelston Mount[,] Huxtable Hill[,] Chelston[,] Torquay[,] County Devon[.] Clerk who died 4 March 1909. Probate granted at London 14 May 1909 to John Wheeler. Resealed at Dublin on 26 July 1909. Effects in Ireland £3 4s 0d."

justice." However, with the ascent of the Catholic Mary to the throne, the Articles never got onto the statute books. After Mary's death they were revised into the Thirty-Nine Articles in 1563. The anti-universalist article was dropped in the revision. This, however, should not be taken to indicate any sympathy with universalism on the part of sixteenth-century Anglicans. Nevertheless, it did create a space for later Anglicans to argue that the Articles of Religion—to which priests in Allin's day had to subscribe—allowed room for maneuver on this question.[30]

Factors in the Growing Disquiet over Hell

While there were some rumblings about hell within eighteenth-century Anglicanism, it was in the nineteenth century that the debate really took off. The growing disquiet with the traditional doctrine was fueled by several different factors:

First of all, the growth of the British Empire in the eighteenth and nineteenth centuries, combined with regular reports from the rapidly increasing number of Protestant missionaries across the world, made Christians back in Britain more aware than at any previous time in history just how many non-Christians there were in the world. Given that traditional theology consigned most or all such people to eternal torment, many began to feel a growing discomfort with the notion that God would send *so many* people to hell. In addition to this, there was a growing body of evidence, from the accumulated experiences of many of these missionaries, that preaching hell was not only ineffective in bringing about conversions, it was often positively counterproductive.

Second, the nineteenth century witnessed changing views on punishment. Since the seventeenth century, there had been various significant modification in British law to the kinds of punishment that were deemed appropriate and the kinds of crimes for which they were applicable. In 1689, the English Bill of Rights had excluded "cruel and unusual punishments," meaning torture, and this trajectory continued through the eighteenth and nineteenth centuries. The number of crimes for which one could in theory be executed dropped dramatically, from 220 at the start of the nineteenth century to five by 1861; public executions were stopped in 1868, in spite of their popularity. Some notable

---

[30] Church of England priests now only need to profess the Christian faith, to which the formularies, including the Articles, have born witness.

Introduction to Thomas Allin (1838–1909)

Victorians, such as Charles Dickens and Elizabeth Fry, made the public more aware of the terrible conditions in prisons and applied pressure for prison reform. There was also the growing influence of Jeremy Bentham's utilitarianism. Bentham had argued that the punishment of criminals needed to be justified in terms of its utility—its ability to serve a desirable goal. This led to growing pressure to consider punishment not merely as retributive or a deterrent, but also in terms of how well it helped to *rehabilitate* criminals. Once people started thinking in such ways, questions about hell were immediately raised. Clearly eternal torment with no hope of deliverance was useless in terms of rehabilitation. Indeed, it seemed to be very "cruel and unusual." Furthermore, on reflection, it even seemed to violate the most basic instinct of retribution itself, the very theory on which it was based. The retributive theory of punishment asserted that the punishment should be proportioned to the crime. But how could an infinite punishment be a proportionate response to a finite set of sins?

Third, the nineteenth century was a period of growing religious doubt: the fast-advancing sciences and developments in Germany in the critical study of the Bible served to make old sureties less secure. There was also a growing religious agnosticism, especially amongst certain intellectuals.[31] The doctrine of hell was an obvious target for such critics of religion, and this too set believers on the back foot. The secularist Austin Holyoake, for instance, argued that the doctrine of hell "brutalises all who believe in it"[32] and was useless as a tool of moral improvement. Christianity was being accused of being immoral and some were rejecting the church because of its theology of hell. This provoked some Christians to feel that rethinking hell was a matter of missional urgency.

Diverse Responses to Worries over Hell

These growing worries about eternal torment motivated varying responses. Many simply dug in and retained the traditional view, which they understood to be a matter of divine revelation. In the controversy that arose in light of the publication of *Essays and Reviews* in 1860, nearly 11,000 clergy signed a declaration to the effect that the Church

---

31 Though there is evidence that disquiet over hell was deeply felt among the working classes too. See Rowell, *Hell and the Victorians*, 147–49.

32 Holyoake, *Heaven and Hell*, 8. Quoted in Wheeler, *Heaven, Hell, and the Victorians*, 185.

of England believed that the life and punishment of the age to come were both "everlasting." Indeed, some preachers even seemed to relish in accentuating the horrors of hell. An often quoted example is that of Father Furniss, a Catholic priest with a special ministry to young people, whose booklet *The Sight of Hell* (1861), written to scare children into salvation, sold in vast quantities. He paints vivid pictures the stench of all the rotting bodies of the damned and of children suffering in perpetual torment: a girl in a dress of fire, which ever-burns, but never consumes; a sixteen-year old prostitute forced to stand for eternity on a red hot floor; a teenage boy who went to the theatre and the pub and now suffers with his blood and brain boiling like a kettle. The aim was to scare people away from sinning, yet one cannot help but wonder what a modern psychoanalyst would make of Furniss' vivid "torture porn." More restrained, though no less dreadful, was the influential hellfire preaching of The Salvation Army or Baptists like Charles H. Spurgeon.

However, the direction of public opinion was away from such views, especially literal physical descriptions of the pains of hell. Thus, alongside this traditionalism there were attempts to mitigate the difficulties. Traditionalists increasingly tended to focus on the *spiritual* torments of hell—the sense of loss, of eternal separation from God. Some argued that while hell was everlasting punishing, the number of the lost may be very small, rather than the majority of mankind. This served to make the horror of hell a little less troubling. One thinks here, for instance, of the American Presbyterian minister W. G. T. Shedd, who was emphatic in his defence of hell as eternal torment, but who was also hopeful that in the end the majority of humanity would be saved. The Anglo-Catholic Edward Pusey took a similar line. There were also a small number of attempts to make the experience of those in hell less grim than in traditional accounts. Thus, for instance, Rev. T. R. Birks, of whom we shall say more soon.

More influential, especially among certain Evangelical Anglicans and Congregationalists, was a revival of a belief in hell-as-annihilation. On this view, hell was indeed the final fate of the lost, but while it was a punishment with everlasting effects, it was not a process of punishment that went on forever and ever. Many found this much more easy to reconcile with divine justice, goodness, and victory than the traditional view.

In addition to these responses, a more radical alternative to the traditional hell was on offer: the universalist vision. Many who had leanings this direction were what we may call literary types—poets and novelists (e.g., Alfred Tennyson, the Brontë sisters, George MacDonald, Philip Bailey).33 But there were churchmen and theologians too.

Debates on hell in seventeenth and eighteenth centuries had generated defenders of universalism in orthodox denominations, but its main British defenders in the early part of the nineteenth century were the Unitarians, whose heterodoxy did little to endear the view to the mainstream. It was only from the mid-nineteenth century that such debates reared their head in the Anglican world. We can track the growing disquiet within Anglicanism over hell through a few key debates.

The Controversy over Rev. F. D. Maurice

First, a controversy was stirred up over the publication of Frederick Denison Maurice's *Theological Essays* (1853).[34] Maurice was an Anglican priest who occupied two professorships at King's College London. He had been brought up Unitarian, but converted to Anglicanism, and *Theological Essays* was written to address Unitarian objections to orthodox Christianity. It was the final essay on "Eternal Life and Eternal Death" that was to prove the cause of much controversy. Maurice argued that salvation should not be thought of as salvation from punishment in hell, but as salvation from *sin*. He further argued that *aiōnios* ("eternal") was first and foremost a descriptor of *God* and his own "eternal" life. It has no *temporal* connotations; no sense of duration. So it does not mean "everlasting" or "enduring forever." In Maurice's view, *aiōnios* is a term denoting the *quality* of the divine life, not a *quantity* of life (or punishment). Thus, eternal life means a sharing in God's own life. Eternal death, on the other hand, is a separation from that life; it is the "punishment of being without the knowledge of God, who is love."[35] Being separated from all God's attributes, the lost are indeed in hell because all that remains to them is to be locked in their own sinful ways. On the issue of whether the damned may one day be reached by God's love, Maurice expresses a pious agnosticism, but a deep hope in "an abyss of love which is deeper than the

---

33 On eschatology in Victorian literature, see especially, Wheeler, *Heaven, Hell, and the Victorians*.

34 On the Maurice controversy, see Rowell, *Hell and the Victorians*, 76–89; Laufer, *Hell's Destruction*, 119–24.

35 Maurice, *Theological Essays*, 455.

abyss of death."³⁶ So while Maurice was not a universalist, he did open a door to such a possibility.

The traditional view of hell laid great store in the word *aiōnois* and Maurice's revisionary understanding threatened one of the planks upon which this theology was built.³⁷ It was therefore no surprise that the publication of the book led to complaints to R. W. Jelf, the principal of King's College, and the setting up by Jelf of what amounted to an inquisition against Maurice. Jelf was simply unable to understand the position being advocated by Maurice and despite Maurice's regular insistence that he was not teaching that all would be saved and that his views were fully consistent with everything required of Anglican orthodoxy, Jelf and the council thought that Maurice was deliberately fudging the issue and that in reality he was a universalist. He was therefore dismissed from his position at the college.

The Controversy over Rev. H. B. Wilson

Second, a massive controversy erupted after the publication of the seven Broad-Church essays in the volume *Essays and Reviews* (1860), edited by John William Parker.³⁸ One of the two most controversial was Rev. H. B. Wilson's essay on eternal punishment. Wilson believed that few people died in a state ready for God's presence in heaven. But this does not mean that the majority are doomed to hell. Rather, there is room for spiritual progress in the afterlife after the great day of judgment. The dead are like seeds sent to "nurseries as it were and seed-grounds, where the undeveloped may grow up under new conditions—the stunted may become strong, and the perverted restored." He goes on to say that when Christ "shall have surrendered His kingdom to the Great Father [an allusion to 1 Cor 15:28]—all, both small and great, shall find refuge in the bosom of the Universal Parent, to repose, or be quickened into higher life, in ages to come, according to His Will."³⁹ This sounds like some version of hope for universal salvation. His liberal views on hell were challenged in the

---

36 Ibid., 476.

37 In fact, controversy about the meaning of *aiōnios* long predated Maurice, as can be witnessed in universalist works from the seventeenth and eighteenth centuries.

38 On the debate about *Essays and Reviews*, see Rowell, *Hell and the Victorians*, 116–23; Laufer, *Hell's Destruction*, 124–26.

39 H. B. Wilson in Parker (ed.), *Essays and Reviews*, 205–6.

church courts. In 1862 the judgment was delivered that Wilson's view was incompatible with the plain sense of the Athanasian Creed (with its comments on "everlasting fire"), to which all Anglican clergy had to subscribe. He was also guilty of making one's future fate depend wholly on moral conduct, irrespective of one's religious belief. Wilson was given a year's suspension of his living. He appealed the judgment and in 1864 the appeal was allowed. The judgment declared

> We are not at liberty to express any opinion upon the mysterious question of the final punishment, further than to say that we do not find in the [Anglican] Formularies . . . any such distinct declaration of our Church upon the subject as to require us to condemn as penal the expression of hope by a clergyman, that even the ultimate pardon of the wicked, who are condemned in the day of judgment may be consistent with the will of Almighty God.[40]

This judgment started a firestorm of protest, especially from Evangelicals and Anglo-Catholics. They feared that this level of latitude over the interpretation of creeds opened the door to any and every heresy. They also thought that a weakening of the doctrine of hell removed a key motivator for moral behavior and set society on a road to moral perdition. The Oxford declaration against the essayists, organized by the Anglo-Catholics, was signed by almost 11,000 clergy, as mentioned previously. It proclaimed the historic Anglican belief in everlasting hell. The Archbishops of Canterbury and York also expressed sympathy with the Oxford declaration. However, within a decade, when the subject of hell was again a matter of intense controversy, "not only was the argument conducted against a background of a more decided agnosticism, the general tone of the debate was much calmer. A growing appreciation of the results of biblical criticism did much to weaken the simple appeal to the authority of texts, which had been so frequently employed by the defenders of eternal punishment."[41]

---

40 Quoted in Rowell, *Hell and the Victorians*, 119.
41 Ibid., 122–23.

The Controversy over Rev. T. R. Birks

The third controversy was over Rev. T. R. Birks' *The Victory of Divine Goodness* (1867).[42] Birks was F. D. Maurice's replacement at King's College London and was the secretary of the Evangelical Alliance. His book was an attempt at constructive revisionist theology from within the traditional camp. While he did affirm hell as the eternal conscious fate of the unsaved and as an objective condition of loss, he argued that those in hell were able to contemplate God's goodness and the glory of his restored cosmos and to appreciate it, even as they felt shame over their lives and anguish at the thought of what they have forever rejected. There was no active torture by God (or demons) nor any continuing malice against God by the damned. The problem was that many Evangelicals felt that Birks' revisionary version of hell was simply incompatible with the Evangelical Alliance's confession of faith. Birks thus resigned as Secretary of the EA. Some tried to have him forced to resigned his membership as well, but in this they failed.

The Controversy over the Athanasian Creed

Fourth, in the 1870s controversy raged within the Church of England over the damnation clauses in the Athanasian Creed.[43] The Creed not only ends with a declaration that at the judgment those who have done evil will depart "into everlasting fire," but it also condemns all who do not affirm the faith as set out in the Creed to "perish everlastingly." The Book of Common Prayer required the use of the Athanasian Creed on certain important feast days. In practice this often did not happen, but the Oxford Movement led to a tightening up on such laxity. Increasing numbers of worshippers thus found themselves confronted with and disturbed by this text. In 1867 a Royal Commission looked into the rituals of the Church of England and the issue of this creed became a focus, setting off a wider debate. The fate of those who had never heard the gospel was a particular sticking point. The debate about the merits and demerits of using the Athanasian Creed rumbled on among the clergy through the 1870s. Should it be dropped from the Prayer Book? Should some

---

42 On the debate over Birks, see ibid., 123–29.

43 On the debate about the Athanasian Creed, see Wheeler, *Heaven, Hell, and the Victorians*, 192–94; Laufer, *Hell's Destruction*, 128–30.

explanatory clause be added to qualify its damnation clauses? Passions were high. For some it was an authoritative statement of the catholic faith; for others it was a stumbling block. In the end, no clear resolution was reached, but considerable latitude on its interpretation was allowed. In 1873 a Convocation agreed on a statement that the Church of England affirms the necessity of the saved holding fast to the catholic faith, and the peril of not doing so. But this allowed plenty of room for maneuver on hell. By the 1890s the Archbishop of Canterbury declared, perhaps a little hyperbolically, that no one in the Church of England took the hell clauses in the Athanasian Creed literally any longer.

The Controversy over Rev. F. W. Farrar

Finally, at the end of 1877, the archdeacon of Westminster, F. W. Farrar, preached a series of sermons on eternal punishment, published the following year as *Eternal Hope*.[44] The book was perhaps clearer in what it denied than in what it affirmed. It denied a doctrine of endless hell, which Farrar, himself a student of F. D. Maurice, judged to be built upon a mistranslation of the Greek word *aiōnios* ("eternal") in certain biblical passages. If not eternal hell, then what? He did not opt for annihilation or purgatory as an alternative, so was he a universalist? Farrar certainly rejected the idea that death was the point at which one's fate was forever sealed, but he emphatically denied being a universalist. Instead, he took the stance, as Maurice before him, of pious agnosticism. But protest as he might, many believed that he was in fact a universalist.

Farrar's work generated some hostility, as would be expected, but also a lot of sympathy. *The Contemporary Review* commissioned a series of reflections on it by thinking churchmen who took differing views on the subject. The most important response, however, came from Edward Pusey, the celebrated Oxford Anglo-Catholic. Pusey was deeply concerned by Farrar's abandoning hell, fearing that it would open the floodgates of immorality by removing an important incentive to avoid sin. In 1880 he published his reply in a scholarly work entitled *What Is of Faith*

---

44 On the Farrar/Pusey debate, see Rowell, *Hell and the Victorians*, 139–52; Laufer, *Hell's Destruction*, 137–39. For those interested in trivia, it is perhaps of interest to note that it was Farrar who arranged for Darwin to be buried at Westminster Abbey, and at the funeral served as a pallbearer and preached the sermon.

as to Everlasting Punishment? Unlike many defences of eternal hell, this one took the more unusual line of arguing that much of the perceived problem with hell was generated by the Protestant two-destiny view of the afterlife. The idea that everyone was destined for heaven or hell did not seem to match our experience of real people with all their shades of grey. Purgatory as a preparation ground for heaven helped deal with this. Pusey also expressed his view that we have no solid grounds for supposing that the majority of humanity would be damned, so we can reasonably hope for the salvation of the bulk of the human race. However, he did see our choices in this life as the only opportunity we have to avoid eternal damnation.

Farrar was pushed into writing a more scholarly book in response to Pusey, entitled *Mercy and Judgment* (1882). He still denied being a universalist, but did declare that all but the most reprobate would make spiritual progress in the intermediate state.

Farrar went a little further than Maurice, his teacher, in his eschatological hope. And Maurice's brother-in-law, Rev. Edward Plumptre, to whom *Eternal Hope* was dedicated, went further still.[45] While Maurice and Farrar might be described as open to the possibility of universalism, though reverently agnostic as to its truth or falsity, Plumptre, yet another professor at King's College London(!), was very much more overt in his universalism. That Farrar and Plumptre's books did not generate the level of furious controversy witnessed in the 1850s through to the 1870s and that, unlike Maurice, they did not lose their jobs (indeed, Farrar later became Dean of Canterbury and Plumptre became Dean of Wells) shows something of the changing temperature of Victorian Anglicanism.

It was in this context of increasingly vocal dissent over the traditional theology of hell that Thomas Allin wrote *Universalism Asserted*.

THOMAS ALLIN'S PATRISTIC VISION

Allin's vision is in many ways of its time. Yet, as Victorian as his theology was, it was also a "welcome discovery" to find that "not a little of what is supposed to be modern in religious thought is really the most ancient

---

45 Edward H. Plumptre, *The Spirits in Prison and Other Studies on the Life After Death*. London: 1884.

and venerable of all . . . ."[46] A key part of what he is at pains to demonstrate in this book is that universalist theology is not grounded in some modern Victorian sentiment, even if it has some resonance with that, but that its roots lie in the ancient Christian theology of the first few centuries of the church. What he is pleading for is not a new theology, but the revival of a *very old* theology.

Allin is not only a Victorian with an interest in patristics; he is also an Anglican. His implied readers are also Anglicans, as is clear from references to *"our* church" (meaning the Church of England) and *"our* Prayer Book" (meaning the 1662 Book of Common Prayer), and note the weight he expects his comments on issues that "the English church" accepts or does not accept to carry. For instance, that the English church only accepts the authority of the first four ecumenical councils means that the decisions of the fifth council need not be considered binding. His Anglicanism is also revealed in the large number of bishops he appeals to and, most especially, in his attempt to see universalist instincts in the Prayer Book. He really believes that universalism fulfills the deepest instincts of the Church of England, even though few of its ministers have embraced such a creed.

But Allin's Anglicanism runs deeper than all this. Indeed, the very *structure* of this book is shaped by his Anglican instinct that theological reflection needs to take seriously what Richard Hooker (1554–1600) called the "three-legged stool" of Scripture, tradition, and reason. The original title (the subtitle in this edition) makes this clear. Allin begins with reason, works through tradition, and ends with Scripture. But his burden all along is to show that these three witnesses are deeply interrelated, mutually reinforcing, and are in complete harmony. The original title page of his book contained a quotation from Ecclesiastes to drive home this point: "A threefold cord is not quickly broken" (Eccl 4:12).

Yet, Anglican as Allin is, he is not uncritical of his church. He is well aware that it is at heart "Latin" in its theology and that most Anglican priests preach a gospel that is, in his view, compromised to one degree or another by this heritage. He is also very open to discerning God's truth wherever it is found, even outside the boundaries of the church.

Allin does not easily fit into the various Church of England parties of his day. Was he Liberal? Was he Rationalist? Was he Evangelical? Was he Anglo-Catholic? No and yes. *No*, in that he did not self-identify with any

---

46 Allin, *Race and Religion*, 4.

of the groups who claimed these labels. In his mind, all of them were too indebted to "Latin" thinking. *Yes*, in that he thought that, properly understood, the terms "liberal," "rationalist," "evangelical," and "catholic" identified noble and important ideals for the church to aspire to. We should be "rationalist" in that we seek to render allegiance to the Eternal Reason (the *Logos*) that was incarnate as Jesus Christ. We should be "liberal" in that we recognize the dignity of the individual and do not seek to impose rigid conformity from above—rather, we should embody a "freer spirit" than that exemplified by the "Latin" desire to prescribe from above the details for every aspect of theology. We should be "evangelical" in that we are gospel-focused and in that we acknowledge the critical role that Holy Scripture plays in our Christian life and faith; we should be "catholic" by seeking to be in true continuity with the ancient and universal tradition of Hellenistic, creedally orthodox Christianity (the mode of Christianity that was dominant before the Latin West came into its own).[47]

It was not uncommon to hear universalists accused of believing heresy, but Allin was as concerned to avoid heresy as anyone. Indeed, one could see the whole of his argument in *Universalism Asserted* as an attempt to turn this accusation back against the believers in hell. It is *they*, not the universalists, who are in the greatest danger of heresy!

Now at first blush this suggestion sounds absurd. Clearly belief in hell is not formally heretical, and most of the great orthodox theologians in the past fifteen hundred years have been believers in an eternal perdition. So how could belief in hell possibly be flirting with heresy!?

Perhaps an example from Allin's arguments will help us to see what he is getting at. Allin argues that if hell continues to all eternity then sinners continue in their resistance to God for all eternity, sin continues forever, evil continues forever. As such, we end up with an everlasting cosmic dualism in which good and evil are co-eternal. Even if God can imprison sin in an eternal chamber in some corner of creation, he has merely contained it, *not* undone and defeated it. Yet such an idea threatens to undermine some central Christian convictions about God and evil.

Allin also argues that a hell from which there is no ultimate restoration—whether that hell be eternal torment or annihilation—would undermine the doctrine of God (his love, his justice, his goodness, his

---

47 Allin, *Race and Religion*, 10–11, 79, 160–61. Allin also argues for an expanded sense of catholicity. He sees his vision as catholic (i.e., universal) in that one day *all* humanity will be embraced. Anything less, he thinks, is inadequately "catholic."

omnipotence), the victory of Christ, the power of the atonement, and so on and so forth.

Of course, those who believe in hell also affirm God's love and justice, omnipotence, the atonement, divine victory, etc. But, Allin's point is that when they do so they either (a) have to add in qualifications that serve to undermine the very beliefs that they affirm or (b) they have to simply ignore the contradictions in their belief set and talk out of both sides of their mouth at the same time.

So the doctrine of hell, in Allin's view, is perhaps a little like a cuckoo in the nest of Christian theology: it is a real and present danger to the genuine chicks. Given the oft-heard, though incorrect, assertion that universalism is heretical, what is interesting is that the heart of Allin's case, though he does not put it in these words, is that to maintain a consistent and healthy Christian orthodoxy we ought to jettison belief in eternal hell. *Hell, in other words, is bad for orthodoxy.* Who said Anglicans were wishy-washy!

I have no intention of outlining the arguments of the book. However, in conclusion, I will pick out a few features that I consider to be some of its strengths and weaknesses. What Allin clearly grasps is that universalism is not simply a doctrine about some subset of theology known as eschatology. Christian theology is a seamless garment, with all the parts interconnecting and interpenetrating each other. As such, the final universal glorification of all humans is as much a doctrine about creation or atonement or resurrection or indeed the being and nature of God as it is a doctrine about what will happen in the end.

The book contains numerous terrific passages and arguments. It is perhaps best known for introducing readers to a wealth of patristic evidence for the antiquity and "ubiquity" of universalism. These discussions are not above criticism, but, on the whole, the case he builds is well documented and convincing.

The biblical material (chapters 4–6) also contains great strengths. His discussions on the meaning of *aiōnios*, judgment, death, wrath, fire, punishment, and so forth are, in my opinion, generally compelling. Also interesting is the cumulative case he builds in chapter 4 for universalism, a case that is not usually taken with the seriousness it deserves. He drives home the point that the Bible repeatedly and emphatically speaks of Christ as the *actual* Saviour of *the whole world*. He argues that the doctrine of hell has blurred our vision and stopped us seeing the obvious meaning of such texts. We do not even notice the irony of affirming that Christ is the Saviour of all, while at the very same time denying it.

I also think the first three chapters are terrific. He unleashes a whole arsenal of weapons against hell that still threaten "traditional" theology (though see a caveat below). In particular, Allin's concern, mentioned a little earlier, that traditional hell entails an eternal cosmic dualism of good and evil—a perpetuation of sin into eternity—is a very weighty concern that ought to give the traditionalist serious pause for thought.

However, the work is not without its weaknesses. First, in his zeal to restore some of the often unknown or overlooked aspects of ancient Christian theology—e.g., the constructive role of judgment, death, and wrath—he ends up giving disproportionate space to these matters and relatively meagre comment on some critical doctrines, such as creation, atonement, and so on.

Second, there are areas that cry out for further theological comment, but do not receive it. For instance, while Allin clearly believes that the cross is at the heart of the gospel story of God's reconciling the world to himself, he does not seem to have a clear account of how it serves this role. In chapter 6, the only atonement theory that he mentions is penal substitution (which he argues requires a doctrine of universalism, unless one embraces limited atonement), but he does not make any comments on the truth, or otherwise, of this model. In *Race and Religion* he is openly critical of penal substitution models of the atonement, or at least the *centrality* of such models. He criticizes the "open dualism between Justice and Mercy" often set up within God by this model, such that God becomes internally conflicted, wanting to forgive humanity (in his love), but unable to (in his justice).[48] He finds the notion that God is angry at humans and needs a blood sacrifice to propitiate his wrath before he can forgive to be, at best, unbalanced. "I do not mean to deny that elements of truth exist in the Latin conception, but it seized on that which is at best but secondary, and made it the pivot of Christianity."[49] Sometimes he is more critical. He is scathing about the suggestion that "it is not possible for God freely to forgive man"; that God, like Shakespeare's Shylock, must have his pound of flesh to make sure that

---

48 Ibid., 122.
49 Ibid., 110.

his *honour* is satisfied.⁵⁰ The *focus* of a theology of salvation, he says, with perhaps an echo of F. D. Maurice, is not the escape from penalty, but freedom from the power of sin and death.⁵¹ So Allin is reluctant to dismiss penal substitution models as simply false, but he is vague about what, if any, value they have. What he is clear about is that they do not capture what is central in the salvation story. In which case, the obvious question is: *what does the cross do in the drama of salvation?* Allin owes us an answer to this question, but does not really offer one.

Third, Allin's expertise is clearly in the area of patristics, so the discussion of the biblical texts, while full of interest and insight, is weaker. There is very little engagement with the then-contemporary scholarship on the biblical texts, and some critical exegetical issues are passed over without comment. In many ways, Allin is reading the Bible *through* the Fathers. This is fine, but there is a lot more that needs to be said about the biblical texts than Allin says.

Fourth, Allin's general hostility to Tertullian, Augustine, Calvin, and the Western tradition, while not without warrant, is unbalanced. Although he is willing to acknowledge that there is much good in Latin Christianity, he tends not to look for the good and so to pass over it. His focus is rather on what is wrong. While I appreciate that he saw himself as offering a sharp corrective, I find this myopic. I agree with Allin that the doctrine of hell in the West has been indefensible and has been integrated with other problematic elements, but there is great theological wealth in the work of Augustine and Calvin, to name his two main nemeses. Indeed, I think that Allin would do better to treat the Western tradition as a whole in the way that he treats Anglicanism—as essentially good, yet as infected with a theological virus. The alien virus and the body it infects are in conflict. The virus attempts to integrate and insinuate itself into the body, but it cannot do so successfully. The body fights back. To focus on what is good in the Western tradition and to use it to expose the alien nature of the virus is a better road to healing than passing over the likes of Augustine with a quick sideways glance and a snarl.⁵² Indeed, I have

---

50 Ibid., 120.

51 Which is not to deny that there may be some place for escape from penalty.

52 To be fair to Allin, his *final* book, *The Augustinian Revolution in Theology*, did devote a lot of space to a consideration of some of Augustine's teaching. But its focus was on what Allin sees as the errant and harmful teachings in Augustine. He had little

Introduction to Thomas Allin (1838–1909)

long thought that there is a book to be written on great theologians in the Western tradition whose own theology might lend itself to universalism in ways that they themselves failed to perceive. Perhaps there is a case to be made for universalism from the principles of Augustinianism or Calvinism or Edwardsianism, or Thomism, or whatever. Maybe I am naive, but I think that there is enough profound insight in the work of all these thinkers to warrant treating them with respect, even as we critique what is horrible in their theology—and I agree with Allin that there is some very horrible material in it.

Finally, one of the things that strikes me as odd, given Allin's love of Hellenistic Christianity and his qualified sympathy with Christian Platonism, is that his understanding of language about God operates at a somewhat naive level. He rightly rejects the radical equivocity of those who deny that goodness or love in God is anything like goodness or love in humans. This approach, if pursued with integrity, would lead to radical agnosticism and unweave Christian theology. However, Allin assumes that the only alternative to this equivocity is a bland univocity in which words used of God mean *exactly the same thing* as when they are used of creatures. The danger here is that sometimes God comes across in Allin's thought as if he were simply a giant version of a human—as though the move from reflection on human creatures to drawing conclusions about God is simple and straightforward. God is like us, just a lot bigger and better. All my Christian Platonist and Thomistic hackles rise at this. Thomas Aquinas' doctrine of analogy long ago charted a middle way between the Scylla of equivocity and the Charybdis of univocity. Some such middle way seems to be to me more or less requisite for those who wish to pursue the Christian Hellenism that Allin so aspires to. It would admittedly complicate some of his argument strategies, as the route from our understanding of creation to our understanding of God would be less direct. It would require some more caution and some more nuance, but I think that his case would still be strong.

So Allin's book is not perfect. Nevertheless, it is a classic, and with good reason. Much of it remains as fresh and relevant as it was when it first appeared in 1885. I trust that this new edition will make a positive contribution to ongoing discussions within Christian theology.

---

interest in considering what is good and beautiful and true in Augustine's work. He recognizes that there is such material, but then ignores it.

Foreword to the Annotated Edition

In a chapter entitled "Universalistic Trends in the Evangelical Tradition: An Historical Perspective," David Hilborn and Don Horrocks point out that "for most evangelicals, and for many non-evangelicals besides, the very concept [of *evangelical universalism*] . . . is an oxymoron." Why so? Because however "conservative a person's background and theological formation may have been, the historic evangelical norm is that once that person embraces universalism, he or she *de facto* forfeits any authentic claim to the description 'evangelical.'"[1]

But why so much concern over the usage of a given label? According to one widely acknowledged group of evangelical Christians (the Arminians), it is a clear and obvious teaching of Scripture that all human sinners are equal objects of God's redemptive love; and according to another such group (the Calvinists), it is a clear and obvious teaching of Scripture that God will in the end reconcile to himself every object of his redemptive love. Does it not seem utterly arbitrary, therefore, to stipulate that a *true* evangelical can accept either one of these supposedly clear and obvious teachings, but not both of them together? Nor would such a stipulation have any relevance, in any case, to a single substantive theological or exegetical dispute. I emphasize this point because Thomas Allin, the nineteenth-century author of *Universalism Asserted* (sometimes retitled as *Christ Triumphant*), accepted both the doctrine of the Trinity, on the one hand, and the absolute authority of Scripture, on the other. So to insist that his affirmation of universalism (and that alone) would suffice to undermine "any authentic claim to the description 'evangelical,'" had he wished to adopt such a label, would most likely constitute a lazy person's

---

1 In *Universal Salvation? The Current Debate*, edited by Robin A. Parry and Christopher H. Partridge (Carlisle, UK: Paternoster, 2003), 238.

Foreword to the Annotated Edition

way of ignoring the important theological, exegetical, and hermeneutical issues raised in this long-neglected classic.

Accordingly, we all owe Editor Robin Parry and Wipf and Stock Publishers a debt of gratitude for bringing back into print a book that, quite frankly, few evangelical presses today would likely have the courage to publish. Fans of George MacDonald in particular should greatly appreciate this volume. For even as MacDonald vigorously challenged the idea that justice and mercy are distinct (and very different) attributes of God, so Allin argued that "God's essential unity is destroyed when we assign to him conflicting actions, as though his love demanded one course of action, and his justice another; as though God the Saviour were one person, and God the Judge a wholly different one." And even as MacDonald often described God's love as a consuming fire (see Heb 12:29), so Allin asked how "but by love can . . . [God's] fires be kindled? They are, in fact, the very flame of love; and so we have the key to the words: 'Your God is *a consuming fire*' and 'Your God is *a merciful God*' (Deut 4:24–31)." As for the popular (albeit confused) objection that a doctrine of universal restoration minimizes the seriousness of sin and the depth of God's opposition to it, Allin and MacDonald both turned that objection on its head, so to speak. According to the traditional understanding, after all, God will eventually confine sinners to a particular region of his creation, a region known as hell, but he will never destroy their sin altogether. So it is the traditional understanding, Allin insisted, that minimizes the seriousness of sin; as he put it himself, "no system so effectually affirms God's hatred of sin as that which teaches that he cannot tolerate its existence for ever." Allin thus drew a contrast between two very different ways of thinking about God:

> Whenever judgment comes, it comes on love's errand, if it comes from God. Here is the spiritual watershed between the two theologies. There is the popular theology that says, God loves his enemies, *till they die*. His love then turns into hate and vengeance. His love is, in fact, a question of chronology, or, if one will, of geography, i.e., bounded to this world. And there is the truer theology that teaches with the Bible that God is love [1 John 4:8]—love unchanging and eternal in all his ways.

Foreword to the Annotated Edition

I have found no evidence, by the way, in either Allin or MacDonald, that the two of them ever interacted with each other, despite their overlapping lifespans and the similarity of their theological ideas. But their approaches also differed in a way that makes this annotated version of Allin's work a most welcome companion to MacDonald's sermons. For even though MacDonald saturated his sermons with the results of his careful study of the Bible in its original languages, he preferred not to make a great show of citing chapter and verse; as a result, people sometimes fail to appreciate just how accurate he was in matters of exegetical detail. For his own part, however, Allin sought to provide in one volume a more systematic and thorough discussion of the two biblical themes most relevant to the topic of universal reconciliation, that of Christ's ultimate victory and triumph over sin, on the one hand, and that of divine judgment, on the other. In an effort to demonstrate just how well these superficially different themes in fact fit together, he thus tried to account for the most important biblical texts (along with important patristic commentary upon them) that might pertain to either of these themes.

With respect to the Greek words *aiōn* and *aiōnios*, for example, Allin showed conclusively that nowhere in either the New Testament or the Septuagint do these words carry any implication of unending *temporal* duration; and with respect to the image of fire, he rightly contended that throughout the Bible this image symbolizes a kind of divine judgment that, however severe it may be, nonetheless purifies and restores as well. Concerning 1 Corinthians 3:12–15, he thus wrote: "And so the 'fire is to try *every man's* work.' He whose work fails is saved (mark the word *saved*), *not damned* 'so as by fire,' for God's fire, by consuming what is evil, saves and refines." As further support for this interpretation, he also cited such clear Old Testament texts as Zephaniah 3:8–9 and Malachi 3:2–3, in effect inviting us to compare Paul's own language with that of Malachi, who likewise associated "the Day" of judgment with a fire that purifies and restores. That so many commentators have ignored altogether the similarity of Paul's own language to that of Malachi, preferring instead to interpret Paul as if he had in mind something akin to "being saved by the skin of one's teeth," is remarkable, to say the least. For Paul nowhere treated salvation as if it were a kind of "fire insurance," like "a brand snatched from the fire" (Amos 4:11); he thought of it instead as a complete destruction of the old person, which seems to render the whole idea of "being saved by the skin of one's teeth" utterly unintelligible. But

Foreword to the Annotated Edition

in any event, regardless of their perspective on universal reconciliation, thoughtful Christians should find much in Allin's work that will reward further reflection and careful study.

Finally, Allin's Victorian writing style, which can at times seem a trifle longwinded and repetitive, is on full display in this work. But the editor's added section headings make this annotated edition easy to navigate, and a wonderful set of annotations make it a rich source of historical information. All of that along with the author's own penchant for thoroughness have resulted in a most valuable guidebook for anyone seeking to understand how Christian universalists interpret various biblical themes, especially the crucial one of divine judgment.

Thomas Talbott
Emeritus Professor of Philosophy
Willamette University

23rd April 2015

Foreword to the Fourth Edition

UNIVERSALISM ASSERTED seems to me to fill a great want of the day. A book was needed which should face fairly and thoroughly, the subject of future punishment, for although there are many works on the subject, they either face one aspect of the matter only, or they are written for scholars only, not for the multitude. Mr. Allin's writing is emphatically writing which can be understood of the people, and surely his book must kill the false accusation so often made that, those who believe in the ultimate triumph of Christ, and in the redemption of the world, make light of sin.

Far from being a weak sentimentalist who shrinks from the thought of suffering, the universalist, as Mr. Allin shows very conclusively in his second and third chapters, is convinced that every sin meets with its just and remedial punishment; he points out, too, how very injurious is the moral tendency of the popular belief in the everlasting existence of evil, in a purposeless suffering, in an unjust and revolting system of torture. And all this is written calmly and thoughtfully, with a view to meeting the difficulties of those who are in doubt on the subject.

Perhaps the most interesting part of the book is that which shows how throughout the entire history of the church the belief in universal salvation has been held by many of the best and truest of Christ's followers. And to my mind one of the finest touches is the description given in chapter 1 of the position of those who, shrinking from the current notions of hell, and dissatisfied with that most unsatisfying theory—conditional immortality, take refuge in saying that nothing can be definitely known, and that they are content to wait in uncertainty.

The sympathetic way in which the writer meets their position, and his fearless exposure of the dangerous vagueness which lurks beneath its apparent humility is beyond praise. How is it possible that those who know the depths of sin and ignorance, those who hear the character of

God slandered by believers and unbelievers, those who love the ones who pass unrepentant into the unseen—how is it possible that they should rest satisfied, while retaining in their hearts even a shadow of a doubt that, "as in Adam all die, so in Christ shall all be made alive"?

The old merciless teaching is still taught; there yet remains in many a nursery, as well, alas, as in many a missionary school abroad, a well-known book called *Peep of Day*. In this, little children are allowed to read such doggerel as the following:

> Now if I fight, or scratch, or bite,
> In passion fall, or bad names call,
> Full well I know where I shall go.
> Satan is glad when I am bad,
> And hopes that I with him shall lie,
> In fire and chains, and dreadful pains.
> All liars dwell with him in hell,
> And many more, who cursed and swore,
> And all who did what God forbid.

Surely it is time that everyone who believes that the Everlasting Father lovingly, eternally, educates all His children should speak out plainly, and not be ashamed to confess with the psalmist, "My trust is in the tender mercy of God for ever and ever."

Edna Lyall,[1]
Eastbourne,
16th December, 1890

---

[1] Editor: Edna Lyall was the pen name of Ada Ellen Bayley (1857–1903), author of eighteen novels.

Preface to the Annotated Edition

For the sake of the purists I shall say a few words about some of the changes I have made for this new annotated edition of Allin's book. Before I could get to the changes, however, the original book had to be scanned and the text converted to a Word file using optical character recognition software. This provides a text that can be worked on and retypeset. The problem is that the process generates a *lot* of errors and one needs to go through the new text, carefully comparing it with the original, to eradicate these. I think that I have restored the text to its original form, but it is inevitable that some alterations will have sneaked through. If you find one, please don't tell me—I may cry.

Right—to the changes. Starting with the *title:* I have relegated the title that Allin gave to his book (*Universalism Asserted on the* . . .) to a subtitle and have adopted the title by which the book is perhaps best-known today (*Christ Triumphant*). I do not know who made this title switch or when, but it certainly captures the heart of the book well, and has the benefit of sounding better.

Second, the chapters in the original book are just solid blocks of text and this can make it hard to trace the progression of Allin's argument and to see the forest for the trees. So I have added a lot of *subtitles* to help readers navigate the text, and to more easily locate sections that interest them.

Third, I have also made some small changes to the *chapter titles* in order to clarify their content. Thus, I added subtitles to all the chapters, except for 1, 6, 7, and 10. In the case of chapter 6, I changed the whole title. Allin designated it as a chapter on creation, but even a cursory glance at it will reveal that only the first short section deals with creation. So I renamed it "Universalism and Doctrine."

Preface to the Annotated Edition

Fourth, to further help readers appreciate the overall argument of the book, I broke it down into three parts—dealing with reason, tradition, and Scripture. The book itself already has this shape, but I added section dividers to draw attention to it. Chapter 6 is something of a transition chapter between the tradition and Scripture sections and could have been located in either. (It was not even included in the first edition of Allin's book.) I have chosen to include it as an introduction to the Scripture section. Readers[1] can decide for themselves on the merits of that decision.

Fifth, and most obviously, I have added *annotations*. These are intended to provide useful background information should readers feel the need of it.

Sixth, I tried to source all the quotations and allusions that Allin makes. His own referencing system was very haphazard and something of a dog's dinner. Sometimes he gives no clue as to who he is quoting; sometimes he will mention a surname only; sometimes he will add an abbreviated fragment of a part of a title; and sometimes he will provide a full title. So, wherever possible I have hunted down his *sources*. Many of these books went through numerous editions, and, of course, for the most part I do not know which editions Allin was using. In such cases, I provided information on the first edition, so readers will at least know when the book was first penned. I have also created a *bibliography* of the texts Allin quotes from or references.

Seventh, with regard to Allin's many patristic sources, I have updated his *abbreviations of early church texts* so that modern scholars may more easily recognize them. I have also provided a *list of these abbreviations*. There were a small number of his abbreviations that resisted my attempts at identification, but for the most part I was able to track them down.

Eighth, I made various small adaptations to the main text itself: (a) I changed all the many Roman numerals in biblical and patristic references to *Arabic numerals* for the sake of modern readers. In addition I conformed his abbreviations for biblical books to *The SBL Handbook of Style*. I also placed all his Bible references in brackets, rather than in the main text following a dash. This seems more visually appealing; (b) Allin's book follows the conventions of the time by capping any words that get within the orbit of God. Modern conventions tend to be much

---

[1] My youngest daughter, Jessica, comments that this assumes there will be more than one reader of this book. Cheeky imp!

more minimalist in the *use of caps*. So I modernized the text in this way too; (c) I retained Allin's British spelling—for this is a very British book, as you'll see—but I did follow American conventions for in-text dashes and more modern typesetting conventions. For instance, I typeset long quotes as block quotations; (d) I broke up some of the very long paragraphs in the original in order to make the reading somewhat easier; (e) on rare occasions I changed a word in the text if the original was too obscure for modern readers (and I did change a fair few instances of "which" to "that"). Sometimes, for clarity, I inserted words into the text in square brackets. I also updated the biblical quotations to change old language (thee, thou, thine, etc.) to more modern equivalents. I was tempted to change Allin's use of "man" for "humanity," but this would have required a much more substantive updating of Allin's words, and my goal was to be minimalist in the modifications I made to the text; (f) Allin provided quite a few dates for the folk he refers to. However, for some reason, these were not date ranges, but single dates that appeared to be randomly chosen for some point between birth and death. I have changed all these to date ranges or, in some cases, date of death; (g) I updated some of Allin's older punctuation conventions to make the book flow a little more easily for a modern reader.

Ninth, this edition includes *an introduction* to the elusive Thomas Allin. It aims to provide some historical background to help readers locate the book in its Victorian Anglican context.

Tenth, and finally, there is a new foreword from Professor Thomas Talbott. Tom has himself played a key role in the modest revival in Christian universalism in recent years, and I was struck over and over again how many of his own views are prefigured here in Allin's work. I would like to thank him for taking the time to read this book and to write the foreword for it. I would also like to express my thanks to those who kindly endorsed it—Rev. Dr. Andrew Davison and Fr. Aidan Kimel.

I did not ever plan on creating this new edition. I was simply researching for a book that I am co-authoring with Ilaria Ramelli on Christian universalism from the Reformation to the Present Day. As I was doing that I thought to myself: "I know! I'll do a new edition of Allin's book. That will only take a few weeks." Well, that moment of madness led me down a track that involved a *lot* more work than I had naively anticipated. Indeed, there were times when the process seemed like eternal conscious torment. However, I am sure that it was a purifying pain and that I am a better person for having wrestled with Thomas Allin.

Purists may lament any modifications to the text at all, but they can always go and stick their head down a toilet . . . I mean, they can always go and read the original book. This edition is an attempt at retaining the original while refreshing it for a new audience. I hope that the balance is about right.

May God use the words of this classic book to provide provocation and encouragement.

    Robin A. Parry
    Easter Day
    April 2015

Preface to the Second Edition

The question of questions to which an answer is attempted in the following pages, is essentially this: can evil triumph finally over good? If we answer affirmatively with the popular creed, we are practically falling into dualism; if we reply negatively, we are teaching universalism. Such are the issues really involved. The more often and the more clearly this is stated as the turning point of the entire controversy about the larger hope, the better for those who write, and for those who read. The Calvinist settled this question by, in fact, affirming that if evil triumphs it is because *God* so orders (i.e., because *God* decrees to evil an eternal existence); thus saving or trying to save God's omnipotence, but at no less a cost than that of blackening his character, nay, of virtually making *him* a partner in evil. But the popular creed saves neither the omnipotence of God, nor yet preserves his character. Sin, the one thing most utterly hateful in his sight, he tolerates forever and ever, poisoning and defiling his works, and defying his power—satisfied, if in this brief life he cannot have obedience and righteousness—satisfied with endless disobedience and sin hereafter! He appears before all creation as trying to dislodge sin, only to fail; as sending his Divine Son to save all men in order that he may return rejected, baffled, vanquished. And so the curtain falls on the great drama of creation and redemption, presenting such a picture as this—a baffled Savior, a victorious devil, a ruined creation, sin triumphant—and so to continue forever—a heaven wholly base, a hell wholly miserable.

Strong as these words are, they are not strong enough, for the horrors and the contradictions of the popular creed alike defy description. And these horrors are taught, these contradictions are believed in the face of the plainest teaching of God's two revelations: his primary revelation to our moral sense; his written revelation in Holy Scripture. Of the former and its teachings, it is needless to speak here; of the latter I have spoken at some length, and have tried to show that from its first page to its last the Bible is the story of one who is our Father—one whose "wrath" and "fire" and "judgment" are at once most real, and yet one and all are the expressions of that essential *Love* which he is; one who being almighty is sending his Son to assured victory, to reconcile to himself all things, "whatsoever and wheresoever they be." I know how eagerly men strive to save the popular creed by various modifications, by diminishing the number of the lost, by softening their torments, by asserting their annihilation, etc. What are all these but so many tacit confessions that men everywhere feel it impossible to maintain the creed still generally professed? What are they but in fact so many vain attempts to disguise the awful fact of God's defeat, to hide if it may be the victory of the Evil One? For so long as sin lingers in a single heart, so long as a single child of the Great Parent perishes eternally, whether annihilated, or sent to hell, so long is the cross a failure, and the devil practically victor.

Letter from Canon Wilberforce to the Author

The Deanery,
Southampton,
August 6, 1890.

My dear Sir,

I am deeply grateful to you for your *noble* book, *Universalism Asserted*. I am greatly indebted to it, not only for the inspiration, but even for the very thoughts in some instances, of the two sermons enclosed. It is the very best compendium of the glorious truth of modern times.

May Our Father continue to send you forth to vindicate His character against the slander of atheists on the one hand, and conventionalists on the other.

I am, faithfully, &c,

Basil Wilberforce[1]

---

1 Editor: Basil Wilberforce (1841–1916) was an Anglican priest and, at the time he wrote this letter, Rector of St. Mary's in Southampton and Honorary Canon of Winchester Cathedral. He was a son of Bishop Samuel Wilberforce (1805–73) and grandson of William Wilberforce (1759–1833), the great campaigner against the slave trade.

List of Abbreviations

Apostolic Fathers
1 Clem.	*1 Clement*
Barn.	*Barnabas*
Herm. Sim.	*Shepherd of Hermas, Similitude*
Ign. *Smyrn.*	Ignatius, *To the Smyrnaeans*
Ign. *Trall.*	Ignatius, *To the Trallians*
Pol. *Phil.*	Polycarp, *To the Philippians*

Ambrose
Bon. mort.	*De bono mortis* (Death as a Good)
Cain	*De Cain et Abel* (Cain and Abel)
De fide Res.	*De fide resurrectionis* (On the Resurrection)
Ep.	*Epistula* (Letters)
Exp. in Ps.	*Expositio Psalmos* (Exposition of the Psalms)
Exp. Luc.	*Expositio Evangelii Lucan* (Exposition on the Gospel of Luke)
Fid.	*De fide* (The Faith)
Incarn.	*De incarnationis dominicae sacramento* (The Sacrament of the Incarnation of the Lord)
In Ps.	*In Psalmos* (On Pslams)
Jac.	*De Jacob et vita beata* (Jacob and the Happy Life)
Paen.	*De Paenitentia* (Repentance)
Sacr.	*De Sacramentis* (The Sacraments)

Ambrosiaster
Comm. in Col.	*Comentarii in S. Pauli epistulam ad Colossiai* (Commentary on Colossians)
Comm. in Heb.	*Comentarii in S. Pauli epistulam ad Hebraeos* (Commentary on Hebrews)

List of Abbreviations

In Rom.	*In S. Pauli Apostoli epistulam ad Romanos* (On Romans)
In I Tim	*In S. Pauli Apostoli epistulam primam ad Timotheum* (On 1 Timothy)

Arnobius
Adv. gen. — *Adversus gentes* (Against the Gentiles)

Asterius of Amasea
Hom. — *Holimae* (Homilies)

Athanasius

Comm. essent.	*De communi essentia Patris et Filii et Spiritus* (On the Essence of the Father and Son and Spirit)
Ep. Drac.	*Epistula ad Dracontium* (Letter to Dracontius)
Exp. Ps.	*Expositiones Psalmos* (Expositions on the Psalms)
Inc.	*De incarnatione* (The Incarnation)
In Illud	*In Illud: Omnia mihi tradita sunt* (Homily on Matthew 11:27)

(Pseudo) Athanasius
De pass. et cruce Dom. — *De Passione et Cruce Domini* (The Passion and Cross of the Lord)

Athenagoras
Res. — *De resurrectione* (On the Resurrection)

Augustine

Conf.	*Confessionum* (Confessions)
Contin.	*De continentia* (Continence)
Enchir.	*Enchiridion de fide, spe, et caritate* (Handbook on Faith, Hope, and Love)
Man.	*De Moribus Manichaeorum* (The Morals of the Manichaeans)

Basil of Caesarea

C. Eun	*Contra Eunomium* (Against Eunomius)
Comm. in Is.	*Commentarii in Isaiam* (Commentary on Isaiah)
Ep.	*Epistula* (Letter)
Hom.	*Homilae* (Homilies)

List of Abbreviations

Hom. in Ps.	*Homiliae in Psalmos* (Homilies on the Psalms)
Quod Dens	*Quod Dens non est auct mal* (God is Not the Author of Evil)

Basil of Seleucia
In sanc. Pascha	*In sanctum Pascha* (Holy Easter)

Bernard of Clairvaux
Ad. Eug.	*Ad Eugenium* (Letter to Eugenium)

Caesarius of Nazianzus
Dial.	*Dialogus* (Dialogues)

Clement of Alexandria
De Ador.	*De Adoratione in Spiritu et Veritate* (Worship in Spirit and Truth)
In 1 John	*In Primam S. Joannis Epistolam* (Comments of the First Epistle of John)
Paed.	*Paedagogus* ([Christ] the Educator)
Strom.	*Stromata* (Miscellanies)

Cyril of Alexandria
De adorat.	*De adoratione et cultu in spiritu et veritate* (Adoration and Worship in Spirit and Truth)
Glaphy. in Ex.	*Glaphyra in Exodum* (Glaphyra on Exodus)
Glaphy. in Gen.	*Glaphyra in Genesim* (Glaphyra on Genesis)
Hom. Pasch.	*Homiliae Paschales* (Paschal Homilies)
In 1 Io	*In Primam S. Joannis Epistolam* (On 1 John)
In Hos.	*In Hosea* (On Hosea)

Didymus of Alexandria
Adv. Man.	*Adversus Manichaeos* (Against the Manichaes)
Comm. in Ps.	*Comentarii in Psalmos* (Commentary on the Psalms)
De Spir. S.	*De Spiritu Sancto* (The Holy Spirit)
De Trin.	*De Trinitate* (On the Trinity)
In 1 John	*In Primam S. Joannis Epistolam* (On 1 John)
In 1 Peter	*In Primam S. Petri Epistolam* (On the First Epistle of Peter)

liii

List of Abbreviations

Dionysius of Alexandria
On St. Luke   Epistle on St. Luke

(Pseudo) Dionysius
De div. nom.   *De divinis nominibus* (On the Divine Names)

Ephrem the Syrian
De sanc. Cruce   *Opera omnia de sancta cruce* (The Works of the Holy Cross)
Serm.   *Sermones* (Sermons)

Epiphanius
AH   *Adversus Haereses* (Against Heresies)
Anc.   *Ancoratus* (The Anchored)
Pan.   *Panarion* (aka *Adversus haereses*) (Medicine Chest, aka Against Heresies)
In Assump. Christi   *Homilia in assumptionem Christi* (Homily on the Assumption of Christ)
In Res. Christi   *Homilia in Christi resurrectionem* (Homily on Christ's Resurrection)

Eusebius
Comm. Isa.   *Commentarius in Isaiam* (Commentary on Isaiah)
Dem. ev.   *Demonstratio evangelica* (Demonstration of the Gospel)
Eccl. theol.   *de ecclesiastica theologia* (Ecclesiastical Theology)
Hist. eccl.   *Historia ecclesiastica* (Ecclesiastical History)

Facundus
Pro def. tr. cap.   *Pro defensione trium capitulor* (For the Defense of the Three Chapters)

Gennadius
Comm. in Rom.   *Comentarii in S. Pauli epistulam ad Romanos* (Commentary on Romans)

Gregory of Nazianzus
Ad Deum.   *Ad Deum* (To God)
Carm.   *Carmina* (Poems)
Or.   *Oratio* (Oration)

List of Abbreviations

Gregory of Nyssa
De an. — *De anima et resurrectione* (On the Soul and the Resurrection)
De mort. — *De mortius non esse dolendum* (The dead should not be grieved)
In Illud — *In illud: Tunc et Ipse Filus* (On 1 Cor 15:28: "Then the Son himself...")
In Ps. — *In Psalmos* (On Psalms)
In Pulch. — *Oratio in Pulcheriam* (Funeral Oration for Pulcheria)
Or. Cat. — *Oratio catechetica* (Catechetical Oration)

Hilary of Poitiers
Comm. in Matt. — *Commentarii in Evangelium Matthaeum* (Commentary on Matthew)
Tr. Ps. — *Tractatus super Psalmos* (Treaty on the Psalms)
Trin. — *De Trinitate* (On the Trinity)

Irenaeus
Haer. — *Adversus haereses* (Against Heresies)

Jerome
Comm. Am. — *Commentariorum in Amos* (On Amos)
Comm. Eph. — *Commentariorum in Epistulam ad Ephesios* (On Ephesians)
Comm. Ezech. — *Commentariorum in Ezechielem* (On Ezekiel)
Comm. Gal. — *Commentariorum in Epistulam ad Galatas* (On Galatians)
Comm. Habac. — *Commentariorum in Habacuc* (On Habakkuk)
Comm. Hos. — *Commentariorum in Hosea* (On Hosea)
Comm. in Jon. — *Commentariorum in Jonah* (On Jonah)
Comm. in Ier. — *Commentariorum in Ieremiam* (On Jeremiah)
Comm. Isa. — *Commentariorum in Isaiam* (On Isaiah)
Comm. Joel — *Commentariorum in Joelem* (On Joel)
Comm. Mich. — *Commentariorum in Michaeum* (On Micah)
Comm. Nah. — *Commentariorum in Nahum* (On Nahum)
Comm. Obad. — *Commentariorum in Obadiah* (On Obadiah)
Comm. Ps. — *Commentarioli in Psalmos* (On Psalms)
Comm. Zach. — *Commentariorum in Zachariam* (On Zechariah)
Comm. Zeph. — *Commentariorum in Zephaniah* (On Zephaniah)

List of Abbreviations

De Res. Dom.	*De resurrectione Domini* (On the Resurrection of the Lord)
Epist.	*Epistulae* (Letters)
Ruf.	*Adversus Rufinum* (Against Rufinus)

John Cassian

Coll.	*Collationes patrum in scetica eremo* (Conferences of the Desert Fathers)

John Chrysostom

De sanc. Trin.	*De sancta Trinitatis* (The Holy Trinity)
Ep.	*Epistula* (Letter)
Hom.	*Homiliae* (Homilies)
Hom. 1 Cor.	*Homiliae in S. Pauli apostolic epistulam i ad Corinthios* (1 Corinthians)
Hom. Gen.	*Homiliae in Genesim* (Homilies in Genesis)
Hom Jo.	*Homiliae in Joannem* (Homilies in John)
Hom. Phil.	*Homiliae in S. Pauli apostolic epistulam ad Philippenses* (Homilies in Philippians)
Hom. Rom.	*Homiliae in S. Pauli apostolic epistulam ad Romanos* (Homilies in Romans)
In Col.	*In S. Pauli Apostoli epistulam epistulam ad Colossiai* (On Colossians)
In Eph.	*In S. Pauli Apostoli epistulam ad Ephesios* (On Ephesians)
In. Hebr.	*In epistulam ad Hebraeos* (On Hebrews)
In Matt.	*In Evangelium secundum Matthaeum* (On Matthew)
In. Ps.	*In Psalmos* (On the Psalms)
In S. Pascha	*In Sanctum pascha* (On Holy Easter)
Sac.	*De sacerdotio* (priesthood)
Ser.	*Sermones* (Sermons)

John Scotus Eriugena

De div. nat.	*De divisione natura* (The Division of Nature)

Justin Martyr

2 Apol.	*Apologia ii* (Second Apology)
Dial.	*Dialogus cum Tryphone* (Dialogue with Trypho)

List of Abbreviations

Leo the Great
Serm.   *Sermones* (Sermons)

Macarius Magnes
Apoc.   *Apocrites*

Marcellus of Ancyra
Cont. Mar.   *Contra Marcellum* (Against Marcellum)

Marius Victorinus
Adv. Ar.   *Adversus Arium* (Against Arius)
De phys.   *De physicis* (Of Physics)
In Eph.   *In S. Pauli Apostoli epistulam ad Ephesios* (On Ephesians)

Maximus the Confessor
Amb.   *Ambigua* (Doubtful Points)
Cap. theol.   *Capita Theologica et Oecumenica* (Ecumenical Theological Chapters)
Q. et dub.   *Quaestiones et dubia* (Questions and Dubious Points)
Schol.   *Scholia*

Maximus of Turin
Serm.   *Sermones* (Sermons)
Serm. in Pent.   *Sermone in Pentecosten* (Sermon on Pentecost)

Origen
Comm. Rom.   *Commentarii in Romanos* (Commentary on Romans)
Cont. Cel.   *Contra Celsum* (Against Celsus)
Hom. in Ier.   *Homiliae in Ieremiam* (Homilies on Jeremiah)
Hom. in Ies. Nav.   *Homiliae in Iesum Nave* (Homilies on Joshua)
Hom. in Lev.   *Homiliae in Leviticum* (Homilies on Leviticus)
Princ.   *De principiis (peri archôn)* (On First Principles)

Paulinus
Car.   *Carmina* (Poems)
Ep. ad Aman.   *Epistula ad Amandus* (Letter to Amandus)

List of Abbreviations

Peter Chrysologus
Serm.   *Sermones* (Sermons)

Photius
Bibl. Cod.   *Bibliotheca Codex* (Library Codex)

Proclus of Constantinople
In san. Pasch.   *In Sanctum pascha* (On Holy Easter)
Or.   *Oratio* (Oration)

Prudentius
Hymn   *Hymn*

Rufinus
Apol. c. Hier.   *Apologia contra Hieronymum* (Apology against Jerome)
Symb.   *Commentarius in symbolum apostolorum* (Commentary on the Apostles Creed)

Serapion
Adv. Man.   *Adversus Manichaeos* (Against the Manichaes)

Tertullian
An.   *De anima* (The Soul)
Pud.   *De pudicitia* (Modesty)
Spect.   *De spectaculis* (The Shows)

Theodore of Mopsuestia
Comm. in Rom.   *Comentarii in S. Pauli epistulam ad Romanos* (On Romans)
Cont. pecc. orig.   *Contra defensores peccati, originalis* (Against the Defenders of Original Sin)
De prov. Or.   *De Providencia Oratio* (On Divine Providence)
In Eph.   *In S. Pauli Apostoli epistulam ad Ephesios* (On Ephesians)
In. Ps.   *In Psalmos* (On the Psalms)
In Rom.   *In S. Pauli Apostoli epistulam ad Romanos* (On Romans)

List of Abbreviations

Theodoret
Comm. in Col. — *Comentarii in S. Pauli epistulam ad Colossiai* (On Colossians)
Comm. in Eph. — *Comentarii in S. Pauli epistulam ad Ephesios* (On Ephesians)
Comm. in Hebr. — *Comentarii in epistulam ad Hebraeos* (On Hebrews)
Comm. in Ier. — *Commentariorum in Ieremiam* (On Jeremiah)
Comm. in Rom. — *Comentarii in S. Pauli epistulam ad Romanos* (On Romans)
Comm. Zach. — *Commentariorum in Zachariam* (On Zechariah)
De prov. Or. — *De Providencia Oratio* (On Divine Providence)
Haer. fab comp. — *Haereticarum fabularum compendium* (Compendium of Heretic False Stories)
In Is. — *In Isaiam* (On Isaiah)
Quaes. in Oct. — *Quaestiones in Octateuchum* (Questions on the Octateuch)

Theophilus
Autol. — *Ad Autolycum* (To Autolycus)

Titus of Bostra
Adv. Man. — *Adversus Manichaeos* (Against the Manichaeans)

Victor of Antioch
Cat. Marc. — *Catena in Marcum* (on Mark's Gospel)

PART ONE

*Universalism Asserted
on the Authority of Reason*

1

The Question Stated

"SHALL NOT THE JUDGE OF ALL THE EARTH DO RIGHT"
GENESIS 18:25

Introduction

THE following pages are written under the pressure of a deep conviction that the views generally held as to the future punishment of the ungodly wholly fail to satisfy the plain statements of Holy Scripture. All forms of partial salvation are but so many different ways of saying that evil is in the long run too strong for God. The popular creed has maintained itself on a scriptural basis solely, I believe, by hardening into dogma mere figures of oriental imagery; by mistranslations and misconceptions of the sense of the original (to which our Authorized Version largely contributes); and finally, by completely ignoring a vast body of evidence in favour of the salvation of all men, furnished, as will be shown, by very numerous passages of the New Testament, no less than by the great principles that pervade the teaching of all revelation. Again, I write, because persuaded that, however loudly asserted and widely held, the popular belief is at best a tradition, is not an article of faith in the catholic church, is accepted by no general council, nay, is distinctly opposed to the views of not a few of the holiest and wisest Fathers of the church in

Part One—Universalism Asserted on the Authority of Reason

primitive times; who, in so teaching, expressed the belief of very many, if not the majority, of Christians in their days.

Further, I write, because deeply and painfully convinced of the very serious mischief that has been, and is being, produced by the views generally held. They in fact tend, as nothing else ever has, to cause—I had almost said, to justify—the scepticism now so widely spread; they effect this because they so utterly conflict with any conception we can form of common justice and equity.

Therefore of mercy I shall say little in these pages: it is enough to appeal, when speaking of moral considerations, to that sense of right and wrong which is God's voice speaking within us. Indeed, among the many misconceptions with which all higher views of the gospel are assailed, few are more unfounded than that which asserts that thus God's justice is forgotten in the prominence assigned to his mercy. This objection merely shows a complete misapprehension of the views here advocated. For these views do in fact appeal to, and by this appeal recognize, first of all, the justice of God. It is precisely the sense of natural equity, which God has planted within us, that the popular belief in endless evil and pain most deeply wounds.

Common Objections to Those Who Question Hell

And these considerations are in fact a complete answer to some other objections often heard. "Why disturb men's minds," it is said, "why unsettle their faith; why not let well alone?" By all means, I reply, let well alone, but never let ill alone. Men's minds are already disturbed: it is because they are already disturbed that we would calm them, and would restore the doubters to faith, by pointing them to a larger hope,[1] to a truer Christianity.

A graver objection arises, but, like the former, wholly without foundation in fact. It is said, "By this larger hope you, in fact, either weaken or wholly remove all belief in future punishment. You explain away the guilt of sin." The very opposite is surely the truth, for you establish future punishment, and with it that sense of the reality of sin (to which conscience testifies), on a firm basis only when you teach a plan of retribution that

---

1 Editor: Allin is very fond of the phrase "the larger hope" to designate his position. It is used by Lord Alfred Tennyson in his famous poem *In Memoriam*. The relevant section is reproduced at the front of this edition.

is itself reasonable and credible. A penalty that to our reason and moral sense seems shocking and monstrous loses all force as a threat. It has ever been thus in the case of human punishments. And so in the case of hell. Outwardly believed, it has ceased to touch the conscience, or greatly to influence the life of Christians. To the mass of men it has become a name and little more (not seldom a jest); to the sceptic it has furnished the choicest of his weapons; to the man of science, and to the more thoughtful of all ranks, a mark for loathing and scorn: while, alas, to many a sad and drooping heart that longs to follow Christ more closely, it is the chief woe and burden of life. But the conscience, when no longer wounded by extravagant dogmas, is most ready to acquiesce in any measure of retribution (however sharp it may be) that yet does not shock the moral sense and conflict with its deepest convictions. And so the larger hope most fully recognizes at once the guilt of sin and the need of fitting retribution: nay, it may be claimed for it *that it alone places both on a firm and solid basis*, by bringing them into harmony with the verdict of reason, of conscience, and of Holy Scripture.

The Traditional Hell

It is better now, for clearness sake, to define that popular view of future punishment of which I shall often speak. It is briefly this: that the ungodly finally pass into a state of endless evil, of endless torments; that from this suffering there is no hope of escape; that of this evil there is no possible alleviation. That when imagination has called up a series of ages, in apparently endless succession, all these ages of sin and of agony, undergone by the lost, have diminished their cup of suffering by not so much as one single drop; their pain is then no nearer ending than before. Those who hold this terrible doctrine to be a part of the "glad tidings of great joy" to men from their Father in heaven, differ indeed as to the number of the finally lost: some make them to be a majority of mankind, some a minority, even a very small minority. This division of views is instructive, as illustrating the ceaseless revolt of the human heart and conscience against a cruel dogma.

For the Bible is clearly against any such alleviation when read *from their own standpoint*. The texts on which they rely, if they teach the popular creed at all, teach *just as clearly* that the lost shall be the majority of men. "Many are called but *few* are chosen." "Fear not, *little* flock."

Part One—Universalism Asserted on the Authority of Reason

"Narrow is the way that leads to life and *few there be that find it.*" These are our Lord's own words. They present no difficulty to those who grasp the true meaning of "life," and "death," and "election," the true working of the purpose of redemption throughout the ages to come.[2] But they present an insuperable difficulty to that very common form of the traditional creed[3] that seeks to lighten the horror of endless evil by narrowing its range.[4] Indeed, it seems perfectly clear that the popular view requires us to believe in the final loss of the vast majority of our race. For it is only the truly converted in this life (as it asserts), who reach heaven; and it is beyond all fair question that of professing Christians only a small portion are truly converted; to say nothing of the myriads and myriads of those who have died in paganism.

But even waiving this point, the objections to the popular creed are in no way really lightened by our belief as to the relative numbers of the lost and the saved. The real difficulty consists in the infliction of any such penalty, and not in the number who are doomed to it. Nor need we forget how inconceivably vast must be that number, on the most lenient hypothesis. Take the lowest estimate; and when you remember the innumerable myriads of our race who have passed away, those now living, and those yet unborn, it becomes clear that the number of the lost must be something in its vastness defying all calculation; and of these, all, be it remembered, children of the great Parent; all made in his image; all redeemed by the lifeblood of his Son; and all shut up for ever and ever (words of whose awful meaning no man has, or can have, the very faintest conception) in blackness of darkness, in despair, and in the company of devils.

Let me next show what this hell of the popular creed really means, so far as human words can dimly convey its horrors, and for this purpose I subjoin the following extracts:

2 Editor: Allin is referring, of course, to universalists.

3 Editor: By "traditional creed" Allin does not, of course, refer to the Nicene Creed or other such creeds. He means the view that some will not be saved, but will face hell (whether understood as eternal torment or annihilation).

4 Editor: There were a few theologians in the nineteenth century who maintained a belief in hell as eternal conscious punishment, but who argued that relatively few people would suffer such a fate; the majority of mankind would be saved. One thinks, for instance, of the American Calvinist theologian William G. T. Shedd (1820–94) and the Anglo-Catholic Edward Pusey (1800–1882). In the twenty-first century such a view has been tentatively defended by the Reformed theologian Oliver Crisp.

Little child, if you go to hell there will be a devil at your side to strike you. He will *go on striking you* every minute *for ever and ever* without stopping. The first stroke will make your body as bad as the body of Job, covered, from head to foot, with sores and ulcers. The second stroke will make your body twice as bad as the body of Job. The third stroke will make your body three times as bad as the body of Job. The fourth stroke will make your body four times as bad as the body of Job. How, then, will your body be after the devil has been striking it every moment for a hundred million of years without stopping? Perhaps at this moment, seven o'clock in the evening, a child is just going into hell. Tomorrow evening, at seven o'clock, go and knock at the gates of hell and ask what the child is doing. The devils will go and look. They will come back again and say, *the child is burning.* Go in a week and ask what the child is doing; you will get the same answer, *it is burning.* Go in a year and ask, the same answer comes—*it is burning.* Go in a million of years and ask the same question, the answer is just the same—*it is burning.* So, if you go for ever and ever, you will always get the same answer—*it is burning in the fire.*
—Rev. J. Furniss[5]

The fifth dungeon is the red hot oven. The little child is in the red hot oven. Hear how *it screams to come out;* see how *it turns and twists itself about in the fire. It beats its head against the roof of the oven. It stamps its little feet on the floor.*
—Rev. J. Furniss

Gather in one, in your mind, an assembly of all those men or women, from whom, whether in history or in fiction, your memory most shrinks, gather in mind all that is most loathsome, most revolting[;] ... conceive the fierce, fiery eyes of hate, spite, frenzied rage, ever fixed on thee, looking thee through and through with hate[;] ... hear those yells of blaspheming, concentrated hate, as they echo along the lurid vault of hell; everyone hating everyone. ... Yet a fixedness in that state in which the hardened malignant sinner dies, involves, without any further retribution of God, this endless misery.
—Rev. E. B. Pusey[6]

---

5 Rev. John Furniss, C.S.S.R., *The Sight of Hell.* (Dublin: 1870). This was a Catholic book aimed at youth.

6 Editor: Edward Bouverie Pusey (1800–1882) was an English churchman, Regius Professor of Hebrew at Christchurch in Oxford, and one of the leaders of the

Part One—Universalism Asserted on the Authority of Reason

> When you die your soul will be tormented alone; that will be a hell for it: but at the day of judgment your body will join your soul, and then you wilt have twin hells, your soul sweating drops of blood, and your body suffused with agony. In fire, exactly like that we have on earth, your body will lie, asbestos like, for ever unconsumed, all your veins roads for the feet of pain to travel on, every nerve a string, on which the devil shall for ever play his diabolical tune of hell's unutterable lament.
> —Rev. Charles H. Spurgeon[7]

Awful as are these quotations, I must repeat that they give no adequate idea at all of the horrors of hell; for that which is the very sting of its terrors—their unendingness—is beyond our power really to conceive, even approximately, so totally incommensurable are the ideas of time and of endless duration.

It will be said, "we no longer believe in a material hell—no longer teach a lake of real fire." I might well ask, on your theory of interpreting Scripture, what right have you so to teach? But let me rather welcome this change of creed, so far as it is a sign of an awakening moral sense. Yet this plea, in mitigation of the horror your doctrines inspire, cannot be admitted; for when you offer for acceptance a spiritual, rather than a material flame, who is there that cannot see that the real difficulty is the same in either case. If evil in any form is perpetuated then the central difficulty of the traditional creed remains.

Alternatives to Traditional Hell

Conditional Immortality and Annihilation?

Merely to state the traditional doctrine in any form is to refute it for very many minds. So deeply does it wound what is best and holiest in us; indeed, as I shall try to show further on, it is, for all practical purposes, found incredible, even by those who honestly profess to believe it.

Anglo-Catholic Oxford Movement. The quote is from a sermon on Matthew 25:46.

7 Editor: Charles Haddon Spurgeon (1834–92) was a very influential Calvinistic Baptist minister, known as the "Prince of Preachers." The sermon quoted here is sermon 66, on the resurrection of the dead, delivered on Sunday 17 February, 1856, at New Park Street Chapel (later the Metropolitan Tabernacle) in Southwark.

This terrible difficulty, felt and acknowledged in all ages, has been largely met for the Roman Catholic by the doctrine of purgatory, which became developed as the belief in endless torment gradually supplanted that earlier and better faith, which alone finds expression in the two really catholic and ancient creeds,[8] faith in *everlasting life*. How immense must have been the relief thus afforded is evident when we remember that the least sorrow, however imperfect, the very slightest desire for reconciliation with God, though deferred to the last moment of existence, was believed to free the dying sinner from the pains of hell, no matter how aggravated his sins may have been.[9]

Among the Reformed communions this difficulty [with the traditional doctrine of hell] was met, no doubt, by a silent incredulity—often unconscious, yet ever increasing—on the part of the great majority: indeed, some divines have at all times, both in England and on the Continent, openly avowed their disbelief in endless torments.

This growing incredulity has found, in our day, open expression in a remarkable theory, that of conditional immortality (itself a revival of an earlier belief). This doctrine, briefly stated, teaches that man is naturally mortal, that only in Jesus Christ is immortality conferred on the righteous—that the ungodly shall be judged, and, after due punishment, annihilated.

Of this dogma[10] I shall at once say that, while it degrades man, it fails to vindicate God.

> It is that most wretched and cowardly of all theories, which supposes the soul to be naturally mortal, and that God will

---

8 Editor: The Nicene Creed and the Apostles Creed.

9 Editor: Allin's point is that as the doctrine of eternal torment came to predominate in the Western church after the sixth century, the pressure exerted by the shocking nature of the doctrine found some partial release in the development of the doctrine of purgatory. Purgatory is not to be confused with hell in Catholic theology. Purgatory is a postmortem state in which Christians—those destined for heaven—are purified of the remaining sin in their lives and made ready for God's presence in heaven. Hell is for those who do not die in a state of grace and are not destined for heaven. In traditional Catholic theology, purgatory is a temporary state, while hell is an eternal and irreversible state.

10. Is annihilation possible? "Nulla enim natura potest corrumpit ut penitus non sit, et ad nihilum redigatur" (Eriugena, *De div. nat.*, book v). [Editor: John Scotus Eriugena (c.815–c.877) was an unusually gifted scholar, teacher, and churchman from Ireland. His sophisticated philosophical theology was in the Neoplatonic and Origenian tradition. The quotation translates as something like "No nature can be undone so that it ceases to exist and returns to nothing."]

Part One—Universalism Asserted on the Authority of Reason

resuscitate the wicked to torment them for a time, and then finally extinguish them. I can see no ground for this view in Scripture but in mistaken interpretations; and it does not meet the real difficulty at all, for it supposes that evil has in such cases finally triumphed, and that God had no resource but to punish and extinguish it: which is essentially the very difficulty felt by the sceptical mind. I have called it cowardly, for it surrenders the true nobility of man, his natural immortality, in a panic at an objection; and like all cowardice, fails in securing safety.
—John Quarry.[11]

Further, let me reply thus; (1) "I believe in one God the Father Almighty, who wills not the death of a sinner." If, then, even one sinner die finally, God's will is not done, i.e., God is so far defeated and evil victorious. Annihilation is the triumph of death over life: it is the very antithesis to the gospel, which asserts the triumph of Christ over every form of death. It is strange indeed that able men, who write elaborate treatises advocating this view, should overlook the fact that all schemes of partial salvation involve a compromise with evil on God's part.

(2) No less strange is the assertion that the moral sense is not shocked by God, who is absolutely free, yet forcing the gift of life on those whom he knows to be in fact destined to become the prey of evil so completely that they either rot away of sheer wickedness; or, being hopelessly corrupt, are extinguished by their Father.

(3) Death[12] nowhere in Holy Scripture implies annihilation, for earthly destruction is, especially in the case of the Old Testament, that which is denoted by the term, death: but as a rule this term has a wider significance, and one far deeper. Nay, as I hope to point out (chapter 6 on death), there is in scriptural usage, especially in the New Testament, a deep spiritual connection between death and life; death becomes the path to, and the very condition of, life.

11. Editor: John Quarry, *Religious Belief: Its Difficulties in Ancient and Modern Times Compared and Considered* (London: 1880). The exegetical case for conditional immortality is, in fact, considerably stronger than Quarry or Allin recognize. And the exegetical case for humanity's "natural immortality" is very weak. That said, Allin's chief objection to annihilationism—that it would constitute a *failure* for God—is not so easy to refute.

12 Editor: One of the strands in the case for hell-as-annihilation is that the biblical language used of it—death, destruction, perishing, being consumed, etc.—naturally implies *cessation of existence*. The argument is that the language is misunderstood when it is stretched to refer to everlasting existence in torment. Allin is arguing that the *biblical use* of such language does not imply cessation of existence.

The Question Stated

(4) Further, this theory wholly breaks down in practice. So far from "perishing" implying final ruin,[13] Christ came specially to save that which has "perished" (*to apololos*), the "lost," "ruined," "destroyed"; the original term is the same which is often translated "destroy," and on which the theory of annihilation is so largely built. The same word occurs in Luke 15, and there is applied to the sheep [15:4, 6], the coin [15:9], the prodigal son [15:24, 32]—all of which are thus "destroyed," "lost," *and yet finally saved*. In Matthew 10:39 and 16:25, to "lose" (destroy) one's life is stated as the condition of finding it. So Christ is sent to save the "lost" (destroyed) sheep of Israel [Matt 10:6; 15:24; cf. Luke 19:10]. So Sodom and Gomorrah are destroyed, and yet have a special promise of restoration (Ezek 16:53–55). Take the Antediluvians. After they had "died" in their sins they were evangelized by Christ in person (1 Pet 3:19). Hence the unanswerable dilemma: either all these are annihilated or you must give up that sense of "perishing" on which the theory is based.

(5) Probably I have said enough, but yet a very grave difficulty remains. This theory stands in hopeless conflict with the promises to restore all things, to reconcile all things through Christ, which abound in Scripture; nay, which form the very essence of its teaching when describing Christ's empire [see chapter 8]. It seems amazing that able men are found capable of maintaining that a reconciliation that is described as coextensive with all creation (Col 1:15–20) can be equivalent to restoring some (or many) things, only after annihilating, as hopelessly evil, all the rest.

Pious Agnosticism?

Another view adopted by a number, probably extremely large, and increasing, differs altogether from that last stated. Those who hold it have had their eyes opened to the fact that the New Testament contains very many long-neglected texts that teach the salvation of all men. They have also learned enough to have their faith gravely shaken in the popular interpretation of the texts usually quoted in proof of endless pain. The theory of conditional immortality fails to satisfy such men. They see that it is altogether unsuccessful in meeting the real difficulty of the popular creed, i.e., the triumph of evil over good, of Satan over the Saviour of

---

13 Editor: Annihilationists argue that the biblical language about the lost "perishing" (*apollumi*) implies a cessation of existence. Allin disputes this.

Part One—Universalism Asserted on the Authority of Reason

man, and therefore over God. They perceive, too, the narrow and arbitrary basis on which it rests in appealing to Holy Scripture. And so they decline to entertain it as any solution of the question, and say, "We are not able definitely to accept any theory of the future of man, because we do not see that anything has been clearly revealed. Enough has been disclosed to show to us that God is love, and we are content to believe that, happen what will, all will ultimately be shown to be the result of love divine."[14]

It is impossible to avoid sympathy with much of this view at first sight, but only then; for when closely examined it is seen to be open to the charge of grave ambiguity, or far worse. It may mean that in the future God will act as a loving human parent would, and then, I reply, this is precisely the larger hope. Again, it may mean a very different and very dangerous thing. It may mean that at the last my ideas of right and wrong will undergo a complete change—that the things that I now pronounce with the fullest conviction to be cruel and vile will at that day seem to be righteous and just, and that thus God will be fully justified though he inflict endless torment.

---

14 Editor: Pious agnosticism on the ultimate fate of humanity—whether all will in fact be saved in the end or whether some will finally be lost forever—is also very common in the twenty-first century. For many theologians it is more than a simple inability to pick which way to jump—it is a *theologically principled* position. To claim with the universalist that all *will* be saved is considered presumptuous, but so too is the anti-universalist claim that all will *not* be saved. We simply do not and *cannot* know such things. We can and should *hope* that all will be saved, but to try to press beyond hope to certainty is a theological mistake.

This principled agnosticism may be predicated on certain views about divine freedom and the inappropriateness of humans seeking to squeeze God into human systems of thought; it may be because of certain view regarding God's creating space for libertarian human freedom, even when the consequences are finally tragic; it may be because of a felt need to hold in dialectical tension what are considered two strands of biblical teaching—the salvation of all and the damnation of some—that cannot be harmonized in the straightforward way that most theologians, whether universalists or eternal hellers, do.

Allin is responding to a less developed version of agnosticism than this. His agnostics claim to be willing to be corrected at the eschaton as to their provisional understandings of what is right and wrong, good or bad. They now consider eternal torment to be bad, but perhaps they are mistaken. Allin sees such a view as very dangerous. However, Allin's critique would need supplementing to counter some of the more nuanced versions of agnosticism now on offer (or indeed those of F. D. Maurice and F. W. Farrar). For what it is worth, I consider the more sophisticated versions of pious agnosticism to be mistaken, but this is not the place for an analysis of them.

But take this statement to pieces and see what it really means. It means, in effect, practical scepticism. It means blank agnosticism. This is easily shown. For what this view really tells me is that my deepest moral convictions are wholly worthless, because that which they declare to be cruel and revolting, is right and holy, and will so appear at the last. But if this be so, then I have lost my sole measure of right and wrong. What is truth or goodness, I know not. They cease to be realities; they are, for all I know, mere phantoms. Religion, therefore, is impossible. Conscience ceases to be a reliable guide. Revelation is a mere blank, for all revelation presupposes the *trustworthiness* of that moral sense to which it is addressed. Thus the above plea, plausible as it seems, is wholly ambiguous, and does in fact lead either to the larger hope, or to mere unbelief.

Universalism?

In opposition to both these theories stand the views here advocated, which have been always held by some in the catholic church; nay, which represent, I believe, most nearly its primitive teaching. These views are, I know, now widely held by the learned, the devout, and the thoughtful in our own and in other communions. Briefly stated, they amount to this: that we have ample warrant—alike from reason, from the observed facts and analogies of human life, from our best and truest moral instincts, from a great body of primitive teaching, and from Holy Scripture itself— to entertain a firm hope that God our Father's design and purpose is, and has ever been, to save every child of Adam's race.

Therefore I have called this book *Universalism Asserted*. But let there be no mistake. I assert this not as a dogma,[15] but *as a hope:*[16] as that which after many years of thought and study seems to me to be the true meaning of Holy Scripture, as it is certainly in harmony with our moral sense, and has been taught by so many saints in the early church. The term,

---

15 Editor: By "dogma" Allin means a teaching of the church that one is required to affirm (or at least, forbidden to deny) in order to be considered an orthodox Christian. Universalism has never had that status in the church.

16 Editor: Allin is not to be confused what is now sometimes called a "hopeful universalist" (see fn 14). "Hope" here is not a mere expression of something that he'd *like* to happen and which he thinks *may* happen, but a *conviction* about what *will* happen; the stronger "hope that does not disappoint" (Rom 5:5). But he calls it "hope" to contrast it with the more central notion of "dogma." It is solidly grounded, but does not ascend to the level of dogma.

Part One—Universalism Asserted on the Authority of Reason

"universalism,"[17] may not, indeed, commend itself to some, but I retain it advisedly. It seems to convey an essential truth. "The kingdom of Christ ... is in the fullest sense ... universal."[18] It is a universal remedy to meet a universal evil. While sin is universal, and sorrow and pain universal, shall not our hope be universal too? Shall not life be as universal as death, and salvation as universal as sin? Can we even think of a divine life and a divine love as other than in their very essence universal?

---

17 Editor: Some are suspicious of "universal*ism*" because they think that God is being squeezed into human systems and *a priori* categories. "God *has* to be like this because my system demands it of him." But God is free and *self*-determined—he is not subject to any created constraints. However, this critique is in danger of getting hot and bothered about a word. What really matters is the theological view being designated by the word. It is the specific views, with all their nuances, that should be the subject of reflection and critique.

18 Editor: The quotation is from Joseph Barber Lightfoot (1828–89), an English New Testament scholar, the Lady Margaret Professor of Divinity in Durham, and Bishop of Durham. I do not know which book the quotation is from.

2

The Popular Creed Wholly Untenable

Part 1

"These questions ... educated men and women of all classes and denominations are asking, and will ask more and more till they receive an answer. And if we of the clergy cannot give them an answer, which accords with their conscience and reason ... then evil times will come, both for the clergy and the Christian religion, for many a year henceforth."
—Canon Charles Kingsley[1]

"The answer which the popular theology has been tendering for centuries past will not be accepted much longer. ... I disclaim any desire to uphold that theology which I have never aided in propagating."
—Rev. Dr. Richard Littledale[2]

1 Editor: Charles Kingsley (1819–75) was an Anglican priest, Regius Professor of Modern History at the University of Cambridge (1860–69), and a canon of Chester Cathedral (1870–73). His most famous book was *The Water Babies* (1863). Allin quotes from *The Water of Life and Other Sermons* (London: 1867). The quotation is from Sermon VI: The Shaking of the Heavens and the Earth.

2 Editor: The quotation is from *The Contemporary Review*, a magazine founded

PART ONE—Universalism Asserted on the Authority of Reason

Introduction

At the outset let me protest against the common and ignorant prejudice that connects universalism with lax views of sin or of dogma. As to the first, I shall have occasion bye and bye to point out that no system so effectually affirms God's hatred of sin as that which teaches that he cannot tolerate its existence for ever. Again, as to the second, I shall largely base my argument for universalism on the fullest acceptance of the great catholic verities. A narrow catholicism is a contradiction in terms.

To this point I shall return, confining myself here to the remark that a partial salvation aims a blow at both the incarnation and the atonement. For a vital part of the incarnation is the taking of the race of man, *as an organic whole*, into God through Jesus Christ, the second Adam. But with this fundamental idea, a partial salvation is in hopeless contradiction. No less vital is the blow aimed by the popular creed at the atonement. First it dishonors the cross by limiting its power to save to the brief moments of earthly life. Further, it virtually teaches that the cross is a stupendous failure. This is easily shown. For plainly that which misses its end is a failure. And if the end aimed at be noble, then in proportion is the failure greater and vital. But the scriptural evidence is overwhelming that the object of Christ's death was to save the *world*. "The Father sent the Son to be the Saviour of the world." He came that the world through him might be saved; i.e., the world in all its extent, not a part of it, however large. If, then, this end be not gained, if the world be not in fact saved, the atonement is so far a failure. Disguise the fact as men may, the dilemma is inevitable. Answer, or evasion, there is none.

The next step will be to state more in detail the various considerations that render it impossible to accept the traditional view of future punishment; or any modification of it that teaches the endless duration of evil, moral or physical, in even a solitary instance; a fact essential to bear in mind when I refer to the traditional creed, or the popular creed, anywhere in this book.

---

in 1866 by a group of intellectuals to promote informed and thoughtful opinion on the great issues of the day. Rev. Richard Frederick Littledale (1833–90) was a regular contributor.

Hell Undermines Christian Ethics

My first appeal shall be to that primary revelation of himself which God has implanted in the heart and conscience of man. I am merely expressing the deepest and most mature, though often unspoken, convictions of millions of earnest Christian men and women, when I assert that to reconcile the popular creed, or any similar belief in endless evil and pain, with the most elementary ideas of justice, equity, and goodness (not even to mention mercy), is wholly and absolutely impossible. Thus, this belief destroys the *only ground* on which it is possible to erect any religion at all, for it sets aside the primary convictions of the moral sense; and thus paralyses that by which alone we are capable of religion. If human reason be incompetent to decide positively that certain acts assigned to God are evil and cruel, then it is equally incompetent to decide that certain acts of his are just and merciful. Therefore, if God be not good, just, and true, *in the human acceptation of these terms*, then the whole basis of revelation vanishes. For if God be not good in our human sense of the word, I have no guarantee that he is true in our sense of truth. If that which the Bible calls goodness in God should prove to be that which we call badness in man, then how can I be assured that what is called truth in God may not really be that which in man is called falsehood? Thus no valid communication—no revelation—from God to man is possible; for no reliance can, on this view, be placed on his veracity.

"We dare not," says the Bishop of London, "let go the truth, that the holiness, the goodness, the justice, the righteousness, which the eternal moral law imposes on us as a supreme command, are identical in essential substance, in our minds and in His."[3]

"*We dare not!*" Why? Precisely because, if we do, the foundations of religion collapse—perishing as the moral order perishes. We are worshipping once more the unknown God. Mere scepticism is our sole refuge. We have lost our standard of right and wrong, and are wandering in a pathless desert, creedless, homeless, hopeless, mocked all the while by phantoms of virtues that are probably vices, and of vices that are probably virtues. For let me repeat that if goodness in becoming infinite turns

---

3 Editor: The quotation is from Frederick William Temple (1821–1902), Bishop of London (1885–96) and later Archbishop of Canterbury (1896–1902). While Bishop of London he gave the prestigious Bampton Lectures (1884) on the theme of *The Relations between Religion and Science* (London: 1884). The quotation is from Lecture II: The Origin and Nature of Religious Beliefs.

PART ONE—Universalism Asserted on the Authority of Reason

into evil—if infinite love may be consistent with what we call cruelty—then, for all we know, truth may turn into falsehood, justice into flagrant wrong, light into darkness. Therefore, *we dare not* let go the truth that in our moral nature we have a true revelation of the divine mind, i.e., that the ideas of right and wrong are in their essence *the same* in our minds and in God's—that they are true *universally;* as true beyond the grave as here and now. But if so, then that which so flatly contradicts all our deepest moral convictions, as does the dogma of endless sin (a dogma which, however modified, no imaginable hypothesis can reconcile with either justice or mercy) must be absolutely *false*, and in teaching it we are but libeling God.

Further, if endless evil may be defended, in even a solitary case, it may be defended logically in every case. This follows strictly from the ground taken by advocates of the traditional creed. "They say we cannot judge what is cruel or the reverse on God's part." Be it so, for argument's sake. Then it follows that if every human being fall under the sway of evil for ever, and God be thus left face to face with a universal pandemonium, then we should have no right even to murmur, for we have [no] right to judge, having no faculties adequate to the task.

But in fact we are not alone justified in arguing from our own minds to God's; we are *forced* to do so, or to remain agnostics. It is from our minds that we gain a knowledge of the divine mind, from the working of our intelligence and will that we gain a knowledge of God's will and intelligence. This is the pathway God has traced, the foundation he has laid. And there is no other possible. "Ils ont beau me crier: souments ta raison. . . . *Il me faut des raisons pour soumettre ma raison.*"4

We smile at the ignorant savage who mutilates his body, thinking thereby to please his God. Are not we far worse who think to please our God by mutilating our noblest part, and to *hear him better by silencing his voice in us?* But our opponents do not forbid the argument from our nature to God: they only forbid the argument from what is best in our nature to his. They are ready to ascribe certain base qualities of humanity

4 Editor: The quotation is from Book IV of Jean-Jaques Rousseau's (1712–78) treatise on education and the nature of humanity, *Émile* (1762). Here it is in its wider context, with the quoted words in italics: "Let's truly look for the truth then, paying no heed to birthright or the authority of fathers or pastors, but let's come back to the examination of conscience and ideas of right and wrong, everything they taught us from our childhood. In vain *they shout at me, they cry: 'Bring your reason to heel';* they can keep on saying this. What trips me up is: *I need reasons to bring my reason to heel.*" (Translation Beckie Cox.)

to God. Because we delight in vengeance, so does God. Because we are cruel, God must be so. But eighteen hundred years have not taught the mass of Christians to credit their heavenly Father with even so much love for his children as a frail woman can feel for her offspring.

Hell Undermines the Doctrine of God's Goodness

The mode in which the ordinary creed does its hateful work of hardening the sceptic, and saddening the most devout, may be shown by two brief extracts. "All the attempts yet made," says a stern moralist, "to reconcile this doctrine with divine justice and mercy, are calculated to make us blush, alike for the human heart that can strive to justify such a creed, and for the human intellect that can delude itself into a belief that it has succeeded in such justification."[5]

"Nothing," says the late General Gordon,

> can be more abject and miserable than the usual conception of God.... Imagine to yourself what pleasure it would be to Him to burn us, or to torture us. Can we believe any human being capable of creating us for such a purpose? We credit God with attributes which are utterly hateful to the meanest of men.... I say that Christian Pharisees deny Christ.... A hard, cruel set they are, from high to low. When one thinks of the real agony one has gone through in consequence of false teaching, it makes human nature angry with the teachers who have added to the bitterness of life.[6]

The popular view is familiar, and most men do not realize its true bearing, or the light in which it really presents the *character* of God. But consider how this dogma of endless evil must strike an inquirer after God, one outside the pale of Christianity, but sincerely desirous of learning the truth. There are such men—there are many such. You tell this inquirer that God is not almighty only, but all good; that God is indeed love; that

---

5 Editor: The quotation is from William Rathbone Greg (1809–81), *The Creed of Christendom: Its Foundations and Superstructure* (London: 1851), chapter 17. Greg was an English essayist.

6 Editor: General Charles George Gordon (1833–85) was a highly respected army officer, best known for his service in China and Africa. The quotation is from *Colonel Gordon in Central Africa, 1874–1879*, edited by George Birkbeck Hill (London: 1881), from a document written in Khartoum, Sudan, and dated 15 November 1878.

PART ONE—Universalism Asserted on the Authority of Reason

God is his Father. But these terms are words *without any justification at all*, if they have not their common ordinary sense when applied to God.

Such a man will say, "You tell me God is good, but what acts are these you assign to him? He is a father; but he brings into being myriads of hapless creatures, knowing that there is in store for them a doom unutterably awful. He calls into existence these creatures, whether they will or no; though the bottomless pit is yawning to receive them, and the flames ready to devour them. The question is not, whether they might have escaped; the real questions are, *do they in fact escape?* and *does God know* that they will not escape? and, knowing this, does he, *acting freely, yet create* them? And you assure me that this Great Being is almighty, is love essential, is the Parent or the Creator (here the terms are practically equivalent) of every one of these creatures who are doomed and damned." What fair answer do you propose to give to these questions if addressed to you? I may put the inquiry in the words of a well-known poet. A lost soul asks:

> Father of mercies, why from silent earth
> Did You awake, and curse me into birth?
> —*Night Thoughts*.[7]

Unsuccessful Attempts to Avoid the Problem

Attempt 1: God Will Try His Best

Pressed by the irresistible weight of these arguments many take refuge in ambiguous and evasive phrases, e.g., "Be sure God will do the best he can for every man." Ambiguous and evasive words, I repeat, as used by the advocates of endless torment and evil. For if they really mean that the *best* an Almighty Being can do for countless myriads of his children is to bestow on them—practically to force on them, whether they will or not—an existence, stained with sin from the womb, knowing that in fact

---

[7] Editor: Allin has wrongly attributed this poetic line. *The Complaint: Or, Night Thoughts on Life, Death, and Immortality* is a long poem written by Edward Young (1683–1765) and published between 1742 and 1745. It was highly regarded in its day. However, the line quoted by Allin is from another of Young's poems, "The Last Day: A Poem in Three Books" (1713). The line is from Book III and is part of a poetic paraphrase of the book of Job.

this sin will ripen into endless misery, then such phrases as the above are but so much dust thrown in our eyes; they are as argument beneath refutation. And if they do not mean this, such pleas are worthless as a defense of the ordinary creed. If endless misery is the certain result, known and foreseen, of calling me into existence, then to force on me the gift of life is to do for me not the best, but the worst possible.

Attempt 2: Universalism Has Worse Problems

Others take refuge in the vain assertion that the larger hope implies the escape of the wicked from all punishment, and places the sinner on a level with the saint. Let me once for all reply that no statement can be more unfounded. For the very method of healing the finally impenitent, as taught by the larger hope, is the severity of the divine judgment, is that consuming fire, which must burn up all iniquity. Thus the larger hope is especially *bound to teach* for the obstinate sinner the certainty of retribution, for in God's judgments it sees the mode of cure (see chapter 6), the mode in which the grace of the atonement often reaches the touched heart. Thus, unrepented sin leads to awful future penalty, to penalty proportioned to the guilt of the sinner and continued till he repent. The larger hope—so falsely called "sentimental"—thus not merely accepts, but *emphasizes* for the ungodly the dread warning of wrath to come—of the fires of Gehenna—for in these it sees not a wanton revenge, but at once a just retribution; and a discipline that heals the obstinate sinner.

Attempt 3: Hell is Needed to Warn Aliens(!)

Again, it is said that perhaps the flames of hell may be needed to terrorize some far distant sinful orb; that rebels against God in some other planet may read, by the light of hellfire, the dangers of sin. Yes, it has been gravely alleged that a Being, whose name is Love, will light, and keep alight through unending ages, a ghastly living torch for such a purpose as this—a torch, each atom of which is composed of a lost soul, once his child, once made in his image, once redeemed by the cross of his dear Son! You know this has been taught, and yet you actually complain that men are sceptical, and that thoughtful artisans reject such a creed with scorn.

Part One—Universalism Asserted on the Authority of Reason

Attempt 4 & 5: The Horrors of Hell Are Spiritual and Only for a Minority of People

Many, too, but in vain, seek to mitigate the just horror and loathing that the popular creed inspires, by saying that the torments of hell are not material but spiritual; and by asserting further (contrary to the plainest teachings of experience) that somehow the majority do really turn to God in this life, or at the last moment of half conscious existence. I say nothing of the bribe thus offered to the selfish instincts of the majority, by the assurance that somehow they will shuffle into heaven, and that only a worthless few perish. But this shabby plea is (1) false from the standpoint of those who teach it (chapter 1), and (2) does not, if true, even touch the central difficulty of the popular creed. For whether our Father *permits* (to use the softest term) the endless misery and evil of countless myriads upon myriads of his own children, or of thousands only; whether hell receives 50, or 5, or only 1 percent of the sons of God, of the brothers of Christ Jesus: and again, whether its torments are applied to their bodies, or to their spirits, all these are points that, however decided, do not even *touch* the central question, i.e., can evil be stronger than God, ever, under any circumstances?—can a Father permit the endless, hopeless sin and woe of even one of his children, and look on calmly for ever and ever unmoved and unsympathising—can the Bible be mocking us when it teaches a restitution of all things, and that a time is coming when God shall be "all in all" [1 Cor 15:28].

Attempt 6: Humans Cannot Judge God's Ways

Some will, no doubt, say that we have no right to measure God's ways by our private judgments, no right to seem to dictate what he will or will not, can or cannot do. I reply that this objection rests on a complete misapprehension. We do not presume to discuss what God, in the abstract, can or cannot do, still less to dictate to him. The argument employed in these pages is open to no such objection as the above, for it is simply this—that God has, both in his primary[8] revelation of himself to our moral sense

---

8 Editor: By speaking of divine revelation to the conscience as "primary," I do not take Allin to mean that it is more important or more reliable than divine revelation in Christ or in Scripture, but that it is more *direct* and that it is the *first* source of divine revelation an individual has, because it is innate. The issues surrounding claims to innate knowledge of God or of ethics are somewhat murkier than Allin appreciates.

and in his written word, distinctly and emphatically declared against the doctrine of endless evil. Because God has so spoken, we therefore speak.

Attempt 7: Hell Is a Natural Consequence of Sin

Others again assert that endless misery is sufficiently accounted for by saying that it comes as the natural result of sin, and not as arbitrarily decreed. I am wholly unable to see how this in the very least alters the divine promise to restore all things, or annuls the work of Christ, which is to "put away sin by the sacrifice of himself" [Heb 9:26]. Surely the more *natural* the tie between sin and misery, the more assured is the destruction of both; for the closer the bond, the more certain it becomes that to put away (i.e., to abolish) (Heb 9:26) the one is to abolish the other.

Attempt 8: People Who Choose Sin in This Life Will Always Choose Sin

But the law of continuity, however, it is said, forbids universalism. Those who go on to the close of life impenitent must be presumed to continue impenitent hereafter. But why? They will continue so only if the forces working for impenitence hereafter are stronger than the forces making for good. And the conditions under which these forces will work in a future state will certainly be very unlike those now obtaining, and very much more favourable to conversion.

> In that other life there will be no room for unbelief, when Christ has been seen. Then that great source of evil which is in the flesh, will be at an end; no inner lust will remain: no external food for vice: no temptation to concupiscence, to ambition, to avarice, will survive. How then the lost can for ever cling to sin, unless divinely hardened, I fail to see.
> —Thomas Burnet[9]

I may add that beyond the grave illusions will cease. Here men are blinded; and most often, if not always, follow evil not as being evil, but as a fancied good. "Had they [i.e., the rulers of this age] known, they would

---

9 Editor: The quotation is from Thomas Burnet, *De Statue Mortuorum et Resurgentium* (London: 1720) [On the State of the Dead and the Resurrection]. Burnet (1635–1715) was an English writer on theology and cosmogeny. His book on the dead was, perhaps fittingly, published after his death.

Part One—Universalism Asserted on the Authority of Reason

not have crucified the Lord of Glory" (1 Cor 2:8)—pregnant words. In fact, this objection seems but a roundabout way of saying that the devil is stronger in the long run than God. Surely the presumption, even apart from a revealed promise of the restoration of all things, is that evil, being an intruder and an alien, and the world being under divine government, this government can never cease working till order and right wholly replace disorder and wrong. Why are we to assume that God means to share his throne for ever with the powers of evil, or that he has, in any case, exhausted his means of cure in the present brief life?

In fact, we totally err in our estimate of the relative strength of good and evil when we treat the latter as though it were on a par with the former in fibre, in duration, or in essence. For this there is no shadow of excuse: it is dualism thinly disguised. It is this degrading heresy to which the traditional creed is ever tending. I deny, then, any presumption that because evil has gone on for years it will go on always. The logical and moral presumption is precisely the other way, viz., that the weaker will in the long run yield to the stronger; the usurper to the lawful owner; the evil one to God.

Further, the facts of the physical and spiritual worlds are alike fatal to any such narrow theory of continuity. What is the creation but a striking breach of continuity? So, too, was the deluge; so is every earthquake, etc., etc. And it is worth careful noting that the only appeal in Scripture to the laws of physical continuity comes from the unbeliever, and is made *in the interests of scepticism* (2 Pet 3:4). I admit that there probably is a higher continuity than any we can at present trace. The very breaks in the established order may be but parts of a higher order, and may thus range themselves on the side of, and not against, a true continuity. But it is impossible to argue that, merely because a certain order of things continues for long unbroken, it will therefore go on for ever. If so, there could be no creation, no resurrection, no final judgment. It is merely suicidal for a Christian to argue as the objection requires.

Attempt 9: For Life to Be a Real Test It Requires the Possibility of Ultimate Failure

I turn to consider a further objection frequently alleged against the larger hope. It is said that probation, in order to be real, involves the possibility of some utterly failing. Note first, the ambiguity of this plausible plea. It

The Popular Creed Wholly Untenable

speaks only of a possibility of failure; I ask, then, *must* some be lost finally, if all are put to a real trial? Unless this be so, the objection does not help the traditional creed; for if 1,000 persons can be tested without a single failure, why not 10,000 or 100,000? Why not all?

But if a real probation of all involves endless evil in some cases, then I reply such probation is an immoral thing. For probation is but a means to an end, viz., the promotion of a higher standard of virtue than if men were not tested. Now it is immoral to use an instrument that brings to some men a higher standard at the cost of the endless ruin of others. A higher type of virtue in the saved would be an evil, if gained practically at such a price as the hopeless degradation of the lost, and the perpetuation of evil in the universe.

Meantime, all the difficulty arises from men's believing *probation* to be an adequate description of our position under God's moral government—an assumption *absolutely groundless*. Such conceptions imply a radical and most mischievous error, viz., that God's relation to us is like that of a head engineer testing his works, or a police inspector on a vast scale. But God is "our Father," and if so, the central fact is, and must be, his *education* of his children. True, we are being tested, but only as a part of our *education*—which is the real conception of our position as God's children. Realize this truth, and how absurd becomes the objection we are discussing: how truly absurd it becomes to say "*God's education cannot be real unless some of his pupils go the devil for ever*"; or, there cannot be a second probation—which really means that God cannot continue and complete his work of education.

Attempt 10: Why Bother Asking about Human Destiny? We'll Never Know the Answers

Some again say—"Why try to solve a question that is probably insoluble, viz., the problem of man's destiny?" In reply we ask what the objection really means. Are we to give up every great question because we can only partly solve it? To do so would be to give up all questions, to bid farewell to all knowledge. For every great question contains an insoluble element. Take, for example, the problems of life, of matter, etc. Take such questions as the Trinity, or the incarnation. Are we to give them all up? All human knowledge is in fact the knowledge of things partly known, partly insoluble at present. To act as the objection requires would simply land us

Part One—Universalism Asserted on the Authority of Reason

in agnosticism, scientific and religious. Lastly, the objection lies equally against the traditional creed, for that decides this so-called insoluble question quite as much as does universalism—a fact that the objectors quietly ignore.

Attempt 11: Universalism Undermines Public Morality

A further plausible argument against universalism is the alleged danger of teaching the larger hope. Those who so argue surely forget what their words involve if true. They involve a serious reflection on the Creator (a) who permits his children, made in his image, to descend to such an abyss of degradation that only an endless hell can restrain them from sin; and who, (b) knowing this, yet conceals, or permits to be concealed, from the vast majority of men this necessary antidote to sin; and who, (c) in the Old Testament, gave a special revelation of himself, and said nothing or almost nothing of it. And this cry of danger has been used against every improvement, moral, social, or scientific.

Having premised this, I meet the objection frankly by saying—look at the verdict of history. Its answer is decisive. Never did lust and vice in every guise so rage and riot as when in the Middle Ages this dogma was most firmly held. Hellfire bred a veritable hell on earth. Those who talk of universalism as antinomian do not face the facts of history. Better were it if they did so, and then were to look at home, and remember the awful danger of teaching a creed whose fruits are so often those well described in the following striking words, in which a Roman Catholic priest states twenty years' experience in the confessional:

> The dogma of hell, except in the rarest cases, did no moral good. It never affected the right persons. It tortured innocent young women and virtuous boys. It appealed to the lowest motives and the lowest characters. *It never, except in the rarest instances, deterred from the commission of sin.* It caused unceasing mental and moral difficulties. ... It always influenced the wrong people, and in a wrong way. It caused infidelity to some, temptations to others, and misery without virtue to most.
> —Rudolph Suffield[10]

10 Editor: The quotation is from Rev. Rudolph Suffield, a former Catholic priest. The comments are from a statement he made during the controversy that arose after the publication in *The Contemporary Review* (April 1873) of a speech by Lord Lilford Thomas Littleton (1833-96), given at Sion College, London.

What, I ask, has the dogma of endless pain and sin really effected? Has it checked the growth of heathenism in our cities? Has it kept the artisan in the fold of Christ? Can a single sin be named which it has banished from our midst? Has the gospel of fear evangelized thoroughly a solitary English family?

Hellfire is preached inside the church, while outside the baptized harlot plies her trade, and the burglar weaves his plot. What wonder, so long as we preach to the fallen a God nominally loving, but in fact a God whose acts towards myriads of his children would excite horror even amid the outcast and the lost. Ineffective always, such teaching is more than ever so in these days, because the intelligent are by it forced into open revolt; and because experience clearly teaches that gigantic penalties go hand in hand with gigantic crimes, and penalties diminished to a reasonable amount with diminished sin. Such has been the result in our penal code. Such has been the result in Norfolk Island,[11] in Western Australia, in Germany, in Spain, etc. Excessive terrorism provokes not only incredulity, but mirth. Even in days far more credulous than ours, Satan, in the religious dramas, soon subsided into a clown; his appearance provoked shouts of laughter.

But true universalism deters from sin, because it preaches a righteous retribution with unequaled force and certainty: on this its creed largely hinges. Restoration is taught *because* of retribution, a fact on which too much stress cannot be laid. "You, Lord, are merciful for you render to every man according to his work" (Ps 62:12).

Attempt 12: A Freewill Defence of Hell

But probably the way in which most people satisfy their own minds, when doubts arise as to the endless nature of future torment, is this: "Endless pain and torment is but the result of sin freely chosen and finally persisted in by the sinner."[12]

---

11 Editor: A small island in the Pacific Ocean.

12 Editor: The relative space that Allin gives to the freewill defence of hell indicates its significance in his own day. It remains a key apologetic for hell in twenty-first-century theology. The key contemporary Christian universalist critics of it are Thomas Talbott in *The Inescapable Love of God*, especially chapter 11, and John Kronen and Eric Reitan, *God's Final Victory*, chapters 7–8. Also of note is the work of Marilyn McCord Adams, "Hell and the God of Justice"; Adams, "The Problem of Hell: A Problem of Evil for Christians." It is interesting to note that many of the points that these

Part One—Universalism Asserted on the Authority of Reason

First, before discussing this, let me ask—*why* all this stress laid on man's will to ruin himself, rather than on God's will to save? Is man the pivot on which all hinges? To me it seems bad philosophy, and worse theology, not to recognize God as center, and his will and purpose as supreme. But to resume:

(1) I would point out one consequence of defending endless evil and misery on the plea of man's free choice, viz., that if this plea avail in any one case to excuse endless evil, it would avail, logically, in every case: and it would justify a universe in which every reasonable being should choose evil finally, and God should remain presiding over a universal hell.

(2) Again, if endless sin be repugnant to every true conception of God, if it be repugnant to morality for God freely to create any being for whom such a doom is reserved, then you do not alter this fact by any possible theory as to the power of the human will. That which is incapable of defense morally, remains indefensible still.

(3) Next, you cannot fairly oppose a mere theory to a revealed assurance of the reconciliation of all things to God finally. Your theory indeed proves a *possibility* of the final choice of evil: you cannot reasonably oppose a [logical] possibility, to a direct statement of him who made the human will.[13]

(4) Next let me add, that the very term "free will" is ambiguous; it may mean a will partly or a will wholly free. If it mean the former, I am most willing to admit man's freedom. But if the latter be meant, then let me remind my readers that the acts of a will wholly free, i.e., undetermined by motive, *would have no moral value whatever.*

(5) Doubtless the problems of freedom and necessity contain an insoluble element. But we can look at them practically. You insist that everything depends on human choice. I reply, see how on the contrary man's choice is limited at every hand. First, man is born in sin; that is certainly not wholly free. Take, next, the facts of life. In the first place man can exercise no choice at all as to the time and place of his birth—facts all important in deciding his religious belief, and through that his character; no choice as to the very many and very complex hereditary influences moulding his entire life, though most often he knows it not; affecting for good or for evil every thought, every word, every act of his; no choice at

---

Christian philosophers develop are found in seed form here in Allin's work.

13 Editor: It is perhaps worth noting that some recent universalist philosophers have argued that freely choosing to reject God forever is not even a logical possibility. See Talbott, *Inescapable Love of God*; Kronen and Reitan, *God's Final Victory*.

all as to the original weakness of his nature, and its inherent tendency to evil. More, still, man can exercise no choice at all on this *vital* question, whether he will or will not have laid on him the awful perils, in which, on the popular view, the mere fact of life involves him. Further, man can exercise no choice at all as to the strength of that will he receives; no choice at all as to the circumstances that surround him in infancy and childhood, and which colour his whole life; man has no choice as to the moral atmosphere he must imbibe in those early years of training, which colour almost of necessity, the whole after life. "But a creature cannot" you reply, "choose these things, from the very nature of the case." That, I answer, only proves my point, that a creature cannot be wholly free, from the very nature of the case. What the facts point to is that God grants a limited freedom, intending to train man, his child, for the enjoyment hereafter of perfect freedom.

(6) The vast extent of human ignorance also confirms the view that the final destinies of the universe are not placed in man's keeping. We know nothing absolutely, we know but appearances—phenomena. We are acquainted with the outsides of things at most, with the insides never. We talk of life, of matter, but these and all other things are in themselves to us unknown and unknowable. Everything we do, every object we see, every natural operation is to us incomprehensible. Are these the hands to which a wise Creator is likely to commit absolutely the awful issues of endless sin, the ruin of creation?

(7) But it is said that if man be not wholly free, his goodness is but a mechanical thing. If so, I reply, better ten thousandfold mechanical goodness that keeps one at the side of God for ever, than a wholly unrestrained freedom that leads to the devil. But the assertion is in fact as hollow as it is plausible. Man is not a machine because the power of defying God finally is not granted to him. Freedom enough is granted to resist God for ages; freedom to suffer, and to struggle; to reap what has been sown, till, taught by experience, the will of the creature is bent to the will of the Creator. If all this does not involve a freedom that is real, though limited, then human words are vain as a vehicle for human thought.

(8) A reasonable theory of human free will is in perfect accord with universalism: so true is this, that the greatest advocates of the larger hope have been the most earnest champions of free will, *and often base on it their teachings*;[14] while the advocates of endless sin and hell, like

---

14 Editor: In regard to this observation, and in light of the often-made claim

PART ONE—Universalism Asserted on the Authority of Reason

Augustine and Calvin, have been enemies to free will.[15] Indeed, man's rescue depends on his freedom.

(9) Further, this pleading for endless sin in hell on the ground that it is freely chosen by man, would, if true, but enhance the great difficulty of the popular creed—the victory of evil; for plainly, the more free on man's part, the more willful his choice of sin, so much the more complete is the triumph of evil, so much the more absolute is the failure of the cross. What is this plea but in fact seeking to vindicate the Almighty by laying stress on his defeat, seeking to justify Omnipotence by emphasizing his impotence?

(10) This plea contradicts itself; for to assert that because of man's freedom he can go on for ever choosing evil, is, in fact, to plead not for human freedom, but for servitude, the basest, the most degrading. Take the assertion to pieces and it comes to this. To preserve man's dignity he must be permitted to become the slave of evil if he will, the associate of devils for ever—to secure his prerogative of freedom he must be allowed to sink into hopeless servitude to sin. What would you say were an earthly father to reason thus?—I will permit my child to become a hopeless drunkard for the sake of preserving his sobriety; I will permit my daughter to sink into vice for the sake of preserving her chastity. Under these circumstances, it is mere rhetoric to talk of "forcing" the will. The will yields, because it is free, and because good is finally the strongest force in an universe ruled by God.

(11) Nay, the only condition of true freedom for man is the divine control. The seeming paradox is true—constraint of man's will, because it is weak and evil, is his emancipation. "If the Son make you free, then

---

that universalism is inconsistent with freewill, it is interesting to observe that all the patristic defenders of universalism were staunch advocates of human freewill. For instance, freewill was at the core of Origen's polemic against Valentinian Gnosticism and Stoic versions of *apokatastasis*. But freewill, in their estimation, was not incompatible with universal restoration: "I do not deny in the least that the rational nature will always keep its free will, but I declare that the power and effectiveness of Christ's cross and of his death . . . are so great as to be enough to set right and save, not only the present and the future aeon, but also all the past ones, and not only for this order of humans, but also for the heavenly orders and powers" (Origen, *Comm. in Rom.* 4.10).

15 Editor: While Augustine and Calvin thought that sin deeply compromised freedom, such that humans are unable to choose God, they acknowledged that even sinful humans had *some* degree of freedom. They did, however, oppose understandings of human freedom that are incompatible with a very strong view of divine sovereignty. Modern philosophers might describe them as compatibilists.

shall you be free indeed" [John 8:36]—*"Deo servire est libertas."*[16] To plead against this constraint of the divine grace, as annulling human freedom, is as unreasonable as it would be on the part of the friends of some fever-stricken patient to object to the restraints of the sick room and the physician. A lunatic is to be restrained; a criminal to be imprisoned; an incendiary to be arrested; but the moral criminal, the spiritual incendiary, these are not to be constrained, even by grace divine! They are to gravitate slowly to perpetual *bondage*—in the name, I repeat, of *Liberty*? God's will is to be set at naught permanently, in order that the devil's will may be done.

(12) Next, is it not strange that this claim to be independent of God, to defy his control finally, is made for man in one direction only, i.e., precisely when and where it may do to him irreparable mischief? We cannot add so much as a cubit to our stature, cannot determine so much as the length of an eyelash. We cannot of ourselves take a single step heavenwards. But we can, on this theory, take as many steps hellwards as we please. We cannot save ourselves, but we can damn ourselves.

(13) But again, it obviously follows that if man is in this sense free, i.e., is free to defy God finally, then either (a) God does not in any real sense will the salvation of all men, but does will man's absolute freedom, at the cost of his salvation (if the two conflict), or (b) he does will it, but is unable to accomplish it. And, if so, then [God] is not free. He wills but his will is useless to save; it is fettered and bound. And what is this but a virtual denial of the true God? Whoever such a being may be, he is not the God of the Bible. To the *very essence* of God it pertains to be sovereign and supreme over all wills and all things whatsoever. "I appeal to the tribunal of a sovereign judge," says Canon Westcott, "whose will is right, and whose will must prevail." And again, "It is enough for us to acknowledge the supreme triumph of divine love from first to last—one will of one God reconciling the world to Himself in Jesus Christ His only Son."[17]

(14) It is impossible to quote more than a fraction of the passages in which Scripture, while *recognizing in man a power of choice*, so that

---

16 Editor: "Serving God is freedom."

17 Editor: Brooke Foss Wescott, *The Historic Faith: Short Lectures on the Apostles Creed* (London: 1883). The quotation is from Lecture 5 on the birth, suffering, and death of Christ. B. F. Wescott (1825–1901) was a biblical scholar and churchman, serving as a canon in both Peterborough and Westminster and, from 1890, Bishop of Durham.

PART ONE—Universalism Asserted on the Authority of Reason

no one is saved against his will, but by God's working in him a good will, yet points distinctly to God's will as supreme, as certain finally to prevail.

> "My counsel shall stand, and I will do all my pleasure." (Isa 46:10)
> "Whatever the Lord pleased, that did he, in heaven and on earth." (Ps 135:6)
> "He does according to his will, in the armies of heaven and among the inhabitants of earth." (Dan 4:35; 5:21; 4:3, 17; 7:14; Prov 19:21; 21:1; Pss 69:13; 99:1; 103:19; 10:16; 29:10, etc., etc.)

Nay, Scripture goes further still. It tells us plainly that the creature (creation) has been made "subject to vanity [sin and imperfection], not willingly, but by reason of him who has subjected the same in hope" (Rom 8:20). Again, "God has shut up all unto disobedience that he might have mercy upon all" (Rom 11:32). And so of salvation we are plainly told that it is "*not of him who wills, but of God who shows mercy*" (Rom 9:16). "You are saved *not of yourselves*," says St. Paul (Eph 2:8). And St. John assures us that the sons of God are born *not of the will of man, but of God*" (John 1:13). "You," says a greater than St. John, "have *not* chosen me, but *I have chosen you*" (John 15:16). So the gospel is the proclamation of his kingdom. "Your kingdom come," not your salvation, but your *rule*. We are to work (and so far are free), but behind and above and beneath our work, there rules and works the will of God.

"Work out your own salvation," says the apostle [Phil 2:12]; but *why*? Not because here is a sphere outside the divine will, but, precisely because here too God rules, *"for* it is *he* [i.e., God] who works in you, both to will and to do." It is *"not* according to our works" that he calls and saves (2 Tim 1:9), but "according to his own purpose"; "according to the counsel of his own will" (Eph 1:11). This divine supremacy is ever in Saint Paul's thoughts in passages too numerous to quote. And so our Lord does not hesitate to say "compel"—literally *necessitate—*"them to come in" (Luke 14:23). For "the Lord God omnipotent reigns" (Rev 19:6).

Men fear the reproach of Calvinism, which is quite another creed from this; and so have lost all true conception of a divine sovereignty, which is universal love. Nor is man a machine, because God is and must be Master in his own house. Man *can resist*, but God's grace is stronger. Perhaps the strongest assertion the New Testament contains of human freewill is Matthew 23:37, "You would not"; but, reading on, we learn that even they, who would not, are one day to say, "Blessed is he that comes in the name of the Lord."

The exigencies of controversy must be great to induce men to teach, on the authority of the New Testament, that the clay can absolutely defy the great Potter. May I remind our opponents that, when controversy is forgotten, we all in fact admit this divine supremacy. So the [Anglican] Prayer Book tells us that God can *"order the unruly wills of sinful men,"*[18] evidently teaching that he will do this. It states that he disposes the hearts of kings (and if so, of all) as it seems best—not to human freewill—but to his will and governance.[19]

That which Scripture so plainly affirms, the very idea of redemption implies. For redemption is either an empty sound, or it implies setting free the will of man, i.e., bringing it into harmony with God's will. "The bondage I groan under is a bondage of the will, and that has led me to acknowledge God as emphatically the redeemer of the will; . . . but if of my will then of all wills."[20]

I have stated my glad acquiescence in human freedom, only preserving God's freedom and sovereignty. For if consciousness assure me of a freedom very real in its own sphere, yet there is another side: a Divinity that "shapes our ends, rough-hew them how we will"[21]—words that may fitly sum up this controversy.

---

18 Editor: This is the collect for the fourth Sunday after Easter in the Book of Common Prayer (1662): "O Almighty God, who alone canst order the unruly wills and affections of sinful men: Grant unto thy people, that they may love the thing which thou commandest, and desire that which thou dost promise; that so, among the sundry and manifold changes of the world, our hearts may surely there be fixed, where true joys are to be found; through Jesus Christ our Lord. Amen."

19 Editor: This is in the prayer for the monarch, which begins: "Almighty and everlasting God, we are taught by thy holy Word, that the hearts of kings are in thy rule and governance, and that thou dost dispose and turn them as it seemeth best to thy godly wisdom . . . ."

20 Editor: The quotation is from a letter by F. D. Maurice to "a Lady" written on 4 May 1864. Frederick Denison Maurice (1805–72) was a well-known theologian and Christian Socialist. From 1840–53 he held professorships in English history and literature and then in divinity at King's College London. However, he was forced out as a result of theological controversy about his views about "eternal" punishment. Maurice was not a universalist, but he did reject traditional views of hell as everlasting torment.

21 Editor: These are the words of Hamlet to Horatio in Shakespeare's *Hamlet* (Act V, scene 2). It is an acknowledgment of divine providence at work behind the human choices we make, no matter how roughly cut they are.

PART ONE—Universalism Asserted on the Authority of Reason

Challenges for Traditional Hell

The God of Traditional Hell is Ungodly

In resuming, let me draw an argument from the fact of creation, a subject to which I shall return in a future chapter. "Nothing," says Bishop Newton, "is more contrariant to the divine nature and attributes than for God to bestow existence on any being, whose destiny He foreknows must terminate in wretchedness without recovery."[22] Let us take an illustration that we may see this more clearly.

> A frail and narrow bridge swings across a gulf, fearful and fathomless. On this, as it rocks wildly in the winds, a father places his young child. Beyond, on the other side of the gulf, he has placed a prize beyond estimate, which he promises to the child if he passes the bridge safely, and then compels him to go, commanding him to look neither to the right nor left.... The boy, heedless and disobedient, hesitates, reels, the bridge quivers for a moment, swings from under him, and hurled into the gulf, he is caught and impaled on a sharp rock down the abyss. There he hangs for long and weary years, agonizing and writhing in torture, and crying to his father for help and deliverance. But his father turns a deaf ear to all his entreaties, wholly indifferent to the horrible sufferings of his child, and justifies himself by saying, "The boy might have passed the bridge safely, he was warned, and he suffers justly." Admitting the possibility of passing safely, yet all men would pronounce this father a monster and a fiend. And shall God place me on the frail and narrow bridge of life, stretched over the awful and flaming abyss of endless perdition, with the possibility of a heaven beyond, and then leave me there to cross it, swinging fearfully in the winds of temptation, knowing that as a matter of fact I shall, in crossing, be precipitated into the horrible pit, there to lie for ever in hopeless agony?[23]

---

22 Editor: Thomas Newton, *The Posthumous Works of the Right Reverend Thomas Newton* (London: 1787). The essay in question—a dissertation "On the Final State and Condition of Men"—is found at the end of volume VI. Thomas Newton (1704–82) was made Bishop of Bristol in 1761 and Dean of St. Paul's, London, in 1782.

23 Editor: This is an extract from Thomas Baldwin Thayer, *Theology of Universalism: Being an Exposition of Its Doctrines and Teachings, in Their Logical and Moral Relations* (Boston: 1862). Thomas Thayer (1812–86) was a universalist theologian and

Who would not cry out with the poet already quoted—

> And canst Thou then look down from perfect bliss
> And see me plunging in this dark abyss,
> *Calling Thee Father in a sea fire,*
> *Or pouring blasphemies at Thy desire?*[24]

Yes, the question is essentially this, and no argument can evade this inquiry: is God good, and is he a just God, as men use these terms, or is he not? Indeed, if the God we worship be not good, as we call goodness, it were better for us not to worship him at all; better for us to worship nothing at all, than to worship an evil deity. But the popular view represents God as doing that which the most degraded human being would not do. "This view," says the Rev. Dr. Littledale, "puts God on a moral level with the devisers of the most savagely malignant revenge known to history"[25]—words that fall far short of the truth.

Hell: Satan Triumphant

To this in fact it comes, that the popular view, while admitting God's power and goodness to be infinite, yet teaches that evil shall ultimately prevail—a position obviously untenable, and indeed absurd. "Order and right cannot but prevail finally in a universe under His government."[26] For argue as you please, refine, explain away, it continues still an *insuperable* difficulty, on the popular view, or any mere modification of it, that the devil is victor, and triumphs over God and goodness. It is nothing at all to the purpose to allege, either that those who perish finally have chosen evil of their own will, or that all evil beings are shut up in chains and torment: it is the very permanence of evil in any shape: its continued presence—*no*

---

pastor from New England who ministered both there and in New York.

24 Editor: The poet is Edward Young. See fn. 7 above.

25 Editor: The quotation is from *The Contemporary Review*. On which, see fn. 2 above.

26 Editor: Joseph Butler, *The Analogy of Religion, Natural and Revealed, to the Constitution and Course of Nature* (London: 1736). Joseph Butler (1692–1752) was an English theologian, philosopher, and churchman; a convert to the Church of England from Nonconformity. From 1738 he was Bishop of Bristol and in 1750 he was Bishop of Durham. The *Analogy of Religion* was an influential text in which Butler argues that the analogy between the principles of divine government as seen in Scripture and as perceived in nature lead us to conclude that the same God is author of both. In the context of the controversy over deism, Butler makes out a case for orthodoxy.

matter from what cause—that constitutes the triumph of the evil one. "To suppose," says Canon Wesccott, "that evil once introduced into the world is for ever, appears to be at variance with the essential conception of God as revealed to us."[27] I repeat that if evil be as strong as God, as enduring as God himself, there is no escape from the conclusion that you proclaim in so teaching the triumph of the evil one. You are proclaiming, not the catholic faith, but a dualism. You blot from the faith of Christendom its fundamental article, "I believe in one God the Father *Almighty.*"

What are all heresies, all errors, that have stained the church of God, compared with this supreme heresy, this dualism, which seats evil on the throne of the universe, a power enduring as God himself? The torments, physical and mental, of the popular hell, awful as they are, recede into almost nothing as compared with the far more awful spectacle of God vanquished, of God trying to save but failing, and watching his children as they slowly sink beneath the endless sway of evil; of God's Son returning, not in triumph, but in defeat; of the cross so far prostrate, paralyzed, vanquished.

Again, so revolting to our moral nature is the popular creed, that it, more than any other cause, as has been said, produces the most widespreading unbelief. "Compared with this," remarks J. S. Mill, "all objections to Christianity sink into insignificance."[28]

The Crippling Missional Effects of Hell

Let me speak plainly. Too long—far too long—have the clergy been silent; content to complain of a scepticism, of which a main cause is a doctrine

---

27 Editor: B. F. Westcott, *The Historic Faith*. See fn. 17 above.

28 John Stuart Mill (1806–73) was an exceptionally influential British philosopher, political and economic thinker, and civil servant. He was one of the key defenders of utilitarianism, refining the moral theory developed by Jeremy Bentham (1748–1832). The quotation is from Mill's "The Utility of Religion," one of his *Three Essays on Religion* (1874). Here are the words in fuller context: "The recognition, for example, of the object of highest worship, in a being who could make a Hell; and who could create countless generations of human beings with the certain foreknowledge that he was creating them for this fate. Is there any moral enormity which might not be justified by imitation of such a Deity? And is it possible to adore such a one without a frightful distortion of the standard of right and wrong? Any other of the outrages to the most ordinary justice and humanity involved in the common Christian conception of the moral character of God, sinks into insignificance beside this dreadful idealization of wickedness."

they continue to teach (without, I believe in many cases, more than a languid and merely traditional acceptance of it). And as this doctrine is the parent of unbelief at home, so abroad in the mission field it is a grievous hindrance to the spread of the gospel. The very heathen are shocked by a dogma more cruel and horrible than anything of which they have ever heard; the more so when they are asked to receive this awful teaching as part of the message of good news. There is certainly a chapter of missionary work yet unwritten, which would, if frankly told, surprise the friends of the traditional creed. This is a chapter that any thoughtful person can construct, if he will try to place himself in the position of an intelligent heathen, when he learns that the *good news* of the missionary contains a revelation often more ghastly and cruel than any that has crossed his mind. A cruel gospel produces a scanty harvest. I repeat that no thoughtful man can believe a doctrine condemned by the conscience; and so men will seek a refuge in scepticism when they hear the clergy teaching these evil traditions (for they are no more) as part of the revelation of that God whose blessed Son tasted death for every man. Yes, the peculiar horror of the popular creed is that it sets up evil as an object of worship—of reverence—of love.

Traditional Hell and the Unforgivable Sin

Nor let us forget the insult offered to God by the traditional creed. Amid the crowd of sins there stands out one in sad preeminence because it has not forgiveness "for the age" (*eis ton aiōna*),[29] its forgiveness demands ages—demands a period indefinitely long [Matt 12:31–32]. Now, from our Lord's own words we may understand in what lay the essence of this awful sin. It lay in confounding the good and evil Spirit, in ascribing to the one the works of the other. If, then, any one whose conscience whispers that endless misery can only be inflicted by an evil being on his own children, still persists in ascribing its infliction to God, does not such a one incur sad and awful risk of committing this greatest of all sins? I invite your earnest attention to this. Does your conscience say I cannot reconcile this awful doctrine with any idea I can form of love, of justice, or of goodness; and yet I believe it? If so, then beware lest in ascribing such things to God, you come perilously near to, if indeed you are not

---

29 Editor: strictly speaking Matthew 12:32 says that the one who blasphemes against the Spirit "will not be forgiven, either in this age or in the age to come."

guilty of, this sin, which is of all sins the greatest (known in the popular creed as the unpardonable sin).

An Existential Challenge

Yes, the question of all questions is: Is God indeed love? Is the gospel really good news, not possible but *actual* glad tidings to all? All around us thoughtful men are more than ever reflecting on these points; what answer do you propose to give? They are thus inquiring—pondering—of themselves, of their lot, of their hopes and fears in the future: "I find myself in this world"—so run the thoughts of each inquirer—"on me are laid, *whether I will or no*, the awful responsibilities of time and of eternity. Sin has from the very womb crippled me, before any power of choice was possible for me. For this calamity, too often, I receive blame and not pity. Is it fair or just to bestow sympathy on a body naturally crooked, and to have no pity, but wrath, for a spirit naturally crooked? At my entrance on life I received a nature already fallen; and that for no fault of mine; stained, and that with no sin of mine. And to this nature so weak, so fallen, come, in every variety, temptations, wiles, and allurements such that no man has wholly withstood, or can withstand, their subtle power. Now, if this be a part of my training, if it be a path to better things, I can in submission—nay, in gladness even—bend to my Creator's will: I can take courage, and though faint, still pursue the narrow path that leads to life. But how can I believe that a loving Father—all powerful as he is all good, and absolutely free—does so arrange, does so permit, that for any one soul, this sad and fallen estate of human nature shall prove but the portal to endless woe; that the gift of life, which providence has forced on me, shall ripen to endless woe and sin?"

So men reason. I do not wonder, I rejoice, that they have ceased to believe that a divine parent can do that which an earthly parent could not do without eternal infamy. For imagine any possible degree of folly and sin that can stain human nature, to be accumulated on the head of some sinful child of man; and I ask, can you believe that any human father, any mother, that once loved that child, could bring herself calmly to sentence her offspring to an endless hell; nay, herself to keep that child there in evil that never shall terminate?

Evacuating Claims for Christ's Salvific Work of Content

Take next a clear exposure of the traditional creed from another point of view. Christ, we know from the Bible, is the Saviour of the world. He is, therefore, on the popular view, the Saviour of those whom in fact he does not save.[30] This evidently follows. But this principle once admitted, it is wholly immaterial, as a matter of reasoning, what the percentage of the lost may be. Although out of the countless myriads of our race but a few hundreds were saved, God would still *save every man*. Indeed, though *not even one solitary soul* were saved, God would still, on the principle popularly held, save *every* man. For that principle is this, that to offer salvation, though the offer come to nothing, is to save. Hence it undoubtedly follows that God might be the Saviour of the whole race of men, *though not one soul were in fact saved*. All might be *saved* on this principle, though all were in fact *damned!*

Christ Is Not Saviour of the Most Sinful

But there is a further difficulty in the way of the popular creed. Who are those whom it represents as finally unsaved?—the finally impenitent, the most obstinate sinners. And what is that but to say, in so many words, that those precisely whose case furnished the strongest reason for the Saviour's mission are unsaved? Admit their guilt, recognize as we do to the very utmost the need and certainty of retribution; still, when all this has been said, it remains true that Christ came to save the "lost," and if so, the more "lost" any are, the more Christ came to seek and to save them, and if he fails, the more marked his failure.

Thus, on the ordinary view, precisely those for whom Christ especially came receive no salvation; those whose claims are strongest perish, those whose claims on a Saviour are weakest, are rescued. For the fullest admission of the guilt of sin must not blind us to the sinner's claim

---

30 Editor: The critique in this section would not apply to classical Calvinism. Classical Calvinists would not claim that Christ died for all people or for the whole world. Instead he died only for the elect. The "all" in question are not all individual people but all *types* of people from all over the world. This position has its own exegetical and theological problems, but it is not vulnerable to Allin's critique here. However, free-will theism, whether of classical Arminian or Open Theistic varieties, is susceptible to Allin's argument, for it does claim that Christ is the Saviour of those who are not, in the end, saved. Allin's argument is that this view is in danger of evacuating the claim that Christ is Saviour of meaning.

Part One—Universalism Asserted on the Authority of Reason

on our sympathy. Sin abounding calls out grace much more abounding [Rom 5:20]; such is the great principle enunciated by Saint Paul. Are we to say with the traditional creed, sin abounding beyond certain limits (obstinate sin) ceases to call out grace?

Let us apply this consideration to a plea often used to disguise, if that may be, the awful fact of endless torment by teaching that but few, comparatively, will share this horrible lot. Elsewhere I have shown the futility of this plea, on other grounds—but here I desire to press this aspect of the case that these few are precisely those whose case appeals most of all to a Saviour. Hence, so to argue, implies a misconception of the very essence of the gospel.

Am I to say the Good Physician can heal all, except those who need him most? He came to save *sinners* (emphatically sinners) [1 Tim 1:15]. Am I to read the passage thus: he came to save all sinners *except the greatest?*

Hell as a Justification for Torture

And let us not forget how much the traditional creed has fostered in man a spirit of cruelty. It is sad, but true, to recollect how much of the suffering inflicted by man on his brother man has been due, directly or indirectly, to the belief in an endless hell. It gave to torture an apparent divine sanction—"In every prison the crucifix and the rack stood side by side." Mediaeval torments have a character peculiar to themselves "They represent a condition of thought, in which men had pondered long and carefully on all the forms of suffering; had combined, and compared, the different forms of torture, till they had become the most consummate masters of their art."[31] For if men believed that God would light up the gloomy fires of hell and keep them blazing to all eternity, it was an easy and a natural step, to set up in his name a little copy of his justice, and thus, as it were, to anticipate God's sentence. "As the souls of heretics are hereafter to be eternally burning in hell," such was the reasoning of Queen Mary in defense of her awful persecution, "there can be nothing

---

31 Editor: This is a quotation from W. E. H. Lecky, *History of the Rise and Influence of the Spirit of Rationalism in Europe*, vol. 1 (London: 1865). William Edward Hartpole Lecky (1832–1903) was an Irishman who abandoned his original intentions of training for the Anglican priesthood to become a historian.

more proper than for me to imitate the divine vengeance, by burning them here on earth."[32]

I say, that however familiar this may be, it is necessary to ponder well the sad facts, for, by awaking a righteous horror and indignation, we may often most effectually combat such dogmas. And more must be said, not alone have the popular doctrines done all this, but they have greatly influenced for evil the general course of human legislation, and human thought. Many pages might be filled in enumerating the horrors and anguish added to human life by these doctrines. Let me only add that they have poisoned the very fount of pity and love, by representing him, whose we are, and before whom we bow, as calmly looking on, during the endless cycles of eternity, at the sin and agony of myriads upon myriads of his creatures.

Hell and Spiritual and Moral Deformation

Thus it is that by this shocking creed the moral tone is lowered all round, wherever it is accepted. Men are familiarized with the idea of suffering and sin as permanent facts. They have even in some sort learned to consider heaven as dependent upon the belief in an endless hell. The very holiest men believing the popular creed are unconsciously depraved, morally and spiritually. You will find for instance, even one like Keble, pleading for endless torment (see hymn for second Sunday in Lent[33]) on the ground that if this were not true, then endless bliss in heaven would also not be true.

> [And is there in God's world so drear a place
>   Where the loud bitter cry is raised in vain?
> Where tears of penance come too late for grace,
>   As on the uprooted flower the genial rain?

---

32 Editor: This comment is attributed to Mary Tudor (1516–58, queen from 1553–58). After becoming queen, Mary sought to reverse the English Reformation and return England to Catholicism. Under the Heresy Acts, which she revived, 283 Protestants were executed, most by burning. The burnings were unpopular, but Mary pursued them with determination. This earned her the nickname Bloody Mary.

33 John Keble (1792–1866) was an Anglo-Catholic churchman and a leading member of the influential Oxford Movement; his 1833 Assize Sermon on "National Apostasy" giving the movement its kick-start. The hymn in question is found in Keble's most famous work, *The Christian Year* (1827). The hymn has been inserted into the main text in this edition so readers can see what Allin is referring to.

Part One—Universalism Asserted on the Authority of Reason

'Tis even so: the sovereign Lord of souls
  Stores in the dungeon of His boundless realm
Each bolt that o'er the sinner vainly rolls,
  With gathered wrath the reprobate to whelm.

Will the storm hear the sailor's piteous cry,
  Taught so mistrust, too late, the tempting wave,
When all around he sees but sea and sky,
  A God in anger, a self-chosen grave?

Or will the thorns, that strew intemperance' bed,
  Turn with a wish to down? will late remorse
Recall the shaft the murderer's hand has sped,
  Or from the guiltless bosom turn its course?

Then may the unbodied soul in safety fleet
  Through the dark curtains of the world above,
Fresh from the stain of crime; nor fear to meet
  The God whom here she would not learn to love;

Then is there hope for such as die unblest,
  That angel wings may waft them to the shore,
Nor need the unready virgin strike her breast,
  Nor wait desponding round the bridegroom's door.

But where is then the stay of contrite hearts?
  Of old they leaned on Thy eternal word,
But with the sinner's fear their hope departs,
  Fast linked as Thy great Name to Thee, O Lord:

That Name, by which Thy faithful oath is past,
  That we should endless be, for joy or woe:
And if the treasures of Thy wrath could waste,
  Thy lovers must their promised Heaven forego.

But ask of elder days, earth's vernal hour,
  When in familiar talk God's voice was heard,
When at the Patriarch's call the fiery shower
  Propitious o'er the turf-built shrine appeared.

Watch by our father Isaac's pastoral door—
  The birthright sold, the blessing lost and won;

> Tell, Heaven has wrath that can relent no more;
>   The Grave, dark deeds that cannot be undone.
>
> We barter life for pottage; sell true bliss
>   For wealth or power, for pleasure or renown;
> Thus, Esau-like, our Father's blessing miss,
>   Then wash with fruitless tears our faded crown.
>
> Our faded crown, despised and flung aside,
>   Shall on some brother's brow immortal bloom;
> No partial hand the blessing may misguide,
>   No flattering fancy change our Monarch's doom:
>
> His righteous doom, that meek true-hearted Love
>   The everlasting birthright should receive,
> The softest dews drop on her from above,
>   The richest green her mountain garland weave:
>
> Her brethren, mightiest, wisest, eldest-born,
>   Bow to her sway, and move at her behest;
> Isaac's fond blessing may not fall on scorn,
>   Nor Balaam's curse on Love, which God hath blest.]

To put it plainly, he would, as I understand his words, purchase heaven's unending bliss at the terrible cost of the endless, hopeless, torture of the lost! Here I will only say that I know not whether his logic or his moral tone be more unsound. Compare the spirit of Keble with, I will not say the spirit of Christ, but with that of St. Paul, who wished himself accursed from Christ, if thereby he could save his brethren [Rom 9:1–3]. As to Keble's argument, that will be, I trust, fully answered in considering, in a later chapter, Matthew 25:46. Meantime, as a further illustration, I copy the following from a periodical lying before me:

> I was talking the other day with a very learned Catholic ecclesiastic, who told me that he had been called on to give the last sacraments to a poor Irishman. He found his penitent with some freethinking friend, who was arguing that there was no hell. The dying Celt raised himself up with much indignation; "no hell," he exclaimed, "then where is the poor man's consolation?"
> —*The Church Reformer*[34]

34 Editor: *The Church Reformer* was a monthly newspaper published by The Guild

PART ONE—Universalism Asserted on the Authority of Reason

Hell and the State of the Redeemed in Heaven

THE PROBLEM OF THE JOY OF THE REDEEMED

Let us take another point. We cannot reasonably suppose that the saints in heaven are without any memory of the past. Even Dives, in the flames of Hades, remembers with pity his brethren [Luke 16:27]. But unless you make the impossible supposition that the blessed lose all memory in heaven, then they must either suffer keenly at the thoughts of the torments of their dear ones lost in hell, and tormented for ever and ever; or they must be on a *lower level*, morally and spiritually, than was even *Dives*—choose which alternative you please. To this dilemma no answer has ever been given, for no answer is possible.[35] If Hades kindles the sympathy of the lost, shall heaven kill the sympathy of the blessed? If the blessed sympathize with the torments of the lost, can they enjoy even a momentary happiness? If they fail to sympathize, are they not sunk in selfishness and debased? Or shall we say that God actually maims his redeemed, depriving them of knowledge and memory, lest they should miss their lost ones? On this view God's ways are so awful that if known they would wither up the very joys of heaven, and so he shuts out pity, and wraps the blessed in a mantle of selfish ignorance. I know nothing more degrading or revolting in the traditional creed than the baseness of its heavenly state. Fancy a mother thrilled through with bliss while (near, or far off, it matters not) her child is in the grip of devils; a wife joining in the angelic harmonies, while her husband for ever blasphemes!

---

of St. Matthew in London. This was a group of clergy and laity who were Christian Socialists with Anglo-Catholic sympathies. Its editor, from 1884 to 1895, was Rev. Stewart Duckworth Headlam (1847–1924), a polemical figure frequently involved in controversy.

35 Editor: This argument was previously deployed by the German Reformed theologian Friedrich Schleiermacher (1768–1834). Allin was aware of Schleiermacher's universalist sympathies, but it appears he had not read his work. He never quotes from Schleiermacher and, apart from this argument here, he never draws on ideas from Schleiermacher's work, even when discussing issues (e.g., election) where they would have proved helpful. The argument against hell from the happiness of the redeemed is today best associated with the Christian universalist philosopher Thomas Talbott.

The Redeemed Rejoicing in the Suffering of the Damned

Such is the heaven of the ordinary creed; if it be not something worse still, an exulting over the torments of the lost. To show that this is no mere figure of speech, I append a few extracts. They are from sources so widely apart as a medieval school man, and a modern puritan.

> That the saints may *enjoy* their beatitude more thoroughly, and give more abundant thanks for it to God, *a perfect sight* of the punishment of the damned is granted them.
> —St. Thomas Aquinas[36]

Take another instance from Peter Lombard:

> Therefore the elect shall go forth to see the torments of the impious, seeing which they will not be grieved, but will be *satiated with joy* . . . at the sight of the *unutterable* calamity of the impious.
> —Peter Lombard[37]

Again, hear another from a modern divine:

> The *view of the misery of the damned* will *double* the ardor of the love and gratitude of the saints in heaven.

This is the opinion of the once famous Jonathan Edwards.[38] Another American divine uses even stronger language: "This display of the divine character," said Samuel Hopkins,

---

36 Editor: Thomas Aquinas (1225–74), an Italian Dominican friar, is considered by many to be one of the greatest theologians in the history of the church. He philosophical theology was in the Augustinian tradition, but it represented a significant development of that tradition in light of the rediscovery in the West of the works of Aristotle. The quotation is from Aquinas' most famous work, *The Summa Theologica III*, Question 94, Article 2.

37 Editor: Peter Lombard (c. 1096–1164) was a great Italian scholar who studied in Reims and Paris. He taught at the Cathedral school in Notre Dame and for a brief time before his death was the Bishop of Paris. His greatest work was *Libri Quatuor Sententiarum* (*Four Books of Sentences*), written around 1150—a compilation of biblical texts and passages from the church fathers and mediaeval thinkers on the whole theological curriculum. For four hundred years it was the most influential book in medieval universities, aside from the Bible itself. The quotation is from Book 4:50.

38 Editor: Jonathan Edwards (1703–58) was an influential Puritan pastor in Northampton, Massachusetts, famed for his preaching. He played an important role in the religious revivals of the First Great Awakening (1733–35) and was one of the truly great and original American intellectuals. The quotation is from a sermon on Matthew 25:46 entitled "The Eternity of Hell Torments," dated April 1739. Sadly Edwards is

PART ONE—Universalism Asserted on the Authority of Reason

> will be most *entertaining* to all who love God—will give them the *highest and most ineffable pleasure. Should the fire of this eternal punishment cease, it would in a great measure obscure the light of heaven, and put an end to a great part of the happiness and glory of the blessed.*
> —Samuel Hopkins[39]

To this the popular creed has degraded the ministers of Christ, to penning passages like the above (easily to be multiplied)—passages than which all literature does not contain anything more revolting. It is easy to be shocked at all this, and to repudiate it, but *how is it possible* for the friends of God to be otherwise than *pleased with his judgments?*

I must ask you, as a relief, to read the following touching picture:

> What if a soul redeemed, a spirit that loved
> While yet on earth, and was beloved in turn,
> And still remembered every look and tone
> Of that dear earthly sister, who was left
> Among the unwise virgins at the gate:
> Itself admitted with the bridegroom's train—
> What if this spirit redeemed, amid the host
> Of chanting angels, in some transient lull
> Of the eternal anthem, heard the cry
> Of its lost darling, whom in evil hour
> Some wilder pulse of nature led astray,
> And left an outcast in a world of fire,
> Condemned to be the sport of cruel fiends,
> Sleepless, unpitying, masters of the skill
> To wring the maddest ecstasies of pain,
> From worn-out souls that only ask to die—
> *Would it not long to leave the bliss of heaven,*
> *Bearing a little water in its hand,*
> *To moisten those poor lips that plead in vain;*

---

best known for a rhetorically powerful and infamous sermon entitled "Sinners in the Hands of an Angry God" (1741). But it would be a mistake to dismiss his sophisticated theology out of hand on the basis of that sermon or sentiments such as those expressed in the quotation Allin selects.

39 Editor: Samuel Hopkins (1721–1803) studied divinity with Jonathan Edwards (see previous fn) and served as a Congregationalist minister in Massachusetts from 1743–69 and in Rhode Island from 1770–1803. Along with Jonathan Edwards he is considered to be a founder of so-called New England Theology, a kind of "consistent Calvinism." The quotation is from *An Inquiry concerning the Future State of Those Who Die in Their Sins* (Rhode Island: 1783), Section IV, sermon 8, on the reason for the doctrine of endless punishment.

With Him we call our Father?
 —O. W. Holmes[40]

Traditional Hell Makes Light of Sin

Hell as God's Eternal Toleration of Sin

I say next that the popular creed does in fact teach men to think lightly of sin. This seems a paradox, and no doubt you wonder: but consider for a moment what the fact is. Tell me that God will permit an eternal hell, with its miserable population of the lost, to go on sinning to all eternity; and what idea is it you really convey to me? It is, I reply, the *toleration of sin*. Have you ever thought of this? "Nothing so effectually teaches men to bear with sin as the popular creed, because we profess to believe that God will bear with it for ever."[41]

Hell and God's Toleration of Sin in This Life

Further, I say that the practical effect of the ordinary creed is to teach men to think lightly of sin in a very large class of cases, for example, where a careless and ungodly life has been lived, and no apparent repentance has marked the closing scene. For to those who believe that the few days or moments remaining of life on a sick bed, are the sole period in which salvation is possible, how irresistible must be the temptation to patch up a hollow peace, to accept anything in lieu of a genuine repentance. And so not the thoughtless, but teachers grave and holy—e.g., Dr. Pusey—do in fact, as they endeavor to escape the awful difficulties of the ordinary creed, lay stress on the possibility or probability of men leading a wicked life, up to the very last moment of existence, and in that last moment receiving the divine grace. Can any teaching be at once more repugnant

---

40 Editor: Oliver Wendell Holmes, Sr. (1809–94) was a well-known American physician, lecturer, and a celebrated poet who lived and worked in Boston. He was friends with other literary luminaries such as H. W. Longfellow and Ralph Waldo Emerson. The quotation is from *The Poet at the Breakfast Table* (Boston: 1872), a work that combines fiction and nonfiction, prose and poetry.

41 Editor: I have been unable to source this quotation.

PART ONE—Universalism Asserted on the Authority of Reason

to all experience, more contrary to all reason, and more likely to cause the young and the careless to make light of sin?

Indeed, it is often precisely those who most deeply feel the taint and evil of sin who reject most completely the popular creed; for in proportion to their horror at sin, is the depth of their conviction that sin cannot go on for ever.

Hell and the Infinite Increase of Sin

There is, too, this further question: if sin is to endure for ever in hell, must it not increase and go on increasing for ever and ever? Think to what point of horror the accumulated sin of the myriads of the lost will have reached, when even a few of the cycles of eternity are over: and this vast and inconceivable horror and taint is to go *on*, and *on*, and *on*, for *ever*, and *ever*, and *ever* increasing, under the rule of him who is of purer eyes than to behold iniquity. Think of endless blasphemy and rottenness: of moral foulness tainting God's universe: the leprosy of undying evil poisoning all around: cries of endless agony blending with the angelic choir. God knows how painful such thoughts are to write down. But it is a duty to try and bring home to men's minds what the traditional creed really means.

> Think, too, how grotesque a parody of the divine justice it is to say, as the popular creed does, that God requires obedience and righteousness here, but if he cannot have these, He will be satisfied with endless disobedience and sin hereafter as a substitute. We are gravely told that if the wrong be not righted within a specified time, justice will be satisfied to increase the wrong infinitely, and perpetuate it to all eternity.[42]

I repeat that the powers of imagination, if taxed to the utmost, could hardly conceive any more ludicrous parody of justice than the above.

---

42 Editor: I have been unable to source this quotation. The last sentence appears in Thomas B. Thayer, *Theology of Universalism*, section V. It reads, "All agree that sin is a wrong a great wrong. This being so, what has justice to do in the case? what are its demands? what will satisfy them? We are told that if the wrong be not righted within a specified time, justice will be satisfied to increase the wrong infinitely, and perpetuate it to all eternity! Can anything be more unjust than such justice?" Thomas Thayer (1812–86) was a prominent nineteenth-century universalist theologian.

The Human Incapacity to Suffer Hell

But there is this further difficulty. For we must ask—how is this perpetuation of evil possible? Can a literal fire for ever prey on the hapless limbs, and never consume them? Can nature support this for ever? Are we to return to the hideous conception (of some early writers) of the "intelligent fire," which renews, as it consumes, in order to make the agony endless? Or if we take a more spiritual view of future punishment, can degradation be perpetual? Must not such a process end at some time from its very nature?

The Problems of Infinite Punishment

THE INJUSTICE OF INFINITE PUNISHMENT FOR FINITE SINS

Further, all sin, be it never so black (and God forbid that I should even seem to weaken its blackness), is but finite. Yet, for these finite sins, I am told, an infinite punishment is the due penalty. But finite and infinite are wholly incommensurable terms. Have you ever set yourself seriously to realize what punishment protracted *for ever and ever* indeed means? In fact, the idea of illimitable time mocks our utmost efforts to grasp it.

> The imagination can come to a stand nowhere or ever. On the mind goes, heaping up its millions and billions and quadrillions of millions. It is to no purpose—time, without a beginning—without an end—still confronts it. As thus thought of, the mind recoils from the contemplation, horrified, paralyzed with terror.[43]

If we grasp ever so faintly the idea of what an *infinite* punishment means, it becomes clear that no proposition more revolting to the idea of

---

43 Allin is here slightly modifying a quotation from another universalist text: Alexander Harvey, *Good the Final Goal of All, Or The Better Life: Four Letters to the Ven, Archdeacon Farrar, D.D.* (London: 1883). The quotations comes from the Fourth Letter. The original reads: "The imagination can come to a stand nowhere or ever. On the mind goes, heaping up its millions and billions and quadrillions of millions. It is to no purpose. Time and space still confront it. Awful reachings-after they are! Illimitable space! Time without a beginning—without an end! Time eternal! Space boundless! As thus thought of, the mind recoils from the contemplation, horrified,—paralyzed with terror."

justice can be stated than this, that finite sins deserve an infinite penalty. Expand the finite as you will, and it still falls infinitely short of infinity. Hence, it is but the sober statement of sober fact to assert that a single sentence of unending torment would outweigh the whole sins of the *whole human race*. To prove this I need but assume that to which every conscience responds, that what is finite can in justice receive only a finite punishment. But any possible number of finite sins put together will still fall short (nay, infinitely short) of infinity—of infinite guilt.[44]

Add together all sins ever committed, be their blackness what it may, be their horrors never so great; still the sum of all, because the guilt of finite mortals is but finite, and unless all justice is to be outraged, would deserve a sentence that, however awful, would be finite. Hence it follows that a single sentence of *infinite misery* would undoubtedly outweigh, if there be such a thing as justice, the sins of all men who have ever lived, and who shall ever live.

Infinite Punishment Undermines the Purpose of Punishment

There is again, a difficulty—an impossibility rather—in reconciling endless penalties with the view, which either Holy Scripture or reason give of punishment—its object and nature. This most important topic, with the kindred question of the scriptural doctrine of forgiveness, needs our best attention. Let us briefly consider the latter first.

Infinite punishment and the God of Jesus

Doubtless God always accepted the penitent. But a wholly novel duty of forgiving has emerged since Christ said, "Love your *enemies*, do good to them which hate [are hating, keep hating] you" (Luke 6:27). No doubt

---

44 If it is said that there may be some infinite evil in sin, that, even if true (which nobody knows and Scripture nowhere teaches), does not make human guilt infinite. For on any just principle, guilt is determined by the capacities and powers of the agent, and all these are in man strictly finite. Nay, the Bible, so far from taking this view, tells us that Israel has received from the Lord's hand *double* for all her sins, which involves a direct contradiction of any such theory of infinite guilt (Isa 40:2; Jer 16:18). Besides, does not endless punishment prove, if true, that the judge never obtains satisfaction? [Editor: The reason being that on the "traditional creed" the debt is never actually paid off—which is why it must continue forever—and so *justice is never actually satisfied*.]

in this novel view we have a distinct revelation of the divine character. But if so, is it possible to suppose that the gospel presents us with two contradictory pictures of God, i.e., a God who does good to his enemies only for the few years they spend on earth, and then proceeds to do them all possible evil in hell? If God's attitude towards his worst foes is love, that attitude is permanent, is eternal; nay, must be so. Whatever be the sin of his enemies, he must be to them the same unchanging God of love, and never more so than when he most inexorably punishes. Note the emphatic *"But I say* to you, love your enemies." Here is the very heart of God disclosed; here is the dividing line; here the spiritual watershed between a true and a false theology.

Infinite punishment is pointless and vindictive

Next I say that endless penalties contradict the true end of punishment. Apart from all question of its justice—apart, too, from the horror it excites—endless torment is a useless and therefore a wanton infliction: it is a mere barbarity, because it is only vindictive, and in no sense remedial. There is something positively sickening in the thought of the cruelty, combined with the uselessness, of penalty prolonged, when all hope of amendment is over, and when retribution has been fully exacted. To go on punishing for ever, simply for punishment sake, shocks every sentiment of justice. And the case is so much the worse when, as remarked, the punishment is really the prolongation of evil, when it is but making evil endless. But the true view of punishment is not to oppose, but to combine its retributive and remedial aspects, for through retribution it aims at amendment.

Our day has seen a complete revolution in the ideas men form of punishment and its end: in few things has the advance been more marked over the past than in our recognition of the true object of penalty. But let me ask, to whom is due this marked change for the better in our ideas of punishment? Surely to that Great Being who guides and orders by his providence all human things. This being so, it is wholly incredible to assign to the divine punishments this very character of mere vindictiveness, which men have in all enlightened systems abandoned. This is, I repeat, impossible to believe, for when God chastises it is *for our profit*, as the Bible says. He punishes, as an old Father puts it, medicinally. Yes, it is impossible to believe the ordinary dogma; for if God does indeed by

PART ONE—Universalism Asserted on the Authority of Reason

his providence—by his Spirit—direct and enlighten men's minds, leading them to higher and truer thoughts on this subject (as on all others), then to suppose that his own punishments are regulated on the very system that he has taught us to abandon is truly impossible.[45] Nor can I discuss this subject without remarking that there is a highly significant expression found in that very passage, most often on the lips of the defenders of endless pain, which yet, curiously enough, furnishes the material for an answer to their creed; I speak of Matthew 25:46. The term there applied to the punishment of the ungodly is not the ordinary Greek word to denote penalty or vengeance (*timoria*), but it is a term (*kolasis*) denoting, literally, pruning, i.e., a corrective chastisement—an age-long (but reformatory) punishment.[46]

It is most important to gain clear conceptions as to the true function of punishment. Three stages may be clearly distinguished—though united by a period of transition, through which men's minds have passed in their treatment of crime. At first all penalties are purely vindictive and personal; in the rudest stage of society we have the wild justice of revenge, an eye for an eye, a tooth for a tooth.[47] This idea lingers yet in some semi-barbarous districts, e.g., the Corsican vendetta.[48] Next comes a higher conception, in which the wrong done to the state replaces the wrong done to the individual. Society exacts the penalty; the tribunal takes the place of the knife. In this stage our ideas have rested for centuries. But this stage

---

45 Editor: It is hard to miss Allin's typically Victorian belief in ever-advancing human progress, albeit understood in terms of divine providence.

46 Editor: This understanding of the word *kolasis* is based upon its usage in the work of Plato and Aristotle. Aristotle says that *kolasis* "is inflicted in the interest of the sufferer," while *timoria* is inflicted "in the interest of him who inflict it, that he may obtain satisfaction" (*Rhetoric* 1369b13). Plato makes the same point (*Gorgias* 476A–477A). Aristotle and Plato do not seem to be innovating by crafting a new meaning for a word, but simply clarifying standard usage. However, later usage does not seem to have neatly retained this distinction and Allin ought not to reply on it. Thus, the LXX uses *kolasis* as a simple generic word for punishment, even when it is not remedial.

47 Editor: in fairness to the Mosaic law, it ought to be noted that the so-called *lex talionis* (law of the talon) was not, in fact, the "purely vindictive . . . wild justice of revenge." It was intended as a means of placing *restrictions* on vengeance—*only* an eye for an eye, not more; *only* a tooth for a tooth, not more. It was, in other words, the principle of making the punishment *proportionate to* the crime.

48 Editor: According to Ferdinand Gregorovius (1821–91), *Wanderings in Corsica: Its History and Its Heroes* (Edinburgh: 1855), vendetta was a social code that required Corsicans to kill anyone who wronged the family honour. Around 4,300 murders were perpetrated in Corsica between 1821 and 1852.

we now see to be, at least, wholly imperfect. It repeats the wrong, and thus tends to perpetuate it: it thinks little of the criminal's amendment, content to rest mainly on the vindictive idea; differing from the rudest stage in this chiefly, that the revenge is exacted in the name, not of the individual, but of the state.

At length we are on the verge of a truer conception of penalty: we are beginning to dwell most of all on the amendment of the criminal. The main idea is not the wrong done to the injured person, as in the first stage; nor the wrong done to society, as in the second; but it is rather the wrong done to the criminal himself by his crime. This is the reformatory age on which we are now entering with steady, if slow, steps.

Need I add that the relation of all this to theology is the closest possible? When we seize on—as perhaps the central idea of sin—the wrong done by the sinner to himself, and not merely the offense against God, *true as that is*, we can better estimate the true function of punishment as retributive indeed, but in its essence remedial. Nor does any sentimentality lurk here, for we recognize the need of stern retribution, and enforce the penalty: but our aim is different. Through suffering we would always heal. The end aimed at is the extinction of sin, and the restoration of the sinner; for no other end is worthy of God, and of man made in his image and likeness.

3

The Popular Creed Wholly Untenable

Part 2

"Far be it from me to make light of the demerit of sin. But endless punishment—I admit my inability (I would say it reverently) to admit this belief together with a belief in the divine goodness—the belief that God is Love, that His tender mercies are over all His works."
—John Foster[1]

Hell as a Brutal Anachronism

THE considerations just stated illustrate well the growth of morality. In fact, we have still vast arrears to make up, for the growth of our moral conceptions has been at once very slow, and very one-sided. In the fierce struggle for success the intellectual faculties have been sharpened, while the sympathetic tendencies have been dwarfed. Even yet we

---

1. Editor: John Foster, *Letter of the Celebrated John Foster to a Young Minister on the Duration of Future Punishment* (1841). John Foster (1770–1843) was an English Baptist minister and essayist. In this relatively short letter Foster rejected eternal torment, though did not take a stance on the alternative views of annihilation or final restoration.

have hardly begun to realize what that saying means, "You shall love your neighbor as *yourself*" [Matt 22:39].

Take an illustration. All Christendom is a vast camp: all Europe is armed to the teeth. What does all this mean?—this at any rate, that our whole life is still permeated with a spirit of revenge. These armaments preach the gospel of hatred of our enemies. They are schools ever open, in which the obvious lessons are a formal contradiction of the Sermon on the Mount. Whatever reasonable excuses may be offered, certain it is that all this reacts on our opinions. It blinds us to the idea of love as supreme, and of humanity as one family. It sets up resentment as an ideal of duty. And if this be so still, how much more was it the case in those ages in which war was the chief occupation, and the chief glory of civilized(?) human beings? Men living in such a state were wholly incapable of rising to true Christian teaching. They held half, or more than half, their neighbors in bondage as mere chattels. They tortured their criminals: they burned them, or boiled them alive; their foes they massacred. Now precisely through such channels as these very much of current theology has filtered down: it is, in fact, an anachronism. We are still drinking largely from poisoned wells. But if our awakening be slow it is sure. A cruel Deity watching unmoved to all eternity the agonies, moral or physical, of his creatures will seem to our children but an evil dream. Is it credible that, when torture has been banished from human justice, divine justice shall stand alone in consigning offenders to torture without any end?

Hell as Unworthy of God

Hell Makes God a Failure

Pursuing our remarks, I must also remind you of another feature of the popular belief that seems to present a great difficulty; it is what I must call its paltriness, its unworthiness of God. Let us for the moment not think of God as a good, loving, and righteous Being. Let us now simply regard him as great, as irresistible, as almighty. Viewed thus, how difficult is it to accept that account which the ordinary creed gives us of this Being's attempt at the rescue of his fallen creature, man. An almighty Being puts forth every effort to gain a certain end; sends inspired men to teach others; works miracles, signs, wonders in heaven and on earth, all for this end of man's safety; nay, at the last, sends forth his own Son—very God—himself almighty. The almighty Son stoops not alone to take our nature on him, but lower still—far lower—stoops to degradation; meekly accepts insults and scourging, bends to the bitter cross even, and all this to gain a certain end. And yet, we are told, this end is not gained after all, man is not saved, for countless myriads are in fact left to hopeless, endless misery; and that, though for every one of these lost ones, so to speak, has been shed the lifeblood of God's own Son. Now, if I may be permitted to speak freely, it is wholly inconceivable that the definite plan of an almighty Being should end in failure—that this should be the result of the agony of the Eternal Son. God has, in the face of angels and of men, before the universe and its gaze of wonder, entered himself into the arena, become himself a combatant, has wrestled with the foe, and has been defeated. I can bring myself to imagine those who reject the deity of Christ as believing in his defeat; but it is passing strange that those who believe him to be "very God Almighty," are loudest in asserting his failure.

Hell Makes the Final "End" of Creation Tragic and Undesirable

To continue this thought—if we think of God at all worthily, we cannot help thinking of him as working for high and worthy ends. Therefore we cannot help thinking of him, as in creation, working for some end worthy of himself. But what end does the popular creed assign to him? A creation mutilated, ruined, and that for ever. A creation ending in misery and endless sin to infinite numbers of the created; and all this misery and horror brought into sharper relief by a vain and fruitless attempt to save all: by a purpose of love declared to all, and yet not in fact reaching all: a creation which is but the portal to hell for so many of the created. And you gravely ask thoughtful inquirers to believe this; to believe that, contemplating these horrors destined never to cease, the morning stars are described as singing together, and all the sons of God shouting for joy on the morning of creation [Job 38:7].

The sons of God shouted for joy, as they contemplated creation; but they should have wept had the popular creed been true. For that creed represents the present life as darkened by the prospect of evil triumphant; our present sorrows made keener by the prospect of a future life, which will be, not to the wicked merely, but to the whole race of man, an evil and a curse—a life that every good man would, if he could, bring to an instant end. To prove this, I will take a definite example. Further, I will concede to the advocates of the popular creed one point of very considerable importance (to which they have no right), i.e., that the number of the saved greatly exceeds the lost.

> Suppose it were offered to the father of three children to take his choice whether two should be received into heaven and one condemned to hell, or the whole should be annihilated in death. What would a parent say? Where is the father who would dare to secure the bliss of two children at the cost of the endless misery of one? Which of the family would he select as the victim, whose undying pain should secure his brother's immortal joy? Is there any one living who would not suffer himself and his children to sink back again into nothingness, rather than purchase heaven at such a price? Now, if so, if we should so act in the case of our own children, *we are bound morally* to make the same choice with respect to every one. No moral being would consent to purchase eternal happiness at the price of another's eternal woe. Hence it follows that a future life, on the popular view, is an evil to the human race, *not to the wicked, but to all*. For if annihilation of the whole race should be tendered as the alternative, no moral being could, as has been shown, refuse to accept it.
> —James W. Barlow[2]

Thus, there is, I repeat, if the popular creed be true, no alternative, no escape from the conclusion that creation is an evil thing, and a future life a curse to the whole human family. What is to be our answer to the scorn of the sceptic, to the challenge of the atheist? So long as we cling to an immoral creed there is none—absolutely none. What awful mockery is a gospel whose message is, in fact, damnation to countless myriads; whose issue is endless sin—sin ever ripening, ever progressing. And I am to accept such a gospel as good news, as glad tidings of great joy—glad tidings of never ending pain and curse and sin.

---

2 Editor: James William Barlow, *Eternal Punishment and Eternal Death: An Essay* (London: 1865). James Barlow (1826–1913) was a Fellow and Tutor at Trinity College, Dublin—where Allin himself had been an undergraduate. Barlow rejected the doctrine of everlasting punishing, but was not a universalist. His view was that punishment in the afterlife was reformative, but that if restoration of a sinner proves impossible in any particular case then God will annihilate that sinner. Aside from theology, Barlow also published a science fiction novel (*History of a World of Immortals without a God*, 1891).

PART ONE—Universalism Asserted on the Authority of Reason

Does Anyone *Really* Believe in Traditional Hell?

Again, there comes this very serious obstacle to accepting the popular creed. I shall state it thus, either this creed is true or false If false—the question is ended. If true, can this strange fact be explained—that *nobody acts as if he believed it*? I say this, for any man who so believed, and who possessed but a spark of common humanity—to say nothing of charity—could not rest, day or night, so long as one sinner remained who might be saved. To this all would give place—pleasure, learning, business, art, literature; nay, life itself would be too short for the terrible warnings, the burning entreaties, the earnest pleadings, that would be needed to rouse sinners from their apathy, and to pluck them from endless tortures. Ask me what you will, but do not ask me to believe that any human being, who is convinced that perhaps his own child, his wife, his friend, his neighbor, even his enemy, is in danger of endless torment, could, if *really* persuaded of this, live as men now live, even the best men: who can avoid the inevitable conclusion that its warmest adherents really, though unconsciously, find their dogmas absolutely incredible? In fact these men (and it is the best thing to be said for them) teach their creed without real conviction. Their best eulogy is that they are self-deceivers.

These remarks also explain an obvious difficulty, viz., it has been shown how the popular creed cuts at the root of all religion, poisoning the very fountains whence we draw our conceptions of love, of righteousness, of truth. But if so, it may be fairly asked, how is it that society subsists, that morality is not extinct? Because, I reply unhesitatingly, because no society, no individual, can possibly act, or has in fact acted, on such a creed, in the real business of life. It is simply impossible: who would dare so much as to smile, if he really believed endless torments were certain to be the portion of some member of his household—it may be of himself? Marriage would be a crime; each birth the occasion of an awful dread. The shadow of a possible hell would darken every home, sadden every family hearth. All this becomes evident when we reflect that to perpetuate the race would be to help on the perpetuation of moral evil. For if this creed be true, out of all the yearly births a steady current is flowing on to help to fill the abyss of hell, to make larger and vaster the total of moral evil which is to endure for ever. "The world would be *one vast madhouse*," says the American scholar Hallsted, "if a realizing and continued pressure of such a doctrine was present."[3] Remark again how this doctrine

---

[3] Editor: I have been unable to source this quotation.

breaks down the moment it is really put to the test. Take a common case: a man dies—active, benevolent, useful in life, but not a religious man, not devout. By the popular creed, such a man has gone to hell for ever. But who really believes that? nay, instinctively our words grow softer when we speak of the dead in all cases. Do even the clergy really believe what they profess? I cannot refrain from most serious doubt on this point. If they believe, why are they so often silent? Habitual silence would be impossible to any one believing the traditional creed in earnest. The awful future would dwarf all other topics, would compel incessant appeals. But what do we find? Everything, I reply, that marks a declining faith in endless evil—silence; excuses; modifications; evasions of the true issue.

Hell and the Majority—Those between Virtue and Vice

Take next a grave difficulty that arises on the popular view. How can you on any such principle deal equitably with the mass of men? Let us speak plainly: do tell me who and what are the great, nay, the *overwhelming* majority of the baptized? They are assuredly neither wholly bad, nor wholly good; they are neither bad enough for hell, nor good enough for heaven. Now how can you adapt your theory to this state of things, which is, I think, quite impossible to deny? Look around you, survey the mass of mankind: of how few, how very few, can you affirm that they are truly devout, converted, Christ-like; take which term you please. Can you affirm this of one in ten, in twenty, in a hundred even, of those baptized into Jesus Christ? Take as an illustration any English parish you please.[4] Take

---

4 Editor: The Church of England's influence was in decline in the period in which Allin wrote, but it was still significant. To give a vague sense of the complicated picture, 90.7% of all marriages were Anglican in 1844, but only 64.24% in 1904. On the other hand, baptisms increased from 62.35% in 1885 to 65.8% in 1902. The picture also varied from region to region and among the different classes. One of the more secular places was London, where only 15–20% of the working class (cf. 40% in Bristol, nearer to where Allin lived) attended church, and 40% of the middle class (cf. 66% in Bristol). The nineteenth century had seen a massive scheme for building new Anglican churches (over six hundred built between 1818 and 1884) and a big increase in clergy numbers (14,613 in 1841 to 24,232 in 1891), but filling the churches was more of a challenge. The current context in the UK is much changed. In 2012, just 800,000 worshippers attended a Church of England church on an average Sunday, the majority of them being over sixty-five. That is a mere 1.25% of the British population. Of course, the picture is more complex. A residual cultural Christianity continues, though much diminished from Allin's day, with attendance for marriages, baptisms, funerals, and special feasts, especially Christmas, drawing in a bigger numbers.

any village, or select some one of our English towns, muster its whole population in imagination, how many true, holy servants of Jesus Christ will you find there? The *mass*—what are they? Let us meet this question, and look the facts straight in the face. What is to be the doom of the mass of baptized Christians; they are not holy, but are they bad? Nobody out of the pulpit—and seldom there in these days—ventures to assert any such thing. For in truth there is abundant good in this crowd of human beings; and still more, there is almost infinite capacity for goodness amid the evil.

Everywhere you will find unselfish parents, hard workers, loving sisters, true friends; everywhere traces, distinct enough amid all the sin, nay, traces in abundance of goodness, patience, self-sacrifice, sometimes carried even to great lengths. Let an emergency arise, let sickness come, what devotion does it not call forth, what love unstinted, what self-forgetfulness? Now your system, that which you call the good news brought from heaven by Jesus Christ, forces you to believe that God will consign all these hapless children of his, because unconverted in this life, to a doom, which in its lightest form is awful beyond all powers of imagination, to the company of devils for ever and ever.

Permit me one question more, would not any creed, or no creed, be a positive relief from such *a gospel* as this of yours? Can there be a mockery more solemn, more emphatic, than to call this any part of the glad tidings of great joy? Is it not time for the clergy, not merely in private to ponder these things, convinced or half convinced of their truth, but to speak out as in God's name—as God's ministers?

Hell and Our Natural Instincts

Our Instinctive Joy at Childbirth

And while I am speaking of men as they are, and of the life they lead, let me add here a statement of another very grave difficulty in the way of accepting an endless hell as the doom of any man, the issue of any life. Wherever human beings exist, in what form of community it matters not, in what climate or under what conditions of life soever, there is found everywhere a deep spontaneous belief, call it feeling, instinct, what you please, that connects the marriage tie and the birth day with joyful associations, with mirth and gladness. Now why is this—has it no meaning? So deep an instinct, one so truly natural and spontaneous as this, comes surely from the Creator of all. His voice it is that bids the bridegroom rejoice over the bride, that bids the heart of the mother overflow with tenderness towards her babe. This being so, again let me put the question, and ask, why has this been so ordered? It is God who has so ordered; do you think he has had no purpose in so doing, no message to convey to those who have ears to hear? Is it possible that our Heavenly Father should bid his creatures everywhere to rejoice with a special joy at the marriage feast, at the natal hour, if these births were in fact destined to add largely to the ranks of hell, to the hosts of evil? Do think over the matter calmly, and ask yourself if that is possible, if you can believe any such thing? And as you think it over, take with you these words of Jesus Christ (that hint so much). They remind us how the mother in the "perilous birth" has sorrow; but add, that all that sorrow is swallowed up in joy—"joy that a man is born into the world."[5]

Dwell on these words, that you may grasp all they convey. Indeed, it may almost be said that in this lies the whole matter. It is a *joy* that a man—any man—should be born into the world. See how wide the words are. If you tell me that this joy is but a blind instinct of the mother: yes, I reply, it is this very blindness, as you call it, of the instinct that constitutes its force, for it thus betrays its origin; it is implanted, and by whom? by the Great Parent, for it is spontaneous and betrays his hand. Do you ask me to believe that he has done this without a meaning, without a certain purpose of good? Can I believe that our Father bids any mother's heart to stir with joy at the sight of her infant, while he knows that this infant is destined to be, will be, in fact, shut up into endless torment and sin?

Our Instinctive Desire for Happiness

And again, can you reconcile the theory of endless evil awaiting so large a portion of our race with that natural thirst for joy, that longing for happiness each one finds within? It matters not whether this has been slowly developed or created at one stroke, all that matters to this argument is its *naturalness*, its *universality*. This longing for happiness cannot then have

---

5 Editor: "A woman when she is in travail hath sorrow, because her hour is come; but as soon as she is delivered of the child, she remembereth no more the anguish, for joy that a man is born into the world" (John 16:21, KJV).

PART ONE—Universalism Asserted on the Authority of Reason

been accidental, there must be in it a design on the Creator's part. Now, what was that design? To delude us?—is that possible?

> If the popular theory of future endless torment were true, what sublime mockery would there be in placing poor wretches first upon earth, where are heard the merry shouts of careless children, the joyous song of birds, where above our heads "with constant kindly smile, the sleepless stars keep everlasting watch," where beneath our feet the delicate beauty of flowers of every tint gladdens the eye. What would have been thought of the propriety of placing a hundred bright and cheerful objects, suggestive of peace and happiness, in the anteroom to the torture chamber of the inquisition? It deserves, too, to be noted that man, the only animal that laughs, has of all animals, according to the popular theory, least cause to laugh.
> —Rev. N. G. Wilkins[6]

The Natural Potential for Spiritual and Mental Growth

THE NATURAL POTENTIAL FOR GROWTH

But there is much to be said beyond remarking on our natural thirst for joy and happiness, and the difficulty of explaining why it was ever implanted in man, except with a design that it should one day be gratified, fully and freely. There is this to be said: there is stored in every man a vast possibility of growth, of expansion, mental and intellectual, no less than spiritual. There are almost infinite germs in man, so to speak, latent as yet, but capable of a development perhaps practically boundless: they are probably unsuspected by the majority, and it is only at intervals, and as it

---

6 Rev. N. G. Wilkins, *Errors and Terrors of Blind Guides: The Popular Doctrine of Everlasting Pain, Refuted* (London: 1880). Rev. Wilkins, an Anglican clergyman, was chaplain to the American and English residents of Hanover in Germany. The book was first self-published in Hanover in 1875. The British edition contained an additional chapter. The author opines that in the five years between the first and third edition there had been a "very considerable change of opinion" among eminent men in the Anglican, Wesleyan, Congregationalist, and Presbyterian denominations on the matter of hell. He says that his own experience now suggests that the "better educated" member of the Church of England "have now generally ceased to hold the dogma" (Preface to the Third Edition). Allin's own book was a part of this spreading Victorian disquiet over the traditional doctrine of hell.

were by chance, that we gain a passing glance at them. But undoubtedly they exist, and their existence, like that of all other natural facts, requires an explanation. *Why* do they exist—who planted within us these powers, and for what end? They have been given to all, not to the good merely, but to man as man. I cannot but see in the very fact of their existence a silent prophecy, an intimation that the spark shall not be quenched in any case. Are they not a very message to man from God, a *hint*, eloquent by its very silence, eloquent, and instinct with hope?

The Problem of Death as a Cut-off Point for Growth

Consider next how strongly the analogy of nature, which is, after all, a very real revelation of God, bears against the popular view, which limits to the few moments of our present life all our chances of discipline, amendment, and probation; and that though "all reason, all experience, all Scripture unite in this, that the divine work of teaching goes on behind, as well as before, the veil."[7] To teach that the mere fact of dying is the signal for a total change from all that has gone before, is to contradict all that we know of God's ways from analogy. Consider this, and say whether any view that interposes so wide a gulf as that commonly held does between our present and our future life can be true. In all God's dealings with us no sharp break intervenes between the successive stages of life: each condition of being is developed out of a prior and closely related stage. Now this being so, can I believe that in another age all this is reversed, and that men, with capacities for good still existing, are to be at one bound consigned to hopeless sin, to endless torture? And the difficulty (surely an enormous one) of believing that our Father will deliberately crush out all the lingering tendencies to good in his own children, is increased by the following consideration, viz., that the whole of our human life here is so manifestly incomplete, so momentary, that in very many cases it has not afforded a satisfactory time of training, and in not a few cases no training at all.

This thought may be pursued further thus: An old proverb says very wisely, "the mills of God grind slowly,"[8] and this divine slowness, or long

---

7 Editor: I have been unable to source this quotation.

8 Editor: The saying goes back at least as far as the philosopher Sextus Empiricus in the late second or early third century AD: "The mills of the gods grind slowly, but they grind exceedingly fine." The point being that justice may not be fast in coming,

Part One—Universalism Asserted on the Authority of Reason

suffering, is very conspicuous in God's ways. How very slowly has he been fitting this earth for man's habitation, and by what a long continued succession of stages, age succeeding age.[9] At length man steps on the earth. Now, is all the divine slowness to be at once changed—and why should it be? Man is to live for ever and ever: we are apt to forget what this means, and how altogether impossible it is to assign any proportion between the fleeting moments of earthly life, and the life that stretches away for ever and ever. If we compare a human life of average duration to one second of time, and compare endless duration to the aggregate of all the seconds that have passed since time was, and that shall pass while time endures, still we assign to human life a proportionate duration infinitely too long.

Am I then to believe that the same God who expends millions of years in slowly fitting this earth for man's habitation, will only allow to man himself a few fleeting years, or months, or hours, as it may be, as his sole preparation time for eternity? To settle questions so unspeakably great in their issue—questions stretching away to a horizon so far distant that no power of thought can follow them—in such hot haste, does seem quite at variance with our heavenly Father's ways. Is God's action outside man so slow, and within man so hurried? Is the husk of far more value than the seed? Are millions of years allotted to fashioning man's earthly home, while for man's spiritual training for eternity, but a few brief years are given, and these so largely broken up by sleep, by work, by disease, by ignorance? What should we say—to take a homely illustration—of an arrangement allotting 10,000 years to fashioning a man's coat, or building his house, while assigning to his whole education but a few hours?

Besides, if we look around, a mass of facts point to the same conclusion—that the present life is rather the initial stage of human training, than its conclusion. The *vast majority* of men have not so much as heard of Christ. In Christian countries very many die in infancy: some are lunatic, or half witted; many wholly uneducated; very many grow up in virtual heathenism, from no fault of their own; or are born in a state

---

but be assured, *it will come, and it will be thorough, missing nothing.*

9 Editor: Consciousness of the vast age of the earth was relatively recent. The earth had long been believed to be only 6,000 to 10,000 years old, as a literal interpretation of parts of Genesis might suggest, but in the mid-eighteenth century the developing field of what became known as Geology pushed this age to 75,000 years, and by Allin's time it had been pushed up to several million years—by the early twentieth century the figure was standing at two billion years. Allin was one of many churchmen to use this developing science to aid his theological reflection.

where evil surroundings aggravate evil tendencies, inherited and innate. Are they—these untold myriads of myriads of hapless creatures—first to hear of Christ at the day of judgment? Perhaps I should speak soberly in asserting that not one in a thousand of the total mass of humanity is at this moment living in the true fear and love of God.

Immunization against Scriptural Teachings

Immunization

Next let us pass to Holy Scripture for a moment only, reserving a full examination of its testimony to later chapters. Here we are at once confronted by a difficulty so grave, that I confess it seems to me quite decisive against the popular view. This difficulty is that you are thus forced absolutely to *suppress* a very large part of the Bible—a very numerous class of passages that clearly hold out a promise of universal restitution, or at least imply a distinct hope for all men. The view generally held is, in short, one-sided, and therefore wholly unfair; it is as though a judge should base a decision of the most weighty importance on one set of witnesses merely, neglecting the others who testify in a directly opposite sense.

> Only imagine the book of nature being studied in this way, with one class of facts systematically ignored; with one law, say of gravitation, fully laid down, while the opposite law of centrifugal motion was altogether overlooked, what results in science could follow from such a method? Yet this is the way in which not a few yet read the Scriptures, taking their first partial sense readings for the truth, and shutting their eyes to all that the same Scripture testifies on the other side.
> —Andrew Jukes[10]

10 Editor: The quotation is from Andrew Jukes, *Catholic Eschatology Examined: A Reply to the Rev. H. N. Oxenham's Recent Papers in The Contemporary Review* (London: 1876). The essay was original published in *The Contemporary Review* in July 1876 under the title "The Restitution of All Things—The Teaching of Scripture and the Church." Andrew Jukes (1815–1901) was an Anglican curate in Hull who found that he could not consent to everything in the Book of Common Prayer. His curacy was suspended and he left the Church of England. For twenty-five years led an independent congregation in Hull before returning to the Anglican church. His most influential and controversial book was *The Restitution of All Things* (1876), which remains a classic defence of Christian universalism.

PART ONE—Universalism Asserted on the Authority of Reason

A most weighty charge, made with absolute truth, as I believe (see chapters 7 and 8).

An interesting illustration of the fact that the New Testament is full of passages teaching the larger hope is furnished by the undoubted, but often unperceived, occurrence over and over again, in the works of those who hold the popular creed, of language that, if fairly understood, involves the salvation of all men. This no doubt arises from the fact that phrases are used freely, while a traditional creed does, as so often, blind men to the real force of the expressions they employ—blind them in fact to everything outside the line of thought that they are taught to believe constitutes the truth.

Perhaps the best illustration that can be given of what I mean will be gained by quoting from some collection of popular hymns. I take, then, the well-known *Hymns, Ancient and Modern*,[11] and quote a few passages as instances of my meaning.

Hymn 43 has this verse:

> Thou, sorrowing at the helpless cry,
> Of all creation doomed to die,
> Did'st save our lost and guilty race
> [and grant us gifts of heavenly grace][12]

But this is universal salvation: the *race* of man saved, if words have any meaning. And this thought—the race saved—finds frequent expression elsewhere in these hymns; nor let any man who regards honesty of speech, and common truthfulness, say that to offer salvation merely, is, or can be, the same thing as to save. (See hymns 56 vv. 3, 4, 5, 6; 57 v. 3; 81 v. 3; 200 v. 6, etc.) Again, listen to these solemn words and tell me what they mean: hymn 97, part 2, v. 2:

> Precious blood which all creation
> From the stain of sin hath freed.

---

11 Editor: *Hymns Ancient and Modern* was a hymn book widely used in the Church of England. It arose from the Oxford Movement in the 1830s, but blended hymns from across the traditions of the Church of England. The first trial edition appeared in 1860, with the first full edition in 1861.

12 Editor: This is verse 2 of "Creator of the Starry Height," J. M. Neale's 1851 translation of a sixth-century Latin hymn.

And again, v. 5:

> That a shipwrecked race for ever
> Might a port of refuge gain.[13]

And hymn 103, v. 5:

> So a ransomed world shall ever,
> Praise Thee, its redeeming Lord.[14]

Can it be right to talk of a ransomed world forever praising its Redeemer, and yet to mean that all the time the world is not actually ransomed, and perhaps half, perhaps more, of its population are groaning in endless pain? Is this consistent with truth? Again, other hymns call on all creation to sing God's praise. Shall this praise then echo from hell? I might well quote, in proof of this address to all creation to praise God, the familiar doxology, but I will only notice here a well-known hymn:

> O day for which creation
> And all its tribes were made;
> O joy for all its former woes,
> A thousand times repaid.[15]

I will simply ask what these words mean: all creation is to have all its woes a thousand times repaid: if this is not universalism, what is universalism? The same lips that assure us from the pulpit that half creation goes to the devil, bid us sing that all creation has been freed from sin! Again, over and over, Christ is said to have vanquished sin, death, and Satan (hymns 147 v. 2; 148 v. 2; 196 v. 3, etc.). But how can this be true on the traditional creed? To say that sin is vanquished, and death and Satan too, while hell receives its myriads of the lost, is worse than absurd. For example, take this line from hymn 196: "Death of death, and hell's destruction,"[16] and say if the universalist's creed could be more distinctly stated: his utmost hopes have never gone beyond a vision of death abol-

---

13 Editor: This is "Sing, My Tongue, the Glorious Battle," another of John Mason Neal's 1851 translations, also of a sixth-century Latin hymn.

14 Editor: This is "Now, My Soul, Thy Voice Upraising," a nineteenth-century translation by Henry W. Baker and John Chandler of an ancient Latin hymn.

15 Editor: This is from verse 2 of "Ten Thousand Times Ten Thousand" by Henry Alford (1867).

16 Editor: This is from verse 3 of "Guide Me, O Thou Great Jehovah," a Welsh hymn by William Williams Pantycelyn published in 1762. The English translation by Peter Williams was published first in 1771.

ished, and hell destroyed? To pursue this further is needless, though it would be easy, and indeed full of interest to add quotation to quotation: but I may point out how significant it is to find the very opponents of the larger hope *forced*, unconsciously, to employ language directly teaching universal salvation. The explanation is simply that they have been using the words and ideas of Scripture, while the fair, honest meaning of their own words is obscured for them by the spell of a narrow traditional creed.

Hell and Speaking Falsely

Before passing on, let me remark once more on the injurious moral tendency of the popular creed. Not merely has it fostered in man a spirit of cruelty; not alone does it promise a heaven that is one of utter selfishness; not merely does it point to evil as finally triumphant, but it scatters broadcast lessons of equivocation and untruth. For if to say one thing, while meaning something totally different, be falsehood, then with falsehood is the popular religious literature honeycombed from end to end. Everywhere it repeats that the race of man is saved, that Christ is the Saviour of mankind, while it really means that half mankind is damned. It tells us, I quote *The Record* (Easter, 1885), how "Satan is utterly subdued," "his empire completely demolished," "his power for ever fallen."[17] This teaching it repeats in a thousand forms, in countless hymns, in sermons, tracts, books; but it really means that Satan is triumphant, and his empire as enduring as God himself. Well may the sceptic exult, and the thoughtful Christian mourn at this duplicity, which stains our religious literature: this terrible perversion, in the holiest matters, of those words by which we shall be judged.

Suppressing Clear Universalist Texts

Again, there are, apart from all direct promises, certain tendencies in the gospel, whose drift and character are impossible to mistake. That these tendencies exist, I am far more certain than I can be of the meaning of any number of highly figurative texts, alleged to prove endless evil. Now these tendencies are too clear, too distinct, to be considered accidental.

17 Editor: *The Record* was a Church of England broadsheet paper, founded in 1828, representing the views of Evangelical Anglicans. During the 1880s it was published weekly. (In 1949 it merged with the *Church of England Newspaper*.)

So far from being a product of the age in which the New Testament was written, they are in conflict with the spirit of that age, and in advance of it. They must therefore represent something inherent in the Author of Christianity, and something essential to his design. I put the case very moderately in saying how extremely difficult it is to reconcile the popular creed with these undoubted tendencies of the New Testament. Can I reasonably believe that a system that, beyond all other creeds, has been distinguished by promoting mercy, goodness, love, and tenderness for body and soul—a system of which these qualities are the very essence—does indeed teach a doctrine of punishment so shocking, so horrible, that if really believed, it would turn this earth into a charnel house,[18] and spread over all nature lamentation, mourning, and woe? Who can believe that a creed that has banished every form of cruelty, so far as its influence is felt, in the present life, yet contains a special revelation of terrible cruelty in the life to come?

Hell Incompatible with Two Key Revealed Truths

Let me next show that certain great principles of revelation conflict with the popular creed. "I am sure," says a thoughtful writer, "these are the two fundamental features of the Christian revelation, of which all its utterances are the manifold expression, viz.: (1) The parental love of the Father. (2) The solidarity of mankind to be conformed to the image of His Son" (*Letters from a Mystic*).[19]

Truth One: God as Father

(1) No one can deny that the New Testament contains a special revelation of the parental tie uniting us to God. When we pray and say, "our Father," these two words convey the spirit of the whole gospel. Now, it is not too much to assert that the view generally held is an absolute negation of all that the parental tie implies. It robs the relation of all meaning. We have the very spirit of popular Christianity conveyed in the well-known

---

18 Editor: A charnel house is a building for the storing of human skeletal remains.

19 Editor: Rowland William Corbett, *Letters from a Mystic of the Present Day* (London: 1883). Rowland Corbett (1839–1919) was an Anglo-Catholic priest who founded the Brotherhood of the Holy Spirit in rural Shropshire. He later disbanded the Brotherhood and became a mystic with a popular speaking ministry.

Part One—Universalism Asserted on the Authority of Reason

line which tells us that we are "ever in the great Taskmaster's eye."[20] *The great Taskmaster*—note the term, for it reduces to mockery the divine Fatherhood, though that is of the very essence of Christianity.[21] What, for instance, shall we say of such a Father's appeal to those who, as he knows, will never hear? To God there is no future—all is present; the "lost" are lost, and yet he calls them; they are, on the traditional creed, virtually damned; and he knows it, and yet invites them to come and be saved. But all this difficulty comes from uniting two things absolutely irreconcilable—endless love and power, and yet endless evil. If we want to retain endless sin, let us return to the God of Calvin:[22] nowhere else shall we find solid footing. This God at least is Lord and Master. He issues no invitations, knowing them to be in fact futile. He saves all whom he wants to save. His will must prevail. His Son sheds no drop of blood in vain. All for whom he dies are in fact saved, while the rest go to the devil.[23] All this is hard—nay, cruel; but it is at least logical, intelligible. Contrast with this system the flabby creed of our pseudo-orthodoxy. Long ago it was shrewdly said by an old Calvinist, "universal salvation is credible, if universal redemption be true."[24] For it shocks the reason to be told of a

---

20 Editor: This is the last line of John Milton's Sonnet VII (probably written on 9 Dec 1631, first published in 1645). John Milton (1608–74) was a well-known poet, author, and civil servant under Oliver Cromwell. His greatest work was *Paradise Lost* (1667).

21 Editor: The theme of the universal Fatherhood of God was not uncommon in nineteenth-century theology.

22 Editor: John Calvin (1509–64) was a French pastor and a major figure in the Protestant Reformation. He was a minister and preacher based briefly in Strasbourg, but for the most part in Geneva, where he exerted considerable influence. It was here that he published his massively important *Institutes of the Christian Religion* (1536, with expanded editions in 1539, 1543, and the final edition of 1559). He is without doubt one of the great theologians of Christian history. When Allin refers disparagingly to "the God of Calvin" he is referring to the strongly predestinarian view of divine providence that Calvin held. It was Calvin's belief that everything that ever happens is ordained by God, that God chooses to redeem some creatures (the elect), on whom he bestows his love, while he chooses to consign other creatures to eternal torment for their sins.

23 Editor: Allin here refers to the Calvinist doctrine of "limited atonement"—the belief that Christ died only for the elect, not for all people. The theological motivation for this doctrine was the attempt to hold together two convictions: (a) all for whom Christ died will be saved, and (b) only the elect will be saved. As a matter of logic it seems to many (though not all) Calvinists that this conjunction requires a limited atonement.

24 Editor: It is unclear which old Calvinist Allin has in mind, but it is true that

universal redemption, when all that is meant is *an attempt* at the redemption of all the race, which fails; it shocks the reason no less to be told of an unchanging love that wholly ceases the moment the last breath leaves the frail body.

I repeat, the essence of Christianity perishes in the virtual denial of any true Fatherhood of our race on God's part. Follow out this thought, for it is of primary importance. We lose sight of the value of the individual soul, when dealing with the countless millions who have peopled this earth and passed away. What is one among so many? we are tempted to say, forgetting that the value of each human being is not in the least thereby altered. Each soul is of infinite value, as if it stood alone, in the eyes of God its Father.

And more than this, we are altogether apt to forget another *vital* point, to forget whose the loss is, if any one soul perishes—it is the man's own loss, says our popular creed. But is this all? No, a thousand times no. It is God's loss: it is the Father who loses his child. The straying sheep of the parable is the Great Shepherd's loss [Luke 15:4–7]: the missing coin is the Owner's loss [Luke 15:8–10]. In this very fact lies the pledge that he will seek on and on till he find it [Luke 15:4]. For only think of the value he sets on each soul. He has stamped each in his own image: has conferred on each a share of his own immortality—of himself: do but realize these things; put them into plain words till you come thoroughly to believe them; and you must see how impossible it becomes to credit that unworthy theology, which tells you that such a Father can ever permit the work of his own fingers, his own offspring, to perish finally.

One step further to make this clearer: how has he shown his sense of the value of the human spirit? The incarnation must say. It is human life taken into closest alliance with the divine—man and God meeting in the God-man. And then follows the atonement, proof on proof of the same truth, when he tasted death for every man, he in whose death all died. Such is the chain, whose golden links I have been endeavouring to follow and trace, whose links bind to the Father above every human soul; *every human soul*, be it distinctly affirmed. Or stay, is there not yet wanting

---

many Calvinists have made the point that if God wanted to redeem all people and sent Christ to die for all people *then all people would be redeemed*. The Calvinist objection to universalism is not an *a priori* objection to the idea of universal salvation. God is free to do whatever God desires—it just so happens that, in the opinion of most Calvinists, he does not desire to save all. Our role is not to question his decision, but to accept it.

the final link to complete this chain? That link is to be found in the great truth, which completes what I have been saying, the truth of the oneness of the human race, its organic unity. Let us consider this.

Truth Two: The Unity of Humanity

(2) The principle of the organic unity of our race is that which underlies the whole divine work, alike in creation, and in the incarnation. It is the divine idea, so to speak, to regard humanity *as one organic whole*, one body summed up in Adam, summed up anew in the second Adam—a whole that must stand or fall together. All this, too, is very legible in the divinely-given symbolism of the old law, and is reflected in the gospel with perfect clearness.

What but this is the teaching of the "first fruits," and the "firstborn" in Scripture? These imply and include, the one, the whole harvest; the other, the whole family, and not less. Now Christ is the "first fruits" (1 Cor 15:23) and Christ is the "firstborn" (Col 1:18). And what follows let St. Paul say, "If the 'first fruits' be holy, the 'lump' is also holy" [Rom 11:16], the whole race. Thus this principle is affirmed in the great central doctrine of the incarnation. For in Christ, who is the "first fruits," mankind (i.e., the aggregate of humanity) is taken into God. And so in his death all died, as the New Testament assures us, and in his resurrection all rise, nay, are risen. In other words, Christ's relation, as the last Adam, is not to individuals, but to the race. Further, it is an actual, not a possible or a potential relation; an actual relation giving salvation to all, in a sense as real as the first Adam gave death and ruin to all.[25]

> Once introduce the belief in Christ's divine nature, and His death and resurrection are no longer of the individual but of the race. It was on this belief the Church was founded and built up. The belief was not indeed drawn out with exact precision, yet it was always implied in the relation, which the believer was supposed to hold toward God. The formula of Baptism, which has never changed, is unintelligible without it. The

---

25 Editor: This point was the very heart of the idiosyncratic Calvinistic universalist system set forth by James Relly (1722–78) in his 1759 book *Union: Or, A Treatise on the Consanguinity and Affinity between Christ and His Church* and in his *Epistles: Or, the Great Salvation Contemplated* (1776). It is not clear whether Allin had read Relly, though he does refer in passing to *Union* in chapter 5. Their universalisms are certainly different in some important respects, but here accord perfectly.

> Eucharist is emptied of the blessing which every age has sought in that holy Sacrament, if it be taken away. If Christ took our nature upon Him, as we believe, by an act of love, it was not that of one, but of all. He was not one man only among men, but in Him *all humanity are gathered up:* and thus now as at all time, *mankind* are, so to speak, *organically united with Him.*
> —B. F. Wescott[26]

And it is this union of the race of man with himself that Jesus Christ would teach in one of his many pregnant hints, by always speaking of himself in his redeeming work as the Son, not of the Jew, not of the Gentile, not of Mary, not of the carpenter, but the Son *of Man.*[27]

Yes, the organic unity of mankind is a principle that, from the fall to the story of the incarnation, runs through the texture of Holy Scripture. Have you ever quietly thought over the very strange fact of what is called original sin? Have you asked yourself what it means, that you are suffering for something done thousands of years before your birth? All the questions raised by this inquiry we need not try to settle, but we may say that it means at least this, that in the divine plan the race falls and rises together; that mankind is not a collection of separate units, but an organized whole. Each individual is not, so to speak, complete in himself, but is a living stone in the great building—is so truly a member of one great body that, if withdrawn, there would ensue no less than a mutilation of the body. And so Adam's sin sent a shock through the whole race, exactly as when a hurt to any part sends a shock through our present body. This is the painful side, but it is only one side; and unfortunately the popular creed, as so often, persists in looking at one side only, and that the dark side, and in looking away from the bright side; or at least in so looking at it, as to miss its real aspect. But here the New Testament comes to our rescue and assures us that "as in Adam all die, so in the new and better Adam all shall be made alive" [1 Cor 15:22, modified]. The race is fallen; true, but the race is risen; quite as true. Both facts strictly correspond; but, if so,

> Of two such lessons why forget
> The nobler and the Christlier one?[28]

---

26 Editor: B. F. Wescott, *The Gospel of the Resurrection: Thoughts on Its Relation to Reason and History* (London: 1866).

27 Editor: Italics added.

28 Editor: I have not been able to source this quotation.

Part One—Universalism Asserted on the Authority of Reason

A partial salvation is thus in absolute conflict with this fundamental principle which the fall affirms, and to which the incarnation testifies; the organic indivisible unity of mankind. A partial salvation is no less in direct opposition to the great truth put by St. Paul so clearly:

> For if many died through one man's [i.e. Adam's] trespass, much more have the grace of God and the free gift by the grace of that one man Jesus Christ abounded for many. . . . Therefore, as one trespass led to condemnation for all men, so one act of righteousness leads to justification and life for all men. (Rom 5:15–18)[29]

Observe, the offense is a thing actually imparted to, actually staining, ruining all men. And Jesus Christ came to bring to every man, to humanity, a salvation that shall be to mankind *much more* than the fall. But the popular view reads *much less*; and in millions of cases, as much less as hell is less than heaven.

I may in passing point out the tendency of modern scientific thought towards the conception of a unity underlying all the various forms of life. The facts of evolution and the facts of heredity confirm this.[30] Individual responsibility is not the less true, because it requires to be supplemented by another fact, that of organic unity. Individuality does not contradict, but is complementary to solidarity. The individual is a whole; but the race is a whole as truly. The individual is truly free and responsible, and yet truly bound by those myriad ties of inherited capacity and character that link each inseparably to the whole. We are "members one of another" in the fullest sense, i.e., parts of a whole from which no act of will can sever us.

This far-reaching conception of a unity of the race is St. Paul's too. See a striking passage, 1 Timothy 2:4–5, where he bases universal salvation not on God's love, but on God's *unity*. The connection is worth tracing: "God wills *all* to be saved. For he is *one*"; such is the apostle's assertion.[31] The meaning is—as an ultimate fact we have unity. It is the

---

29 Editor: I inserted the KJV, as Allin's semi-paraphrase was a bit of a mess.

30 Editor: Charles Darwin's *On the Origen of Species by Means of Natural Selection* was published in November 1859. This reference to evolution does not appear in the first edition of Allin's book, but was added in the third edition (1888). Allin was among many Victorian churchmen who incorporated Darwin's theory into their theology.

31 Editor: ". . . God our Saviour, who desires all people to be saved and to come to the knowledge of the truth. For there is one God . . ." (ESV). Allin takes *eis gar theos* to speak not of the number of Gods (for there is *one* God), but of the unity of God (for God is *one*).

law of creation. The "all" run up into and are bound together into unity by his will, who is *"one."*

I may here briefly note how scientific researches illustrate human solidarity. "The definite result of these researches—and the point is so important, that it must be again and again repeated—is that heredity is identity as far as is possible: it is one being in many."[32]

This law may be traced everywhere. Not a sentiment or a desire exists: not an excellence or defect, bodily or mental, which is not capable of transmission, and actually transmitted. Why is this? "The cause of this heredity," says Heckel, "is the partial *identity* of the materials which constitute the organism of the parent and child."[33] This shows how vast a part heredity plays, and how close its relation to morality. We assert freely the facts of individuality; we forget the less obvious, but no less true, facts of heredity; we fail to see all that is involved in the apostle's words, "we are members one of another" [Rom 12:5].

Hell and Divine Immutability

But again, the traditional view conflicts with another great principle, viz., the unchangeableness of God.

> If God be unchangeable, then what we see of Him at any moment, must be true of Him at every moment of time; true of Him also both before and after all the moments of time; always and for ever true of Him. If His purpose be to save mankind, that purpose stands firm for ever, unaffected by man's sin, unshaken by the fact of death, unaltered and unalterable by men, by angels, by naught conceivable.
> —Samuel Cox[34]

Redemption is no afterthought, it was planned in the full knowledge of all the extent of man's sin: knowing all, God declared his purpose to

---

32 Editor: Th. Ridot, *Heredity: A Psychological Study of Its Phenomena, Its Laws, Its Causes, and Its Consequences.* Translated from the French (London: 1875), 280.

33 Editor: Ernst Haeckel (1834–1919) was a German biologist who promoted and popularized Darwin's work in Germany and developed a controversial theory according to which the biological development of an individual organism recapitulated the evolutionary development of the species. I have not been able to ascertain which of Haeckel's publications Allin is quoting from.

34 Editor: Samuel Cox, *Salvator Mundi: Or, Is Christ the Saviour of All Men?* (London: 1877). Samuel Cox (1826–93) was a British Baptist Minister and universalist. *Salvator Mundi* was his most influential publication.

Part One—Universalism Asserted on the Authority of Reason

save the race. Redemption, then, is something indefeasible, except indeed God can change, or the will of the created be stronger than the will of the Creator. "The gifts and calling of God are irrevocable"[35] (Rom 11:29). That is, what God wills must be done; those whom God calls must obey finally. And this unchangeable purpose of God is stated afresh in the words that describe Jesus Christ as "the same yesterday, today, and for ever" [Heb 13:8]—words deeply significant, and yet, whose true teaching so very often escapes attention.

And here let me illustrate this part of my argument by introducing a story, for whose truth I vouch, to show how practical these considerations really are: In a certain quarter of London, one of the many evangelists employed for that purpose had gone forth to preach to the people. When he had concluded an eloquent address, he was thus accosted by one of his hearers: "Sir," said the man, "may I ask you one or two questions?" "Surely," said the preacher. "You have told us that God's love for us is very great and very strong." "Yes," "That he sent his Son on purpose to save us, and that I may be saved this moment, if I will." "Yes," "But, that if I go away without an immediate acceptance of this offer, and if, a few minutes after I were to be by any accident killed on my way home, I should find myself in hell for ever and ever." "Yes." "Then," said the man, "if so, I don't want to have anything to do with a Being *whose love for me can change so completely in five minutes.*"

"God so loved the world"—dwell on these words. The world, then, must have been in some real sense worthy of love. He cannot *love*—he may pity—the unlovely. Has he ceased to love it? *If so, when?* I challenge a reply. "Love is not love that alters, where it alteration finds";[36] even human love, if true, never changes. Yet this love is but a faint, far-off, reflection of our Father's love. God is not love and justice, or love and anger. He is love, i.e., love essential [1 John 4:8]. Therefore his wrath and vengeance, while very real, are the ministers of his love. To say that God cannot change is to say that his love cannot change. Hence his love, being changeless, pursues the sinner to the outer darkness, and, being almighty, draws him thence. An earthly parent, who, being able to help, should sit unmoved, month after month, year after year, watching, but never helping, the agonies of his own offspring is a picture more hideous than any the records of

---

35 Editor: I changed the original "without repentance" to the more modern translation "irrevocable" to avoid any misunderstanding of Allin's point.

36 Editor: Shakespeare, Sonnet 116 (1609).

crime can furnish. What shall we say to those who heighten enormously, infinitely, all that is shocking in such a picture, until its blackest details become light itself; and then tell us that the parent in this ghastly scene is one who is love, love infinite, almighty, and our Father?

God is Love

And this brings us face to face with a blunder of our traditional creed, which is radical. It talks of God's love as though that stood merely on a par with his justice, [as] though it were something belonging to him which he puts on or off. It is hardly possible to open a religious book in which this fatal error is not found; fatal, because it virtually strikes out of the gospel its fundamental truth—that GOD IS LOVE. The terms are equivalent. They can be interchanged. God is not anger, though he can be angry; God is not vengeance, though he does avenge. These are attributes; love is essence. Therefore, God is unchangeably love. Therefore, in judgment he is love, in wrath he is love, in vengeance he is love—"love first, and last, and midst, and without end."[37]

But in fact the traditional creed knows nothing of what love really is. For love is simply the strongest thing in the universe, the most awful, the most inexorable, while the most tender. Further, when love is thus seen in its true colours, there is less than ever an excuse for the mistake still so common, which virtually places at the center of our moral system sin and not grace. This it is which the traditional dualism has for centuries been doing, and is still doing. Doubtless retribution is a most vital truth. Universalists rejoice to admit it; nay, largely to *base* on it their system; but there is a greater truth—which controls, and dominates the whole: the truth of love. We must not, in common phrase, put the theological cart before the horse. Retribution must not come first, while love brings up the rear; nor must we put the idea of probation, before that of God's education of his human family. In a word, to arrive at truth is hopeless, so long as men virtually believe in a quasi-trinity—God and the devil, and the will of man.

---

37 Editor: This is an allusion to John Milton, *Paradise Lost*, Book V, lines 164–65: "On earth join all ye creatures to extol / Him first, Him last, Him midst, and without end." This line from Milton is picked up by William Wordsworth in *The Prelude or, Growth of a Poet's Mind*, Book VI, "Cambridge and the Alps," lines 639–40: "The types and symbols of Eternity,/ Of first, and last, and midst, and without end."

PART ONE—Universalism Asserted on the Authority of Reason

In Closing

I desire in closing these chapters to point out that in proportion to the excellence of Christianity, are its corruptions especially vile—*corruptio optimi pessima*.[38] These flow mainly from the characteristic unwillingness of theologians to accept as *fundamental* the dictates of the moral sense; a reluctance which is the opprobrium of the noble science of theology. Those versed in the great controversy (so imperfectly discussed in these pages) must have noticed how constantly the advocates of endless evil *evade the great moral issues*. They will not face the question of the utter injustice of visiting finite guilt with an infinite penalty. They prefer to observe a discreet silence. They practically ignore the clear evidence of experts, which shows that moderate penalties are far more effective in repressing crime and reforming the sinner than are excessive punishments. They will not meet the arguments that prove that the true conception of penalty is one that, recognizing the need of retribution, yet lays the chief stress on its reformatory character.

They, in fact, substitute the "Great Taskmaster" for "Our Father," thereby obscuring, nay, almost denying, the fundamental fact of Christianity. They are strangely blind to the *vital* question of the dualism virtually involved in teaching eternal evil. They do not seem aware that so to teach is to proclaim the defeat of Jesus Christ. They forget how indefensible is a dogma that, in fact, divides God into two Beings, which represents the unchanging One as changing from love here [in this life], to wrath hereafter. They have never explained *when* God who "so loved the world" has ceased to love it, or how such a change is possible to him who never can change. They attempt no answer when the moral degradation is pointed out, which a heaven involves, where we are to rejoice while our dear ones, or our fellowmen, for ever agonize. They are dumb when asked to explain how sympathy can expire at the very gate of heaven; or how, if sympathy with the lost survive, the blessed can know a moment's true joy. They do not explain how a process of degradation in hell can be endless: how moral rottenness can share the dignity of immortality: or how God can go on punishing his own children for ever, when all hope of amendment is past. They will not face the awful difficulty involved in God's free creation, in his own image, of myriads whom such a doom as hell to his certain knowledge awaits. They evade the difficulty, no less great, of conceiving a God, who is love, as watching to all eternity, unmoved and

---

38 Editor: The Latin translates as, *the corruption of the best is the worst of all.*

unloving, the agonies of his own children. They will not tell us why the savage is wrong, who mutilates his body to please his God; and the Christian is right, who mutilates his moral sense, his noblest part, by calling those acts good in God which he loathes in his fellowman.

This list, incomplete as it is, is sufficient to explain why those who would gladly [remain silent], dare not. God's honour is at stake; God's truth is at stake, when, in place of the gospel, horrors are taught that especially wound that which is best within us, horrors that contradict alike man's conscience, primitive Christianity, and the express teaching of Holy Scripture

Part Two

*Universalism Asserted
on the Authority of Tradition*

4

What the Church Teaches

From the second to the fourth century

"JUST AS ANY TEACHER IN CHRISTIANITY TOWERED ALOFT, SO IN PROPORTION DID HE THE MORE HOLD AND DEFEND THE TERMINATION OF PENALTIES AT SOME TIME IN THE FUTURE."
—D. J. C. DOEDERLIN[1]

"Indeed, beside Origen, Gregory of Nyssa also, Gregory of Nazianzus, Basil, Ambrose himself, and Jerome, taught everywhere the universal restitution of things, asserting simultaneously with it, an end of eternal punishment."
—C. B. Schlüter[2]

"The ultimate restoration of the lost was an opinion held by very many Jewish teachers, and some of the Fathers."
—Pfaf[3]

1 Editor: D. Johann Christoph Doederlein, *Institutio theologi christiani in capitibus religionis theoreticis, nostris temporibus accomodata* (Nuremberg: 1780). Doederlein (1745–92) was a German Protestant, and from 1782 he was Professor of Theology in Jena.

2 Editor: Christoph Bernhard Schlüter's Preface to John Scotus Eriugena, *De divisione naturae*, translated by C. B. Schlüter (Münster: 1838). Reprinted in J. P. Migne's *Patralogia Latina*, vol. 122 (Paris: 1853), 101–26. Schlüter (1801–84) was Professor of Philosophy at the Academy of Münster, writing mostly on Christian theology.

3 *Frag. Anec.* [Editor: This may refer to Christoph Matthaeus Pfaf (1668–1760), a

Part Two—Universalism Asserted on the Authority of Tradition

"The doctrine of a general restoration of all rational creatures has been recommended by very many of the greatest thinkers of the ancient church, and of modern times."
—Édouard Reuss[4]

"From two theological schools there went forth an opposition to the doctrine of everlasting punishment."
—Augustus Neander[5]

"The dogma of Origen had many, and these the most celebrated defenders."
—Pagi[6]

"The school of Antioch had no hesitation in hoping for an end of the pains of the other world."
—Münter[7]

"Universalism in the fourth century drove its roots down deeply, alike in the East and West, and had very many defenders."
—Dietelmaier[8]

German Lutheran lecturer at Tübingen and discoverer of various fragments of previously unavailable patristic texts.]

4 Editor: Édouard Reuss, *Historie de la Théologie Chrétienne au Siècle Apostolique*. 2 vols. (Strasbourg: 1852). Reuss (1804–91) was a Liberal Lutheran and a professor of theology in the Protestant faculty of Strasbourg. He mediated German scholarship into the French Protestant world.

5 Editor: Augustus Neander, *General History of the Christian Religion and Church*. Translated by Joseph Torrey. 2nd ed. 4 vols. (London: 1853; German original, 1843; the first German edition was published in four volumes from 1825–42), 4.444. Johann Augustus Wilhelm Neander (1789–1850) was a German church historian, a student of Friedrich Schleiermacher in Halle, and a professor of theology in Berlin. The "two theological schools" Neander refers to are the catechetical schools in Alexandria and Antioch.

6 Editor: The following is all the information I have been able to gather: Pagi, *Critice in Baronium*, Ann. AD 410, p. 103.

7 Editor: This is quite possibly Bishop Friedrich Münter (1761–1830), a professor of theology in Copenhagen and a church historian.

8 Editor: This may be J. A. Dietelmeier, author of *Historia Dogmatis do Descensu Christi ad Inferos* (1762). Allin refers to the source as *Comm fanat. de res. omn. αποκατ. hist.* I have been unable to locate this source.

> "The belief in the inalienable power of amendment in all rational creatures, and the limited duration of future punishment was general, even in the West."
> —J. C. I. Gieseler[9]

Introduction

I TRUST the candid reader will weigh the above testimonies with all care, coming as they do, so far as I know, in almost every case from those who are not friendly to universalism.[10] We shall see how they are supported by a vast body of evidence, from all quarters, in the earliest centuries; and confirmed by the express testimony (which I shall quote) of co-temporary witnesses so famous as Augustine, Jerome, Basil, and Domitian of Ancyra, who attest the very wide diffusion of the larger hope in their age. The following pages will, I hope, show clearly how groundless is the widespread opinion that represents universalism as the outcome of modern sentimentality, and will establish clearly:

(1) That it prevailed very widely in the primitive church, especially in the earliest centuries, often in a form embracing all fallen spirits.

(2) That those who believed and taught it, more or less openly, or held kindred views, were among the most eminent and the most holy of the Christian Fathers.

(3) That it not only has never been condemned by the church, but is, far more than any other view, in harmony with the ancient catholic creeds.

(4) That in our Prayer Book[11] are some passages that show a leaning towards universalism.

---

9 Editor: J. C. I. Gieseler, *Text-Book of Ecclesiastical History*. 3 vols. Translated from the third German edition by Francis Cunningham. 3 vols. (Philadelphia: 1836), 1:212. Gieseler was a professor of theology in Göttingen. His work on church history was very highly regarded by his peers.

10 The learned and candid Huet names several Fathers as in sympathy with the larger hope [Editor: P. D. Huet, *Origeniana*. 3 vols. (Cologne: 1685), 2:159, 205. Pierre Daniel Huet (1630–1721) was a French scholar, founder of the Academie du Physique in Caen (1662–72), and Bishop of Soissons (1685–89). Huet translated some of Origen's works into Latin.]

11 Editor: Allin is speaking of the Church of England's Book of Common Prayer (1662).

Part Two—Universalism Asserted on the Authority of Tradition

Such an inquiry seems indispensable, not alone because this branch of the question has been usually neglected, and the argument for universalism thereby weakened; nor because to many minds the Fathers speak with special weight, as a link connecting us with the apostolic age, and preserving apostolic tradition; but on grounds common to every serious student. For all such will surely admit that in dealing with a historic faith like Christianity, its doctrines cannot be adequately treated, their growth and development rightly comprehended or studied with intelligence, except when viewed from the standpoint of history, as well as of the moral sense, and of Holy Scripture. Further, if this historical inquiry were not entered on, we should have no sufficient answer to a very possible, and very fair objection, viz.: why, if the larger hope be in the Bible, did not those great minds of old find it there? And our faith in the larger hope will gain fresh vigor as we see it very widely taught by many of the wisest and best men in primitive times, and taught (a) not alone on the direct authority of the Bible, but (b) by those especially to whom Greek was a living tongue, was indeed their native tongue. It is a striking fact that the weight of opposition to universalism in primitive times is found in the Latin church, is found most vigorous where, as in Augustine's case, the Greek language was never really mastered.

The period into which I propose to inquire will fall naturally into three divisions: (1) down to the opening years of the fourth century; (2) thence during the church's "Augustan era," to the year 430 or 440 AD; (3) from that period to the eleventh or twelfth century. The two earlier divisions may be said to include all that is of most value and originality in patristic literature. These centuries are especially characterized by the preponderance of the Eastern theologians, and their broad and hopeful teaching. All the early influences that moulded Christian thought are of the East, and not of the West. The language hallowed by the New Testament, carried to the East by the tide of conquest and colonization, and there naturalized, continued for several centuries the language of theology. The earliest Christian writings, even in the church of Rome, are in Greek. The great councils that fixed the creed of the church were all held in the East,[12] and there, too, were the early schools of theology—centers of Christian light and learning.[13] At first the East was active, while the West

---

12 Editor: Nicea (I—325; II—787), Constantinople (I—381; II—553; III—680), Ephesus (431), Chalcedon (451).

13 Editor: The catechetical schools in Alexandria and Antioch.

(North Africa excepted) slumbered: Italy, Spain, and Greece were sunk in theological torpor, while Alexandria and Caesarea were vigorous and active. Not only what is Roman, but in a wider sense what is Latin, counted at first as almost nothing in the theological scale, till the fatal genius of an African turned the balance, and the dark shadow of St. Augustine's cruel and novel theology fell as a blight on the whole Western church.

The Moral and Social Context of Patristic Universalism

Before we can hope to understand the Fathers, or rightly to estimate the force of the testimony they bear to universalism, we must try to place ourselves mentally where they stood. The church was born into a world of whose moral rottenness few have, or can have, any idea. Even the sober historians of the later Roman empire have their pages tainted with scenes impossible to translate. Lusts the foulest, debauchery to us happily inconceivable, raged on every side. To assert even faintly the final redemption of all this rottenness, whose depths we dare not try to sound, required the firmest faith in the larger hope as an *essential* part of the gospel. But this is not all: in a peculiar sense the church was militant in the early centuries. It was engaged in, at times, and always liable to, a struggle for life or death, with a relentless persecution. Thus it must have seemed in that age almost an act of treason to the cross to teach that, though dying unrepentant, the bitter persecutor, or the votary of abominable lusts, should yet in the ages to come find salvation. Such considerations help us to see *the extreme weight attaching even to the very least expression in the Fathers that involves sympathy with the larger hope*—a fact to be kept in mind in reading these pages. Especially so when we consider that the idea of mercy was then but little known (and that truth, as we conceive it, was not then esteemed a duty).

As the vices of the early centuries were great, so were their punishments cruel. The early fathers wrote when the wild beasts of the arena tore alike the innocent and the guilty, limb from limb, amid the applause even of gently nurtured women; they wrote when the cross, with its living burden of agony, was a common sight, and evoked no protest. They wrote when every minister of justice was a torturer, and almost every criminal court a petty inquisition: when every household of the better class, even among Christians, swarmed with slaves, liable to torture, to scourging, to mutilation, at the caprice of a master or the frown of a mistress. Let

PART TWO—Universalism Asserted on the Authority of Tradition

all these facts be fully weighed, and a conviction arises irresistibly that, in such an age, no idea of universalism could have originated, unless inspired from above. If, now, when criminals are shielded from suffering with an almost morbid care, men, the best men, think with very little concern of the unutterable woe of the lost, *how, I ask, could universalism have arisen of itself in an age like that of the Fathers?*

Consider further. The larger hope is not—we are informed—in the Bible; it is not we know in the heart of man naturally: still less was it there in days such as those we have described, when mercy was unknown, when the dearest interest of the church forbad its avowal. But it is found in many, in very many, ancient Fathers, and often in the very broadest form, *embracing every fallen spirit. Where, then, did they find it? Whence did they import this idea*, not taught in the Old Testament and forbidden by the New Testament, as we are assured: totally out of harmony with every prevailing belief: totally at variance with the obvious interests of the gospel in such days? *Whence, I repeat the question, whence did this idea come?* Can we doubt that the Fathers could only have drawn it, as their writings testify, from the Bible itself?

I am aware that it will be said that patristic teaching is often not consistent on the question of the larger hope. This inconsistency, so far as it exists, it may be confidently said in reply, (a) is *precisely what we must expect under the circumstances;* (b) is very largely apparent only, and due to the use of ambiguous phrases that are misunderstood; (c) and where it is real, it is amply accounted for by the remarkable doctrine of reserve. These propositions I hope now to establish clearly, taking the last first.

Pious Deception in the Fathers

It is the fashion to confine the doctrine of reserve to the duty of suppressing a truth deemed inexpedient to disclose. I am prepared to show by the Fathers' own words that it went very much farther, e.g., to the advocacy of falsehood as a distinct duty, *when the supposed interests of piety were at stake*, a limitation to be carefully noted.

In considering this doctrine, we must remember that the principle of a so-called *fraus pia* [pious fraud] pervaded the whole legislation of antiquity. So great a teacher as Plato regarded falsehood as a kind of moral medicine.[14] Thence this teaching passed to Philo;[15] thence in turn to Alexandria, the birthplace of theology. The fruits of such teaching are only too apparent in the early centuries. A swarm of apocryphal gospels and forged writings appear;[16] fraudulent oracles, acts and canons of councils, gospels, legends abound. Writings were interpolated, glossed, mutilated, even wholly forged. "For a good end," says an eminent scholar (speaking of the innocent primitive times), "they made no great scruple to forge whole books."[17] The illustrious scholar Casaubon speaks very strongly:

> This vehemently moves me, that I see in the first times of the Church how many there were, who thought it a palmary deed that heavenly truth should be aided by their own figments. These *falsehoods* they call *dutiful*, excogitated with a good end; from which fountain, without doubt, sprang 600 books, which that and the next age saw published, under the name even of the Lord Jesus, and other saints."
> —Isaac Casaubon[18]

Of the fourth century Mosheim says, an error, almost publicly adopted, was "that *to deceive and lie is a virtue*, when religion can be promoted by it,"[19] words that not unfairly describe the teaching prevalent

---

14 Editor: Allin seems to be referring to Socrates' teaching concerning the "noble lie" (Plato, *Republic*, Book 3, 414e-415d). This is a deliberate falsehood—in Socrates' case, a myth concerning the origins of the different groups within society—told to the populous by its leaders for the benefit of the people. As such it functioned as a kind of medicine, though one that should be administered by the "physicians" (i.e., the leaders), and even they may only lie for the public good, not for private benefit.

15 Editor: Philo of Alexandria (c.25 BCE–c.50 AD) was a Jewish philosopher who blended the Hebrew and Hellenistic traditions of thought into a potent and sophisticated brew. Plato's philosophy was a massive influence in his own system. His thought was very influential on certain sections of early Christianity.

16 Editor: During the second and third centuries numerous gospels were written claiming to be by significant figures in earliest Christianity (Peter, Thomas, James, Nicodemus, Bartholomew, etc.), though it is universally agreed that they were not. Similarly pseudepigraphaic epistles, written under the names of famous early Christians, also appeared.

17 Editor: Johannes Dallaeus, *De usu Patrum* (1646. Geneva: 1686). Jean Daillé (Johannes Dalleus) (1594–1670) was a French Huguenot minister. He was critical of those who made the Fathers a final authority, claiming that the thought of the Fathers was often confused and the texts were often corrupt.

18 Editor: Isaac Casaubon, *Exercrationes in Baronium (App. in Ann.)* (London: 1614). Isaac Casaubon (1559–1614) was a French Huguenot scholar of the classics who worked in Switzerland, France, and England

19 Editor: Johann Lorenz von Mosheim, *An Ecclesiastical History: From the Birth*

PART TWO—Universalism Asserted on the Authority of Tradition

in the early centuries. Thus, Epiphanius[20] tells us that Catholics blotted out from St. Luke's Gospel a statement "that Jesus wept" (*Anc.* 31). I cite this story, which may not be true, as clear proof that Catholics were thought capable of most fraudulent usage of Holy Scripture itself.

At Carthage, 419 AD, Faustinus tendered the canons of Sardica as though genuine canons of the Council of Nicea.[21] Only thirty years later Leo attempted the same fraud.[22] Cassian,[23] a friend of Chrysostom,[24] is author of a collection of spiritual precepts; one of his chapters bears this striking heading: "Even the apostles teach us that *falsehood is very often permissible, and the truth hurtful!*" (*Coll.* 17.20). St. Chrysostom openly advocates deceit (*apate*) as a spiritual medicine (*Sac.* books 1 and 2), and having planned and carried out a fraud, and thus entrapped his friend Basil into ordination, he exults in his success, and defends by Scripture his deceit.[25] He also maintains that St. Peter and St. Paul were merely dissembling in the scene recorded in Galatians 2. And this was the common opinion since Origen's time [i.e., the late second/early third century], and is asserted by St. Jerome very earnestly. He even says, writing to Augustine, "Tu veritatis tuae saltem *unum adstipulatorem* proferre debebis"

---

of Christ to the Beginning of the Eighteenth Century . . . 2 vols. Translated by Archibald Maclaine (London: 1842), 1:357. Johann Mosheim (1693–1755) was a German Lutheran church historian, Professor Ordinarius at the University of Helmstedt then Chancellor of the University of Göttingen.

20 Editor: Epiphanius (c.315–403) was Bishop of Salamis and is remembered as a defender of Christian orthodoxy.

21 Editor: Apiarius, a deposed African priest, had appealed to the Bishop of Rome, which angered the African bishops. An African synod in 418 forbade such appeals overseas. Legates from Rome came to Africa in 419 to work matters out. Faustinus, the Roman legate, cited the canons of Sardica (343/4), which regulated the appeals of bishops and allowed the Bishop of Rome to function as a court of appeals in the Western church, as canons passed at Nicea, thus as canons universally binding. In fact, they had not been passed at Nicea. The questions is whether Faustinus was simply mistaken or whether he lied.

22 Editor: Pope Leo the Great (c.400–461) also tried to impose the canons of the Council of Sardica, which were accepted as binding in Rome, on the African bishops on the grounds that they had ecumenical approval and were universally binding.

23 Editor: John Cassian (c.360–435) was a monk in Palestine, Egypt, Constantinople, Antioch, and Gaul.

24 Editor: John Chrysostom (c.349–407) was Patriarch of Constantinople. In 399 Chrysostom actually offered protection to John Cassian when he fled, with about three hundred other Origenist monks, from Theophilus, Archbishop of Alexandria.

25 Editor: The issues surrounding the ordination of Basil of Caesarea (c.329–379) are not entirely clear, though it was surrounded by accusations of illegality.

(*Epist.* 112),²⁶ words that any comment would weaken. What is this but to attribute a lie to the apostle, and, in some sense, a partnership in lying to the Spirit of inspiration?

Nor is this strange, for several Fathers do not hesitate to attribute dissimulation to our Lord himself; e.g., the author of ninety-two sermons found in some editions of St. Ambrose (possibly Maximus of Turin, 422 AD), says of Christ, "sitire se *simulat*"²⁷ (*Ser.* xxx): this he repeats, adding that Christ circumvented the devil by *fraud* (*Ser.* xxxv). Compare a striking passage in an old writer (*De sanc. Trin.* in St. Chrysostom's works). St. Gregory of Nyssa²⁸ remarks that our Lord used deceit for purposes of salvation (*Or. Cat* 26). St. Hilary²⁹ asserts that Christ, in saying he was ignorant of that day, was not in fact ignorant of it (*Trin.* book 9), and that Christ's fear and sadness and suffering in his Passion were not real (*Trin.* book 10). St. Ambrose³⁰ says,

> Neque faflitur Pater neque fallit Filius, verum ea est in Scripturis consuetudo ... Ut Deus dissimulet se scire quod novit. Et in hoc ergo unitas divinitatis in Patrer ... probatur et Filio, si quemadniodum Deus Pater cognita dissimulat, ita Filius, etiam in hoc imago Dei, que sibi sunt nota dissimulet."³¹
> —*Fid.* 5:8

---

26 Editor: Jerome (c.347–420) was a priest and scholar in the Latin-speaking church. He was responding to Augustine's critique of his interpretation of a passage in Galatians. Jerome calls forth the great Christian theologians whose interpretation he was following, and he challenges Augustine, saying: "You will have to bring forward at least one witness in defence of your truth/interpretation."

27 Editor: Christ "pretends to thirst."

28 Editor: Gregory (c.335–c.395), Bishop of Nyssa, was a respected theologian who defended Nicene orthodoxy.

29 Editor: Hilary (c.300–c.368) was Bishop of Poitiers and known for his opposition to Arianism.

30 Editor: Aurelius Ambrosius (c.340–397) was Bishop of Milan.

31 Editor: This says, "Neither is the Father deceived nor the Son a deceiver, although this is the customary way of putting things in the Scriptures. ... So that God pretends that he doesn't know what he does know. And so in this way is proved to exist a unity of divinity and a unity of disposition in Father and Son [Allin omitted some Latin here], since just as God the Father hides what he knows so the Son, also the image of God in this respect, hides what is known to him." (My thanks to Daniel Hill for this translation.)

Part Two—Universalism Asserted on the Authority of Tradition

The Son of God *se fingit infantem*[32]—St. Zeno[33] (book 2. *tract* 8). St. Basil[34] teaches that Christ pretends ignorance (*Ep.* 141; *C. Eun. hom.* 4) and he expressly commends fraud employed for a good end (*Hom.* 12).

From this evidence (which might be easily increased) it plainly follows, that such writers would have had no scruple whatever in employing threats, which were not true, to terrify obstinate sinners.[35]

Finally, let me place side by side the two following views of this doctrine:

St. Hilary	Dr. E. B. Pusey
Commenting on Psalm 15:2: "And speaks the truth in his heart," this Father, after enforcing the duty of truth, proceeds thus: "But this is difficult by reason of the sins and vices of the age. For *a lie is very often necessary (Est enim neccesarium plerumque mendacium)*, and *sometimes falsehood is useful;* as when we tell a lie to an assassin lying in wait, or upset evidence on behalf of one who is in danger, or deceive a sick man as to the difficulty of cure."	"The principle of accommodation was that of our Lord. 'I have many things to say unto you, but you cannot bear them now' . . . its limit was in not declaring as yet all the truth on a given subject, never in saying what was untrue."
Hilary, *Tr. Ps.* 15.2	E. B. Pusey, *What is of Faith as to Everlasting Punishment?* 250

32 Editor: The Son of God "made himself an impersonator of an infant."

33 Editor: St. Zeno of Verona (c.300–371 or 380) is shrouded in mystery, but was a monk and may have been Bishop of Verona and a martyr.

34 Editor: St. Basil (329/30–379) was the Bishop of Caesarea. He was one of the so-called Cappadocian Fathers, an influential defender of the Nicene faith.

35 Those desiring further information may consult Fabricius, *Bibliothèque Grecque*—"Tot fraudes a preposterâ pietate profectae" [which means something like "so many delusions in the past came from a preposterous piety"]; Henry Hart Milman, *History of Christianity to the Abolition of Paganism in the Roman Empire* (London: 1840), 3:358; Gregory of Nazianzus, *Or.* 36; Tertullian, *Pud.* 19; Rufinus, *Symb.*; Dionysius of Alexandria, *On St. Luke* 22; Marius Victorinus, *De phys.* books 23–26; Proclus, *Or.* 8; Leo, *Serm.* 2; *Serm.* 17; Huet, *Origeniana* 2 prop. fin. and 3:2–3; Henry Dodwell. "De paucitate martyrum" 13 and 8; August Neander, *General History of the Christian Religion and Church*, 6:325; J. C. I. Gieseler, *Text-Book of Ecclesiastical History* 1:298; Hugo Grotius, *De Jure Belli ac Pacis* (Paris: 1625), 3:1. In fact, the evidence seems clearly to show that dissimulation was regarded as perfectly legitimate, and even as a duty, when (as in the case of the larger hope) the good of others seemed to require it. I am not for a moment charging the Fathers with a general advocacy of lying. I am but stating, in their own words, the limits they set to the duty of truth in one particular direction, and *in that only*.

Dr. Pusey's book is so often quoted by those who do not read the Fathers, that a striking instance of the way he has done his work will be useful. I might add *much more*, but forbear, desiring no controversy with an honoured name, and letting facts speak for themselves.[36]

The Terminology of *Aiōnois* in the Fathers

I turn next to show the wholly inconclusive nature of the arguments drawn from the patristic use of such epithets as *aiōnios*, etc., when applied to future punishment.[37] The least reflection will suffice to show that everything depends upon the sense in which these terms are used. No early universalist hesitates to use *aiōnios*, which the Bible admittedly uses of future punishment. So far is this from proving the traditional creed, that it is even asserted—by both Caesarius[38] (*Dial.* 3) and by Leontius— that Origen and his adherents *argued from the very term aiōnios, as being finite, that future punishments were temporary.*[39] In fact, we should remember what our own experience amply teaches. Almost every conversation we take part in, every book we read, offers ample proof that such terms as "for ever," "eternal," "ceaseless," etc., are habitually used in a purely conventional sense, *without so much as a thought of absolute endlessness*. And this is even more true of the Fathers, whose training was largely rhetorical; whose whole habit of mind was totally unscientific.

To come to definite proofs: just as the prophet calls that incurable, of which in a moment after he asserts the cure (Jer 30:12, 17), just so do

---

36 Editor: What is perhaps surprising about Allin's discussion on pious deception in the Fathers is that while he establishes that it is very *possible to imagine* the Fathers not speaking the whole truth on the matter of the wider hope in certain circumstances, he does not at this point cite any texts in which they *explicitly* speak of concealing the full truth *on this issue*. However, such texts exists (e.g., Origen, *Comm. Rom.* 5:1.7). So some of the Fathers explicitly tell us that for pastoral reasons one should be very cautious who one tells about ultimate salvation for all. And in numerous Fathers who we know embraced a belief in the salvation of all we can also find texts in which they speak of hell as the fate of sinners. *In those rhetorical and pastoral contexts* they withheld the further claim that hell was only the *penultimate* fate of sinner.

37 Editor: By Allin's time, the interpretation of the term *aiōnios* was a central issue in the hell debates, though it had been raised by universalists since at least the seventeenth century.

38 Editor: Caesarius of Nazianzus (c.331–368) was the younger brother of Gregory of Nazianzus. He was medic and involved in the world of Byzantine politics.

39 Huet, *Origeniana* 2:161.

PART TWO—Universalism Asserted on the Authority of Tradition

the Fathers often employ, in a limited sense, words that seem to assert the opposite. Thus, St. Jerome, commenting on Zephaniah 2:9, explains the *eternal* desolation of Amon as ending in their conversion.[40] See, too, his comment to the same effect on Ezekiel 25:4. Of Jerusalem, he says on Ezekiel 24, that the city was burnt with *eternal* fire by Hadrian. He says Israel is delivered over to *eternal* woe (*Comm. Am.* 8): a flame is kindled against them which shall not he quenched (*Comm. Ier.* 7.20); yet he asserts repeatedly the final salvation of Israel (*Comm. Hos.* 8, *Comm. Zeph.* 3, *Comm. Ezech.* 39, 21, 35, etc.). Again, he says that Edom is to be banished to *eternal* desolation (*Comm. Ezech.* 35), that Edom and the host of Egypt are to lie (slain) in a *perpetual* sleep (*Comm. Ezech.* 32): And God is angry with Esau (Edom) *for ever*, a fact St. Jerome repeats three times over; yet Edom is to be finally converted (*Comm. Obad.* 1): And Egypt is represented as restored and converted (*Comm. Ezech.* 29). To St. Jerome the "outer darkness" permits an escape; and after "the uttermost farthing" is paid, salvation comes (*Comm. Mich.* 7:8). Nay, Jonah's three days' imprisonment in the whale is *"eternal"* night! (*Comm. in Jon.* 2). And the very fire of "hell" (Gehenna) cleanses (and is, therefore, temporary) (*Comm. Nah.* 3). In St. Jerome's works I have noted many cases in which *eternus* (etc.) means in fact temporary.

Nay, so wholly ambiguous and inconclusive are such terms that we shall see Origen asserting that obstinate sins are to be *extinguished* by the *"eternal fire."* So, the ancient author of the second Sybilline book[41] tells us (in words that recall the statement in Rev 20:14, about the second death) that "hell" (Hades) and all things and persons are cast into "unquenchable fire" for cleansing. The author of the sermons printed in St. Ambrose's works,[42] who bids his hearers consider "the day of judgment" and the *"unquenchable"* flames of hell, yet says that baptism extinguishes the flame of hell, and opens Tartarus (*Ser.* 31). So Domitianus says those assigned to *eternal* punishment are saved (*Fac, Pro def. tr. cap.* 4.4). Another old writer, as we shall see, tells us that the worm "that dieth not" dies.

40 Editor: All the following references in brackets indicate Jerome's comments on the biblical texts in question. They can be found in his biblical commentaries.

41 Editor: The Sibylline Oracles are a collection of prophetic oracles, written between the second and sixth centuries, and ascribed to the Sibyls (women in ancient Greece, located at holy sites, believed to possess divinely inspired prophetic powers). The oracles contain a lot of Jewish and Christian material. Book 2, to which Allin refers, may have been Christian (or Jewish with Christian modifications).

42 Ed. Paris, 1569.

Leo (Augustus)[43] says *eternal* prisoners were released from Hades by Christ (*Or.* 7). Eusebius twice calls *unquenchable* the brief fire that consumes a martyr (*Hist. eccl.* 6.41). Origen calls, without hesitation, that fire *eternal* which he believed to be finite. He even says that obstinate sins are to be extinguished by the *eternal* fires (*Hom. in Lev.* 14: So de la Rue,[44] his best editor, reads), a sentiment he repeats in *Homiliae in Iesum Nave* 8. Again, in the rival school of Antioch, Theodore of Mopsuestia[45] (a strong opponent of Origen) agreed with him in calling "eternal" that future penalty which he taught would be in all cases *temporary*. Or if we take other words we may find a similar usage: thus to Pamphilus,[46] "*limitless*" ages, and to Rufinus,[47] "*infinite*" ages have an end (*Apol. c. Hier.*): as also to St. Jerome (*Comm. in Jon.* 3). St. Gregory of Nazianzus,[48] calls ceaseless (*apaustos*) that which is terminable (*Or.* 9). Next, let us take St. Ambrose:[49] he says—Christ freed the dead from *perpetual* chains (*Exp. in Ps.* 44 *ad fin.*) and says the rejection of the Jews is their *perpetual* death (*Exp in Ps.* 119.9–10). And he very strikingly teaches deliverance from *the eternal fire prepared for the devil and his angels*, for he says that Dives[50] is to be set free (*Exp in Ps.* 119): and teaches distinctly that Dives was in this very fire (*Exp. in Ps.* 119.17). An old author in Epiphanius' Works says that *eternal* bars and *eternal* gates are shattered (*In. sep. Christi*). Patristic usage, again, is well illustrated by no less an authority than St. Athanasius,[51] who calls the sin against the Holy Ghost *"unpardonable,"* and its punishment *"eternal"*; and yet asserts that this *"unpardonable"* and *"eternal"* sin

---

43 Editor: Leo I the Thracian (401–474) was Byzantine Emperor from 457 to 474.

44 Editor: Charles de la Rue (1643–1725) was a French Jesuit. He edited all the works of Origen except the Hexapla.

45 Editor: Theodore (350–328) was Bishop of Mopsuestia (392–328).

46 Editor: By Pamphilus, Allin most likely intends the third-century presbyter of that name from Caesarea (d. 309). He was a biblical commentator and the teacher of Eusebius.

47 Editor: Rufinus of Aquileia (340/45–410) was a monk and a translator and defender of Origen in the Latin West.

48 Editor: Gregory (c.329–390) was Archbishop of Constantinople and a significant theologian.

49 Editor: Ambrose (c.340–397) was Bishop of Milan.

50 Editor: Dives is the name given by tradition to the rich man from the parable in Luke 16:19–31. He died and found himself in torment in Hades, with an impassable chasm separating him from Abraham and the poor man.

51 Editor: Athanasius (c.296/98–373) was Bishop of Alexandria and an opponent of Arianism.

Part Two—Universalism Asserted on the Authority of Tradition

might, on repentance, be pardoned.[52] And let us carefully note that the eminent writer [Joseph Bingham] states that this was the *general opinion* of the Ancients—a very suggestive fact. The author of *Christus Patiens*[53] begs to be loosed from bonds which *"cannot be loosed"* (v.2540). A similar instance may be found in Athanasius (*Rescrip. ad. Lib.*). So Clement of Alexandria[54] calls that *incurable* which he goes on to show may be cured (*Strom.* 1). Theodoret[55] intimates that *"eternal"* death admits an escape (*Comm. in Zach.* 9), and that *"eternal"* disgrace may be only temporary (*Comm. in Ier.* 23). St. Hilary, like St. Jerome, says Jonah escaped from *"eternal"* bars (*Tr. Ps.* 69). And such teaching is common as to the meaning of "eternal." St. Gregory of Nyssa calls an *interval limitless*, and says it can be crossed over (*In Ps.* 14); and he calls an interval which has an end, and a beginning *eternal* (*In Ps.* 1:7). He describes even the "second death" as cleansing (*De an.*) and in two passages, in the same work, plainly treats "the eternal fire" as purifying.[56] St. Basil teaches that "sins unto *death*" admit a cure (*Comm. in Is.* 4.4) and that God's wrath, that "will *not* cease," ceases on repentance (*Comm. in Is.* 1.24). He teaches also that where it is said, Moab shall be shut out *"eternally"* (from God), this "eternal" is not really more than temporal (*Hom. in Ps.* 60:8).

We have seen St. Jerome calling the flame of Gehenna, purifying, and St. Gregory of Nyssa teaching the same of "eternal" fire: and Origen asserting that these fires extinguished sin. So does St. Chrysostom term *incurable* what may be cured in many passages (e.g., *In Ps.* 145.8–9 and 110; *In Gen.* 6 *Hom.* 22). He calls perpetual (*dienekes*) what is temporary (*In Hebr.* 2 *Hom.* 4, and *In Eph.* 4 *Hom.* 13). He also calls the fire which destroyed Sodom (the *eternal* fire of St. Jude [v. 7]) beneficial (*In Ps.* 111).

---

52 See Bingh. 2:970. [Editor: This is presumably Joseph Bingham, *Origines ecclesiasticae, or The Antiquities of the Christian Church*. 10 vols. (London: 1708–22), 2:970. Rev. Joseph Bingham (1668–1723) was a tutor at Oxford University, but was compelled to leave after giving a controversial sermon. He moved to the country, near Winchester, and began work on his magnum opus, intended to organize the mass of data on the early Christian writings into topics, so that readers could see the range of views presented on the topic in question.]

53 Editor: *Christus Patiens* was originally thought to be by Gregory of Nazianzus, but is now considered to come from the Middle Ages, and several hundred years after his time.

54 Editor: Clement (c.150–c.215) taught at the catechetical school in Alexandria. He was a pioneer in the synthesis of Greek philosophy and Christian theology.

55 Editor: Theodoret (c.393–c.458/466) was Bishop of Cyrus and a theologian at the School of Antioch.

56 On pp. 658, 691, ed. Paris, 1615.

What the Church Teaches

Similar phrases occur in the ancient homilies printed in most editions of this Father, e.g., the sleepless (i.e., undying) worm is said to die (*In trid. Res.*). An old commentator on the Psalter (in St. Jerome's works) calls the *eternal* blotting out of the wicked their conversion. Prudentius (348–c.413)[57] calls the brief darkness at the crucifixion *eternal* (*Hymn* 9) and the gloom of a martyr's prison *eternal* (*Hymn ad Vincent*).

I have not exhausted the instances I might adduce: but I have brought very ample evidence to show how *absolutely groundless* is the argument still commonly urged in favour of endless penalty, from the mere use of terms like *aiōnios*, etc., etc. If the "eternal" can be finite, if the "incurable" can be cured, if the "undying" worm does in fact die, if hell (Gehenna) cleanses, *how vain* to build on the mere use of such terms a proof in favour of a penalty literally endless.

Canon Farrar gives good reasons for thinking that even the terrible threats of such writers as Dr. Watts,[58] the poet Young,[59] and Jeremy Taylor[60] cannot be literally pressed.[61] I will give a stronger instance, viz., Dr. Burnet, after teaching the larger hope, uses these significant words:

> Whatever your opinion is within yourself, and in your own breast concerning these punishments, whether they are eternal or not, yet always with the people, and when you preach to the people, use the received doctrine, and the received words in the sense in which the people receive them.[62]

These considerations fully dispose of very many passages quoted as proof that the Fathers teach endless penalty. They no less apply to any similar expressions that may be brought forward from those Fathers I

57 Editor: Prudentius was a Christian poet from what is now northern Spain.

58 Editor: F. W. Farrar was referring to Isaac Watts (1674–1748), the famous hymn writer. He cites the following verse:
> There is a dreadful hell,
> And everlasting pains,
> Where sinners must with devils dwell,
> In darkness, fire, and chains

59 Editor: Farrar was speaking of Edward Young (1683–1765), the author of *Night Thoughts* (1742–45).

60 Editor: Farrar was referring to Jeremy Taylor (1613–67), Anglican Bishop of Down and Connor in Ireland.

61 Editor: F. W. Farrar, *Mercy and Judgement: Last Words on Christian Eschatology with Reference to Dr. Pusey's "What Is of Faith?"* 2nd ed. (London: 1882), 275–76, 401.

62 Editor: Thomas Burnet, *De Statue Mortuorum et Resurgentium* (London: 1720) [On the State of the Dead and the Resurrection], 366.

Part Two—Universalism Asserted on the Authority of Tradition

am about to claim as universalists. And if any passages remain that seem too positive to admit of this explanation, I point at once to the doctrine of reserve, which quite distinctly authorized dissimulation, and specially applied to such questions as the larger hope. And this is to state the case moderately and to refrain from pressing this doctrine to its legitimate bounds. For plainly, anyone holding it may *continuously deny universalism, and yet secretly believe it*. But I merely apply it to cases of so-called inconsistency, i.e., where the larger hope is apparently at once held, and yet contradicted by the same Fathers. Such I claim as universalists, because no other view can possibly explain all the facts. Therefore, I feel obliged to lay down this simple rule as the fair test of the Father's real meaning, viz., that *no hypothesis other than strong conviction of its truth can account for universalistic teaching*; while the desire to terrify sinners, added to the ambiguous character of most or all of the terms they employ, and lastly the doctrine of reserve, easily account for apparent, or even real, inconsistency which we find in certain of the Fathers.

I may sum up by saying that the method usually employed in case of these writers seems to *violate every rule of fair criticism*. Practically it takes account of but a single factor in their writings, and misunderstands that; e.g., if *aiōnios* or kindred terms are applied to future punishment, such a writer is at once labeled as teaching endless sin and pain. But (i) this is (very often) to neglect that most important indication, viz., a writer's tone and general drift. Next (ii) this is to assume that such terms are used in a strict and extreme sense, which, as we have seen, is certainly not (necessarily) the case, or even usually so. Professed universalists have no hesitation in using such terms. (iii) It is to ignore the highly significant doctrine of reserve; (iv) and it is no less to ignore the great mass of evidence, direct and indirect, in so many Fathers, which *admits of no explanation other than sympathy with, or belief in, the larger hope*. This I shall now adduce; premising that evidence abundant enough to fill a volume must, I fear, suffer in cogency when compressed into a few pages. The quotations I shall make will fall under these heads: (a) showing a drift and tone of thought totally out of harmony with the perpetuity of evil; (b) involving the larger hope by fair inference; (c) or by direct statement; (d) at times teaching the restoration of every fallen spirit.

Annihilation in the Early Church

First, it is well to note a fact, which it seems to me vain to deny, viz., that some very early writers appear to have held the final annihilation of the wicked.[63] Thus Clemens (Romanus)[64] seems to confine the resurrection to the righteous. "Can we think it strange," he asks, "if the Maker of *all* shall cause a resurrection of those *who serve him holily*" (1 *Clem.* 26; compare a passage in 1 *Clem.* 1). The epistle of the *Pseudo-Barnabas* (120 AD) seems to teach annihilation. Perhaps the most decisive passage is that in which he says that "the wicked shall perish with the wicked one" (*Barn.* 21), meaning apparently the cessation of existence. There are also passages in the Ignatian epistles (Ign. *Smyrn.* 7; Ign. *Trall.* 9) and in St. Polycarp (Pol. *Phil.* 2 and 5) that seem to indicate that they expected a resurrection of the just only. The *Didachē tōn Apostolōn*, while devoting a considerable space to eschatology, seems to speak of the resurrection of the righteous only. This is perhaps the teaching of Hermas (Herm. *Sim.* 6.11–13; 8.54, 59, 63, 68, 69, etc.).

Justin Martyr (100–165)[65] also almost certainly takes this view; for though his language is hardly consistent, yet the terms applied by him to the lot of the wicked seem to imply their final extinction. God delays the destruction of the world, he says, "by which wicked angels, and demons, and men shall cease to exist" (2 *Apol.* ch. 7). "Some which have appeared worthy of God never die, others are punished so long as God wills them to exist" (*Dial.* 5). "Souls both die, and are punished" (*Dial.* 5). "The soul partakes of life since God wills it to live. Thus, then, it will not even partake of life, when God does not will it to live" (*Dial.* 6). A fragment (*Ex Leont. Adv. Eut.* 2) seems to take the same view. Irenaeus also, I believe, teaches annihilation: it is true that he ascribes a natural immortality to the human soul and spirit (*Haer.* 5:4.7, 13), perhaps as surviving the body. For elsewhere he argues in a way that involves the final annihilation of the evil: e.g., souls and spirits endure "as long as God wills," he who rejects life "deprives himself of continuance for ever" (*Haer.* 2:34; see also the argument 3:19, *ad fin.*; 5:2 *ad fin.*; and 5:27).[66]

63 Editor: All the texts referred to in this paragraph are found in the collection known as the Apostolic Fathers.

64 Editor: Clement of Rome was listed as Bishop of Rome (from 92–99) by both Irenaeus and Tertullian.

65 Editor: Justin was a pagan convert to Christianity, who became an early Christian defender of the faith against its pagan and Jewish critics. He was martyred.

66 Editor: For an alternative interpretation of Irenaeus, see Ilaria Ramelli's

PART TWO—Universalism Asserted on the Authority of Tradition

Further proof of the existence in very early times of a belief in conditional immortality is afforded by Origen's words, which are given by Epiphanius (310/20–403)[67] (*AH* 64.10). To the early writers who teach the final extinction of the wicked should be added Hermogenes.[68] I may point out that Theodoret (referred to by Neander) adds that Hermogenes taught the final extinction of all evil spirits (*Haer. fab. comp.* 1.19). And I believe Theophilus of Antioch (d. 181) to have maintained the final extinction of the wicked (*Autol.* 2:26–27). The Clementine homilies, though inconsistent, teach in one or two passages the annihilation of the wicked (e.g., *Hom.* 3.6). Arnobius[69] (d. 330 AD) is the latest writer whom I can name as holding similar opinions. He speaks at length on this subject (*Adv. gen.* 2:14, 19, 31–36, etc.). The soul is, according to him, of intermediate quality, i.e., not naturally immortal, yet capable of immortality by God's grace, cut off from which it perishes absolutely. This phase of opinion, though short-lived, and confined to but few writers, is of interest, because appearing at such an early date: and because it affords fresh and distinct evidence of the very slender claims that the dogma of endless evil has to being the genuine representative of primitive teaching. The annihilation of the wicked was, it may be noted, the teaching of certain Jewish rabbis in our Lord's day and later. If dogmatic considerations were not so certain to warp the judgment, I believe no doubt would be thrown on the existence of *this remarkable phase of early teaching*.

Universalism in the Early Church

I now turn to the task of adducing a portion, and it can only be a portion (on account of my limited space), of the mass of evidence that exists, both direct and indirect, in favour of primitive universalism.

Christian Doctrine of Apokatastasis, 89–107. Ramelli argues that Irenaeus was, in effect, a proto-universalist. "Irenaeus does not formulate a doctrine of universal salvation, nor a theory of universal *apokatastasis*. However, he does introduce elements that point to the doctrine of *apokatastasis* and very probably inspired those who formulated it after him, such as Clement and Origen" (ibid., 106).

67 Editor: Epiphanius was Bishop of Salamis in Cyprus.

68 August Neander, *General History of the Christian Religion and Church*, 2:350. [Editor: Allin may refer to Hermagoras (third century), Bishop of Aquileia in Italy.]

69 Editor: Arnobius was a Christian apologist.

Christ's Descent into Hades

Our first class of proofs shall be drawn from the very remarkable doctrine of Christ's descent into Hades. The number of texts formerly alleged in proof of this was very large, e.g., from the Old Testament were quoted Isaiah 9:2; 45:2, 3; 49:9, 25, Zechariah 9:11–12; Psalms 68:18; 69:33; 107:16. From the New Testament, not only St. Peter's famous statement, 1 Peter 3:21, but also Matthew 12:29; Philippians 2:9–10; Colossians 2:15; Ephesians 4:8–9, were alleged. Very striking is the contrast between the universal acceptance of this doctrine in primitive days, and its universal disregards in our days.[70] Very instructive, too, is this contrast; for, doubtless, the explanation is that the gospel preached to the dead, and still more to those who were in life *disobedient* to direct preaching (and who died so), was felt instinctively to strike a blow fatal to the traditional creed. To us this doctrine is thus of the highest interest; the more so when we regard the widespread belief of antiquity in the liberation from Hades[71] of *all souls* by Christ. It is surely impossible to deny that this involves universalism as a necessary conclusion. For if all the dead, without any exception, were delivered by the preaching of Jesus Christ; then, as an eminent writer has tersely put the case, "it argues absolute *fatuity* to suppose that those who lived after the Incarnation can be worse off than if they had lived before it."[72] I do not mean that this view was everywhere held, nor do I mean that all the writers holding it were themselves universalists. It is enough for our argument to show that the doctrine so held does logically involve universalism.

A very early statement of this doctrine is that of the *Gospel of Nicodemus* (perhaps of the second century[73]).

> Of course, to us, this fiction speaks with an authority no greater than that of the *Pilgrim's Progress*. But just as from Bunyan's great allegory we might very safely infer what

---

70 For although adopted by nearly all commentators, it has never passed into the current theology of the day. [Editor: the doctrine of the descent of Christ into Hades, while very strong throughout most of church history, was all but absent in the English Protestantism of the nineteenth century. Allin is one of few who sought to revive it.]

71 Both Jews and early Christians seem to have taught that the spirits of the departed were in one common abode (*sheol—Hades—apud infernos*), though with separate regions for the just and the unjust. Tertullian, *An.* 55; Origen *Hom.* 2; etc.

72 Editor: I do not know which eminent author Allin quotes here.

73 Editor: the scholarly consensus now is that the final redaction of the work was some time in the fourth century.

PART TWO—Universalism Asserted on the Authority of Tradition

> the puritan conception of the Christian life was in the seventeenth century, so from this Gospel of Nicodemus, we may very safely infer what conception the Christians of the second century formed of Christ's descent into Hades.
> —Samuel Cox[74]

The story is told dramatically. A great voice echoes through Hades, crying, "Lift up your heads, you gates, and the King of glory shall come in." Immediately the brazen gates are shattered, and all those bound come out; and Hades (personified) exclaims, "*Not one* of the dead has been left in me." Jesus then turns to Adam, extending his right hand and raising him. Then to the rest he says, "Come *all* with me, as many as have died through the tree which he [Adam] touched, for behold I raise you all up through the tree of the cross."[75]

We may note also that the ancient (so-called) *Acts of the Apostle Thomas*[76] addressed Christ as the "Saviour of *every creature*. . . . You who went down even to Hades . . . and did bring out thence those shut in for many ages." A statement, perhaps even earlier, of the same fact is given by Eusebius, as found by him at Edessa, in the archives, to the effect that Christ had descended into Hades . . . and brought up the dead. Origen, on Psalm 68:18, says, that Christ drew up and set free from the recesses of Hades, the souls that were held in captivity. I quote next from an interesting homily, probably by Eusebius of Alexandria.[77] He supposes that John the Baptist announced in Hades the descent of Christ (*Hom.* 8).[78] Another homily says "Christ will descend in order that *all*, both on earth and in heaven and in Hades, may obtain salvation from him" (*Hom.* 12). Eusebius of Caesarea[79] (260/65–339/340) writes as follows: "Christ, caring

---

74 Cox, *Salvator Mundi: Or, Is Christ the Saviour of All Men?* (London: 1877).

75 See also chs. 6, 7, Latin version (and a contradictory passage ch. 9, 2nd Latin vers). ed. Edinburgh, 1870.

76 Editor: The *Acts of Thomas* is a third-century Syrian work that is part of the New Testament apocrypha.

77 Editor: Very little is known about Eusebius of Alexandria, though he was likely about in the fifth century. The homilies in question are very possibly not from Eusebius.

78 This opinion is almost peculiar to Greek Fathers. Some writers teach that the apostles also preached in Hades, e.g., Clement, *Strom.* 2:379; and 6:637; *Hermas* 3:9. 156. Some say that the Blessed Virgin did the same. Some even say that Symeon went before Christ to Hades (Photius [810–93], *fide*; Leo, ALL). An old writer in Epiphanius's works asserts the same of the archangels Gabriel and Michael (*In sep. Christi*—this curious homily is worth perusal)

79 Editor: Eusebius was Bishop of Caesarea. He is best known for his important

for the salvation of *all* . . . and bursting the eternal gates, opened a way of return to life for the dead bound in chains of death" (*Dem. ev.* 4:12). To St. Athanasius is ascribed a treatise (certainly very ancient)—*De passione et cruce Domini*. It says, "While the devil thought to kill one he is deprived of all cast out of Hades, and sitting by the gates, sees *all* the fettered beings led forth by the courage of the Saviour." In a treatise, certainly genuine, this Father tells how Christ broke the bonds of the souls detained in Hades (*Inc.*).

I quote next an ancient homily—perhaps by Basil of Seleucia (d. 458/60).[80] "That which happened to the visible tomb [of Christ— i.e., its being *emptied* on his rising], the same happened to Hades the invisible" (*In sanc. Pascha.*).[81] I take next St. Hilary (c.300–c.368), who says, "Christ ascending on high . . . took [captured] those who had been captured by the devil" (*Tr. Ps.* 68.18). M. F. Victorinus[82] (360), says, "The Saviour descends into Hades by that Passion of the cross in order that he may set free *every soul*" (*In Eph.* 4). In a translation, or paraphrase, of Didymus (313–398)—*De Spiritu Sancto*, by St. Ambrose—are these words: "In the liberation of all no one remains a captive; at the time of the Lord's Passion he alone [the devil] was injured, who lost *all* the captives he was keeping." St. Basil (329/30–379) seems to teach this universal liberation, for he says the true Shepherd brought out of the prison of Hades, and handed over to the holy angels, the sheep for whom he died (*Hom. in Ps.* 49.14). But Christ died for all.

St. Ephrem (Syrus) (306–373), as will be seen in the note on him in this chapter, teaches the liberation of all from Hades. From St. Gregory of Nazianzus (c.329–390) I take the following: "Until Christ loosed by his blood *all* who groan under Tartarean chains" (*Carm.* 35.9).[83] In this Father's works a remarkable poem is usually printed, entitled *Christus Patiens;* it is of ancient, but uncertain, authorship. Speaking of Christ's descent, it says: "*all* of whom (i.e., the dead) you shall bring forth as your spoils from Hades" (vv. 1391–92). So again: "I believe you will bring forth from Hades as many mortals as it has imprisoned" (vv. 1934–35). From St. Ambrose (c.340–397) I take the following: "The Lord descends to the

Ecclesiastical History.

80 Editor: Basil was a fifth-century Bishop of Seleucia.

81 In the writings of Athanasius (ed. Cologne, 1686).

82 Editor: Marius Fabius Victorinus was a fourth-century African Christian who taught rhetoric, philosophy, and theology in Rome.

83 Ed. Lyons, 1840.

Part Two—Universalism Asserted on the Authority of Tradition

infernal world, in order that even those who were in the infernal abodes should be set free from their *perpetual* bonds" (*In Ps.* 44). Here note that perpetual bonds are really temporary. Elsewhere St. Ambrose says, Christ, when amongst the dead, "gave pardon to those in the infernal abodes, destroying the law of death" (*Incarn.* 5).

Quite as emphatic is the Ambrosiaster[84] in his teaching: "Christ descending to the infernal abodes condemned death, taking from him those whom he was keeping" (*In I Tim.* 2.6–7). "Christ snatched from Hades *all*. . . . [T]he devil, lost, together with Christ, all whom he was keeping" (*In Rom.* 3:22–24).

My next witness shall be an early treatise (wrongly ascribed to St. Ambrose), which says: "Christ went down to the *depths* of *hell* (*Tartarus*) and recalled [the] souls, bound by sin, to life, out of the devil's jaws." The context seems to imply the rescue of all sinners (*De myst. Pasch.*).

Next I take the words of an old writer (Maximus of Turin?) whose sermons are bound in St. Ambrose's works.[85] He says: "hell (*Tartarus*) yields up those it contains to the upper world: the earth sends to heaven those whom it buries" (*Serm.* 3). St. Jerome (c.347–420) bears clear testimony to the same effect: "Our Lord descends . . . and was shut up in [the] eternal bars, in order that he might set free all who had been shut up" (*Comm. in Jon.* 2.6). "In the blood of your Passion you did set free those who were being kept bound in the prison of hell (*inferni*)" (*Comm. Zach.* 9.11). We may note that, in the context, St. Jerome asserts that Dives was kept in this prison; the inference being, that in his opinion, the "great gulf" [Luke 16:26] may be crossed by Christ. Indeed, the words that I next give, seem to say so quite plainly. "The Lord descended to the place of punishment and torment, *in which was the rich man*, in order to liberate the prisoners" (*Comm. Isa.* 45.7). This liberation of all (as it seems) is taught in an old document, perhaps by Caesuras of Aries, printed in St. Jerome's works.[86]

> The *eternal* night of hell (*infernorum*) is illuminated as Christ descends; . . . the bonds of the damned, torn asunder, fell away; every cry of the groaning is still. . . . The captive souls loosed from bonds go forth from hell (*Tartarus*), and the apostle's words come true, i.e., in Jesus' name *every* knee bends of

---

84 Editor: Ambrosiaster is the name given to the author of a commentary on Paul's epistles written some time between 366 and 384. It used to be attributed to Ambrose, hence Ambrosiaster.

85 Ed. Paris, 1569.

86 Ed. Paris, 1623.

things in heaven, and earth, and under the earth.
—*De Res. Dom.*

Here note that the *eternal* night is only temporary—the whole is worth reading as a specimen of early teaching.

An old homily in Epiphanius' works[87] says, "Christ, like a swift-winged hawk, snatched away *all* that he [Christ] had from the beginning, from the devil, and left him deserted" (*In Assump. Christi*). Another homily affirms that "Christ arose, and the prison of Hades was emptied" (*In Res. Christi*).

I take next the testimony of St. Chrysostom (c.349–407) (from whom further evidence will be quoted in the next chapter). He writes: "While the devil imagined that he had got hold of Christ [in Hades], he lost all in fact whom he was keeping" (*In Col.* 2). In this Father's works are usually included some homilies of ancient, but uncertain, authorship. Anonymous writings of this sort, of which I have already quoted a few, afford excellent proof of the beliefs then current among Christians. "The wood of the cross recalls from Hades those who went down thither" (*In S. Pascha*). "I see the earth trembling . . . [the] dead preparing their escape . . . Jesus Christ receives all" (*In S. et magn. Par.*). Another homily teaches that Christ puts forward (pretends) fear to draw on the devil, so that, attacking Christ as man, he should be routed, and all be set free who were held captive by him (*De sanc. Trin.*). This whole description is highly characteristic and suggestive. A passage perhaps even more striking is the following: "The fire of *hell* (Gehenna) *is extinguished*, the sleepless worm [evidently the '*worm that does not die*'] *dies* . . . those who were in Hades are set free from the bonds of the devil" (*In trid. Res.*).

Another witness is St. Asterius, Bishop of Amasea (c.350–c.410), who writes: "Death swallowed up life, and becoming sick, vomited forth even those it had previously swallowed" (*Hom.* 19). Few Fathers have taught the deliverance of all from Hades more clearly than Cyril of Alexandria (c.376–444) (see especially his *Paschal homilies*). He describes Christ as having spoiled Hades, and "left the devil there *solitary* and *deserted*" (*Hom. Pasch.* 7). And again, "Christ, wandering down even to Hades, has *emptied* the dark, hidden, unseen treasuries" (*Glaphy. in Gen.* 2). I understand Maximus of Turin (d. 408/422)[88] to teach the same. "Christ," he says, "carried off to heaven man [mankind] whose cause he undertook,

---

87 Ed. Paris, 1622.
88 Editor: Maximus was an Italian bishop.

Part Two—Universalism Asserted on the Authority of Tradition

snatched from the jaws of Hades" (*Serm. in Pent.* 2). From Theodoret[89] (c.393–458/466) I take the following: Christ says to the devil, "I mean to open the prison of death for the rest, but will shut up you only. You were justly despoiled of all your subjects" (*De prov. Or.* 10). My next quotations are from St. Peter Chrysologus[90] (c.380–c.450): "The rule of hell perishes ... and *all* obtain pardon (?)" (*constat de venia jam totum*) (*Serm.* 74). Proclus[91] (d. 466/467), Archbishop of Constantinople, says: "Today Christ emptied the entire treasury of death" (*Or.* 11). "*All* the dead, wondering at his Passion, cry for joy, 'we are healed by his stripes'" (*Or.* 12).

My readers can now judge of the significance rightly attaching to such a catena of authorities—which I might increase—comprising as it does almost all the greatest names in the first four or five centuries. Fresh evidence might very easily be given down to the tenth or eleventh century, did space permit. I am wholly unable to perceive any reasonable grounds on which can be met the argument that regards universalism as the logical outcome of such teaching. If Christ delivered from Hades *every soul of Adam's race* up to the time of his incarnation; if, for example, every murderer, if every blasphemer and adulterer, though dying unrepentant, were at last evangelized and saved by Christ, then on what grounds can it be fairly or reasonably asserted that less mercy will be extended to that half of our race who differ in this, that by no fault of their own they were born after the incarnation? Is salvation—the final salvation or damnation of millions of immortal spirits—a question of chronology?

Those who are students of this subject may be asked to draw their own inference from the significant silence in which writers on the traditional side (e.g., Dr. Pusey) have left this branch of the question. I have already noticed the very striking fact of the disappearance, practically, in modern days, of this truly primitive and scriptural doctrine; and will now sum up, in the following beautiful lines of Whittier:

> Still Your Love, O Christ arisen,
> Yearns to reach those souls in prison:
> Through all depths of sin and loss,
> Props the plummet of Your Cross;

---

89 Editor: Theodoret was Bishop of Cyrus and a theologian at the School of Antioch.

90 Editor: Peter Chrysologus was Bishop of Ravenna.

91 Editor: Not to be confused with the Neoplatonist philosopher.

Never yet abyss was found
Deeper than that Cross could sound.[92]

The Question of Evil in the Fathers

Before dealing with the more direct evidence for early universalism, I may as well here notice a significant element in many Father's writings, i.e., their attitude towards the question of evil. Pressed by the Manichean[93] controversy, the Fathers were forced to consider this question. Their answers to the difficulty are often very significant; they frequently prove their point, either by asserting that *all evil shall one day cease*, or else that evil is nothing. Even Augustine (354–430) is forced to make admissions that seem to involve the final disappearance of evil.[94] It is a strange sight to see the great dialectician caught in the toils he has himself set. Any struggle seems to me vain against the inevitable conclusion from his own premises, i.e., the final extinction of evil. Evil, he maintains, tends to what is less, and what is less tends to absolute nonexistence. (His arguments may be seen in *De continentia* (2.15), and in the context; and in *De Moribus Manichaeorum* (2.2, etc.). Augustine no doubt denies the extinction of evil. My point is that his denial seems vain on his own theory. So in the dispute between Archelaus and Manes[95] (275 AD), which, if not genuine, is ancient, it is said on the catholic side, "that death *has an end*, as it had a beginning" (*Acta Archelai* 29). So an old commentator (in St. Jerome's works), on Romans 8:20, says: "Vanity is that which at some time *comes to an end*." And so St. Ambrose (337–397) says: "For whatever is of the

---

92 Editor: This is from the poem "The Grave by the Lake" (1865) by John Greenleaf Whittier (1807–92), an American Quaker poet.

93 Editor: Manichaeism was a religion founded by the prophet Mani (216–274) in the third century AD. It is marked by a very stark cosmological dualism in which there is an eternal, equally matched struggle between good and evil, light and darkness. This was contrary to Christian teaching in which evil was a temporary intrusion into a good creation—in the beginning it was not, and in the end it will not be.

94 Editor: Augustine was himself an adherent of Manichaeism for a time, but he found it deeply problematic and eventually rejected it and embraced Christianity. Augustine the Christian was a *very clear* opponent of cosmological dualism. The problem, from Allin's perspective, is that he believes that Augustine's doctrine of hell undermines any opposition to an ultimate dualism of good and evil. Thus, inadvertently, Augustine was feeding the very dragon he sought to slay.

95 Editor: Allin refers to a dispute between Archelaus, Bishop of Caschar in Mesopotamia, and the prophet Mani (216–274).

PART TWO—Universalism Asserted on the Authority of Tradition

devil is nothing, which cannot have any perpetuity nor substance" (*Jac.* 2.5). St. Gregory of Nyssa (335–395) also often asserts the non-perpetuity of evil. From Serapion, the friend of Athanasius, I shall quote a passage to the same effect a few pages further on. Titus of Bostra (d. 378), quoted in this chapter, teaches the same. The passages just given seem conclusive against any creed that teaches the permanence of evil. I have ventured to call the traditional creed a dualism thinly disguised. Thoughtful readers will note its marked affinity with the Manichean heresy, in so far as both agree in the *essential fact of teaching the perpetuity of evil*.

Direct Evidence of Universalism

THE SECOND CENTURY TO THE EARLY FOURTH CENTURY

To the arguments just stated, which are indirect, but, as it seems to me, significant, may be added, as an indication of primitive teaching, the undoubted fact that in the very earliest representations of Christian thought, in the Catacombs, everything is bright and joyous. Terrorism is conspicuously absent. No figures appear indicating pain, or anxiety; not even the cross.[96] Flowers, winged genies, and the play of children; such are the prevailing ornaments.

I will now take the more direct testimony in favour of universalism, which abounds in the writings of the Fathers. The earliest of all Christian authors, Clement of Rome (d. 99), has left us an epistle [1 *Clement*] about as long as St. Mark's Gospel. It is significant that though he devotes three chapters to the resurrection, not a line can be quoted from him in favour of the traditional creed. This, though important, is negative evidence only, but there is a passage in Rufinus (*Apol. c. Hier.*, book 1, *prop. fin.*) from which we may, I think, infer, that Clement, with other Fathers, was a believer in the larger hope. We have already noted that the ancient *Didachē tōn Apostolōn* is silent as to any endless punishment. Again, if we turn to the striking *Epistle to Diognetes*, which probably dates from about the middle of the second century, we shall find the author describing God as one who always was, is, and will be "wrathless" (ch. 8); he describes the

---

96 Editor: The absence of crosses is a striking and unexpected feature of early Christian art. However, a good case can be made for subtle allusions to the cross of Jesus in such art. See Young, *Construing the Cross*, chapter 4.

"eternal" (*aeōnian*) fire as chastising, not "without an end," but "*up to* an end" (*mechri telous*) (ch. 10).

For many years after the apostolic days we possess but scanty records of Christian thought, yet we are able to supply the blank indirectly. Pamphilus, the martyr (d. 309), wrote, in conjunction with Eusebius, an Apology for Origen, which has almost wholly perished; but we possess very valuable information as to its contents. Two early writers, anonymous, it is true, but whose testimony there seems no reason to doubt, agree in stating that this Apology contained *very many testimonies* of Fathers, earlier than Origen, in favour of restitution (and preexistence).[97] Now, as Origen was born about ninety years after St. John's death, these very numerous testimonies would carry back these doctrines very close, or altogether up to, the apostolic age. Nor is this all: Domitianus, Bishop of Ancyra, whose words are quoted farther on, writing in the sixth century, is very positive indeed. He seems to assert the *universality* of such teaching *before* and after Origen's days (184/85–253/54): a very significant statement. To this evidence must be added that of the passage respecting Clement just referred to. Indeed, when the great scantiness of early records during the three first quarters of the second century is considered, it is cause for deep thankfulness that we possess such strong evidence, as that just quoted, of the extreme antiquity of the doctrine of universalism.[98]

Clement of Alexandria (c.150–c.215)

We may be said to emerge into the full daylight of Christian history, with the famous Clement of Alexandria,[99] head of the catechetical school there, and who perhaps may be called the founder of a Christian philosophy. Of the great school of Alexandria I shall not attempt to speak at length, but we should note (a) how early it was founded, (b) how widespread was its influence in leavening Christian thought; existing as it did without a

---

97 Editor: M. J. Routh, ed., *Reliquiae Sacrae*. 5 vols. (Oxford: Oxford University Press, 1815) 3:498.

98 Editor: Ilaria Ramelli finds the component elements of universalism before Origen in a number of texts and Christian thinkers. Origen may have been the first to develop a fully worked out systematic theology of *apokatastasis*, but all the component elements predate his work. See Ramelli, *Christian Doctrine of Apokatastasis*, 1–136.

99 Editor: On Clement, see now Ramelli, *Christian Doctrine of Apokatastasis*, 119–36. See also Harmon, *Every Knee Shall Bow*.

Part Two—Universalism Asserted on the Authority of Tradition

rival practically for 150 years; and (c) how that influence was exercised in favour of the doctrine of restoration. As to Clement, I may say that his nearness to the apostolic age (he speaks of having learned from a disciple of the apostles—*Strom.* 2), his wide and various learning, and his sympathetic spirit combine to give special weight to his teaching. Few, if any, of the Fathers, appeal so little to terrorism, or so uniformly dwell on God's mercy, even in his punishments, as does Clement. "It is manifest," says the learned Dallaeus, "that Clement thought all the punishments God inflicts upon men are salutary, and executed only for reformation."[100] (So Clement's best editor, Potter;[101] so Guericke.[102]) I proceed to quote:

> All men are Christ's, some by knowing him, the rest not yet. . . . He is the Saviour, not of some [only] and of the rest not [i.e., he is actually Saviour of all], for how is he Lord and Saviour if he is not Lord and Saviour of all? . . . But he is indeed Saviour of those who believe . . . while of those who do not believe he is Lord, until having become able to confess him, they obtain through him the benefit appropriate and suitable [to their case]. He by the Father's will directs the salvation of all. For all things have been ordered, both universally and in part, by the Lord of the universe; with a view to the salvation of the universe. . . . But needful correction, by the goodness of the great overseeing Judge, through [by means of] the attendant angels, through various prior judgments, through the final (*pantelous*) judgment, compels even those who have become still more callous to repent.
> —*Strom.* 7[103]

These words seem to teach that all (even those who are callous) are finally restored (a) by correction, (b) or by angelic ministries, (c) by previous judgments, (d) by the final judgment. Thus, he says that the evil, by chastisements far harder, shall be moved, though unwilling, to repentance.

> The universe has become ceaseless light. The Sun of righteousness, who traverses the universe, pervades all humanity alike. Giving us the inalienable inheritance of the Father. . . . Writing his laws on our hearts. What laws are those he thus writes? That *all* shall know God from small to great. It is always the

100 Editor: Johannes Dallaeus, *De usu Patrum* (1646. Geneva: 1686).
101 Editor: Bishop John Potter (c.1674–1747).
102 Editor: H. E. F. Guericke, *De schola quese Alexandrina* (Halle: 1824).
103 Ed. Cologne, 1688, 702–6.

purpose of God to save the human flock [humanity].
—*Adm. ad gent.*

Clement's teaching as to the design of penalty is conceived in the spirit of the larger hope. God's "blame is censure concealed in an artful mode of help, ministering salvation under a veil" (*Paed.* 1:9). And again: "David very plainly states the motives of God's threats [by saying], 'when he slew them they sought him and turned to him'" (*Paed.* 1:9). Commenting on Deuteronomy 32:23–25, where God uses very bitter threats of destruction, Clement says: "The divine nature is not angry, but is at the very farthest from being so, for it is an excellent artifice to affright, in order that we may not sin" (*Paed.* 1:8).

The drift of Clement's teaching may be thus stated. God is training the universe with a resolve to save all. If men are disobedient to the message of salvation, then by discipline and by punishments, he sooner or later brings all to repentance. He says, "So Christ saves all men. Some he converts by penalties, others who follow him of their own will . . . that *every* knee may be bent to him, of those in heaven, on earth, and under the earth, i.e., angels, men, and souls, who, before his coming, passed away from this mortal life" (*In 1 John*).

Before passing on I may point out that Clement, like many of the Fathers, seems to regard death (not of the righteous merely), but death in itself, as a provision designed in mercy for healing sin. He asserts that "when any one falls into *incurable* evil . . . it will be for his good if he is put to death" (*Strom.* 1). Of Sodom, Clement writes: "The just vengeance on the Sodomites became an image of the *salvation* which is well calculated for men" (*Paed.* 3:8).

ATHENAGORAS (C.133–C.190), ETC.

There is much that is interesting in a writer earlier than Clement, Athenegoras.[104] He nowhere alludes to endless penalty, though he speaks of future judgment. His conception of the resurrection seems to be that it is the crown and completion of man's rational nature.[105] "If this [the resur-

---

104 Editor: Athenagoras was a philosopher, possibly a Platonist, from Athens who converted to Christianity.

105 Editor: The doctrines of *apokatastasis* (the final restoration of creation) and *anastasis* (resurrection) were intimately related in the tradition coming down from Origen. The resurrection was the resurrection of the whole human being, both body

rection] takes place [then] an end befitting the nature of man follows also" (*Res.* 25). He speaks of the future body as not liable to suffering (*Res.* 10), and of the resurrection as a change for the better (apparently in every case) (*Res.* 12). Athenagoras, though little known, writes with a grace and vigor too often wanting in more famous names.

Further evidence of early teaching is afforded by a fragment, assigned to Irenaeus by Pfaff,[106] its discoverer, but certainly very ancient. "Christ will come at the end of the times in order to annul everything evil, and to reconcile again all things, that there may be an end of all impurities" (*Frag.* 4). These words fairly express the larger hope.

The Sibylline Oracles

Further proof of the prevalence of universalist views at a very early date in the church may be drawn from the so-called Sibylline books, which were composed (except a certain portion, which is pre-Christian), at various dates, and by various authors, in the second and following centuries. These books furnish us with most valuable evidence as to the beliefs current in those days. It will be seen how sharp is the contrast between them and our modern notions. In one of them a very striking picture is drawn of the end of the world. All things, *even Hades*, are to be melted down in the divine fire in order *to be purified*. All, just and unjust, pass through *unquenchable* fire. The unjust are further committed to *hell* (Gehenna); they are bound in fetters not to be broken; they pray vainly to God; yet these men—apparently all the lost—are finally to be saved at the request of the righteous. They are to be "removed elsewhere to a life eternal for immortals" (book 2, vv. 195–340). Another passage (book 8, 412), seems to teach an universal purification. These verses belong perhaps to the second century; so far from exhibiting any sentimentality, the picture drawn of the end of the world is awful: even infants at the breast wail in the unquenchable fire; how significant then is it to find mercy finally

---

and soul. It was the restoration of human nature. This was understood to transcend any individual human and to apply to all humanity.

   106 Editor: In 1713 C. M. Pfaff published four fragments that he claimed to have found in Turin library. He attributed them to Irenaeus. In 1900, fifteen years after Allin first published this book, Adolf von Harnack (1851–1930) showed the fragments to be a likely fabrication.

triumphing. "The Sibyl asserts that the pains even of the damned are to be terminated."[107] (So, too, say Opsopceus, Masardus, Gallaeus, etc.[108])

In passing, too, we may at any rate note that the *Apocalypse of Moses*—in part, probably very ancient—represents God as saying to Satan: "There shall not be granted to you ear, or wing, or one limb of all which those have whom you have enticed by your wickedness." Even if the primary reference be to Adam and Eve, still the drift and spirit of these words is quite in harmony with the larger hope.

Origen (184/5–253/4)

I give next a few quotations from the famous Origen,[109] born at Alexandria, and when only eighteen called to preside over its school of theology. Writing on 1 Corinthians 15:28, he says: "When the Son is said to be subject to the Father, the perfect restoration of the whole creation is signified" (*Prin.* 3:5.7).[110] And again, speaking of the end, "God will be all ... seeing evil nowhere exists, for God is all things." "When death shall no longer exist, or the sting of death, nor any evil at all, then, verily, God will be all in all" (*Prin.* 3:6.3). "All things shall be reestablished in a state of unity, all rational souls restored" (*Prin.* 3:6.6). "We assert that the Word

---

107 Fabricius, *Bibliothèque Grecque* 1:203 [Editor: The theme of the righteous praying for the postmortem salvation of the damned from the burning lake is not uncommon in the second and third century. It can be found in *The Apocalypse of Peter*, *The Odes of Solomon*, *The Apocalypse of Peter*, *The Life of Adam and Eve*, *The Testament of Zebulon*, *The Acts of Paul and Thecla*, *The Acts of Thomas*, etc. See Ramelli, *Christian Doctrine of Apokatastasis*, 67–87.]

108 Editor: Johannes Opsopaus (1556–96) and Servatius Gallaeus (1627–89) were scholars who worked on the Sibylline texts. I do not know Masardus.

109 Editor: Given the huge significance of Origen in terms of systematizing the theology of *apokatastasis* and in terms of influencing the subsequent Christian tradition on this matter, it is very surprising how little space Allin devotes to him. On Origen, see now Ramelli, *Christian Doctrine of Apokatastasis*, 137–215. See also Harmon, *Every Knee Shall Bow*.

110 Editor: Origen's proposal is that when Christ submits to the Father at "the end" (1 Cor 15:28) he is doing so as the Second Adam, as the representative of humanity and of creation as a whole. So Christ is submitting to God in his humanity on behalf of creation. He can only do this once creation has been subjected to him. This interpretation was intended to avoid the subordinationist reading of Christ's subjection to God. Thus, Christ submits to the Father *in his humanity*, not in his divinity. This interpretation was also defended by Gregory of Nyssa and others in the Origenian tradition.

PART TWO—Universalism Asserted on the Authority of Tradition

will subdue to himself all rational natures, and will change them into his own perfection" (*Cont. Cels.* 8:72).[111]

Such was the teaching that at first leavened all Christendom: the fearless assertion of a restoration embracing not all men merely, but all fallen spirits. Such was the teaching of one who stands perhaps foremost, since the apostle [Paul]'s day, in the union in one person, of genius, learning, industry, holiness, "whose life was one continuous prayer." "Everyone with hardly an exception adhered to Origen."[112] "Provided one had Origen on his side, he believed himself certain to have the truth."[113]

Three points may be briefly noted, (a) the wide diffusion at this early date of the larger hope; (b) the stress Origen frequently lays on the guilt of sin, and the need of retribution; (c) his use of *aiōnios* to express a limited punishment.

Gregory the Wonderworker (c.213–270)

Another ancient universalist, as I think we may conclude, is St. Gregory Thaumaturgus.[114] Born of heathen parents, he was converted by Origen, whose friend and pupil he became. As Bishop of Caesarea, he was distinguished for orthodoxy and numerous (alleged) miracles. He there converted nearly the whole population to Christianity. Bound as he was to Origen by the closest possible ties, he would naturally, in turn, teach the larger hope; and thus, from so important a center as Caesarea, a vast district would in turn be leavened. That St. Gregory did, in fact, so teach,

---

111 Some critics think Origen to have taught a possibility of falling away after restoration. This is not certain, but he certainly taught a universal restoration. [Editor: in Origen, the possibility of *temporarily* falling away after restoration is not to be confused with the possibility of *finally* falling away. Origen may have contemplated the possibility of falling into sin again after restoration in ages *prior to* the final apokatastasis. However, for Origen, the *final* apokatastasis is (a) universal (unlike gnostic versions of restoration) and (b) permanent (unlike Stoic versions of restoration).]

112 Huet, *Origeniana*, 197.

113 Editor: Louis Doucin, *Historie de l'Origénisme* (Paris: 1700). Louis Doucin (1652–1726) was a Jesuit historian and theologian. His comment here is something of an overstatement. While Origen was highly regarded, within his own lifetime there were those who opposed him, and in later centuries his teaching—or better, *alleged* teaching—was a matter of heated controversy.

114 Editor: On Gregory the Wonderworker, see now Ramelli, *Christian Doctrine of Apokatastasis*, 275–77.

we can infer from a passage in Rufinus (*Apol. c. Hier.* 1 *prope fin.*). Of his writings hardly anything has survived.[115]

Methodius (d. c.311)

I have next to cite some extracts from Methodius, Bishop of Tyre, and a martyr (probably).[116] Extracts of his work on the resurrection have been preserved in Epiphanius and Photius. His teachings seem logically to involve universalism. Thus, he asserts that death was given for the destruction of sin in man:

> God for this cause pronounced him mortal and clothed him with mortality, that man might not be an undying evil [i.e., that evil in man might not be endless] ... in order that, by the dissolution of the body, *sin might be destroyed root and branch from beneath*, that there might not be left even the smallest particle of root, from which new shoots of sins might break forth.

He goes on to employ the illustration of a fig tree growing in the walls of a splendid temple, to preserve which the fig tree is torn away by the root and dies. "In the same way also, God, the Builder, dissolved, slaying by the seasonable application of death, man, his own temple, when [man] had fostered sin like a wild fig tree, ... in order that the flesh, after sin is withered and dead, may, like a restored temple, be raised up immortal, while sin is *utterly* destroyed from its foundations" (from Epiphanius, *AH* 64.24–25). He adds that if the Artist wishes that that on which he has bestowed so much pains shall be quite free from injury, it must be broken up and recast, in order that all disfigurements may disappear while the image is restored again. *"For it is impossible for an image under the hands of (kata) the original artist to be lost, even if it be melted down again"* (from

---

115 Editor: It is of interest to note that one of Gregory's disciples was Macrina the Elder, the grandmother of Basil, Gregory of Nyssa, and Macrina the Younger. So there is a direct chain from Origen, through Gregory the Wonderworker, to the Capadocians. The doctrine of *apokatastasis* was very likely passed down this chain.

116 Editor: The claim that Methodius was Bishop of Tyre was made by Jerome, but it does not seem to fit with other evidence that we have. Methodius was an opponent of Origen, albeit one who had much appreciation for him and one whose opposition was arguably based on a misunderstanding of Origen's doctrine of resurrection. But, opponent though he was, he was not an opponent of Origen's universalism. This was the case for all of Origen's early opponents—including Eustathius of Antioch, Apollinarius of Laodicea, and Theophilus of Antioch.

PART TWO—Universalism Asserted on the Authority of Tradition

Epiphanius, *AH* 64.27). He says that what the melting down is to a statue, that is death to man, and the recasting in full beauty is man's resurrection.

It is possible no doubt to minimize and explain away all this, but such teaching as that quoted seems clearly to imply in its natural meaning that God's image cannot be lost, and that death and resurrection (the common lot) involve the cure of sin. To the African school[117] death is simply a penalty. To the great Eastern theologians, death is in fact a mode of cure—a striking difference. I may add that Methodius says in one passage, "Death is good, if it be found like stripes to children for correction"; not the death of sin (sinners?) (in Epiphanius, *AH* 22). He adds that God sent death in order that all sin in man might perish (in Epiphanius, *AH* 22). Photius (810–893)[118] asserts that Methodius maintains that even the power of thinking evil thoughts is eradicated by the presence of natural death (*Bibl.* Cod. 224). "Man, after having been formed for God's worship . . . cannot return to discord and corruption" (*Fragment* 1 from a *Homily on the Cross*). "It is incredible that we, who are the images of God, should be altogether destroyed as being without honour" (*Fragment on Jonah*). Christ was sacrificed and rose again, in order that he might "be by *all created things* equally adored, for to him 'every knee shall bow, of things,'" etc. (*Oration on the Psalms*—This treatise is in one manuscript assigned to St. Chrysostom).

The Early Fourth to Mid-Fifth Century

We may now be said to have entered on the second of those periods into which our inquiry is divided. The years stretching away from the present date to 430 or 440 AD are crowded more than any other with names illustrious in the annals of the church. And it is noteworthy that precisely in this period universalism finds some of its ablest and most outspoken advocates, as we shall see in the course of these pages.

---

117 Editor: Allin speaks here is Augustine of Hippo. However, it must not be forgotten that Alexandria was *also* in Africa.

118 Editor: Photius was the Patriarch of Constantinople.

Eusebius of Caesarea (260/65–339/40)

Eusebius of Caesarea was a notorious Origenist.[119] "He in the most evident manner acquiesced in Origen's tenets" (except on the Trinity[120]) says St. Jerome (*Ruf.* book 2). Commenting on Psalm 2, he says: "The Son's 'breaking in pieces' his enemies is for the sake of remoulding them, as a potter his own work; as Jer 18:6, says: i.e., to restore them once more to their former state." "Even the impious, when the day of the Lord arrives . . . shall cast forth and fling away every false opinion of their mind with regard to idols" (*Comm. Isa.* 2.22)—words that are certainly suggestive when speaking of the universal judgment, as here.

> Christ will therefore subject to himself *everything* [the universe], and this saving subjection it is right to regard as similar to that, according to which the Son himself shall be subjected unto him, who subjected to himself all things. . . . But after the close of everything, he will not dwell in a few, but in all those who are then worthy of the kingdom of heaven. So then shall come to pass [God's being] all in all, when he inhabits as his people all [absolutely, *tous pantas*].
> —*Eccl. theol.* 3.16.

Eusebius has preserved some fragments of the writings of Marcellus of Ancyra (d. 374). I may quote one: "For what else do the words mean, 'Until the times of restitution' [Acts 3:21] but that the apostle [Peter] designed to point out that time, in which all things partake of that perfect restoration" (*Cont. Mar.* 2.4).

---

119 Editor: Eusebius' Origenism and belief in *apokatastasis* was passed down a direct line from Origen to Pierius to Pamphilus to Eusebius. On Eusebius, see now Ramelli, *Christian Doctrine of Apokatastasis*, 307–31.

120 Editor: Origen's trinitarian views were subject to some controversy after his death, largely based on misunderstanding of his work. Origen was, in fact, very loyal to the church's rule of faith and orthodox in his view of Christ and the Trinity. In later controversies some accused Origen of being a subordinationist in his Christology, but he was actually fiercely anti-subordinationist. Eusebius is often thought to have had Arian sympathies, but this too is likely not correct. Indeed, Eusebius was a counsellor to the Emperor Constantine and Ilaria Ramelli speculates that he may have influenced Constantine to introduce the anti-Arian *homoousios* ("of one substance with") clause into the Nicene Creed, inspired by Origen, who used such language of the relationship of the Son to the Father. See Ramelli, "Origen's Anti-Subordinationism and Its Heritage in the Nicene and Cappadocian Line."

PART TWO—Universalism Asserted on the Authority of Tradition

Serapion (fourth century) and Athanasius (296/98–373)

I take next a brief passage from Serapion,[121] Athanasius' friend. His words seems certainly to involve the final extinction of evil. In his view, evil, as consisting in choice merely, has no real existence, and easily passes away, leaving no trace behind. "It is of itself nothing, nor can it of itself exist or exist always; but is in process of vanishing, and by vanishing proved to be unable to exist" (*Adv. Man.* 151.4).

I do not design to discuss St. Athanasius' teaching at any length. It has never been my intention to deny the existence of a school of thought adverse to universalism, in early times. But I do not feel certain, by any means, that Athanasius belonged to this school.[122]

1. There is undoubted evidence seeming to point the other way, e.g., the learned and candid [Joseph] Bingham shows that he teaches the possibility of repentance, and pardon, for even the sin against the Holy Ghost.[123]

2. Of Origen he speaks, more than once, with respect and even admiration.[124]

3. In his treatises, *De Incarnatione* and *In illud* there is much teaching as to Christ's work, etc., that seems in perfect harmony with the larger hope.[125]

    121 Editor: Serapion was Bishop of Thmuis, Egypt, from about 339–360. He had previously been a monk and a companion of the great St. Anthony (one of the pioneers of Christian monasticism and himself a universalist in the Origenian tradition).

    122 Editor: Allin is arguably being too cautious here. Ilaria Ramelli has made a strong case that Athanasius *was* a believer in the final restoration of all intelligent creatures (*The Christian Doctrine of Apokatastasis*, 241–55). The passages usually cited against it are all explicable in terms compatible with universalism (e.g., that *aiōnios* punishment does not mean everlasting punishment).

    123 Joseph Bingham, *Origines ecclesiasticae, or The Antiquities of the Christian Church*.

    124 Editor: Athanasius defended Origen against critics. We also know that Athanasius held some of Origen's disciples in very high regard—in particular, St. Anthony (who *bios* Athanasius wrote), Didymus the Blind (whom Athanasius appointed as head of the catechetical school in Alexandria), Palladius, Evagrius, Theognostus, and Basil of Caesarea. And these, like Origen himself, all seem to have affirmed *apokatastasis*. That Athanasius so esteemed Christians that he knew taught the salvation of all *at very least* suggests that he was not hostile to the notion.

    125 Editor: There are actually numerous texts in Athanasius that speak of the salvation of all creatures. See Ramelli, *Christian Doctrine of Apokatastasis*, 241–55.

What the Church Teaches

4. His teaching as to the descent into Hades is significant. He says that the whole population of the world, which existed in the first ages, and was detained by death, [will] bend the knee as being freed from it. "For he [Christ] spoke to those in bonds, 'Come forth.' ... But that they who were formerly disobedient and resisted God were set free, that Peter showed" (1 Pet 3:18) (*Frag. in verb. Laud. Dom. dracones*). "Christ captured over again the souls captured by the devil, for that he promised in saying, 'I, if I be lifted up, will draw all men to me' [John 12:32]" (*Exp. Ps.* 68.18).

5. Let us note the following: "'But when all things have been subjected to him [Christ], then shall the Son also himself be subject, that God may be all in all' [1 Cor 15:28]: now this is so, when, as he [Paul] says, we all are made subject to the Son, and *are found members of him*." This seems to teach an universal subjection to Christ—a subjection of obedience. Again, elsewhere, after remarking that all things are not yet subject to Christ, for that he is to the Jews a scandal, and to the Gentiles folly. He proceeds, "when, then, the whole creation shall meet the Son in the clouds, and shall be subject to him, then, too, shall the Son himself be subject to the Father, as being a faithful apostle, and high priest of all creation, that God may be all in all."[126]

6. Lastly, I may notice a remarkable comment on Psalm 9:5. "'You have rebuked the nations, you have destroyed the wicked, etc.' The devil is meant since *rebuke (epitimesis)* signifies emendation ... these words may also be understood of the Last Judgment, for then sinners (*ton hamartalon*—all sinners) being rebuked, the devil, who is rightly the wicked one, is destroyed" (*Exp. in Ps.* 9).

Hilary of Poitiers (c.300–c.368)

We now turn to St. Hilary, Bishop of Poitiers,[127] one of the most distinguished champions of orthodoxy. His leaning to Origen is evident, of whom he translated [into Latin], says Jerome, nearly 40,000 lines (*Ruf.*

---

126 Editor: Here Athanasius is closely following Origen's interpretation of 1 Cor 15, and we should note that in both cases the interpretations affirms the final restoration of all.

127 Editor: On Hilary of Poitiers, see now Ramelli, *Christian Doctrine of Apokatastasis*, 237–41.

Part Two—Universalism Asserted on the Authority of Tradition

1).[128] Of Luke 15:4, he says, "This one sheep is man, and by one man *the entire race is to be understood* ... the ninety and nine are the heavenly angels ... and by us [i.e., mankind] who *are all one*, the number of the heavenly church is to be filled up. And therefore it is that every creature awaits the revelation of the sons of God" (*Comm. in Matt.* 18). This extract, in its obvious sense, teaches universalism. The whole human race, *who are one*, are the one lost sheep, which is destined to be found by the Good Shepherd.[129]

Again, St. Hilary has a long and interesting comment on Psalm 2:8–9, pervaded by the spirit of the larger hope. In giving to Christ the ends of the earth as his possession is meant, he says, a dominion, absolutely universal, one to be summed up in St. Paul's words, which teach "that every knee of things in heaven, and earth, and under the earth, are to bend in Jesus' name." And as to the nature of this supremacy over all, St. Hilary proceeds to say that by Christ's "ruling the nations with a rod of iron" is indeed meant the care of the Good Shepherd; and by "breaking them in pieces like a potter's vessel" is really signified the vessel's *restoration*. "In this way God will bruise and break the nations of his inheritance, so as to reform them." And the breaking of the vessel, he says, takes place "when the body, being dissolved by death, and thus broken up, the restoration shall be effected by the artificer's will." This surely is the same process as that in Revelation 19:15, where Christ smites the nations and rules them with his rod of iron, "treading the winepress of the fierceness of the wrath of Almighty God." But if all this means *salvation*, do we not arrive at the larger hope? By God's slaying sinners, he says that their *conversion* is meant.

> "Will you not slay the sinner," can he who came to save that which was lost, and to redeem the sinner, [really] pray that the sinner may be slain? Far be it from him to desire that he should be slain. But the sinner is slain *when he dies to the world*. ... In this way is the sinner slain, when the birth of spiritual life is renewed, by the death of all vices and sins.
> —*Tr. Ps.* 139.19.

128 Editor: Origen's influence was understandably strongest in the East, but he did exert some influence in parts of the Western church, as is evidenced by Hilary and Novation, and later Jerome, Rufinus, Eriugena, and others.

129 Editor: It should be noted that the theme of the ontological unity of the human race, grounded in the unity of human nature, was also a recurring theme in patristic defenders of a universal restoration.

This Father is not easy of quotation, being often diffuse, involved, and at times inconsistent (this latter a fact in perfect harmony with his explicit advocacy of dissimulation), yet his writings convey to me a distinct impression of an inner belief in the larger hope; as, for example, when writing on Psalm 119:159, he says that the psalmist knows a life of immortal glory to have been promised to him by the fact of his being formed in God's image—"an arrangement of *unalterable* truth," he adds, and true of every man. Or again, take the following comment on Christ's words: "'As you have given him power over all flesh in order that he should give eternal life to all that you have given him' [John 17:2], ... so the Father gave all things and the Son accepted all things and, honoured by the Father, was [in turn] to honour the Father, and to employ the power received in *giving eternal life to all flesh* ... now this is life eternal that they may know you," etc. (*Trin.* book 9).[130] "When the poor in spirit shall have been set in the heavenly kingdom, then *every creature*, together groaning and mourning, is to be set free from the bondage of corruption" (*Tr. Ps.* 69:32–33). "Even the abode of hell" (*inferni*) is to praise God, he says (*Tr. Ps.* 5:34).

Victorinus (fourth century)

Our next witness shall be F. M. Victorinus (born about 300), a distinguished rhetorician at Rome (where he was converted to Christianity). Though of African birth, this writer's sympathies are wholly with the Neoplatonic school and its liberal theology. Such a system—whose essence is the outflow of all rational beings from God and their return to God through Christ, who is the Universal Word and Saviour, and who is also the final centre of unity to all creation—leads without doubt to the larger hope. Victorinus' rugged Latinity has prevented due recognition of his merits as a thinker and theologian. "And because Christ is the life, he is that by 'whom all things have been made, and for whom (*in quem*, into whom) all things have been made, for *all things cleansed by him return into eternal life*'" (*Adv. Ar. lib.* 3, 3).

> In assuming our flesh Christ assumed [the position of] universal word (*logos*) of flesh ... and therefore succored all flesh; as is said in Isaiah, "All flesh shall see you the salvation of God"; and in the Psalms, "To you shall all flesh come"; ... for in him were all

130 Ed. Paris, 1652, 206–7.

Part Two—Universalism Asserted on the Authority of Tradition

> things universally—the universal soul and the universal flesh—and these were lifted up on the cross and cleansed by the life-giving God the Word, by [him who is] universally [the Word] of the entire universe. For by him all things were made.
>
> —*Adv. Ar.* 3:3

Victorinus' periods are harsh and involved, but his meaning seems clear. Christ is, he says, *universally* (i.e., to the entire universe at once) and *actually* Creator, Word (*logos*), and Saviour—actually the Saviour; for the whole train of thought excludes any such idea as that of a merely potential salvation. And so, he adds, "he is Jesus Christ because he will save all things unto life" (*Adv. Ar.* 3:8). "Christ fulfilled the mystery in order that *all* life with the flesh [i.e., after the resurrection], filled with eternal light, should return free from all corruption into the heavens" (*Adv. Ar.* 1:57). "*All things* shall be rendered *spiritual* at the consummation of the world" (1 Cor 15:28) (*Adv. Ar.* 1:36). "At the consummation *all things* shall be *one*" (*Adv. Ar.* 1:37).

> Therefore *all things* converted to him *shall become one*, i.e., spiritual. ... [T]hrough the Son all things shall be made one, for all things are by him; ... for all things that exist are *one*, though they be different. For the body of the entire universe is not like a mere heap, which becomes a body only by the contact of its particles; but it is a body chiefly in that—its several parts being closely and mutually bound together—it forms *a continuous chain*. For the chain is this—God: Jesus Christ: the Spirit: the Intellect (*noes*): the Soul: the angelic host, and lastly, *all* subordinate bodily existences.
>
> —*Adv. Ar.* 1:25

To Victorinus, the universe is one organic whole: a living chain clasped and bound together to the very throne of God. "The *Logos* was made 'all in all,' he begot *all things* and saved them" (*Adv. Ar.* 1:26). Again commenting on Ephesians 1:4, he says: "Thus the mystery was completed by the Saviour in order that, perfection having been completed throughout *all things* and in *all things* by Christ, *all universally should be made one through Christ and in Christ*" (*In Eph.* 1.4).

Victorinus' system shows clearly what I have elsewhere maintained, the natural connection between the dogma of Christ's deity and the larger hope.[131]

---

131 Editor: At the time that Allin wrote, the only denomination that affirmed

Titus of Bostra/Basra (d. 378)

The next witness I shall call is Titus, Bishop of Bostra,[132] in whose writings we see the larger hope taught in Arabia by one whom his editor, Caillou, describes as "the most learned among the learned bishops of his age, and a most famous champion of the truth."[133] St. Jerome reckons him as one of those in whom you are at a loss whether to admire most their learning or their knowledge of Holy Scripture.[134] From Eusebius we learn that Origen thrice visited Arabia, and taught there, once certainly at Bostra (*Hist. eccl.* 6:9, 33, 37).

I transcribe a striking passage, in which Titus is speaking of evil spirits.

> The very pit itself is a place of torments and of chastisement, but is *not eternal*. It was made that it might be *a medicine and help to those who sin*. Sacred are the stripes *which are medicine* to those who have sinned. "Therefore we do not complain of the pits [of hell] (*abyssis*), but rather know that they are places of torment, and chastisement, being for the correction [amendment] of those who have sinned."
> —*Adv. Man.* 1:32

Such words are very significant, as seeming to teach the salvation of all evil spirits. Again, his view of death is significant, and quite inconsistent with the doctrine of never-ending punishment, or of annihilation. He teaches that death is universally, and from its very nature, a blessing. Indeed, Titus maintains significantly that "if death were an evil, *blame would rightly fall on him who appointed it* [i.e., God]" (*Adv. Man.* 2:27). He goes on to say that it comes "not as an injury to the just, nor as a vengeance to the unjust, for that *which is natural cannot be a vengeance*, but as an example, or for the chastisement of evils [*otherwise*] incurable" (*Adv. Man.* 2:27). This I believe, from the context and his whole tone, to be Titus' meaning. Thus, he teaches that "Death, which is assigned by

---

universal salvation—the Universalist Church in the USA—was also unitarian in its theology. So clearly an orthodox trinitarian theology was not essential to affirm the wider hope. Nevertheless, Allin is correct that in *historic* Christian universalism the connection between Christ's deity and universal salvation was, as he phrases it, "natural." The two ideas were fully integrated in the Origenian tradition.

132 Editor: On Titus, see now Ramelli, *Christian Doctrine of Apokatastasis*, 575–76.

133 Ed. 1778.

134 On Titus' Origenism, see Huet, *Origeniana* 2:199.

PART TWO—Universalism Asserted on the Authority of Tradition

law to nature, is not evil in what way soever it come: . . . to those who are killed [in war] it brings an end of sin, . . . for as to the unrighteous, death is *an end of unrighteousness,* so also to the righteous . . . it is a beginning of their crown" (*Adv. Man.* 2:12). "Death is not appointed by God to cause men hurt, but is appointed for the greatest benefit, *both to the righteous and the unrighteous*" (*Adv. Man.* 2:16). He goes on to say that death if inflicted on a great number is just the same natural event as in the case of individuals, and even indicates more clearly the divine care: for it *"by the show of indignation (te kata to phainomenon aganaktesei)* [which the death of many causes] *benefits,* as explained, those who die, and converts the living" (*Adv. Man.* 2:16). Thus, as he remarks elsewhere, war is permitted by God to raise a surmise, that it is for the punishment of sin, "while in fact it is to put an end to sin" (*Adv. Man.* 1:12). And thus he teaches that evil has "a beginning *and an end*" (*Adv. Man.* 1:35). I need hardly pause to point out the significance of all this.

Macarius Magnes

I give next a few sentences of a little known author, Macarius Magnes, who flourished about this time.[135] Death was sent to our first parents "in order that, by the dissolution of the body, even all the sin arising from the bond (of body and spirit) should be totally destroyed" (*Not. et. frag.* 19).

Ephrem the Syrian (c.306–373)

Of St. Ephrem (Syrus),[136] it is enough to say that however strong his language may be as to future penalty, yet he teaches very clearly the liberation of all souls from Hades. "Christ burst open the most voracious belly of Hades . . . seeing that Death trembled . . . and sent forth all whom from the first man up to that time he had kept in bonds" (*Serm.* 18. *De sanc. Cruce*[137]).

---

135 Editor: This is the name given to the author of an early-fourth-century Christian apology (because he may possibly be Macarius, Bishop of Magnesia). The manuscript was only discovered in 1867 and published in 1876, not long before Allin's first edition.

136 Editor: On Ephrem the Syrian, see now Ramelli, *Christian Doctrine of Apokatastasis,* 331–44.

137 Ed. Caillou.

What the Church Teaches

GREGORY OF NAZIANZUS (C.329–390)

Another very great name there is whose testimony must be given here, St. Gregory of Nazianzus,[138] president of the second great Ecumenical Council, "the most learned bishop in one of the most learned ages of the Church."[139] With St. Gregory we come to the first of the very celebrated group of teachers, who, in the fourth century, throw luster on the Cappadocian school.

(a) Let us take a few examples of the way in which St. Gregory hints, to say the least, his belief in the final salvation of all men. Speaking of the dead, he tells us that God brings them to life as partakers either of fire or of illuminating light. "But whether *even all* shall hereafter partake of God, let it be elsewhere discussed" (*Carm.* 1:5.548). This striking statement is concealed in the Latin version.[140]

St. Gregory says elsewhere, "I know also a fire not cleansing but penal . . . which, more to be dreaded than all, is conjoined with the undying worm, which is not quenched . . . unless anyone pleases, even in this instance, to understand this more humanely and worthily of him who punishes" (*Orat.* 40). "It is manifest," says Petavius, "that in this place, Gregory doubted about the pains of the damned, whether they would be endless, or whether they are to be estimated rather in accordance with the mercy of God, so as at some time to be brought to an end."[141] It is no less manifest that he, Gregory, who was perhaps the foremost man in all Christendom, evidently knew of no ecclesiastical objection to teaching the widest hope: nay, there is strong reason to think that he himself believed it.

(b) He teaches that when Christ descended into Hades, he liberated not some, but *all* the souls there in prison. This view, as already shown, logically implies universalism. "Until he loosed by his blood *all* who groan under tartarean chains" (*Carm.* 35[142]). "Today salvation has been brought to the universe to *whatsoever* is visible and *whatsoever* is invisible; . . . [today] the gates of Hades are thrown open" (*Or.* 42).

---

138 Editor: On Gregory of Nazianzus, see now Ramelli, *Christian Doctrine of Apokatastasis*, 440–61.

139 Editor: I have been unable to source this quotation, but it is true that Gregory of Nazianzus is regarded as one of the most important theologians in early Christian orthodoxy.

140 Ed. Cologne, 1690.

141 Editor: This is O. Petravius, SJ (1583–1652).

142 Ed. Lyons, 1840.

(c) Again, it is significant that St. Gregory speaks of death as a gain to man, because it puts an end to sin, and of penalty as a mercy. "Adam receives death as a gain, and [thereby] the cutting off of sin; that evil should not be immortal: and so the vengeance turns out a kindness, for thus I am of opinion it is that God punishes" (*Or.* 42). "When you read in Scripture of God's being angry or threatening a sword against the wicked ... understand this rightly and not wrongly. ... How, then, are these metaphors used? Figuratively. In what way? With a view to terrifying the minds *of the simpler sort*" (*Carm.* 21.370–85).

These words recall at once a striking passage of St. Gregory of Nyssa, elsewhere quoted: God's judgment uses threats to the lazy and vain, "but by those who are more intelligent, it [the judgment] is believed to be *a medicine, a cure* from God" (*Or. cat.* 8). I believe such teaching to be most highly significant. St. Basil, too, uses very similar words: "Fear edifies *the simpler ones*," speaking of God's slaying sinners (*Quod Deus*).[143]

(d) Again, St. Gregory seems to treat the human race as made one organic whole by Christ's death, "A few drops of blood renew the whole world, and become for *all* men that which rennet is for milk, uniting and drawing us into one" (*Or.* 42). Again: "Christ, stretching his sacred body to the ends of the earth, brought thence that which is mortal, and bound it into one man" (*Carm.* 2:5.167). Christ is man that he may be "like leaven for the entire mass [of mankind], and having made that which was condemned [or 'damned'] one with himself, frees the whole from condemnation [damnation]" (*Or.* 36).

(e) In a brief iambic poem, he uses language recalling the Neoplatonic view, saying among other things that God is "end of all things" (*Ad Deum*).

(f) Again, having used language that seems to favour the ordinary view [i.e., eternal hell], St. Gregory goes on to say "that everything (*ta panta*) shall be subdued to Christ, and they shall be subdued by a full knowledge (*epignosis*) of him, and by a remodeling. ... Now God will be all in all at the time of restitution" (*Or.* 36).

(g) It is certainly noteworthy again, that this Father speaks of the Novatians[144] (who die in heresy, and in a way not that of Christ) as

---

143 Editor: These are just three of numerous places in which the Fathers note that the threats of divine judgment were useful to guide the "simple," but were not fully understood by them (i.e., they did not appreciate that they were not the end of the story, but a means to an end—i.e., to salvation).

144 Editor: The Novatians were those who, following a Roman priest called

follows: "Perhaps there [in the other world], they shall be baptized with the fire, the last and more laborious and more protracted baptism, which devours the substance like hay, and *consumes the lightness of all evil*" (*Or.* 39). These words are abundantly suggestive. On this "It is clear," says Petavius, "that pains *by no means endless*, though very long, are appointed for the lost . . . and, those dying in heresy."[145] The passages just quoted, if read together, can leave little doubt indeed as to St. Gregory's views, but there remain two pieces of evidence to complete our proof: (i) It is certain that St. Gregory's authority as teaching "restoration" was appealed to by the monks of the New Laura[146] early in the sixth century (*Vit. St. Cyril*, 100.10); (ii) We have, finally, a passage of Rufinus, a contemporary, from which the same may be inferred (*Apol. c. Hier.* 1).

Basil of Caesarea (329/30–379) and Macrina (c.330–379)

Next in the list of Cappadocian teachers are two illustrious names—(brothers) Basil[147] and Gregory, Bishops of Caesarea and Nyssa respectively, to whom should be added a sister, St. Macrina the younger.[148] Basil's teacher in childhood had been another St. Macrina, his grandmother, herself a disciple of that Gregory who was Origen's bosom friend and pupil, and almost without a doubt a universalist.[149] In such a family the larger hope might be expected to find a congenial home. Certain it is that St. Macrina (the younger), to whose holy counsels Basil largely owed his choice of a religious life, was an ardent, nay, an extreme universalist. And no less certain is it that Gregory of Nyssa taught openly and strongly the same creed. I know what may be alleged from Basil's works to prove that he did not share these views; but I also know that one who scruples not expressly to approve pious frauds, and to attribute dissimulation, for

---

Antipope Novatian, took the hard line that those who had buckled under Roman persecution in 250 AD should not be readmitted to the church. The church declared this view heretical.

145   O. Petravius (1583–1652), *De Ang.* 3:7, §13.

146   Editor: The New Laura was a monastery near Jerusalem that was dominated by Origenists.

147   On Basil, see now Ramelli, *Christian Doctrine of Apokatastasis*, 344–72.

148   On Macrina the Younger, see now Ramelli, *Christian Doctrine of Apokatastasis*, 372ff.

149   Editor: Allin is referring to Gregory the Wonderworker.

Part Two—Universalism Asserted on the Authority of Tradition

a good end, even to our Blessed Lord, may be supposed very likely in his own person to copy such a pattern. And I feel also quite unable to reconcile with the doctrine of endless evil such passages as I shall here quote from St. Basil.

Take, for example, these words: "The peace [coming] from the Lord is coextensive with all time [eternity]. For *all* things shall be subject to him, and all things shall acknowledge his empire; and when God shall be all in all, those who now excite discords by revolts, having been quite pacified, [all things] shall praise God in peaceful concord" (*Comm. in Is.* 9.6). Such a prospect is in absolute harmony with the larger hope, and with it only.

"Therefore, since *all* are to be made subject to Christ's rule according to the saying, 'He must reign till he put his enemies under his feet,' [the prophet] said his throne shall be restored, [for] the things made subject to his rule are to *obtain restoration*" (*Comm. in Is.* 16.4–5). That is, Christ's rule is to be one day universal, and this rule involves the restoration of those who come under it (including his enemies).

Again, on Isaiah 2:17, reading thus: "Every man shall be brought low," Basil says it means that "every kind of wickedness in man shall cease"—a very remarkable description of the result of the judgment day, to which the passage refers: he adds on verse 18 the significant words that *"every rational nature* shall bear witness that true loftiness and greatness belongs to God alone." In another passage this Father teaches that "sins . . . unto death . . . require the fire of judgment" for their cure (*Comm. in Is.* 4.4)—a noteworthy statement.

In the same spirit, he explains the words "My fury shall not cease on My enemies" (reading: *ou pausetai mou ho thumos*): "consider the good issue of righteous judgment. . . . *My anger will not cease*, I will burn them. And why is this? In order that *I may purify. Thus it is that God is angry in order to bestow benefits on sinners*" (*Comm. in Is.* 1.24). Here note that *ceaseless anger* on God's part is said to mean mercy.

On Isaiah 2:9, he says, reading, "'I will *not* forgive,' *even this* the Good [Lord] works for beneficence; . . . the not being forgiven is not a hurtful threat, but a saving discipline." This passage refers to the final consummation, it must be remembered (see Basil's comment on verse 2).

On Isaiah 1:28, he says, "'Therefore the sinners and transgressors shall be destroyed [crushed] together,' in order that they may *cease to be disobedient and unruly;* and 'they that forsake the Lord shall be consumed,' i.e., the sin whereby they have offended against God shall no more be committed."

St. Basil goes on to imply that the destruction of the Man of Sin, by Christ at his coming [2 Thess 2:5–12] is the removal of his sin, as Jerome teaches (*Comm. Mich.* 5.8): "For we have often observed that it is the sins that are consumed, not the very persons to whom [the sins] have happened" (*Comm. Mich.* 5.8). St. Basil says on verse 31 that we have once more their case referred to here: first, they are to be consumed, and here it is added they are to be burned. This burning he refers to Gehenna (hell), and the whole context seems to render it clear that he regards this as a healing and purifying fire.

Again, commenting on Psalm 49:1, this Father says that Zephaniah's words about God's wrath devouring the earth at the last day (Zeph 1:8–18) is in order that all men "may call upon the name of the Lord, and serve him under one yoke." With this, he says, such psalms as the present agree, pointing to a time when all things are subdued by Christ, and every knee bends to him (evidently in harmony).

So on Isaiah 9:19, God's burning up the whole earth is, he declares, for the soul's benefit, for its cleansing. Again, on Isaiah 13:19, Babylon's destruction, like that of Gomorrha, is, he says, for its healing. To see the significance of this we must remember (a) that the context threatens Babylon with a final and hopeless ruin (v. 20), and (b) that Sodom and Gomorrha suffer the vengeance of eternal fire (Jude 7).

Before passing on we may relieve the tedium of quotations by noticing a touching family picture,[150] not unworthy to take its place side by side with the famous scene of Augustine and his mother (*Conf.* book 9). St. Macrina (the younger), of whom I have just spoken, is lying on her death bed, to which St. Gregory of Nyssa has come, that they may together mourn for St. Basil, their brother, just taken to his rest. The dying Macrina, strong in faith and in hope, cheers her surviving brother, by noble thoughts and assurances of the true extent of Christ's redemption—as destined to embrace savingly all humanity, destined to blot from the universe every stain of sin. This most remarkable conversation of two famous saints, in which "The Purificatory Nature of the Fire of Hell is Unmistakably Set Forth,"[151] has been recorded by St. Gregory in a well-

---

150 Editor: The deathbed scene was a standard motif in Victorian art and literature, so this setting from Gregory of Nyssas *On the Soul and Resurrection* could strike a special chord with Victorian readers like Allin.

151 Henry Wace and William Smith, eds., *A Dictionary of Christian Biography, Literature, Sects and Doctrines.* 4 vols. (London: 1877–87), 3:780.

known book—*De anima et Resurrectione* [The Soul and Resurrection]. The list of early female saints contains, I think, no name illustrious in so many ways as that of St. Macrina; illustrious at once for wisdom and energy in practical life; for the deepest devoutness; and for intellectual vigor.

Gregory of Nyssa (c.335–c.395)

Our next witness deserves special attention—the famous Gregory of Nyssa,[152] at once the very flower of orthodoxy, and, like his sister, the most unflinching advocate of extreme universalism, which he teaches in almost countless passages.

I proceed to quote in proof of this. St. Gregory, in a remarkable passage, speaks of Christ as "both *freeing mankind* from their wickedness, and healing *the very inventor of wickedness* [the devil]" (*Or. cat.* 26).

In another treatise the same great Father writes, "for it is needful that at some time, *evil shall be removed utterly and entirely* from existence. . . . For since by its very nature evil cannot exist apart from free choice, when free choice becomes in the power of God, shall not evil advance to *utter abolition, so that no receptacle for it shall be left?*" (*De an.*[153]). Here it is quite clear that the saint anticipates the utter extinction of evil at some future day, and bases its extinction largely on man's free will.

Again, writing on Philippians 2:10, St. Gregory says that "in this passage is signified that when *evil has been obliterated* in the long circuits of the ages, nothing shall be left outside the limits of good; but even from them [the demons] shall be unanimously uttered the confession of the Lordship of Christ" (*De an.*[154]). "The word seems to lay down the doctrine of the *perfect obliteration of wickedness,* for if God shall be in all things that exist, obviously wickedness shall not be in existence" (*De an.*[155]).

In another treatise, the *Oratio in* 1 *Cor* 15.28,[156] there is the widest possible assertion of universalism, viz.:

---

152 On Gregory of Nyssa, see now Ramelli, *Christian Doctrine of Apokatastasis,* 372–440. See also Ludow, *Universal Salvation* and Harmon, *Every Knee Should Bow.*

153 Vol. 2:659, Paris, 1615.

154 Vol. 2:644, Paris, 1615.

155 Vol. 2:661, Paris, 1615.

156 Editor: Allin is referring to *In illud: Tunc et Ipse Filus.* The whole homily is well worth reading as a very clear way into early Christian universalism.

> At some time the nature of evil shall pass *to extinction, being fully and completely removed from existence;* and divine unmixed goodness shall embrace in itself *every rational nature*, nothing that has been made by God falling away from the kingdom of God: when all the evil that is blended with existence being consumed by the melting action of the cleansing fire, everything that has had its being from God shall become such as it was at first, when as yet untainted by evil.

In this strain St. Gregory continues all through this treatise. Every form of evil is to lie swept away; every rational creature, *without exception*, shall bow the knee in love and peace to Jesus Christ. "For it is evident that God will, in truth, be 'in all' then, when there shall be *no evil seen in existence.*" And again, "when *every created being* is at harmony with itself . . . and every tongue shall confess that Jesus Christ is Lord; when *every creature* shall have been made one body (then shall the body of Christ be subject to the Father). . . . Now the body of Christ, as I have often said, is *the whole of humanity*" (*pasa hē anthrōpine phusis*) (*In illud*).

Again, in the clearest manner St. Gregory maintains that subjection to God is reconciliation to God. Where it is said that God's enemies shall be subjected to God,

> this is meant that the power of evil shall be taken away, and they who, on account of their disobedience, were called God's enemies, shall *by subjection* be *made God's friends.* When, then, all who once were God's enemies, shall have been made his footstool, because they *shall receive in themselves the divine imprint*, when death shall have been destroyed . . . in the subjection of all, which is not servile humility, but immortality and blessedness, Christ is said, by St. Paul, to be made subject to God.

A favourite doctrine of this Father's is that the resurrection involves restoration—as undoing of all the work of the fall. It brings immortality and incorruption—things, says St. Gregory, peculiar to the divine nature, and in themselves a blessing. There is a long and striking passage to this effect in the *De anima et Resurrectione*. The apostle's words seem to me to imply

> what our definition contains, i.e., that [the] resurrection is nothing else than *the restoration of our nature to its ancient state* [of blessedness]. . . . This corruptible [body] must put on incorruption. But incorruption and honour and glory are confessed to be

Part Two—Universalism Asserted on the Authority of Tradition

> peculiar to the divine nature. . . . So we, too, severally divested of mortality literally—stripped of the form which is like the ear of corn and blended with the earth, are born again in the resurrection after the fashion of our pristine beauty.

Doubtless, he adds, the evil are to look for great severity from the Judge; but after due curative treatment, and when the fire shall have destroyed all foreign matter, then the nature, even of these, shall improve by the copious nurture they receive, and at length they too shall regain the divine impress. In this and in a former passage, this Father expressly attributes cleansing properties to the *"eternal"* fire—a fact concealed in the Latin version.

Let us here note the length to which St. Gregory goes. Universalism, not in isolated sentences, but as the centre of his teaching, and in a form embracing all fallen spirits, characterizes this great Father. And this universalism is as fearless as it is clear. With the Dean of Wells, I say "that St. Gregory claims to be taking his stand on the doctrines of the Church in this teaching, with as much confidence as when he is expounding the mysteries of the divine nature, as set forth in the Creed of Nicaea."[157] Let me proceed to quote:

> By which God shows that neither is sin from eternity, *nor will it last to eternity*. For that which did not always exist shall not last for ever . . . [The Lord] will . . . in his just judgment, destroy the wickedness of sinners, *not the nature.* . . . *[W]ickedness being thus destroyed* and its imprint being left in none, all shall be fashioned after Christ, and in all that one character shall shine, which originally was imprinted on our nature.
> —*In Ps.* 2.8.

On the words, "Arise, O Lord, in your wrath, and be exalted over the end of your enemies" (so the words run in St. Gregory's text): "The term 'wrath,'" he says, "shows the retributive power of the just judge, and that which follows [shows] the *extinction of sin:* for that alone is contrary to nature which is seen to be opposed to good, which is sin, whose end is *extinction* and a *change to nothingness.*" He then goes onto explain that to put an end to the enemies of God, means not to allow to human life any power of turning to evil; for as the end of disease is health "so here

---

157 Editor: Edward Hayes Plumptre, *The Spirits in Prison and Other Studies on the Life After Death* (London: 1884). Edward Plumptre (1821–91), F. D. Maurice's brother-in-law, was chaplain at King's College London and became Dean of Wells in 1881.

the psalmist calls the change of the nature of *mankind, from evil to a state of blessedness, the end of [God's] enemies*" (*In Ps.* 2.10). Here let us notice the stress laid on *wrath, justice,* and *retribution* amid the conclusion so strictly drawn, that these involve the termination of sin. Again, St. Gregory writes on Psalm 57:1:

> For the nature of sin is unstable and *transitory*, . . . nor lasting for ever in the universe; . . . it is like a plant on a house top, *not rooted*, not sown, not ploughed in, and though for the present it may cause trouble with its unsubstantial shoot, yet in the time to come, in the restoration to goodness of all things, it passes away and vanishes. So *not even a trace of the evil, which now* abounds in us, shall remain in the life that is promised as an object of our hope.
> —*In Ps.* 2.14

So too, writing on Psalm 107:42: "And all iniquity shall stop her mouth," this Father says: "How blessed is that life in which the mouths of iniquity shall be for ever stopped. . . . This is the crown of all blessings, the head of all hope . . . that nature shall no longer be troubled by wickedness, but that he shall put a stop to all iniquity, that is to say [to] the very inventor of iniquity [i.e., the devil]" (*In Ps.* 1:8).

Again, on Psalm 150:5: "Praise him upon the high-sounding cymbals," there is a very striking comment.

> These cymbals, joined with cymbals, show the [future] harmony between the human and the angelic natures, when human nature shall have attained its end. One cymbal is the heavenly nature of the angels. The other is the rational creation of mankind; but sin separated the one from the other; when, then, the goodness of God shall have united once more one with the other, then shall both, brought together, chant forth that hymn, as the great apostle [Paul] says, "*Every* tongue, of things in heaven, and on earth, and under the earth, shall confess that Christ is Lord, to the glory of God the Father" [Phil 2:10–11]. Which done, the voice of these cymbals shall chant their song of victory, which arises . . . for the extinction of war: which being *wholly extinguished* and *reduced to nothingness*, ceaselessly shall there be, with like honour, fully rendered by every spirit alike, praise to God *for ever:* for since praise is not comely in the mouth of a sinner, but then there shall be no sinner [sin no more existing], *every spirit* shall by all means praise God for ever.

Part Two—Universalism Asserted on the Authority of Tradition

St. Gregory sums up: such is the meaning of this final psalm

> in which after the complete abolition of sin, praise shall be sung to God; which praise contain [implies] our being *incapable* of turning to sin ... *when every created being shall be harmonized into one choir* ... and when, like a cymbal, the reasonable creation, and that which is now severed by sin ... shall pour forth a pleasing strain, due to mutual harmony. Then comes the praise of every spirit for ever abounding with increase unto eternity.
> —*In Ps.* 1:9

It may be questioned[158] whether a nobler exposition of the true spirit of the Psalter, and the true hope of the gospel, can be anywhere found than the above.

As some readers may not grasp the full significance of this evidence, let me point out that, even if it stood alone, it should dispose of the pleasing fiction, for such it is, that the church of the fourth or fifth centuries was unfriendly to universalism. What are the facts? Very few of his day were so prominent, or so famous, as St. Gregory: none more thoroughly orthodox; a confessor and most able champion of the Nicene faith; next to Gregory of Nazianzus, the most famous member of the General Council of Constantinople; chosen to draw up that creed,[159] which we to this day recite; appealed to by subsequent councils as *a very bulwark of the catholic church.*[160] Such was Gregory, this fearless advocate of universalism; nay, of a universalism *wide enough to embrace every rational being.*

Didymus the Blind (c.313–398)

With the celebrated Didymus,[161] we return to the school of Alexandria, of which he was the last distinguished head. "Didymus," says St. Jerome,

---

158 Dr Pusey thinks it *fair* to describe this Father's teaching as "mists" (of Origenism): such are the ways of theological controversy.

159 Editor: Allin refers here to the Niceno-Constantipolitan Creed, the modified version of the Nicene Creed adopted at the Council of Constantinople in 381. It is the most important creed in the church, being ecumenically agreed by both East and West.

160 Editor: The Seventh Ecumenical Council (787) described Gregory of Nyssa as follows: "Let us then, consider who were the venerable doctors and indomitable champions of the Church ... [including] Gregory Primate of Nyssa, who all have called *the father of fathers*." High praise indeed for a universalist!

161 Editor: On Didymus, see now Ramelli, *Christian Doctrine of Apokatastasis*, 286–307.

a scholar of his, "surpassed all of his day in knowledge of the Scriptures." The same Father styles him "a most avowed advocate of Origen." But a small portion has survived of his numerous writings, and little, if any, in a perfect condition, mostly in translations, or as fragments in *Catena*.

He argues "that as by the Son all things endowed with reason received their being, so by him the salvation of all of them has been wrought out.... For Christ brought peace to all things through the blood of his cross, whether in heaven or on earth.... For as men, by giving up their sins, are made subject to him, so, too, *the higher intelligences*, freed by correction from their willful sins (*correcta spontaneis cupis*) are made subject to him, on the completion of the dispensation ordered for the salvation of all" (*In* 1 *Pet.* 3.22). These words seem to involve the salvation of the fallen angels.

Didymus, elsewhere, speaks of a time when all are to come to the knowledge of the fulness of Christ, i.e., of God made all in all (*In* 1 *John* 3.2). Another passage (the text is unfortunately corrupt), on 1 Peter 1:12, evidently contains a hint as to the salvability of evil spirits. With many Fathers, Didymus, from the fact that sin resides in the will, argues its final abolition; and holds that beings who sin voluntarily are from that very fact not essentially evil. Therefore, even the devils themselves are not *radically* evil; their will has been deflected, but not their substance, not their essential being. Hence all evil spirits are capable of salvation.

On Psalm 10:15, we have a striking comment: "Break you the arm of the wicked," etc. This wicked one, Didymus says, is Satan, whose arm is broken, and his sin is not found, "receiving its end in its very completion, for evil is no substance, but a quality. And so shall come that end for all things, for the sake of which all things came into being"; evidently these words intimate the final extinction of evil. And so he says, "God desires to destroy evil, therefore evil is [one] of those things liable to destruction. Now that which is of those things liable to destruction will be destroyed" (*Adv. Man.* 2).

So we find Didymus earnest in teaching that the destruction of God's enemies is practically their conversion. Thus, when it is said that God burns up his enemies (Ps 97:3), Didymus explains this of the removal of their sins. And so again in Psalm 58:8, the melting away of God's enemies is explained by him of life absorbing death. On Psalm 18:43, where God is said to beat his enemies "small as the dust before the wind," Didymus explains this *of their conversion*. And, he says, God "destroys liars, *so far*

Part Two—Universalism Asserted on the Authority of Tradition

as they are liars" (*Comm. in Ps.* 5.6). On Psalm 9:5, a comment to the same effect will be found, and other passages might readily be quoted from this Father to the same effect.

I may next point to Didymus' teaching on penalty; he argues that divine correction, even vengeance, and promise have the same object in view (*Adv. Man.* ch. 18). I should like to add that he teaches the liberation from Hades of every soul by Christ, for he says that Christ "descends to Hades and brings back the souls, there detained *on account of their sins*" (*Comm. in Ps.* 71:20. See, too, *De Trin.* 3:21, etc.).

I can hardly feel any doubt that Didymus held the final conversion of all evil beings. (So, too, think Basnage,[162] Lucke,[163] and Guericke,[164] cf. Huet.[165])

---

[162] Editor: J. Basnage in *Patrologia Latina*. Edited by J. -P. Migne. 221 vols. (Paris: 1841), 39:176.

[163] Editor: in *Patrologia Latina*. Edited by J. -P. Migne. 221 vols. (Paris: 1841), 39:1740.

[164] Editor: H. E. F. Guericke, *De schola quese Alexandrina* (Halle: 1824), 359, 368, 390.

[165] Huet, *Origeniana*, 199.

5

What the Church Teaches

From the fourth to the nineteenth century

> "The Eastern Church of that time [fourth and fifth centuries] was permeated, from Gregory of Nyssa downwards, with the wider Hope."
> —The Dean of Wells[1]

> "Of course I was aware that several of the Fathers are in favour of a restoration of all things."
> —Cardinal Newman[2]

---

1 Editor: Edward Hayes Plumptre, *The Spirits in Prison and Other Studies on the Life After Death* (London: 1884), ch. 4. Edward Plumptre (1821–91), F. D. Maurice's brother-in-law, was chaplain at King's College London and became Dean of Wells Cathedral in 1881.

2 Editor: John Henry Newman (1801–90). This was a letter to Edward Plumptre, dated August 9, 1871. The quotation continues, "... but such a restoration does not imply probation to stand or fall continuing beyond this life, and this is the point which I doubt in your findings in the Fathers." John Henry Newman was a leading Anglo-Catholic clergyman, nationally known by the 1830s. He was a key player in the Oxford movement, but, to the shock of the nation, he converted to Catholicism in 1845.

Part Two—Universalism Asserted on the Authority of Tradition

The Gradual Eclipse of Eastern Theology in the West

WE have already noticed the dominant influence exercised over early Christian thought, not by Greeks (for Greece itself was singularly barren theologically), but by Eastern theology, couched in the language of the New Testament. Even at Rome the church continued, down to the end of the second century, or later, a Greek-speaking body—reared under Oriental influences—and whose earliest teachers, like Clement and Hermas, wrote in Greek, as St. Paul had written to them, and not in Latin: indeed the very name "pope" is Greek.[3]

This influence is very marked in the "writings of the Latin Fathers, excluding North Africa, of the first four centuries. Ambrose and the Ambrosiaster, Hilary, Victorinus, Jerome, alike bear evident traces of the more liberal[4] theology of the East. Doubtless to Alexandria—with its cosmopolitan culture, its varied learning, and its school of theology, at once the most ancient and most famous in the world—is due the largest share in thus moulding Christian thought to a broader and truer catholicity. Its influence may be traced far and near. Thus, when Pamphilus, the martyr, founded towards the end of the third century a library and school at Caesarea—or, perhaps, restored the school founded there by Origen in his exile from Alexandria—we find him giving the place of honour to the works of Origen, transcribing the greater part of them with his own hand—inspired by the influence of Alexandria, where he had studied.

When, again, about the same epoch, the presbyters Dorotheus and Lucian laid the foundation of the celebrated school of Antioch, it is very significant that, though representing a healthy reaction against the allegorizing interpretations of Origen,[5] the new school retained the

---

3 Editor: The Latin *papa* derived from the Greek *pappas*, meaning father.

4 Editor: By "liberal theology" Allin obviously does not mean the patterns of modern theology developed within parts of European Christian from the late eighteen century onwards. These were attempts to contextualize Christianity in an Enlightenment cultural context. Allin simply means that Eastern theology was more tolerant of, among other things, the wider hope.

5 Editor: Origen believed that scriptural texts had three different-but-related senses: a literal/factual/historical sense (akin to the body), a figurative/moral sense (akin to the soul), and a spiritual, revelation-of-God's-plan-in-Christ sense (akin to the spirit). The lower sense (the body) was important, but the higher senses (the soul and spirit of Scripture) were more important. Origen employed allegory in his attempt to discern the soul and spirit of Scripture. The popularity of allegorical interpretation waned with the Renaissance and the Reformation, with their focus on the plain surface meaning of the text.

dogma of restoration. The same advocacy of the larger hope may be found in the famous teachers of Cappadocia,[6] whose spiritual ancestry is to be traced to the first Gregory,[7] Origen's bosom friend and pupil, and so to Alexandria finally.

There is this to be noted and frankly admitted, that if Africa [in Alexandria] gave birth to a theology broad and truly catholic in its sympathies, so it [also] furnished what to some may seem the antidote. North Africa was in a special sense the home of a theology cruel and remorseless in its eschatology. Let us hear Tertullian[8] gloating and reveling over the future torments of the heathen. He is to "laugh," "rejoice," "exult." He tells us why: "when I behold so many kings ... groaning in the lowest darkness; so many magistrates liquefying in fiercer flames than they ever kindled against Christians; ... sapient philosophers blushing as they burn with their disciples: then shall we see the tragedians more tuneful under the fire, ... the charioteer *all red* in his burning car" (*Spect.* 30).

Tertullian rejoices *because* the condemned are for ever burning; we are to rejoice *while* they are burning, even though our nearest and dearest are in those flames! Is the moral difference very great? When, exhausted by faction and strife, this church fell hopelessly before the advance of Islam, the teachings of its greatest bishop[9] not only survived, but gained a wider sphere. Extinct in their birthplace, the cruel doctrines of Augustine flourished as a graft on the Roman stock, thence leavening by slow degrees the whole of Latin Christendom, with an element novel and uncatholic. The moment was auspicious for their success, for now the churches of Italy were fast rising to power. The great Greek Fathers had spoken and passed away: their very language rapidly becoming unknown in the West. Thus no obstacle was left to stem the fast rising tide of Augustinianism, naturally triumphant in an age cruel, corrupt, and superstitious. And so by degrees no less than a doctrinal revolution was accomplished, and the whole framework of Western theology, to its infinite loss, bears to this day the imprint of Africa, and its pitiless creed, which slanders at once God and man, true sign of an ignoble and false theology. The medieval schoolman and the modern puritan alike

---

6 Editor: Basil, Gregory of Nyssa, and Gregory of Nazianzus.

7 Editor: Gregory the Wonderworker.

8 Editor: Tertullian (c. 160–225) was from Carthage, a Roman province in North Africa.

9 Editor: Allin refers to St. Augustine, Bishop of Hippo in North Africa.

wear with complacency the spiritual fetters forged at Hippo, by one who, despite his genius, never so much as fully mastered the language of the New Testament—a fact I commend to those who claim the authority of Scripture for the traditional creed.[10]

The Larger Hope up to the Mid-Fifth Century

Let us now turn to some Latin Fathers, whose works attest plainly this widespread influence of Greek theology.

Ambrose (c.340–397)

I take first a very distinguished name, St. Ambrose of Milan.[11] We shall see what his teaching is on the question of the divine punishment of the wicked. Their very destruction is, in his view, a mode of cure.

> Many ask an important question here, whether Holy Scripture asserts the perishing of our nature, especially because it elsewhere says: "I will beat them small as the dust before the wind. I will destroy them as the mire of the streets" (Ps 18:42).... What, then, hinders our believing that he who is beaten small as the dust is not annihilated, but is *changed for the better;* so that, instead of an earthly man, he is made a spiritual man, and our believing that he who is *destroyed, is so destroyed that all taint is removed,* and there remains but what is pure and clean. And in God's saying to the adversaries of Jerusalem, "they shall be as though they were not,"... you are to understand they shall exist substantially and as *converted* [to God], but shall not exist as [God's] enemies.
> —*In Ps.* 1.

On the words: "I have set you over nations and kingdoms to root up, to destroy, to ruin, to build, and to plant." St. Ambrose says this means Christ's "destroying *every vestige of sin;* ... this it is to destroy and to plant, viz., that what is sinful should be rooted out, and what is better planted in" (*In Ps.* 44[12]).

---

10 Editor: Augustine confessed that he never could get to grips with Greek.

11 Editor: On Ambrose, see now Ramelli, *Christian Doctrine of Apokatastasis*, 616–22.

12 Ed. Paris 1569, p. 1370.

What the Church Teaches

In harmony with this, but in hopeless contradiction to the traditional creed, stands St. Ambrose's teaching as to death, which to him is not a penalty but *a mode of cure*. "Why, then, do we blame death," asks St. Ambrose, "if life is a burden, death is freedom; if life is a punishment, death is a remedy. In every way, then, death is good because it does not change one's state for the worse. We shall find death to be the end of sin. The Lord suffered death to enter in order that guilt might cease" (*Bon. mort.* 4). "Death is a passage to better things, for if the guilty, who will not recall their steps from sin, die even against their will, yet they receive not an end of nature, but of their guilt" (*Cain* 2:10). "God gave death, *not as a penalty, but as a remedy*; death was given for a remedy as the *end of evils*.... God did not appoint death from the beginning, but gave it as a remedy" (*De fide Res.*).

In the next chapter we shall discuss the true meaning of the resurrection, and shall quote St. Ambrose (and many other Fathers) as teaching that it involves restoration, as being a gift of life in Christ to all. (See, for example, *De fide Res.*) Next we see St. Ambrose asserting that from its very nature sin cannot last for ever. "That which is of the devil is nothing, and can have no perpetuity and substance" (*Jac.* 2:5). "How shall the sinner exist in the future, seeing the place of sin cannot be of long continuance?" (*In Ps.* 37). Again, writing of the wickedness of evil spirits: "They will not always remain, nor can their wickedness be perpetual" (*Exp. Luc.* 8).

The next class of quotations consists of those, in which St. Ambrose argues from the divine image in man. "That image may indeed be obscured, but *cannot be destroyed* by reason of its nature" (*per naturam*) (*De fide Res.* [frag.]). For as St. Ambrose asks; "Shall he who has not permitted those things to perish, which belong to man's needs, permit man to perish, whom he made after his own image ?" (*De fide Res.*). "Because God's image is that of the one God, it—like him—starts from one, and is diffused to infinity. And, once again, from an infinite number *all things return into one* as into their end, because God is both beginning and end of all things" (*Epis.* 1.1).

The closing words of the last passage recall that Neoplatonism that we have noticed in Victorinus, and shall see fully elaborated by the so-called Dionysius (the Areopagite) and his imitators.

We shall next quote St. Ambrose's teaching as to the subjection of all things to Christ, which breathes the very spirit of universalism. "How,

Part Two — Universalism Asserted on the Authority of Tradition

then, shall [all things] be subject to Christ? In this very way in which the Lord himself said: 'Take my yoke upon you.' For it is not the untamed who bear the yoke, but the humble and gentle . . . so that in Jesus' name every knee shall bend." St. Ambrose asserts that subjection to Christ is loving submission, and that in this sense all must become Christ's subjects. He proceeds to discuss Christ's subjection to the Father.

> Is this subjection of Christ now completed? Not at all. Because the subjection of Christ consists not in few, *but in all* [becoming obedient]. . . . Christ will be subject to God in us by means of the obedience *of all.* . . . [Then], when vices having been cast away, and sin reduced to submission, one spirit of *all* people, in one sentiment, shall with one accord begin to cleave to God, then God will be all in all; . . . when *all*, then, shall have believed and done the will of God, Christ will be all and in all; and when Christ shall be all in all, [then] God will be all in all.
> —*Fid.* 5:7

Again, on Psalm 119:91, "For all things serve you," he says,

> At present we do not all serve God. But, when Christ shall have delivered his kingdom over to God, then shall *all* things be subject to him, who has subjected the universe to himself; acquiring *the faith of all*, through the Passion of his only begotten Son; . . . when, therefore, all shall have believed in the Lord, then shall *the universe* serve God, so that he may be all and in all.
> —*In Ps.* 119.91

> By a profound design the apostle [Paul] declares that Christ shall be subject to the Father in us, when there shall exist in *all* the fullness of faith. . . . At present he is over all by his power, but it is necessary that he be in *all* by their free will.
> —*In Ps.* 62.1

St. Ambrose, I may add, teaches that the sin against the Holy Ghost may be forgiven (*Paen.* 2:4—a chapter worth reading). Lastly, the following passages show clearly the tone of his theology.

> The mystery of the incarnation is the salvation of the entire creation, . . . as it is elsewhere said, "the *whole creation* shall be set free from the bondage of corruption" (*Fid.* 5:7).

> The Father has committed all judgment to Christ; shall then he be able to condemn you for whom he gave himself? . . . Will not

> he say, "what use is there in my blood if I condemn him whom I have saved?" (*Jac.* 1.6).
>
> *All* nations shall come and worship before you ... "for *all* flesh shall come to you, no longer subject to the world, but united to the spirit" (*De fide Res.*).
>
> The mercy of the Lord is to all flesh, in order that *all flesh* ... may ascend to the Lord (*In Ps.* 119.156).
>
> So the Son of Man came to save that which was lost, i.e., *all*, for as in Adam all die, so, too, in Christ shall all be made alive" (*Exp. Luc.* 15.3).

In St. Ambrose's teaching "death is altogether to be desired, the terrors of the future state almost entirely disappear.... [H]e affirms that, even to the wicked, death is a gain."[13] Thus, while St. Jerome with perfect truth asserts that nearly all of St. Ambrose's books are full of Origenism (*Ruf.* 1), and the learned Huet confirms this,[14] we must note that even Origen lays more stress on sin and future penalty than does St. Ambrose.

I next proceed to quote an early and able writer (not certainly identified), whose works are usually bound with those of St. Ambrose, and who wrote during the popedom of Damasus (366–384) (see his words on 1 Tim 3:14–15). He teaches clearly the liberation of all souls by Christ from Hades. I quote some further specimens of his teaching.

> This seemed good to God ... to manifest in Christ the mystery of his will ... namely, that he should be merciful to all who had strayed, whether in heaven or in earth.... *Every being, then, in the heavens and on earth, while it learns the knowledge of Christ, is being restored to that which it was created.*
> —*In Eph.* 1:9–10.

On the two last verses of the same chapter may be found a striking comment—tracing the salvation of all through Christ to his creation of all. Since *all* were made by Christ, he is to be Head and Lord of all.

> In speaking of the whole church [reading *omnem ecclesiam*], the apostle [Paul] summarily comprehends the *totality of that which exists in heaven and on earth*; ... for when they shall have

---

13 Henry Wace and William Smith, eds., *A Dictionary of Christian Biography, Literature, Sects and Doctrines*. 4 vols. (London: 1877–87).

14 Huet, *Origeniana* 2:159, 199.

Part Two—Universalism Asserted on the Authority of Tradition

returned to the confession of one God, bending the knee to Christ, he is fulfilled in all, so as to be all, for all comes from him.

Again, we find the same argument for universal salvation. "Christ rose that he might create anew once more those things which he had first made; . . . that he should restore all those things which he [God] made through him . . . and *all things* that have been made by him should live in him as in their Author (*In Col.* 1:20).[15]

A striking passage is the following, recalling Victorinus, and the Neoplatonic school:

> The creation was formed by God through Christ, so that . . . it should be, as it were, a chain linked together (*concatenatio*), descending in ordered arrangement to the firmament, so as to form a *united whole*. . . . This, then, is the point aimed at, that the creation (*creatura*) may be brought back to one mind . . . so that it may be harmonious in love of the Creator. . . . For it is rebuilding itself into a temple of the Lord.
> —*In Eph.* 4

On 1 Corinthians 15:27, this writer says:

> When every creature learns that Christ is its Head, and that Christ's Head is God the Father, then God is all in all; that is to say, that *every creature* should believe alike, that with one voice *every* tongue of things in heaven and earth and under the earth, should confess that there is one God from whom are all things.

The following is interesting on Christ's enemies being made his footstool: "They are made to bow under his feet who . . . return to the Lord, and as a footstool to the feet so are bent to his preaching. Without doubt this is said of those enemies who, having been corrected, are set on his right hand" (*In Heb.* 1.13). "The Father has granted to the Son that, after the crucifixion, all things should be saved in the name of the Son" (*In Phil.* 2.10).

In St. Ambrose's works is generally printed a treatise, *De Sacramentis*, assigned by most critics to a contemporary, or it may be, a later author. It is of interest as further tending to show the tone of the current beliefs of Christian antiquity.

"God," it teaches, "desiring to undo everything hurtful . . . sentenced man to death. . . . It was assigned as a remedy that man should die and

---

15 Compare Victorinus' teaching already quoted.

rise again: ... death interposing puts a stop to sin. ... Christ brought in the resurrection. ... We have on our side both [i.e., death and resurrection], because death ends sin, and resurrection is a remolding of our nature" (*Sacr.* 2:6). "What, then, is the resurrection except our rising from death to life" (*Sacr.* 3:1). These words are in harmony with a very large body of primitive teaching (as my readers can see), and are in hopeless antagonism to the views now general, which regard death as essentially penal.

Jerome (c.374–420)

Our next witness shall be one who is, with the exception of Augustine, the most striking figure among the Latin Fathers; one to whom in learning and in critical acumen even Augustine cannot be compared—I mean St. Jerome.[16] It is impossible not to pause as we survey these two great contemporaries, who corresponded, indeed, but never met. In Jerome are represented the tendencies, broad and sympathetic, of Eastern theology (already beginning to wane). In Augustine are summed up the cruel and uncatholic dogmas of the rising school of North Africa. In a true sense St. Jerome is the last of a long line of Latin Fathers, drawing their inspiration from Eastern sources. Augustine is the founder of a new theological dynasty. The lengths to which St. Jerome went in teaching universalism may be seen from what follows.

"Christ will, in the ages to come, show, not to one, but to *the whole number of rational creatures*, his glory, and the riches [of his grace]." He adds that the saints are to reign over *the fallen angels, and the prince of this world, Lucifer, even to them bringing blessing* (*Comm. Eph.* 2.7).

This remarkable passage is followed by one even more explicit and outspoken. Both should be read in the original rather than in my brief summary, especially that which follows.

> In the end of [all] things ... the whole body which had been dissipated and torn into divers parts shall be restored. ... Let us understand *the whole number of rational creatures* under the

---

16 Editor: Not all would share Allin's estimate of the relative acumen of Jerome and Augustine, though all would admit that Jerome was an unusually accomplished scholar. Editor: On Jerome in both his pro- and anti-Origen phases, see now Ramelli, *Christian Doctrine of Apokatastasis*, 627–41.

Part Two—Universalism Asserted on the Authority of Tradition

> figure of a single rational animal; . . . let us imagine this animal to be torn . . . so that no bone adheres to bone, nor nerve to nerve.

Jerome proceeds,

> And then suppose some wonderful physician to come and restore to its place every part. . . . So in the restitution of all things, when the true physician, Jesus Christ, shall have come to heal the body of the whole church, *every one* . . . shall receive his proper place. . . . What I mean is, *the fallen angel will begin to be that which he was created*, and man, who has been expelled from paradise, *will be once more restored to the tilling of paradise*. These things, then, will take place *universally*.
> —*Comm. Eph.* 4.16

What an idea may not unprejudiced readers gain of the breadth of early teaching from these words. If, he says, we see one falling into sin we indeed are sorry, and hasten to rescue him, but we cannot be saddened, knowing that "with God *no rational creature perishes eternally*" (*Comm. Gal.* 5.22). "Death shall come as a *visitor to the impious*; it will *not be perpetual*; it will not annihilate them; but will prolong its visit, *till the impiety which is in them shall be consumed*" (*Comm. Mich.* 5.8).

Again, speaking of the consummation of all things, St. Jerome says, on Zephaniah 3:10:

> The prophet, here aware of the extent of God's mercy, is like the psalmist communing with his heart and asking, "will the Lord cast off for ever?" [Ps 77:7] . . . of which the meaning is—I did think God would abandon sinners for ever, . . . but now I perceive that it was done for this end: . . . to *change everything*, and that he might *show mercy* on those whom *he had before* cast away.

"In the cross and Passion of the Lord, all things have been summed up." He goes on to show what this means. It is, he says, as though one were to lend 100 pence in various sums and get all back in one sum. In other words, Christ is to get back all things (*Comm. Eph.* 1.10). To this idea he returns: "The cross of Christ has benefited not earth only but heaven, . . . and *every creature* has been cleansed by the blood of its Lord" (*Comm. Eph.* 2.16). And on chapter 3:14, he teaches clearly that "by every knee bending in Jesus' name is meant 'the obedience of the heart.'"

> Christ is subject to the Father in those who are faithful, for all who believe, nay, *all the race of man is counted as his members*. But in those who are unbelievers, Jews, heathen, and heretics, Christ is said not to be subject, because a part of his members is not subject to the faith. But in the end of the world, when all his members shall have seen Christ, i.e., their own body, reigning, they, too, shall be subject to Christ, i.e., to their own body, so that *the whole body of Christ* may be subject to God and the Father, that God may be all in all.
> —*Epist. ad Aman.*

This involves the final obedience of all, and teaches that Jews, heathen, and heretics are Christ's members. Nor are these isolated instances: I have found *nearly* 100 passages in his works (and there are doubtless others) indicating St. Jerome's sympathy with universalism.

[However,] we should note that when towards the year 400 AD, St. Jerome took part with Epiphanius and the disreputable Theophilus against Origen (whom he had hitherto extravagantly praised), he, as Huet points out,[17] kept a significant silence on the question of human restoration. "Though you adduce," says Huet, "six hundred testimonies, you thereby only prove that he changed his opinion." But did he ever change his opinion? and if so, how far? Thus, in his *Epistula ad Avitum*, where he goes at length into Origen's errors, he says *nothing of the larger hope; and when charged with Origenism, he refers, twice over, to his commentaries on Ephesians, which teach the most outspoken universalism* (*Epist.* 65; *ad Pam.* 75; *adv. Vigil*).[18] As a specimen of his praise of Origen, he says, in a letter to Paula, that Origen was blamed, "not on account of the *novelty of his doctrines, not on account of heresy, as now mad dogs pretend*," *but from jealousy.*[19] So that to call Origen a heretic is the part of a mad dog! Note this: from the most orthodox Jerome.[20]

---

17 Huet, *Origeniana* 2:159.

18 Editor: It is interesting that the salvation of all humans was not listed as an error in any of the early attacks on Origen's teaching. Many of those who criticized Origen were themselves believers in the final restoration.

19 Editor: Origen's patristic defenders often accused his detractors of being motivated by jealously.

20 Editor: Jerome's U-turn from being an avid supporter of Origen to a fierce critic followed the visit of Atarbius to his monastery; a visit aimed at ferreting out Origenists. Sensing a threat, Jerome agreed to make the requested anti-Origenist profession. From then on Jerome turned on his friend Rufinus, a staunch defender of Origen, and on Origen himself. We do not know Jerome's motivations here, but it is certainly possible

Part Two—Universalism Asserted on the Authority of Tradition

Certain it is, that his works abound in universalistic teaching: I proceed to quote. On Amos 9:2 we have this vivid (and *significant*) description of the fate of the sinful soul *after death:*

> If despairing of safety, it shall try to avoid the eye of the Lord, and to fly to the utmost limits, . . . even there shall the Lord command the old and crooked serpent, the enemy and avenger, and he shall bite it; . . . it shall also be smitten by the sword of the Lord, . . . in order that, by means of tortures and punishment, it may *return to the Lord.*

On Nahum 2:2, this striking comment occurs: at the end of the world Satan and his hosts shall fly in terror—

> Now while they [the devil and his hosts] are thinking over this, *every thing* that they have captured shall be brought forward [i.e., rescued]. . . . Further, *all the substance of the world*, and *all its servants* after they have submitted themselves to Christ, . . . shall be led along in joy and gladness. . . . And then shall be fulfilled that which is spoken (Ps 68:18) of the Saviour's victory, when ascending on high, "He led captivity captive" [Eph 4:8].

Here there seems to be taught the final liberation from Satan of all his captives. In this spirit this Father says that Christ's final coming is "to destroy *sins*" (not sinners) and so, "at the consummation of the world every creature shall have been set free" (*Comm. Habac.* 3:2, 11).

St. Jerome's teaching as to God's vengeance and destruction of his enemies is very significant. "'What shall I do to you, Ephraim? . . . I will destroy you unto dust and ashes.' And when the harsh, nay, cruel sentence has been passed . . . he appeases the austerity of the Judge by the love of the Father, . . . 'for I do *not strike in order to destroy for ever*, but in order to *amend*'" (*Comm. Hos.* 11.8). "The Jews think the original word may be translated, not only 'judgment' but 'gold,' meaning that in the valley of judgment, which they believe to be Gehenna, the taint of sins being purged away, you [the sinner] may remain pure gold" (*Comm. Joel* 3:14)—suggestive words. Again he says, commenting on Zechariah 12:9: "He will destroy, not for their ruin, but for *their amendment*, . . . for if he created all things out of nothing, he did not do so in order to destroy that which he had created, but in order that by his mercy the things created should be saved"—words that recall Victorinus' teaching as to creation.

---

to see his *volta face* as strategic self-preservation.

From an early writer (not certainly identified), whose commentary on the Psalms is bound with St. Jerome's works,[21] I quote some passages, wholly breathing the larger hope.

Thus, on the destruction of God's enemies, he writes: "When the psalmist says, 'Your enemies, O God, shall perish,' ... *every one* who has been your enemy *shall hereafter be made your friend;* the man shall not perish, the enemy shall perish" (*In Ps.* 92.9). No less striking is the comment on Psalm 9:5: "You have blotted out their name *for ever and ever.*" This Father says, in effect, that it means blotting out their sins and *their turning to God.* Here *an eternal blotting out means amending.* So again: "The devil is, as it were, God's executioner. They who walk not rightly are handed over to the devil. Wherefore? That they may perish eternally? And where then is the mercy of God? Where is the tender Father? ... What the apostle [Paul] says is this, 'I have handed over sinners to the devil, that, tormented by him, they may be converted to me' [1 Cor 5:5]" (*In Ps.* 108:9). On the words "His wrath will soon be kindled" (Ps 2:12) this Father (reading *in brevi*) says: "This mean at the death of every one, or, with *a brief wrath* at the day of judgment, as that [verse means] 'sudden destruction shall come on them.'" This involves the opinion that the sudden destruction of the wicked, to which St. Paul refers, would be satisfied by a brief wrath at the day of judgment. A significant passage holds out hope of pardon even to Satan. "You who were first a dragon: ... Look you what the Psalmist says. ... Do you not then despair, *repent* and *straightway you are converted*" (*In Ps.* 148.12).

Diodore (d. 390)

Nor should the name of Diodorus, Bishop of Tarsus, be absent from the roll of early universalists.[22] He was one of the greatest ornaments of the famous school of Antioch, with whose teaching we are now to make acquaintance. In his lifetime he was noted for untiring zeal in defense of the Nicene Faith, and was praised by men like Basil, Theodoret, Chrysostom, and Cyril, and died in universal honour; having, says Theodoret, saved the bark of the church from being submerged under the waves of

---

21 Ed. Paris 1624.

22 Editor: On Diodore, see now Ramelli, *Christian Doctrine of Apokatastasis*, 521–39.

unbelief. Of his numerous writings but mere fragments have survived. The following is from his book *De Oecon*.[23]

> For the wicked there are punishments not perpetual, ... but they are to be tormented for a certain brief period, according to the amount of malice in their works. They shall therefore suffer punishment for a short space, but *immortal blessedness*, having no end, *awaits them;* ... the penalties to be inflicted for their many and grave crimes are very far surpassed by the magnitude of the mercy to be showed them. The resurrection, therefore, is regarded as a blessing, not only to the good, but also to the evil.

Rufinus of Aquileia (340/45–410)

We may next note that Rufinus[24] certainly taught that the future punishment of the wicked would be *temporary*, in his exposition of the Creed. He plainly so teaches, says Huet.[25] He contrasts the *perpetuity* of glory of the just, with a (merely) lengthy punishment of the wicked. There remain two other facts by which we may ascertan Rufinus' views. In his preface to [his Latin translation of] Origen's *De principii*, he states, in effect, that he had removed what was "discordant with our belief" from that book.[26] But he certainly left there *very distinct* assertions of universalism. Again, it seems hardly possible to doubt that in his work on the Creed, he taught the liberation from Hades of all souls by Christ.

---

23 Giuseppe Simone Assemani (1687–1768), *Bibliotheca Orientalis* (Rome: 1719–28) 3:324.

24 Editor: On Rufinus, see now Ramelli, *Christian Doctrine of Apokatastasis*, 636–58.

25 Huet, *Origeniana* 2:160.

26 Editor: It was the case that from very early on people were inserting material into copies of Origen's books and some of this material was of questionable orthodoxy. This practice gave the impression that the interpolated material was from Origen himself, and Origen's early apologists found themselves having to defend Origen on the grounds that some of the material in copies of his works were not from him. Rufinus may have thought that the material he was leaving out was inauthentic, rather than that it was original but dubious.

Paulinus of Nola (c.354–431)

I quote next from St. Paulinus, Bishop of Nola (not attempting to decide what he at heart believed).[27] Paulinus' brother, Delphinus, seems to have died in sin: so far from abandoning his case as quite hopeless, Paulinus begs St. Amandus[28] to pray for him, because *"doubtless* the dew of God's indulgence will penetrate hell (*inferna*), so that those burning there ... may be refreshed" (*Ep. ad Aman.*). He, too, teaches that the destruction of the heathen by Christ is really their *cure*. His iron rod "breaks their hearts as though vessels formed of clay, in order to remake them [for the] better." How far this principle logically goes—for Christ is to have possession of the whole earth—any one can judge (*Par. of Ps. 2*). "A common disobedience shut up all, in order that faith might heal *the whole*; so that *all the world* may be made God's servant" (*Carm. ad Cynth.*[29]).

John Chrysostom (c.349–407)

I take next St. Chrysostom; trained in the school of Antioch, a pupil of Diodorus of Tarsus, his education can hardly have been otherwise than decidedly universalistic in character. When all the evidence is fairly weighed, I think that but little doubt can remain as to his very strong sympathy with, or indeed adoption of, the larger hope; notwithstanding his apparent teaching of the ordinary creed.[30] For, on the theory of his really holding that creed, I can find no explanation of such passages as I shall quote; while his threats of future punishment, however terrible, may be easily explained: (a) as coming from a great preacher in cities stained with horrible vices, like Antioch or Constantinople (e.g., see *Hom.* 9 on

---

27 Editor: On Paulinus, see now Ramelli, *Christian Doctrine of Apokatastasis*, 656–58.

28 Editor: Amandus (d. 431) was Bishop of Bordeaux. He instructed Paulinus prior to Paulinus' baptism.

29 Ed. Antwerp, 1622, 494.

30 Editor: John is very ambiguous on this issue. He did at times seem to teach eternal hell and to distance himself from *apokatastasis*, though other texts seem to point in the exact opposite direction. How to hold all his teaching together is the issue. It may be that he found the threat of hell useful as a motivator for "the simple" (Allin's point (c), above). It is worthy of note that he went out of his way to shelter Origenist monks from Egypt (whom he did not regard as heretical), and suffered exile for doing so. For a discussion of these ambiguities, see Ramelli, *Christian Doctrine of Apokatastasis*, 549–64.

Part Two—Universalism Asserted on the Authority of Tradition

Romans 5, where he speaks of lusts worse than those of Sodom: perhaps civilization has nowhere assumed so base a form as in the Byzantine empire); (b) by the rhetorical and ambiguous character of the terms used;[31] (c) by the notorious advocacy of deceit (*apate*) as a spiritual medicine, which we find in his works.

We may note, too, (i) the fact that he was charged with a leaning to Origenism in the controversy between Jerome (and Epiphanius), and John of Jerusalem.[32] (ii) Again, he sanctions prayers and almsgiving on behalf of those who have died in sin (i.e., unrepentant) (*Hom. Jo. Ser.* 61; *Hom. 1 Cor., Ser.* 41).[33] (iii) Nor should his enthusiastic praise of the universalists Diodorus and Theodorus of Mopsuestia be forgotten.

These facts raise a strong suspicion, at least, of his sympathy with the larger hope. Let us therefore try to gather his views from his own words. Writing on Romans 5:16 (*Ser.* 10), he uses language inconsistent with the perpetuation of evil in hell. St. Paul is speaking of the result of Christ's work; on this Chrysostom comments as follows: "By this is inevitably shown that death is plucked up root and branch; . . . not only was the sin [of Adam] *abolished*, but *also all other sins whatsoever*." Of death "*not a trace remains*, nor *can its shadow* be discerned, as it is *utterly* destroyed." Again, on the words, God shall be "all in all" [1 Cor 15:28] he says: "Some maintain that the apostle [Paul] asserts here *the abolition of evil*, so that *all* shall henceforth willingly yield [to God], and *not one resist or be under the power of* evil, for when sin shall no longer exist, it is evident that God will be all in all." He closes his comment with these words: "For when *evil has been taken away*, much more shall death cease." The abolition of sin is surely a synonym for the larger hope. And so, on Colossians 1 (*Hom.* 3),

31 Editor: For instance, with only a single exception, he never described hell as *aidios* (eternal). It is, instead, *aiōnios* (on which, see ch. 4).

32 Editor: When Jerome was abbot in Bethlehem, he was willingly drawn into a conflict between Bishop Epiphanius from Cyprus and Bishop John II of Jerusalem (c.356–417). Epiphanius preached a sermon in Jerusalem against Origenism, widely seen as a sermon directed against the city's own bishop. He urged Jerome and his friends to separate from John, their bishop. Jerome wrote a fierce polemic against Bishop John, accusing him of supporting Origenism. His hostility to John never waned.

33 Editor: He is worth quoting on the effect of almsgiving for those in hell: "What is more, the spring of almsgiving extinguishes the river of fire [of hell] as though it were a sparkle; it suffocates the worm [of hell] as though it were nothing. Those who have almsgiving do not know the gnashing of teeth. If any drop of water falls onto the chains [of the prison of hell], it destroys them, and even in case it should flow upon the furnaces [of hell], it extinguishes them all" (*Hom. Phil.* 174ff).

What the Church Teaches

where the apostle is speaking of Christ as first creating *all things*, and then reconciling all things, Chrysostom says that it was needful that he should reconcile them *"perfectly*, so that they should never again become his enemies": and on verse 18 says that the church stands for the whole race.

I cannot see any escape from the conclusion that these words involve universalism, in their natural meaning. Again, on Ephesians 1 (*Hom.* 1), this Father says that all, angels and men, are to be brought under one Head. Thus, then, shall there be a unity . . . when *all things* [the universe] shall have been brought under one Head, having a necessary bond of connection from above." On John 12:32: "'I will draw all men unto me.' Had Christ said, 'I will rise,' it is not clear that [he would have implied that] they [all] would believe, but in saying that they shall believe, he combines both."

The following extracts again teach a view of "vengeance" and "penalty" and "death" that seems to point clearly in the direction of the larger hope. "Tell me on what account do you mourn for him that is departed? Is it because he was wicked? But for that very reason you ought to give thanks, because his evil works are put a stop to" (*De dorm. Serm.* 30). "Death has been ordered for our *benefit* by the Lord . . . for such a Master is ours that in his vengeance (*timoria*), no less than in his benefits, he shows his care of us. Had he known that sinning without vengeance, [i.e., with impunity] would make us no worse, he never would have inflicted vengeance on us. . . . To extirpate our wickedness . . . he kindly inflicts vengeance" (*Hom. Gen.* 3, *Hom.* 18). "If punishment were an evil to those who sin, God never would have added evils to evils. . . . It is, then, no evil to the offender to be punished, but that one so acting should not be punished [is an evil], just as for a sick man not to be cured" (*Hom. Rom* 5, *Hom.* 9). "God is *equally* to be praised when he chastises, and when he frees from chastisement. For both spring from goodness. . . . It is right, then, to praise him *equally* both for placing Adam in paradise, and for expelling him, and to give thanks, not alone for the kingdom [of God], but for *hell as well* (Gehenna)" (*In Ps.* 148.10). Note, too, the following: "What great goodness did it not show to restrain from sin those who, at the time of the Deluge, were *incurably* diseased . . . and to employ, as a medicine, the common debt of nature, and to bring on them the easiest death by water" (*In Ps.* 165.8). "God does all things through love, as, for example, to benefit man he set him in paradise, and to benefit him he

PART TWO—Universalism Asserted on the Authority of Tradition

turned him out of paradise. . . . To benefit him he sent that fire on Sodom" (*In Ps.* 111.3—cf. [Sodom's] "eternal" fire in St. Jude 7).

The drift of St. Chrysostom's teaching is further shown by his attitude toward the so-called unpardonable sin, as quite capable of pardon. Many, though guilty of it, were, he tells us, pardoned subsequently on their repentance (*In Matt.* 12, *Hom.* 42). I commend to the thoughtful and unprejudiced to consider the light thrown by this teaching on the patristic use of such terms as "never," "for ever," "eternal" (see pp. 93–98).

Again, I may appeal to Chrysostom's very clear assertion of the liberation of *every soul whatsoever* from Hades by Christ, and of the subversion of Hades itself in consequence. I give a summary of his striking words: Christ, he asserts, not merely opened, but broke in pieces the gates of brass, in order to make the prison useless; where there is neither door, nor bar, *whosoever enters is not detained*. What God destroys, who can set up again? Earthly kings indeed set free prisoners, yet leave untouched the prison gates; but Christ broke in pieces the gates of brass. Christ went to the utterly black and joyless portion of Hades, and turned it into heaven, transferring all its wealth, *the race of man*, into his royal treasury. In this, too, Christ surpasses kings, for they send messengers, but he went in person to set the captives free (*Ser.* 34). So again, he says: "Our Lord, when he was in Hades, set free *all* who were kept prisoners by death" (*Hom.* 30).

Theodore of Mopsuestia (c.350–428)

We now come to the famous Theodore of Mopsuestia,[34] who enjoyed during his lifetime an extraordinary renown as a teacher of the catholic faith. "He was," says Dorner, "the crown and climax of the school of Antioch, and was called the Master of the East from his theological eminence."[35]

Theodore and (perhaps) Diodorus, after they had rested for a century and a quarter in their honoured graves, were condemned as *Nestorians*[36] in the Fifth [Ecumenical] Council (553 AD), an assembly

---

34 Editor: On Theodore, see now Ramelli, *Christian Doctrine of Apokatastasis*, 521–26, 539–48.

35 Editor: Isaac August Dorner, *History of the Development of the Doctrine of the Person of Christ.* Translated by Rev. D. W. Simon. 5 vols. (Edinburgh: 1861–63; first German edition, 1835–39; second, expanded German edition, 1845–56) 1:50. Isaac Dorner (1809–84) was a German Lutheran pastor and a theologian of some renown.

36 Editor: Nestorians were those who followed the teaching of Nestorius, Patriarch of Constantinople (386–450), according to which Jesus is a human nature united to

unrecognized by the English church.[37] *No question of universalism was thereby raised*, for the very promoters of this council *were Origenists*, and intrigued against Theodore *on the very ground of his hostility to Origen.*[38] That Diodorus was condemned is uncertain, for though Photius states that he was, his name does *not occur* in the Acts of the Council.

Certain it is that:

(1) Theodore towered above almost all his contemporaries, and lived and died in honour. See a striking letter full of praise from Chrysostom, addressed to Theodore (*Ep.* 119).

(2) Certainly too, such posthumous attacks by councils of very doubtful authority[39] are most often rooted in paltry jealousy and intrigue.

(3) And it is a painful reflection to compare the impunity enjoyed by those who blacken the divine *character* (e.g., St. Augustine) with the sharp measure meted, too often, to those great men, who—as in Theodore's case—*before* the church has defined the point at issue, write, perhaps, incautiously, but moved with zeal for the truth, about the divine *nature*.

(4) Huet has the candor to confess that if the mere teaching or originating heresy, unconsciously, and with a readiness to abjure it—as distinguished from persisting in it when the church has once spoken—make

---

God the Son, a divine nature. This view was declared heretical on the grounds that it did not do justice to the *unity* of the person of Christ—*one person* with two natures.

37 Editor: The Church of England, like many mainstream Protestant denominations, recognizes the first four Ecumenical Councils as authoritative. However, the Fifth Ecumenical Council is authoritative in the eyes of the Orthodox and Catholics.

38 Editor: This is an odd comment for Allin to make, for the Fifth Ecumenical Council was called by the Emperor Justinian, a fierce anti-Origenist (as were those who advised him and prepared the documentation for him), and is the one associated with the so-called anathemas against "Origen." Nevertheless, Allin is correct that it was Theodore's Christology and *not* his universalist eschatology that was picked out for condemnation. And he is correct to note that there were Origenists at the council. (The posthumous condemnation of Theodore was controversial, because he had died in full communion with the church, whose teaching he had always sought to defend. Furthermore, the issue of the unity of the person of Christ had not been clarified during his lifetime.)

39 Editor: Allin does not explain the basis of his suspicion of the council's authority, unless it simply be that Protestants tend not to see it as binding. However, it may be that he had in mind that the Fifth Ecumenical Council was pushed through by the Emperor Justinian. The pope of the time, Vigilius, and the other bishops did not want the council. Indeed, the pope refused to accept the invitation to attend and had to be brought along by force. He then refused to declare the council open, as was expected of him, forcing Justinian to do so. So perhaps Allin is not convinced that this council was adequately ecumenical.

Part Two—Universalism Asserted on the Authority of Tradition

a heretic, then *very many orthodox fathers* (e.g., Cyprian, Irenaeus, etc.) *may be called heretics*.[40]

(5) And it is certain too that, as his best editor says, "Every accession to our knowledge of Theodore adds strength to the conviction that he was *entirely unconscious of deviating from the catholic church.*"[41]

(6) And to talk of *heretics* is ground most unsafe for the advocates of endless sin. That dogma bears a deeply tarnished escutcheon. Who was its first distinguished advocate? The heretic Tertullian.[42] What were the authors of the Pseudo-Clementines?—heretics, and forgers, and teachers of unending pain?[43] What was Tatian, another very early champion of this doctrine?—a gnostic heretic.[44] What was Lactantius?—an ill-taught layman "hovering ever on the verge of heresy."[45] And who is the true fountain and source of the cruel heresy of Calvin?—no less a name than Augustine himself.[46] And what was Pelagius?—at once a heretic, and a champion of misery without end.[47]

---

40 Huet, *Origeniana*, 2:195. [Editor: Allin's point in (4) and (5) is that a heretic is not one who believes teaching contrary to the teaching of the church, but one who believes such teaching *knowing that* it is contrary to the teaching of the church. However, the faulty Christology that Theodore is said to have affirmed was a matter that the church had not come to a single mind on in his day, so his affirming it would not make him a heretic. His concern was to be true to the teachings of the church and he never knowingly went contrary to it. Thus, even if we can now see faults in some of his ideas, he was no heretic.]

41 Editor: Allin *may* refer to Henry Barclay Swete (1835–1917), Regius Professor of Divinity at Cambridge.

42 Editor: Tertullian is not considered a heretic by the church, though some of his teaching is seen in retrospect to diverge from what the church later came to teach.

43 Editor: Pseudo-Clementine writings purport to come from Pope Clement I and to record conversations between Clement and the apostle Peter.

44 Editor: Tatian (c.120–c.180), according to Irenaeus, was a follower of the gnostic Valentinus. He is best known for his *Diatessaron*, a harmony of the four Gospels.

45 Editor: Lactantius (c.250–c.325) was an advisor to the Emperor Constantine.

46 Augustine is certainly not regarded as a heretic by the church, and while some Orthodox and Catholics consider Calvin a heretic, few Protestants would concur. Allin tries to defend his claim that Augustine was a heretic in *The Augustinian Revolutuon in Theology* (London: 1911).

47 Editor: Pelagius (c.390–418) had taught that humans could choose to perfectly obey God without the need of any special divine assistance. It is ironic that some, including Augustine, believed that Origen was an inspiration for the Pelagian heresy. It was this misunderstanding of Origen that significantly increased the pressure against Origenism during the Pelagian controversy. But in fact Origen would have had no sympathy for Pelagianism.

(7) But did Theodore and Diodorus really teach what is known as Nestorianism? "The Syrian teachers, and Nestorius himself, in the opinion of *every one who understands the case*, are guilty of no error; and the dogmas which are known as Nestorianism have been neither taught by Nestorius, nor approved by the Syrian church."[48] "Theodore," says Neander, "sincerely adopted the doctrine of the church respecting the divine Incarnation."[49] "Of all that the church declared to be of the faith, he was the staunch defender,"[50] says his editor Swete.

(8) Certain it is that, practically, the Anglican Church has abandoned the term (*theotokos*), so strenuously contended for.[51]

(9) And it is also certain that the condemnation of Nestorius brought its nemesis, it helped to pave the way for the cult of the Blessed Virgin,[52] and its terrible abuses, and for the heresy of Eutyches.[53]

Certainly Theodore's immense influence must have spread very widely the larger hope, which lay at the root of his doctrinal system. Nor did his enemies charge him with this as a fault, so far as I have read, a fact to be noted; as is also this, that he calls those penalties *"eternal"*—as being out of time—which he yet taught to be finite (so little does the use of such terms prove).

He lays great stress—with the school of Antioch—on the resurrection as in itself, and to all, a blessing. "Who *is so great a fool* as to think

---

48 Münter, *Staud. u. Tzsch. Archiv.* 1

49 Augustus Neander, *General History of the Christian Religion and Church*. Translated by Joseph Torrey. 2nd ed. 4 vols. (London: 1853), 4:110

50 Editor: Henry Barclay Swete, *Theodori episcopi Mopsuesteni: in epistolas B. Pauli comentarii: the Latin version with the Greek Fragments, with an introduction, notes and indices*. 2 vols. (Cambridge: 1880).

51 Editor: *Theotokos* is a title for Mary, meaning "Mother of God." The reason that the church considered the title so important was because it stressed something critical *about Jesus*—he was God-made-flesh. It was more a claim in Christology than Mariology. However, to many Protestant ears it sounded like an elevation of Mary to semi-divine status; some even thought that it was asserting that Mary was the mother of Jesus' *divinity*, which is emphatically *not* what it asserts. For such reasons it has tended to be dropped by Protestants.

52 Editor: Allin's claim is that whatever the intentions of the term *Theotokos*, it paved the way for an elevation of Mary in the Middle Ages to something close on occasion to an object of worship, in practice, if not in theory.

53 Editor: Eutyches (c.380–c.456) was a fierce opponent of Nestorianism, but erred in the opposite direction. He sought to defend the unity of the person of Christ by arguing that Christ's divine and human natures had merged into a single, new, hybrid nature. His view was condemned at the Council of Ephesus in 451.

that so great a blessing can be to those that arise, the occasion of endless torment?" (*Cont. pecc. orig.*). "All have the hope of rising with Christ so that the body having obtained immortality, thenceforward the proclivity to evil should be removed" (*In Rom* 6:6). Speaking of the resurrection he says, "then, too, shall we be freed from sin, for being rendered immutable by the grace of the Spirit, we shall be set free from sin" (*In Rom* 8:2). God "recapitulated all things in Christ . . . as though making a compendious renewal, and *restoration of the whole creation*, through him. . . . Now this will take place in a future age, when all mankind and *all powers* (*virtutes*) *possessed of reason*, look up to him, as is right, and obtain mutual concord and firm peace" (*In Eph* 1:10).

Cyril of Alexandria (c.376–444)

Cyril of Alexandria frequently teaches the liberation of every soul from Hades by Christ.[54]

> The devil was deprived of all power of being able to do anything for the future. . . . The souls of men who had been caught in his toils to their ruin, came out of the underground gates, and, leaving the hiding places of the pit, escape. (*Hom. pasch.* 6)

> Traversing the *lowest recesses* of the infernal regions, after that he had preached to the spirits there, he led forth the captives in his strength. (*Hom. pasch.* 20)

> For when death devoured him who was the Lamb on behalf of all, it vomited forth *all men* in him and with him. . . . Now when *sin has been destroyed*, how should it be but that death, too, should wholly perish? (*In* 1 *Io* 1.29).

Speaking of the cities of refuge [Num 35:6–28; Deut 19:1–14; Josh 20:7–8] are these words:

> It is, perhaps, not improbable to think, that those who have been entangled in sins are, as it were, homicides of their own souls. . . . So, then, the wretched soul of man is punished by exile from the world and the body, and *residing in the recesses of death as in a city of refuge*, was spending these long ages, but was with difficulty set free when Christ, the High Priest, died, . . . and went

---

54 Editor: On Cyril, see now Ramelli, *Christian Doctrine of Apokatastasis*, 598–602.

down to Hades and loosed their bonds. (*De adorat.* book 8 *ad fin.*)

This picture is suggestive. All sinners who die before Christ's visit to Hades go thither, *as to a city of refuge*, and are by him set free: because, though sinners, yet they have been as it were forced to sin by a nature prone to evil (so he says). But if so, how can you fairly suppose Christ's work less efficacious after his death? On the death of Christ, "all iniquity stopped its mouth, and the rule of death was destroyed, all sin (*tes hamartias*, sin generally) having been taken away, . . . so, then, the sin of *all* having been taken away, we can justly say, 'O death where is your sting?'" (*In Hos.* 13.14). "Through Christ has been saved the holy crowd of the fathers, nay, the whole human race altogether which was earlier in time [than Christ's death], for he died for all, and the death of all was done away in him" (*Glaph. in Ex.* 2 *ad fin.*)

Cyril's teaching as to the final salvation of all men before Christ is fairly clear. I fail to see how this can be logically held apart from the larger hope. I close with the following quotation. "The force of sin has been dissolved—the evil that has grown out of it, i.e., death has been plucked up *from the very root*" (*Hom. pasch.* 24).

Maximus of Turin (d. 408–23)

In St. Ambrose's works,[55] there are included ninety-two sermons, which may be by Maximus of Turin. The author seems to teach (a) the liberation of every soul from Hades, and (b) to take the significant view of God's inflicting death to amend the sinner. "By the resurrection of Christ, hell (*Tartarus*) is opened; . . . hell yields up those it contains; . . . so David invites everything created to the festivity of this day" (*Serm.* 52). It illuminates, he adds, heaven, earth, and *hell*. Christ "destroyed the sins of all believers. He must of necessity have destroyed the sins of all, who bore the sins of all, as says the Evangelist: 'The Lamb of God who takes away the sins of the world'" (*Serm.* 21). "We read in the Scripture that the salvation of the entire human race was won by the redemption of the Saviour, . . . the everlasting safety of the entire world" (*Serm.* 51).

---

55 Ed. Paris, 1569.

PART TWO—Universalism Asserted on the Authority of Tradition

Theodoret of Cyrus (c.393–c.458/66)

I take next Theodoret, the Blessed. This great Father was, I cannot doubt, a universalist. He became Bishop of Cyrus, or Cyrrhus, in Syria, and is the last representative that we shall quote of the school of Antioch. Theodoret was perhaps the most famous, and certainly the most learned teacher of his age; uniting to a noble intellect a character and accomplishments equally noble. We notice in his writings great prominence given to the view that regards the resurrection as being of itself restoration; as essentially a spiritual force, bringing to man's whole nature immortality and glory, and, therefore, immunity from sufferings; a view supported by very many Fathers, but surely fatal to all forms of the traditional creed.

> St. Paul, asserting that "the last enemy to be destroyed is death," and that "he [God] has put all things under Christ's feet," adds finally, *"in order that God may be all in all."* . . . In the present life God is *in all*, for his nature is without limits, but is not *all* in all. . . . But in the future, when [by the resurrection] mortality is at an end and immortality granted, and [consequently] sin has no longer any place, God will be *all in all*. (*Comm. in Eph.* 1.23).

> For Christ has *wholly destroyed* the power of sin by his promise of *immortality;* for it [sin] *cannot trouble immortal bodies.* (*Comm. in Heb.* 9.26).

> In the future life, the body, when it has been made incorruptible, cannot admit the filth of sin. (*Comm. in Col.* 2:11).

On 1 Corinthians 15:20, he writes: "Now the mass shall certainly follow the 'firstfruits.'" This refers to the entire mass of humanity. For, says Theodoret, as all men became mortal through Adam, "so shall the whole nature of mankind [all men] follow the Lord Christ, and be made partaker of the resurrection." The meaning of this is stated in a lengthy comment, of which I can only give a brief summary. No doubt there shall be a difference between good and bad, and so the apostle [Paul] writes: "Every one in his own order" [1 Cor 15:23] (meaning probably a delayed resurrection till judgment has done its cleansing work). Then comes the end, i.e., *the general resurrection*, when Christ delivers up his kingdom, causing all to know God, for he must altogether subdue all men. In what sense? In that indicated by the apostle, "Who shall change our lowly body after the fashion of his glorious body" (Phil 3:21).

But how is the Son to be himself subjected to God? The apostle shows by adding, "that God may be *all in all.*" So the Son is subject in the subjection of mankind (when that is complete).[56] At present God is indeed in all, for in him we live, . . .

> But he is not by obedience in all: for he is by obedience in those fearing him, even in those he is not *all;* for nobody is sinless. . . . But in the future life when corruption is at an end, and immortality granted, there is no place for *suffering (pathē)* but it [suffering] being *totally removed, no form of sin remains at work.* So shall God be all in all, all being out of danger of falling, and *converted to him,* and not admitting an inclination to what is worse.

So on Philippians 3:21 he says, Christ "puts an end to corruption and death . . . causing all to look up to himself." In the same spirit Theodoret writes: "Christ being taken as 'firstfruits,' the whole nature of man [all humanity] shall know the true God, and chant praises for his loving kindness" (*In Ps.* 80:18). "Afterwards the psalmist speaks more plainly: 'All the kings of the earth shall adore him.' Some, indeed, in the present life willingly, but all the rest after the resurrection; for not yet do we see *all things* subject to him, but then every knee shall bow to him" (*In Ps.* 72:11). Here the context shows "all kings" to be used for "all peoples," and the subjection of all to Christ is in Theodoret's view their submission and adoration.

Finally, on two other points, let us note his teaching. First, he explicitly asserts the liberation from Hades of every soul.

> I shall shut up you only. . . . "You," says Christ to Satan, "are justly despoiled of *all* your subjects.' . . . You shall vomit forth *all* that you have already swallowed. . . . I shall free *all* from death . . . for I paid the debt for the *race.*' . . . As the debt has been paid, it is right that those confined on account of it should be set free from their prison.
> —*De prov. Or.* 10

Second, he teaches that *death is a medicine, not a penalty* (*Quaes. in Oct.* 40) and even goes a great deal farther, for he says, that to imagine that God, in anger at a little eating, inflicted death as a penalty, is to copy the abominable heretic Marcion. This statement I commend to my readers' attention. Those who fancy God to have acted from wrath, show, says

---

56 Editor: This is Origen's anti-subordinationist reading of 1 Cor 15:28.

Part Two—Universalism Asserted on the Authority of Tradition

Theodoret, their ignorance of the mystery of the dispensation. Can this teaching be reconciled with any modification of the traditional creed? Take, finally, the following: *"After* his anger, God will bring to an end his judgment; for he will not be angry unto the end, nor keep his wrath to eternity'" (*In Is.* 13).

Peter Chrysologus (c.380–c.450)

From St. Peter Chrysologus (so called from his eloquence[57]), Bishop of Ravenna, I take the following, which refers to the great gulf separating Lazarus and Dives [Luke 16:26]:

> Those assigned to penal custody in Hades cannot be transferred to the repose of the saints, *unless,* having been redeemed by the grace of Christ, they be freed from this hopelessness by the intercession of the holy church: so that what the sentence denies them, the church may gain for them and grace bestow.
> —*Serm.* 123

Suggestive words,[58] coming from one who uses elsewhere such strong language as to the fate of the lost.

Again, explaining the words, "Your kingdom come" [Matt 6:10] he says: "We thus pray for the coming of that time when the author of so great evil [Satan] perishing, *the whole world, the whole creation*, may reign and triumph for the whole glory of Christ only" (*Serm.* 71). "We pray that the devil may perish, that sin may cease, death may die.... This is the kingdom of God, ... when in *all* men God lives, God acts, God reigns, God is everything" (*Serm.* 67). This seems to involve an anticipation that all evil shall in the future wholly cease.

So he says on the parable of the leaven [Matt 13:33]: "In order that, as a woman [Eve] had corrupted the whole mass of the human race in Adam, by the leaven of death, so [a woman] should, by the leaven of the resurrection, restore in Christ *the whole mass of our flesh* [all humanity?]" (*Serm.* 99).

---

57 Editor: Chrysologus means "golden-worded."

58 Editor: Chrysologus is here picking up on a very ancient Christian tradition, dating back to at least the second century, according to which the intercessions of the redeemed in glory are effective in rescuing the damned from hell. His words indicate that this tradition had not died out by the fifth century.

On the parable of the hundred sheep [Luke 15:1–7] he says that the one lost sheep represents *"the whole human race lost in Adam,"* and so the Good Shepherd "follows the one, seeks the one, in order that in the one he may find *all*, in the one he may restore *all*" (*Serm.* 168).

I may finally cite a striking passage on the raising of Lazarus [John 11:1–43]. Hades, personified, is represented as addressing God, to this effect: "If I permit Lazarus to escape, you lose *all* whom I have been keeping." Christ answers: "I, O Father, will pay Adam's debt, in order that those who, through Adam, are perishing in Hades, may, through me, live to you." On this the whole Trinity consent. And Lazarus is ordered to leave the tomb and "hell (*Tartarus*) was ordered to obey, and give up to Christ all the dead" (*Serm.* 65). Surely these teachings involve universalism, if taken logically: at least they may be set over against any passages that seem to teach the ordinary view.

Creeds

I will now ask my readers to consider another very important piece of evidence. Within the first five centuries, the two great creeds—the Apostles' Creed and the Niceno-Constantinopolitan Creed—received their present form, and the first four general [ecumenical] councils were held at Nicea [325], Constantinople [381], Ephesus [431], and Chalcedon [451]. Now it is a highly significant fact that though universalist views were then widely prevalent, no syllable of condemnation was breathed against them at any of these councils. Nobody ever thought of including amongst the articles of the faith a belief in endless punishment; and this, be it remembered, though *the very question of the life to come was distinctly raised* at Constantinople, in the clauses then added to the creed.[59] I say, without fear of contradiction, that this silence would of itself be an argument of irresistible weight in proving that universalism was, as an opinion, perfectly tenable in those days.[60]

---

59 Editor: "We look for the resurrection of the dead and the life of the world to come" was one of the clauses added to the Nicene Creed of 352 at the Council of Constantinople in 381. Indeed, it became the climactic clause of the whole creed.

60 Whatever we may think of the Athanasian Creed—its want of conciliar authority; its comparatively late date; its uncertain origin; its doubtful acceptance in the East—when it speaks of "everlasting," that term can mean no more than the scriptural *aiōnios*, which it represents: and as it is clear that everlasting is not the necessary or even the usual meaning of *aiōnios*, this creed is really quite consistent with the larger

PART TWO—Universalism Asserted on the Authority of Tradition

This is a very small part of the evidence. If the silence of these councils is significant, so are the following facts still more significant. We have the faith of the church defined in two documents, of an authority in its kind quite unique and fundamental: the two creeds—the Apostles' and that we call the Nicene. Rightly to estimate the weight of the testimony they bear, let us remember that in the Second Great Ecumenical Council [381], where the Nicene Creed received its present shape, St. Gregory of Nazianzus (whose opinions are discussed earlier) presided: while the chief agent in the task of adding to the Nicene Creed the new clauses then adopted, and ending with the significant words, "I believe in the life of the world to come" (in the *life*, be it remembered, and in *nothing more*), was, probably, St. Gregory of Nyssa; whose words show him to have been an unhesitating advocate of universal salvation.[61]

What can be more significant of the belief of the church in those primitive days? Look at the facts. To a known and outspoken believer in universal salvation is entrusted principally, by the church in her great

---

hope. [Editor: Allin mentions this creed because it threatens the one who denies the content of the creed as follows: "he undoubtedly perish everlastingly" (Latin: *absque dubio in aeternum peribit*). It also speaks of the evildoers going into everlasting fire (*ignem aeternum*). However, Allin's comment on *aiōnois* in his attempt to defuse this clause is not really relevant, as the creed was most likely composed in Latin, not Greek. *Contra* Allin's comment here, it probably *did* intend to speak of a everlasting loss of the wicked. It seems to be a late fifth- or early sixth-century Western creed. It is considered by the Western church—including Allin's Church of England—to carry authority, but the Eastern church spurns it. It is thus not an ecumenical creed. During the nineteenth century the Athanasian Creed was the subject of intense controversy in the Church of England over its comments on eternal damnation. See my introductory essay. In *Race and Religion*, Allin takes a slightly different stance. There, he considers the Athanasian Creed an instance of "Latin" theology, as opposed to the "Hellenistic" theology of the Nicene Creed. Thus, the Nicene Creed climaxes with faith in "the life everlasting," while the Athanasian Creed climaxes in "everlasting fire" (*Race and Religion*, 134–35). Clearly, he sees the Athanasian Creed as compromised.]

61 Editor: In this regard, it is also worth considering a tentative proposal recently made by Ilaria Ramelli that the Nicene Creed's famous anti-Arian *homoousious* ("of one substance with") clause, describing the relation of the Son to the Father, *may have come from Origen*. Origen used the term to describe the Son being "of one substance with" the Father. The clause was suggested for inclusion in the creed by the Emperor Constantine. Constantine's advisor was Eusebius, who was an ardent Origenist. So it is perfectly plausible, though unprovable, that Eusebius suggested the term to Constantine and that Eusebius had got it from Origen. See Ramelli, "Origen's Anti-Subordinationism and Its Heritage in the Nicene and Cappadocian Line." If this is so, then Origen himself, along with Nazianzus and Nyssa, played a key role in shaping creedal trinitarian orthodoxy.

What the Church Teaches

council, the duty of defining the faith; and that definition runs thus, "I believe in the life of the world to come." *What but the larger hope* could such words, under such circumstances, have conveyed to the council? And mark the position these words occupy in the Creed (as does the corresponding clause in the Apostles' Creed). They close and, as it were, sum up the whole. The Creed opens with a statement of belief in the Great Creator; it speaks of the Father, Son, and Holy Ghost: of the work of salvation: of the incarnation, etc. But the great procession of the Christian verities ends, in both creeds, in the expressive assertion of faith in everlasting life. It is as though both creeds proclaimed—that to this all Christian truth led, in this all Christian hope culminated; in life, and not in death everlasting.

Summary of the Patristic Evidence So Far

We have now reached the close of the second, and most important of the three periods embraced in our inquiry, a point from which it is well to look back over the ground we have traversed. We have seen the tide of universalism, so far from being censured, rising, swelling, and broadening; till in that famous age of the church's story, the period embracing the fourth and the earlier years of the fifth century, universalism seems to have been the creed of the majority of Christians in East and West alike; perhaps even of a large majority. It had gained a footing in the most famous schools of theology: it had leavened Alexandria and its school; had leavened Palestine; had leavened Cappadocia; had even leavened Antioch—where Origen's teaching was directly opposed; it had leavened the early Latin Fathers, and in the roll of its teachers (or those, at least, in sympathy with it), were, as we have seen, most of the greatest names of the greatest age of primitive Christianity.

A crowd of witnesses, from almost every quarter to which the gospel had reached, assure us of their belief that Christ liberated from Hades every soul, without exception. And we have heard teachings that openly assert, or, by fair inference, involve the larger hope, from both East and West, from Gaul as well as from Alexandria; from Rome; from Milan; from Arabia; from Palestine; from Antioch; from Cappadocia; from Cilicia; from Constantinople; from the distant Euphrates. And this teaching, be it noted, is strongest where the language of the New Testament was a living tongue, i.e., in the great Greek Fathers: it is strongest in the church's

Part Two—Universalism Asserted on the Authority of Tradition

greatest era, and declines as knowledge and purity decline. On the other hand, endless penalty is most strongly taught precisely in those quarters where the New Testament was less read in the original, and also in the most corrupt ages of the church.

Note carefully—the point is significant—that this universalism was *essentially and first of all based on Scripture;* on those promises of a "restitution of all things," taught "by all God's holy prophets," repeated so often by the psalmists; and echoed clearly and distinctly in the New Testament.[62]

There is another point, whose importance—in view of some modern teaching—seems to me very great: it is the teaching of so many, and such illustrious Fathers, that death is no penalty, but is, indeed, *a cure*; that it is, in fact, the great Potter remolding his own handiwork to restore it to its pristine beauty, and that the sinner's destruction means but the destruction of the sin—the *sinner* perishes, the man lives. Such teaching would be significant even in a solitary instance; but here we have witness upon witness, to whom Greek was a familiar and a living tongue, repeating the same striking idea; teaching death to be no penalty, but the remolding of our nature by the Heavenly Artist, and designed to cure sin; teaching, too, that the sinner's destruction by God is not loss but gain, is not annihilation, but conversion and reformation. To this point I shall return, and adduce fresh evidence from early writers, in the next chapter.

I have said enough, amply to prove the wide diffusion of universalism in the early centuries, alike in East and West, taught as it was, as in perfect harmony with the catholic faith. But it may be well to call three witnesses (whose testimony it is quite hopeless to gainsay). From St. Basil I quote "The *mass of men* [i.e., of Christians] say that there is to *be an end of punishment* to those who are punished" (quoting Luke 12:47–48)

---

62 Editor: It may be that Allin is directing this claim against those who argue that belief in *apokatastasis* was an alien import into Christianity. It has variously been said to come from Plato, from Gnosticism, and from Stoicism. However, Origen carefully distinguishes the *Christian* doctrine of *apokatastasis* from all of these philosophies. Plato, in fact, denied any universal restoration; the gnostics did not think of the final *apokatastasis* as either including all people (only the elite) or as holistic (bodies were excluded); the Stoics saw *apokatastasis* as characterized by necessity and as being on an eternal loop of fall-restoration-fall-restoration-fall . . . , on and on, *ad infinitum*. The Christian doctrine was distinguished in that it was truly universal, was holistic (salvation of soul *and body*), placed a high value on human freedom, affirmed the *eternal* state of the final restoration, and, as Allin rightly points out, was grounded in Scripture and Christian doctrine.

(*Conc.* 14 *De fut. judic.*). This opinion the writer [Basil] disputes, but his words prove that a terminable penalty was the ordinary view, and *he does not even hint that this view was opposed to the faith*. The passage is from the *Ascetica*, a work interpolated, and I do not claim it as certainly Basil's: its value as ancient *testimony* is, however, not altered.

Again, St. Jerome (and no more competent witness can exist), writing towards the end of the fourth century, says, "I know that *most persons* understand by the story of Nineveh and its king, *the ultimate forgiveness of the devil and all rational creatures*" (*Comm. in Jon.* 3). Now, if *most* believed the ultimate salvation of *every evil spirit*, ought we not to say that all, or nearly all, believed in the more moderate dogma of universal human salvation in St. Jerome's day?

There is another witness of slightly later date, and of equal weight. St. Augustine tells us that, in his days, there were not only some, but *"very many"* or *"the majority"* (*quam plurimi*) "who compassionated the eternal punishment of the damned, and believed that it would not take place" (*Enchir.* 112).

In addition, we have the testimony of Dominitan to be presently quoted, which, if indirect, is perhaps even stronger. The significance of such testimonies is very great indeed. They state precisely the all-important fact that universalism was the belief of half, or *more than half*, of Christendom, even in the West, during the fourth and part of the fifth century. St. Augustine speaks for the West, St. Basil for the East, and Dominitan for the same, while St. Jerome, from his peculiar position, may represent both.[63] How, indeed, shall any fact be attested satisfactorily, if such testimony, backed by the very words of so many Fathers (as quoted) be not decisive? And how hopeless and inveterate must be the prejudice that rejects such testimony because unwelcome. In the succeeding ages as ignorance spread, and superstitions of every kind multiplied, with a wholly corrupt and licentious people, and a clergy venal and grossly ignorant, there is no reason to wonder that, by slow degrees, the earlier and nobler faith decayed everywhere (declining in almost exact proportion as knowledge declined and corruption flourished); a process aided largely in the West by the preponderance of the cruel and uncatholic Augustinian theology, and by the consequent development of the doctrine of purgatory. It would be difficult, and want of space forbids the attempt, to convey to

---

63 Editor: Jerome is closely associated with the Latin, Western church, yet he was also based in Palestine, in the East. He thus straddles the two halves of the empire and of the church.

general readers an adequate idea of the degraded state of learning and morals, when in the tenth century, the climax of darkness was reached in the West.[64] Yet the creed even then current *was mercy itself* compared with our modern traditions, leaving as it did a door of hope widely open, beyond the grave, to all but a few exceptionally great sinners.

The Mid-Fifth Century to the Twelfth Century

I now resume my task of quoting. From what has been said all can understand why in the period into which we now proceed to inquire our quotations are neither so numerous nor so striking as before. This period (the third of the divisions already made, p. 86) extends from about the middle of the fifth century to the eleventh or twelfth.

Facundus and Domitian (Sixth Century)

I may begin by an extract from Facundus, who was a man of considerable eminence, Bishop of Hermiane. To all this is to be added the confession of Domitian of Galatia,[65] formerly Bishop of Ancyra; for in the book which he wrote to Vigilus he says, "they have hastily run out to anathematize most holy and glorious teachers, on account of those doctrines which have been advanced concerning preexistence and restitution; and this, indeed, under pretext of Origen, but thereby anathematizing *all those saints who were before and have been after him*" (*Pro def. tr. cap.* 4.4). It is clear from the context, that Domitian believed in the salvation of all evil spirits—a noteworthy fact—indeed, we shall see this belief existing at a still later period.

There are also three branches of evidence to which I desire here briefly to refer:

(a) First, we know on excellent authority that many of the followers of Nestorius, who were very widely diffused over the East, taught universalism.[66] Nor has their Nestorianism *the very least connection* with this particular opinion, which they drew, *not from Nestorius*, but from the general current of church teaching in that age, and to which they thus

---

64 Editor: Mediaevalists may beg to differ.

65 Editor: Domitian of Ancyra was an Origenist monk who helped to spread Origenism among the monks in Palestine.

66 See Assemanni, *Biboitheque Orientalis*.

become witnesses. "It is obvious," says the Dean of Wells, "that the special point on which Nestorius was condemned had no connection with this or that form of eschatology; and that it was derived by them from those whose orthodoxy, like Gregory of Nyssa, was unquestioned."[67]

(b) But next, it is also certain that in the sixth century, in the monasteries, erected in the wilds lying between Jerusalem and the Dead Sea, there was a strong party, of which Domitian (just quoted) was a leader, teaching (with other tenets of Origen) the restitution of all souls.[68]

(c) Further, several testimonies might be quoted from writers of the period now under discussion, teaching the liberation from Hades, by Christ, of every soul whatsoever. I proceed to quote Gennadius, Patriarch of Constantinople (458 AD): "The first fruits shall obtain the *totality* and the rest of the body shall follow the Head. . . . For, said he, when lifted up, I will draw all men unto myself" (*In Rom* 8:34). Gennadius also seems to hold the opinion shared by many Fathers (see next chapter) which regards the resurrection as in itself involving immunity from sin and suffering. "Thank God who has given us immortality, incorruptibility, and impassability" (*In Rom* 7:24). Finally, as I understand his comments on Romans 8:19, there will be one day an universal regeneration.

Andrew of Caesarea (563–637)

Other passages might be given; but I pass on to quote from Andrew, Bishop of Caesarea. He is describing the great future apocalyptic song of praise, thus: "By *all things* intelligible or sensible [i.e., invisible or visible], both living and simply existing, God is glorified as author of all, in the modes of speech natural [to them]" (*In Rev.* 5:13). Neither Gennadius nor Andrew are consistent writers; and they probably do not design to teach universalism, but such extracts seem noteworthy, and very hard to reconcile with the dogma of endless misery and sin.

---

67 Editor: Edward Hayes Plumptre, *The Spirits in Prison and Other Studies on the Life After Death* (London: 1884).

68 In the sixth century there were indeed Origenist monks in Palestine. Their teaching was a development of Origen's own that took it in directions that the church came to see as particularly problematic. However, these later Origenist views were then anachronistically read back as if they had been the views of Origen and his more faithful interpreters. Thus, Origen himself and the Origenians were tarred with the same brush as the later Origenists.

Part Two—Universalism Asserted on the Authority of Tradition

Pseudo-Dionysius and His Influence

We now approach a striking incident in the history of religious thought. In the sixth century were published the (so-called) works of Dionysius, the Areopagite.[69] The influence exerted by these writings, and their profoundly mystical tone, was extremely great, and has lasted, in a true sense, even to our day. As the worship of the church became more and more material, so contemplative minds gladly turned for relief to a theology that spiritualised, without rejecting, the external symbols. The system these writings embrace recalls the earlier teaching of Alexandria, and its Platonism; and asserting, as they do, that all things come out of God, and return to (or, into) him, cleansed from all stain, they form a storehouse of universalism.

Although challenged when first produced in 533 AD, at Constantinople, yet, in an uncritical age, a belief in their authenticity prevailed. Thus viewed as belonging to the apostolic era, their influence was widely felt, especially in the case of two remarkable men. Of these, one was Maximus, head of a monastery near Constantinople (645 AD), the ablest theologian of his day. The other was John Scotus Eriugena—perhaps the acutest of the schoolmen, if he be not rather their forerunner—who, two centuries later, taught at the Court of Charles the Bald.[70] We thus find the East once more communicating an impulse, vital and fertile, to the colder West, warming with a diviner hope her narrow creed, now touched with a stern Africanism.

I append the following brief extracts to show the tone of the writings of the so-called Dionysius.

> Out of him and through him is every being and life ... every power, every energy ... and [all] are being turned into the good and beautiful. All things—whatsoever exist and are formed—exist and are formed for the sake of beauty and goodness; and he is beginning and end of all things for [out] "of him and through him, and unto him are all things" [Rom 10:36]. (*De div. nom.* 4:10)

> He makes all things, makes perfect all things. He holds together and converts all things [to himself]. (*De div. nom.* 4:10)

---

69 Editor: On Pseudo-Dionysius, see now Ramelli, *Christian Doctrine of Apokatastasis*, 694–721.

70 Editor: Charles the Bald (823–77) was the Holy Roman Emperor, Charles II.

> With God are the causes of evils, they are beneficent powers. (*De div. nom.* 4:30)
>
> Even of all evils, the beginning and *end* is the good, because for the sake of good exist all things, both those which are good, and those which are opposed to it. (*De div. nom.* 4:31)
>
> What is good is the beginning and end of all things. (*De div. nom.* 4:35)
>
> Even to the *demons* that they exist both comes of good and *is* good. (*De div. nom.* 4:34)
>
> God converts and holds together all things, as being the all powerful abode of all, safe guarding all things, nor permitting them to fall away from himself, and perish by departing from the all perfect home. (*De div. nom.* 10:1)
>
> The good [or beautiful] is the beginning and end of all things. (*De div. nom.* 4:7)

All this leads logically and naturally to the larger hope.

Hierotheus and Stephen Bar Sudali

At this point I must ask attention to two names, as teaching the larger hope, whose personality has almost faded away in the mists of time. The first is Hierotheus, who is known only by a few brief extracts, which Dionysius quotes, as from the writings of his master. Hierotheus belongs, probably, to the school of Edessa, sometime in the fifth century. I give two brief specimens. "Towards the supreme love tends the total love flowing from *all* existences" (quoted in *De div. nom.* 4:16). "There is one simple force, self-moved, towards a blending together in unity [flowing] from what is good unto the last of those things that exist" (quoted in *De div. nom.* 4:17). Inadequate as are these brief extracts to represent the man, yet his teaching is evidently in harmony with the Pseudo-Dionysius.

The other name is that of an Abbot of Edessa, Bar Sudali, who, towards the end of the fifth century, taught (under the name of Hierotheus) the broadest universalism. He asserts the termination of all penalties of the future world, and their purifying character. Even the fallen spirits are

PART TWO—Universalism Asserted on the Authority of Tradition

to receive mercy, and all things are to be restored, so that God may be all in all.[71]

Maximus the Confessor (c.580–662)

I now quote briefly from Maximus, Saint and Confessor,[72] to whom I have alluded. Having spoken somewhat unfavourably of Gregory of Nyssa's teaching, be proceeds:

> For it is necessary that as *all* nature is to receive at the resurrection immortality of the flesh, . . . so, too, the fallen powers of the soul must, in the process of the ages, *cast off the memories of sin* implanted in them, and having passed all the ages, *come to God;* and so by the knowledge, not the fruition of good, receive strength and be *restored to their original state.*
> —*Q. et Dub.* 13

Again, in his *Aphorisms*, sec. 20: "the reunion of *all rational essences* with God is established as the final end."[73]

[August Neander] adds that the fundamental ideas of Maximus seem to lead to the doctrine of a final universal restoration—a proposition that is, in my judgment, beyond question true, not only of Maximus, but of the Pseudo-Dionysius and of Eriugena: while we may admit that an absolutely consistent enunciation of this was rendered difficult by the theology current in their days (the language of which Maximus indeed sometimes uses).[74]

In his *Scholia* on Dionysius, we find him teaching that "God is end and measure of all things" (*Schol. De div. nom.* 4:20). "God moves, for

---

71 Assemanni, *Bibloitheque Orientalis* 2:291. [Editor: Bar Sudhali was a Syrian Christian mystic towards the end of the fifth century. He Christian Platonism was of a pantheistic variety. Editor: On Sudhali, see now Ramelli, *Christian Doctrine of Apokatastasis*, 690–94.]

72 Editor: A confessor was one who had been killed for the faith. On Maximus, see now Ramelli, *Christian Doctrine of Apokatastasis*, 738–57.

73 Augustus Neander, *General History of the Christian Religion and Church*, 5:242.

74 Editor: After the Fifth Ecumenical Council, it became widely believed—whether or not it was the case is a different matter—that the church had condemned the hitherto widespread belief in universalism. This meant that those who spoke of such a wider hope had to do so very circumspectly. Consequently, it is more tricky to know whether or not certain thinkers were indeed universalists. If it was too obvious they could have been in trouble, so there was a trend towards more guarded talk around such matters.

he transforms and changes for the better all things . . . as says Dionysius, 'he is beginning and end of all things'" (*Schol. De div. nom.* 5 *ad fin.*). And again, "God is made all in all, embracing all things" (*Amb.* 2), (from Eriugena's version). "All things made by God are gathered into God perpetually and unchangeably" (*Amb.* 2). "The rest—the Sabbath—of God is the full bringing back into himself of the things that are created" (*Cap. theol.* 1:47). Again, with so many Fathers, Maximus teaches that the passing away of the wicked is the passing away of their wickedness. Thus on Psalm 37:36, he says the meaning is that evil will pass away and leave no trace (*Schol. De div. nom.* 4:18). Maximus, as noted above, connects with the resurrection the idea of restoration. I take one more passage: "At the resurrection, through the grace of the incarnate Son, the flesh will be absorbed by the soul" (quoted by Eriugena, *De div. nat.* 5:8).

John Scotus Erigena (c.815–c.877)

Our next witness shall be Eriugena,[75] of whom I have spoken, whose remarkable writings may be heartily commended to every student of theology. Profound thinking—conveyed in clear and vivid style—lends to them an unusual charm.

"It belongs in common to all things that have been made to return—as though by a perishing—into those causes which subsist in God" (*De div nat.* 5:21). In another very characteristic passage (to which I have unfortunately mislaid the reference), he argues that as Christ is maker and cause of all things so "the universal end of the whole creation[76] is the Word of God. . . . Last of all, the universal creation shall be united with the Creator, and shall be one in him, and with him. *And this is the end of all things visible and invisible.*" Again he says, there is to be a return and a gathering together "into that *unity of all things*[77] which is in God and is

---

75 Editor: Eriugena was an Irishman who moved to France and took over the Palatine Academy at the invitation of the Holy Roman Emperor. He was an unusually gifted philosopher in the Christian Platonist tradition, influenced by Augustine, the Capadocians, Pseudo-Dionysius, and Maximus the Confessor. On Eriugena, see now Ramelli, *Christian Doctrine of Apokatastasis*, 773–815.

76 Eriugena guards against pantheism by repudiating any blending in the future life of human and divine (*De div. nat.* 5:8). [Editor: It is sometimes said that Eriugena was a pantheist, but Allin is correct in denying this.]

77 It is true that Eriugena, writing in the Latin church of the ninth century, naturally professes a belief in endless punishment. But this stands in hopeless contradiction to his entire theological system; and the extraordinary process of jugglery with words,

Part Two—Universalism Asserted on the Authority of Tradition

God: so that both all things may be God, and God be all things" (*Pref in Max. Ambig.*).

This passage gives the substance of Maximus' version of the teaching of the Pseudo-Dionysius, and involves Eriugena's agreement with both: "the whole human race has been both redeemed in Christ, and will return into the heavenly Jerusalem" (*De div. nat.* 5:38). "Nothing contrary to the divine goodness, and life, and blessedness can he coeternal with it. Because the divine goodness will destroy evil, eternal life will absorb death, blessedness absorb sin" (*De div. nat.* 5:27). "Sins and iniquities . . . shall be completely brought to nothingness, so that they shall have no existence" (*De div. nat.* 4:4). "Further, if the entire world, and *the entire creation universally*, which has been made by God, is not destined to return into the eternal causes in which it subsists, then the whole of our reasoning so far will fall away, as vain, and completely gone to pieces" (*De div. nat.* 5:28).

There are still writers who (even at dates later than the present) teach the liberation from Hades of all souls, but any direct evidence for universalism is now very rare.[78] The following from Ecumenius (990) shows evident traces of primitive teaching. He writes on the famous words: "That God may be all in all": "The abolition *of evil* (all evil, *tes kakias*) is shown by these words, for when sin (*he hamartia*—all sin) has been taken away, it is evident that God will be all in all, when we are no longer divided between God and passions. Others have so interpreted it, that all things will be brought back to the Father as source" (*In* 1 *Cor*. 15.28).

Theophylact (1055-1107)

Theophylact, Archbishop of Achrida, in Bulgaria, shall be our next witness. By the parable of the ninety-nine and the one lost sheep, he understands the just and sinners. But as the lost sheep of the parable is found, then, if this represent the sinners of mankind, the passage seems logically to involve universalism. But there is more than this:

by which he attempts to teach that a thing can exist, and not exist, at the same time, may be read in the fifth book (*De div. nat.*). A curious and striking passage intimates that perhaps the *eternal punishment* of the devils will be *the universal abolition of their wickedness and impiety* (*De div. nat.* 5:27).

78 Editor: For instance, Lady Julian of Norwich (1342–1416) is one writer who seems to have subtle universalist leanings. On Julian, see Sweetman, "Sin Has Its Place, But All Shall Be Well."

Some, he goes on to say, understand by the one hundred sheep all rational creatures, and by the one lost sheep man (i.e., mankind) and by the lost coin, the lost image of God. "The whole world is cleansed over again from sin, and plainly the lost coin [the royal image] is found." Both interpretations seem to involve the larger hope. On 1 Corinthians 15:28, he says: "some understand by this *the removal of wickedness*, for when sin is no more, plainly God will be all in all."

This seems to show that the larger hope survived up to nearly the end of the eleventh century: it is also noteworthy that Theophylact says nothing against it here. On Ephesians 1:10:

> Things in heaven were cut off from things on earth, and had not one Head. For though by creation all had one God, yet by friendship (*oikeiosis*, domesticity) they had not yet [one God]: and so it was that the Father planned to bring back to one Head the things in heaven and on earth, i.e., to set Christ as Head over all.

On Colossians 1:18–20, he says:

> Paul by the church intends the whole human race. . . . Christ, as first fruits, has even [all] the rest following him (*kai tous loipous*). . . . One sheaf being offered, the whole harvest is sanctified . . . and one body rising, the whole nature [mankind] is deemed worthy of the resurrection. . . . Christ is first begotten [from the dead] as first fruits of the resurrection, because that is regeneration.

The train of thought in these passages is hard to reconcile with the perpetuity of evil, whatever the writer's views may have been.

Universalism Not Fully Extinguished

Nor are later instances wanting. "Both St. Thomas Aquinas and Durandus show us that, even in their day, absolute universalism was not unknown. It was the opinion of the school of Gilbert of Poitiers (Aquinas, *Sent.* 4:45) and 'aliquorum juristarum' (Durandus),"[79] and, probably, of some mystics. Again, a great name, St. Anselm, in the twelfth century, writes thus: "It is quite foreign to God's nature to suffer any reasonable creature wholly to perish" (*Cur Deus Homo* 2:4)—a striking proof of the

---

79 F. W. Farrar, *Mercy and Judgment*.

Part Two—Universalism Asserted on the Authority of Tradition

survival of the earlier hope. "Nor," adds the saint, "is it *possible* for the reasonable mind to think otherwise."

To these testimonies may be added a highly interesting prayer, quoted by the Dean of Wells from an old English manual, *The Fifteen O's*, published by Caxton; and illustrating the dominant tone of religious feeling in England in the age immediately preceding the Reformation:—

> Be merciful to those souls for whom there is no hope . . . in their torment, save that they were made in your image. . . . Put forth your right hand and *free them from the interminable pains and anguish of hell*, and lead them to the fellowship of the citizens on high.

The three periods of the church's history, embraced in the inquiry we have just made, may be said to correspond to early springtime; to summer, brief and bright; to autumn, followed by wintry gloom. After some centuries of conflict and growth, the freedom won for the gospel by Constantine was followed by an outburst of activity, theological and intellectual (such were the church's spring and summertide). But in the very success lay unperceived the seeds of disaster. Elements of evil, repressed in adversity, soon revived; and the crowds who now flocked to Christian teaching brought with them, too often, the superstition, the ignorance, the vices of heathenism. Bitter intestine strife, scandalous intrigues, virulent controversies, began more than ever to exhaust the energies of the church, or to direct them into barren channels. And so the autumn and its decay followed. To the Fathers succeeded—after a period of barrenness—the schoolmen in the West; while, in the East, no successor appeared to the great names of earlier days. Other features of this period I can barely notice; for example, the break up of the Roman empire; the growth of the papacy; the successive inroads of barbarians into Italy; the spread of monasticism; the steady advance of superstition; the decay of learning; the ever-widening divisions between the East and West. Who can pretend to wonder that amid all this "hurly burly," the larger hope—taught so freely in the church's spring and summer time—gained ever fewer adherents in its autumnal decay, and well nigh died out in its dark winter?

The Sixth-Century Condemnation of Origen

Any sketch of universalism would be incomplete without a discussion of the assertion still repeated, though often refuted, that the dogma of the final salvation of all men was condemned, in the person of Origen, at the Fifth [Ecumenical] Council.[80] This assertion is, as will be distinctly shown, untrue. An attempt was indeed made to procure a condemnation of this doctrine—an attempt which *wholly failed;* and which was made, not at the Fifth Council, but at the Home Synod of Constantinople (i.e., a committee of bishops from a small number of sees near Constantinople, who, with some officers of the metropolitan church, formed a standing council for the patriarch).

For a clearer understanding of the facts, which are very generally misunderstood, it must be premised that the larger hope was but a very inconsiderable part of what was known as "Origenism," and quite independent of it, e.g., so that it was strongly held by Origen's determined antagonists in the school of Antioch. Origenism meant a widely spreading system, embracing amongst many other points: (a) certain highly speculative tenets, e.g., preexistence,[81] and also (b) certain views, e.g., on the Trinity, capable at least of easy misrepresentation, (c) and a doctrine of the resurrection, in which this great writer was too far in advance of his day.[82] These it was, the two latter especially, that led Origen into grave disrepute; and *not his belief in the final salvation of all men.* The proofs of this are abundant and decisive.

(1) Those who taught simple universalism perhaps more fully than Origen (e.g., Clement of Alexandria and Gregory of Nyssa, and many

---

80 Editor: On the Origenist controversy and the Fifth Ecumenical Council, see now Ramelli, *Christian Doctrine of Apokatastasis*.

81 Editor: Origen's own speculations on preexistence are somewhat complex and easily misunderstood. Contrary to common belief, he did not believe in the preexistence of disembodied souls (*psuche*) as such, but he did believe in the preexistence of intellectual beings (*logika*) with spiritual bodies (which will be restored in the resurrection). This speculative theology may still be off track, but it is more nuanced that the cartoon presentations of it allow.

82 Editor: Origen was often accused of denying the resurrection of the body. This was a misunderstanding of his view. He was very clear that the resurrection will be a resurrection of the *whole* person, including their body. However, taking his lead from Paul's comment in 1 Corinthians 15 that the resurrected body will be a *spiritual* body, he denied a material substance to this body. Again, his speculation may be inadequate, but it is not the same thing as denying the resurrection of the body.

PART TWO—Universalism Asserted on the Authority of Tradition

others) were held in universal honour, or if some were condemned, like Theodore of Mopsuestia, no condemnation, direct or indirect, was made of their universalism.

(2) The larger hope was, in fact, widely held by those who opposed Origen in nearly everything else (e.g., the school of Antioch). Indeed, the intrigue against Theodore was promoted by Origenists.

(3) We have several lists, more or less complete, of the alleged errors of Origen, from 300 down to 404 AD: *in none of them is any mention of the larger hope.* I may instance the lists[83] of Methodius (300), that given by Pamphilus and Eusebius, in their Apology (310); of Epiphanius (376 and 394); of Theophilus, in a circular letter, and in three Paschal letters of 400, 402, and 404, and more than one of St. Jerome (400). I beg that this most significant fact may be noted, Jerome, Theophilus, and Epiphanius literally scrape together every possible charge against Origen, but *never allude to his teaching of the larger hope as heretical.*

How can any fair mind refuse the inevitable conclusion that this was, at least, a perfectly open question? Again I ask how these facts can be reconciled with the common prejudice, which asserts that Origen's teaching of all men's final salvation was that which brought him into disrepute? Indeed, so far from the larger hope, as we understand it, being something peculiar to Origen, there is reason to believe that—while he certainly taught restoration and the limited duration of all future punishment (and thus gave a great impulse to these opinions)—he himself held them in a peculiar form. I do not mean so much that he taught the final salvation of all evil spirits—a view held by several Fathers, but that he seems to have taught (a) that all human beings would return to exactly the *same level*, so that a prostitute, as St. Jerome says, would finally be the same as the Blessed Virgin; (b) that, thereafter, fresh cycles would ensue, in which even the good angels might fall away, and so on for long periods, or, possibly, even for ever.[84] These views naturally invited opposition on all sides, from the friends of the larger hope, as well as from its enemies.

---

83 Some other early writers against Origen are known, e.g., Eustathius of Antioch (330 AD), Marcellus of Ancyra (320 AD). But none of these touch on the doctrine of restoration. Leo the Great, in a letter (*Ep.* 35) alludes to Origen as condemned for teaching preexistence.

84 Editor: Origen was often accused of teaching never-ending cycles of falls and restorations, as the Stoics taught. Allin here accepts such accusations uncritically. In fact, Origen was strongly opposed to such endless cycles, and was very clear that the final state of *apokatastasis* was eternal.

What the Church Teaches

Thus, from what has been stated, it is absolutely certain that to condemn "Origen" or "Origenism" in general terms, does not involve disapproval of restoration,[85] even as he taught it; still less of the restoration of all human beings—a tenet quite compatible with very strong hostility to Origenism, as in the school of Antioch. I repeat that all the evidence goes to prove that it was speculative tenets—at least tenets wholly unconnected with the larger hope—that brought Origen into disrepute, aided, doubtless, by the jealousies of rivals.

Equally misunderstood are the facts connected with the alleged condemnation of Origen at the Fifth Council, so that it is needful to state briefly the salient points, which are these—In 541 AD (the exact year is not certain), the Emperor Justinian caused the Patriarch Mennas to convene at Constantinople the *Home Synod*, expressly to condemn the larger hope, and certain other opinions attributed to Origen.[86] This is noteworthy, as being the first attempt to procure a distinct condemnation of the larger hope. Mark the result. "This Synod passed fifteen canons, in which various theories of Origen were condemned, but *deliberately omitted*" that concerning the larger hope, i.e., *deliberately refused to condemn it*.[87] Twelve years later was convened the Fifth Council (born in intrigue[88] and unrecognized by the English Church[89]).

It is said, but the fact is disputed by able and impartial writers, to have condemned Origen by name in the eleventh canon, but only in general terms, which, as I have shewn above, proves nothing at all as to the condemnation of the larger hope.[90] Further, special reasons ex-

85 Editor: Or, to condemn Origen*ism* was not to condemn Origen, for Origenism arguably was a somewhat distorted version of what Origen himself had taught. Indeed, arguably Origen himself did not teach *any* of the Origenist errors condemned at the Fifth Ecumenical Council. Sadly, the church at the time made no distinction between what Origen taught in the second/third century and what certain Origenists taught in the sixth century.

86 Editor: Justinian's letter even included the list of anathemas against Origen that he wanted the bishops to sign up to.

87 Editor: This claim is not really correct. The canons did say, "If anyone claims or maintains that the punishment of demons and of impious people is temporary, and that it will cease sooner or later, or that the complete restoration of demons and impious humans will take place, be it anathema." However, whatever this synod had decided, a *local* synod would not have any *universal* authority in the church.

88 Editor: The Pope refused to attend and had to be brought under guard. He then flouted custom by refused to open the proceedings.

89 Editor: i.e., the one true church. (Joke)

90 Editor: Furthermore, Origen's name is almost certainly a later insertion into

Part Two—Universalism Asserted on the Authority of Tradition

ist which render any intention to condemn universalism, on the part of the Fifth Council, in the highest degree unlikely. (a) The promoters *were themselves Origenists*. (b) The object of the council was to condemn certain Nestorian tenets, *quite distinct from universalism*. (c) The council expressly referred to St. Gregory of Nyssa, who was the most outspoken universalist of all the Fathers, as a prop of the faith! Such is the true story of the so-called condemnation of universalism.

The Home Synod distinctly refused to condemn it, even at the Emperor's bidding; while if, as is doubtful, the Fifth Council did condemn Origen, it did so in general terms only, and *it did not thereby condemn the larger hope; nor am I aware that this special point was ever so much as submitted to any ancient general council for decision*.[91] In short, "we have no evidence that the belief in 'restitution,' which prevailed in the fourth and fifth centuries, was *ever* definitely condemned by *any council of the church*."[92] A fact that I must ask my readers to impress most clearly on their minds; a fact further attested by a witness of most strict orthodoxy, in these words: "Whatever the amount, and quality of authority arrayed against Origen's view may be, conciliar decisions make no part of it."[93]

No doubt some will ask, does not the very fact that this belief in an endless hell was permitted to spread so widely, as to have become practically universal, prove its truth? If so, I reply, why not then carry out your theory? Infant communion was universal for centuries;[94] slavery was universally defended from the earliest age of the church.[95] Are we, therefore, to adopt them? The duty of persecution for errors of faith was universally

---

the original document. It appears out of chronological order in a chronological list of heretics, suggesting that it was not part of the original list. We also have the sketch of the list on which anathema 11 was based, and that list does not include Origen. So Origen was probably not condemned in anathema 11. *Thus, Origen was never formally condemned by the church.*

91 Editor: There is an appendix to the main deliberations of the council that includes the Justinian condemnations of apokatastasis. The status of this appendix is not agreed—was it part of the official output of the council or was it added on later? Even if it was part of the council's output, it is important to appreciate that, strictly speaking, what is condemned is not *apokatastasis* per se, but a specific form of *apokatastasis*—i.e., one associated with problematic views on preexistence and pantheism. It should not be interpreted in a more blanket way that would condemn, for instance, the universalist views of Gregory of Nyssa or Athanasius.

92 Edward Plumptre, *Spirits in Prison*, 141.

93 *Church Times*, Feb. 1, 1884.

94 Editor: The practice of giving the Eucharist to infants and children.

95 Editor: With some exceptions, such as Gregory of Nyssa.

held—shall we adopt it? Shall we invoke saints and angels because the practice was once universal, or burn witches for the same cogent reason? It has pleased God to permit in numberless cases error to prevail, and obscure in this present age his truth. This very fact is but a louder call to us to work against all that hides or distorts that truth. Nay, it points not uncertainly to a conclusion in perfect agreement with the larger hope, this namely, that the present is but an initial stage of being; one of many ages, during which God is slowly, very slowly, working out a vast plan, and permits for a moment, as it were, an apparent triumph to error and to evil.

The Wider Hope in England

The Wider Hope and the Church of England

Let us now pass on and see what our own church [i.e., the Church of England] teaches on this point. We shall, I think, find, if we examine it carefully, in our Book of Common Prayer—moulded as it is on primitive lines, and on Scripture—not a few testimonies in favour of the larger hope. Not that I mean to represent the compilers as themselves universalists, far from it. But it is interesting to note the indications of a wider hope that emerge, even where indirect and unintentional.

Take, for instance, the service of Holy Baptism—what is the profession of faith required? "Do you believe in everlasting life after death," and not a *word* or *hint further*. Again, in our Litany, do we not pray God to have mercy, not on some men, but on *all men*? If this were in fact impossible, would it not be very like a sham to address such a prayer to God—just as the Inquisition used to hand over prisoners to the secular courts with a request that they would be merciful?

Do we not also address, in the same Litany, Jesus Christ as the "Lamb of God that takes away the sins of the world," and that twice over? Do we not, in Holy Communion, repeat, *three times* in one prayer, this truly catholic address to Christ, as "taking away the sins of the world?" And here it is right to ask, are words a mere pretense, and that in our holiest moments? How does Christ *take away* the sins of the world, if to all eternity in hell the sins of any men remain not taken away? On this point our Book of Common Prayer is specially emphatic, for in the proper preface for Easter Day we are bidden to remember how Christ *"hath taken away* the sins of the world? and has by His death *destroyed* death." But to abolish death in its Scriptural meaning is surely to abolish all that the fall brought on man. Take next one of the Ember Collects: "To those who shall be ordained, grant Your grace, that they may set forward the salvation of *all* men." Does the salvation of *all* men mean the damnation of *most* men, of *any* man? And so, too, when the church bids us render thanks for a world redeemed, and for our creation, no less than for our redemption, how can this be if creation be not a certain promise of good? If creation does, as a matter of fact, imply an awful, unutterable risk of hell's torment, why bid a man give thanks for that, which may be to him an occasion of endless pains?

I will next ask your attention to a fact perhaps not always remembered, that our church deliberately expunged that article which (adopted in 1552) condemned the belief in the final salvation of all men.[96] "The 42nd article was withdrawn," says the Bishop of Manchester, "because the Church, knowing that men like Origen, Clement, and Gregory of Nyssa, were Universalists, refused to dogmatise on such questions."[97]

Nor are other indications wanting of the hopeful teaching of our Prayer Book. Let us not fail to note the hope expressed for *all* in the Burial Service; the stress laid on the wide extent of the atonement in the Catechism, and in the General Confession; the true force of all this is best seen when our formularies are compared with those of other Reformed communions (a comparison for which I have not space). In a word, the tone of the Book of Common Prayer is frequently that indicated in the Collect for the Sunday before Easter—where the object of Christ's death is described as this: "that *all mankind* should follow the example of His great humility," and in that other prayer, which addresses God as one, "whose property is *always* to have mercy"; words that, if taken in their full meaning, certainly seem to teach the larger hope.

But there is further important evidence of our church's teaching. Of Christ's descent into Hades I have already spoken, and pointed out

---

96 Article 42 of the Forty-Two Articles of Religion proposed as a standard for the English church was a condemnation of universalism. However, before it ever got as far the statute books, the Forty-Two Articles had become the Thirty-Nine Articles, and the condemnation of universalism had been dropped. So the Church of England has never officially required its priests to deny universalism.

97 Editor: Rev. James Moorhouse was Bishop of Melbourne from 1877 to 1885 and Bishop of Manchester from 1886–1903.

What the Church Teaches

that to teach the liberation of all souls thence, is logically at least to teach universalism. And this liberation of *all*, it can, I think, be shown that our church teaches: for the church has intimated her belief in the fact of Christ's descent into Hades, and preaching there, by the selection of 1 Peter 3:19 as the Epistle for Easter Eve, and of Zechariah 9 as the first lesson (see verse 11, and its striking allusion to the "prisoners of hope").[98] Further, in the Homily (*Of the Resurrection*) appointed for Easter Day, we have the result of Christ's preaching in Hades stated in the following words: "He destroyed the devil and *all* his tyranny, and took from him *all his captives*, and hath raised and set them *with Himself among the heavenly citizens* above. His death *destroyed hell and all the damnation thereof*." These words, as I think, teach the liberation of all souls, without exception, from Hades.

The Wider Hope in England

Nor has the larger hope wanted able defenders in English theology since the days of the Prayer Book. It is interesting to note that amid the tumults of the Rebellion[99] and the gross profligacy of the Restoration,[100] there rose and flourished a school of devout men (trained, most of them, at Cambridge); partly Anglican, partly Nonconformists, who held, or sympathized with, the larger hope. One of the earliest was Gerald Winstanley, who taught a complete restoration of the whole creation in *The Mystery of God*, etc., printed 1669.[101] To nearly the same epoch belong two very remarkable names, Ralph Cudworth and Henry More, of the school of Cambridge Platonists, whose sympathies were distinctly in favour of the

---

98 Editor: The issue of Christ's descent into Hades was a matter of some controversy in England during its Reformation period, and this is reflected in the Church of England's engagement with it. The actual statement is carefully worded so as to keep all sides of the disputes happy. See Laufer, *Hell's Destruction*, 92–99.

99 Editor: Allin is referring to the English Civil War (1642–51).

100 Editor: The Restoration of the monarchy in England, after the Interregnum brought about by the Civil War, began in 1660.

101 Editor: Gerald Winstanley, *The mysterie of God concerning the whole creation, mankinde to be made known to every man and woman after seaven dispensations and seasons of time are passed over, according to the councell of God, revealed to his servants* (London: 1649). Gerald Winstanley (1609–86) was a political activist (one of the founders of the True Levellers, aka The Diggers) and a religious reformer. He became a Quaker.

Part Two—Universalism Asserted on the Authority of Tradition

larger hope.[102] More outspoken in his teaching was Peter Sterry, Fellow of Emmanuel College, Cambridge—one of Cromwell's chaplains—whose works published (after his death) in 1683 and 1710, evidence a strong leaning to mysticism, often stated with much beauty of imagery.[103]

I may note next, as of the same school of thought, [John] Sadler, author of *Olbia*,[104] and [Benjamin] Whichcote[105]—a friend of [Ralph] Cudworth and [Henry] More, a Fellow of Emmanuel College, a contemporary of [John] Milton and Jeremy Taylor. Also two less known authors, [Richard] Coppin[106] and [William] Erbury.[107] At this time there also appeared not a few anonymous books, advocating the wider hope, which deserve mention, as illustrating the course of theological inquiry in the seventeenth century, e.g., *Enochian Walks with God*, and *The Revelation of the Everlasting Gospel Message*, by the same author;[108] and *God's Light*

---

102 Editor: Ralph Cudworth (1617-88) was the Master of Claire Hall and Professor of Hebrew in Cambridge; Henry More (1614-87) was also based at Cambridge University. Both were leaders in the seventeenth-century revival of Christian Platonism in Cambridge. Both Cudworth and More expressed some sympathies with universalism, although their exact views are not so clear.

103 Editor: Peter Sterry (1613-72) was a Fellow of Emmanuel College, Cambridge, where he was associated with the Cambridge Platonists. He was a chaplain to Oliver Cromwell, who held Sterry in very high regard. The two posthumous books Allin refers to are presumably *A Discourse on the Freedom of the Will* (London: 1675, not 1710, contra Allin) and *The Rise, Race, and Royalty of the Kingdom of God in the Soul of Man Opened in Several Sermons on Matthew 18:3* (London: 1683). Even more blatant is an unpublished manuscript, *That State of the Wicked Men after This Life Is Mixt of Evil & Good Things*.

104 Editor: John Sadler (1615-74), *Olbia: The New Iland Lately Discovered. With Its Religion and Rites of Worship; Laws, Customs, and Government; Characters and Language; with Education of their Children in their Sciences, Arts and Manufactures . . . By a Christian Pilgrim, Driven by Tempest from Civita Vecchia, or some other Parts about Rome; through the Straits, into the Atlantick Ocean* (London: 1660).

105 Editor: Benjamin Whichcote (1609-83) was a Puritan, Provost of King's College Cambridge, and a leader of the Cambridge Platonists.

106 Editor: Richard Coppin, author of *The Exaltation of All Things in Christ* (London: 1649), was a public defender of universalism. He got in trouble for this and was tried in Worcester then Oxford—the jury found him guilty of blasphemy, but the Judges disagreed. He was set free, and he continued to get into trouble. Even another universalist, albeit it an idiosyncratic one, James Relly, attacked him in one publication.

107 Editor: William Erbury (1604-54) was a Welsh clergyman but was ejected by his Bishop. He became an Independent who openly preached the salvation of all.

108 Editor: These books were not anonymous, but were written by the mystic Jane Leade (1624-1704).

What the Church Teaches

(1653); also *Of the Torments of Hell, the Foundation and Pillars thereof Shaken* (1658) by [Samuel] Richardson.[109]

A more distinguished advocate of the larger hope was Bishop Rust,[110] successor of Jeremy Taylor, author of *De Veritate*, and *A Letter concerning the Opinions of Origen*. Another name almost equally eminent is that of Jeremy White,[111] Fellow of Trinity, Cambridge, chaplain to Cromwell, and author of *The Restoration of all Things*, published (after his death) in 1712; a book, I may add, eloquent, devout, and breathing the deepest reverence for Holy Scripture. Towards the close of the seventeenth century, came R. Stafford[112] and Jane Leade, the latter a mystic, whose works are rare and valuable.[113] To these I may add [John] Tillotson,[114] who seems to have held that God was not bound to execute his threatenings pronounced against sinners; a view in which he was followed more decisively by Bishop Stillingfleet;[115] and by Dr. [Thomas] Burnet,[116] Master of the

---

109 Editor: Samuel Richardson was a Baptist preacher with Cromwell's army and in several London Baptist churches.

110 Editor: George Rust (d. 1670) was one of the Cambridge Platonists and Bishop of Dromore, Ireland, from 1667–70. His *Letter of Resolution concerning Origen and the Chief of His Opinions* (London: 1661) expressed clear universalist leanings, even if not an open declaration of the sentiment.

111 Editor: Jeremiah White (1629–1707) was a friend with some of the Cambridge Platonists and a Nonconformist chaplain to Oliver Cromwell. His defence of universalism, *The Restoration of All Things* (London: 1712), was published five years after his death.

112 Editor: R. Stafford, *Some Thoughts of the Life to Come* (London: 1693).

113 Editor: Jane Leade (1624–1704) was a mystic and leading member of the Philadelphian Society, a short-lived ecumenically-inclined prophetic group influenced by the teaching of Jacob Böhme, the German mystic. Her teachings, especially on universalism, influenced some of the early German pietists, who in turn took universalism across to America.

114 Editor: John Tillotson (1630–94) was Archbishop of Canterbury from 1691–94. When Dean of St. Paul's he preached and published a controversial sermon on Matt 25:46 (1689/90) which speculated that God threatens eternal punishment as a deterrent, but that this does not obligate him to carry out the threat. Perhaps the *actual* fate of the lost will be something between full salvation and hell.

115 Editor: Edward Stillingfleet (1635–99) was Bishop of Worcester and a keen defender of Anglicanism and of orthodox Christianity .

116 Editor: Thomas Burnett (c.1635–1715) wrote on issues of cosmogeny and also on the state of the dead. In his posthumously published book on the latter theme, he examined the teachings of the Fathers and argued that future punishment was corrective. He was Master of Charterhouse School from 1685.

Part Two—Universalism Asserted on the Authority of Tradition

Charter House, a pupil of his at Cambridge, who, in his *De Statu Mortuorum [et Resurgentium]*, teaches universalism openly.

The movement in favour of the larger hope was continued during the eighteenth century by William Whiston,[117] in his *Sermons and Essays* (London: 1707) and by many others. I may name Dr. Cheyne,[118] in his *Discourses*, published 1742, and (probably) Bishop Warburton[119] (see ch. 8 note on Rev. 20:14), Bishop Newton (1750), in a sermon on the "Final State of Man";[120] and William Law[121] (1766) in his *Letters* and *Way to Divine Knowledge*. To the latter may probably be due, ultimately, the whole revival movement in England.[122] To this era belong also two books, little known, *De Vita Functorum Statu*, by J. Windet,[123] and *Glad Tidings to Jews and Gentiles* (1763), by [Richard] Clarke,[124] both published in 1763, and both advocating the larger hope.

Other names of authors, favourable to universalism, in this century, are J. Cooke (London, 1752);[125] [James] Relly (1759);[126] Sir [George]

---

117 Editor: William Whiston (1667–1752) is best known as a translator of Josephus. He worked with and succeeded Isaac Newton at Cambridge as Professor of Mathematics, but was forced to leave the university for being an Arian. He issued three publications against eternal punishment (1709, 1717, 1740), and while not convinced of universal salvation, he hoped it might be so.

118 Editor: Presumably Allin refers to George Cheyne (1671–1743), a physician. He briefly reveals himself as a universalist in *Philosophical Principles of Natural and Revealed Religion* (London: 1715). I am uncertain what *Discourses* (1742) refers to.

119 Editor: William Warburton (1698–1779) was Bishop of Gloucester from 1759 to 1779. He was a literary critic and wrote defences of Christian orthodoxy against Deism.

120 Editor: Thomas Newton (1704–82) was a biblical scholar, literary critic, and Bishop of Bristol from 1761 to 1782.

121 Editor: William Law (1686–1761) was an Anglican priest who refused to swear the oath of allegiance to George I and so lost his position. He was well known for his piety and his mystical writings were widely influential.

122 Editor: This claim that the evangelical revival was ultimately due to William Law is, of course, absurd. However, it is true that Law was a significant influence on key players in that revival, including John and Charles Wesley.

123 Editor: I do not know who J. Windet was.

124 Editor: Richard Clarke, *A Voice of Glad Tidings to Jews and Gentiles* (1763). Richard Clarke was rector of St. Philip's Episcopal Church in Charleston, SC from 1754 to 1759 before returning to Anglican ministry in England. He described himself as "preacher of the everlasting gospel." He proclaimed universalism for almost fifty years.

125 Editor: I do not know who J. Cooke was.

126 Editor: James Relly (c.1722–78) was a Welsh convert of the famous revivalist

Stonehouse (1768);[127] [William] Dudgeon (1765);[128] Rev. [Capel] Berrow (1772);[129] C. Charnay (1784);[130] [Francis] Leicester (1786);[131] [James] Weaver (1792);[132] [John] Browne (1798).[133] About this time Elhanan Winchester, a follower of John Wesley, advocated the larger hope in his *Dialogues*;[134] and, indeed, Wesley himself seems to have finally shared this view,[135] for he published, in 1787, as "one of the most sensible tracts he

---

George Whitfield. He became one of Whitfield's preachers and then converted to his own idiosyncratic brand of Calvinist universalism, becoming an Independent preacher in London. The text Allin refers to is *Union; or a Treatise of the Consanguinity between Christ and His Church* (London: 1759). One of Relly's followers was John Murray (1741–1815), the so-called "Father of Universalism in America."

127 Editor: Sir George Stonehouse was a member of the "Holy Club" at Oxford University with George Whitefield (Calvinist) and the Wesley brothers (Arminians) and was later a vicar in Islington, London. Although they had debated universal salvation at the Holy Club, Stonehouse was disappointed when, after he published his mature and scholarly case for universalism in 1761, neither Whitefield nor the Wesleys made time to reply to his arguments. This spurred him on to publish more. Stonehouse was allegedly proficient in at least thirteen languages.

128 Editor: William Dudgeon (1753?–1813) was a philosophical writer who lived in Berwickshire and wrote on religious philosophy. *The Philosophical Works of Mr. William Dudgeon* was published in 1765.

129 Editor: Capel Berrow (1715–82) was an Anglican clergyman in Rossington, Northamptonshire, who published *Theological Dissertations* (London: 1772), in three of which he defended universalism.

130 Editor: I wonder if Allin was referring to Rev. Charles Chauncy (1705–87), the Congregationalist minister at First Church, Boston. He was a critic of the excesses of the Great Awakening in New England and published two defences of universalism: *Salvation for All Men* (Boston: 1782) and *The Mystery Hid from Ages and Generations* (Boston: 1784). Both are scholarly exegetical works. The latter may be the item Allin's date is intended to pick out.

131 Editor: Francis Leicester, *Christ Glorified in the Salvation and Final Restoration of All Mankind* (London: 1786). Francis Leicester was an Anglican clergyman.

132 Editor: James Weaver, *Free Thoughts on the Universal Restoration of All Lapsed Intelligences from the Ruins of the Fall* (London: 1792).

133 Editor: John Browne, *An Essay on Universal Redemption: : Tending to Prove that the General Sense of Scripture Favours the Opinion of the Final Salvation of All Mankind* (London: 1798). John Browne, M.A. was linked with Sidney Sussex College, Cambridge.

134 Editor: Elhanan Winchester (1751–97) was an American Baptist revivalist preacher and minister who became a key player in the universalist movement, first in Philadelphia and then in London. He was not, contra Allin, a follower of Wesley, but he was a great admirer of Wesley. His best known work was *The Universal Restoration: Exhibited in a Series of Dialogues between a Minister and His Friend* (London: 1788).

135 Editor: The claim that before his death John Wesley became sympathetic to

Part Two—Universalism Asserted on the Authority of Tradition

had ever read," a translation from Bonnet's *Palingenesie Philosophique*,[136] which seems to advocate universalism, e.g., it teaches: "There will be a perpetual advance of all the individuals of humanity towards perfection" in the other life. There is also a considerable American literature advocating universalism.[137]

In the present century the same steady movement continues, with ever-increasing force, in the direction of the larger hope. The name of [Thomas] Erskine[138] of Linlathen will be familiar to many. Again, the late Bishop Wilberforce[139] is stated on high authority to have finally "leaned to the larger hope," which his son[140] now preaches.

Other well known names may be given as openly teaching, or sympathizing with universalism, e.g., [Alfred] Tennyson,[141] [John] Whittier,[142] [William] Bryant,[143] [Robert] Browning and Mrs. [Elizabeth Barrett]

---

universalism is often repeated by universalists, with some supporting evidence, but I have never heard it proposed by a reputable Wesley scholar, so I am strongly inclined to be sceptical.

136 Editor: Charles Bonnet (1720–93) was a Genevan naturalist and philosopher. *La Palingénésie philosophique* [The Philosophical Revival] (Geneva: 1769) considers the past and future of living beings, and supports the idea of the survival of all animals, and the perfecting of their faculties in a future state.

137 Editor: The Universalist denomination in America, founded at the end of the eighteenth century, produced a *vast* number of publications in the nineteenth century. Richard Eddy (*Universalism in America: A History*) notes 2,052 universalist publications in the USA between 1800 and 1889! See the graph in Bressler, *The Universalist Movement in America, 1770–1880*, 55.

138 Editor: Thomas Erskine (1788–1870) was an Anglican lay theologian from Scotland. He was a highly respected theologian who sought to rethink the Reformed tradition from within.

139 Editor: This is a reference to the Bishop of Oxford, Samuel Wilberforce (1805–73), son of William Wilberforce. Allin was presumably told about Samuel's late-in-life sympathies with universalism by Basil Wilberforce, Samuel's son. Samuel is best known for his infamous debate on evolution with T. H. Huxley. The well-known tale of the debate is, according to recent historical studies, a significantly reimagined and mythologized version of the actual event, recast by Huxley for polemical reasons.

140 Editor: Rev. Basil Wilberforce (1841–1916).

141 Editor: Alfred, Lord Tennyson (1809–92) was Poet Laureate during a significant part of Queen Victoria's reign. Like many novelists and poets in the Victorian period, Tennyson has sympathies with "the larger hope." See the section of *In Memoriam* reproduced at the front of this volume.

142 Editor: John Greenleaf Whittier (1807–92) was an American Quaker and a celebrated poet.

143 Editor: Presumably William Curren Bryant (1794–1878), who was the editor of the *New York Evening Post*, a journalist, and a poet. He was unitarian and universalist.

Browning,[144] [Bernard] Whitman,[145] Edna Lyall,[146] George MacDonald,[147] [Oliver Wendell] Holmes,[148] Mrs. Oliphant,[149] James Hinton,[150] [Charlotte] Brontë and her sister Emily,[151] General Gordon,[152] Miss Mulock,[153] Fredericka Bremer,[154] Ellice Hopkins,[155] Hesba Stretton,[156] Florence Nightingale,[157] [Friedrich] Schlegel,[158] Dr. Quincey,[159] [Ralph Waldo]

---

144 Editor: Robert Browning (1812–89) was a well known poet and playwright. Elizabeth Barrett Browning (1806–61) was a very popular Victorian poet.

145 Editor: Bernard Whitman (1796–1834) was an American Unitarian minister, missionary, and apologist.

146 Editor: Edna Lyall (1857–1903) was a popular Victorian novelist. She wrote the foreword to Thomas Allin's book.

147 Editor: George MacDonald (1824–1905) was a well-known Scottish minister, poet, and novelist, best known for his fantasy literature. He reacted against the harsh Calvinism of his upbringing and embraced a kinder view of God. He was a major inspiration for C. S. Lewis.

148 Editor: Oliver Wendell Holmes (1809–94) was one of the most celebrated American authors of his day. He was a member of Boston's literary elite.

149 Editor: Margaret Oliphant (1828–1897) was a well-known Scottish novelist and historian.

150 Editor: James Hinton (1822–75) was a surgeon. (He has been proposed as a candidate for Jack the Ripper—though few find that thesis convincing.)

151 Editor: Charlotte Brontë (1816–55) was a novelist, author of *Jane Eyre*, and Emily Brontë (1818–48) was a novelist and poet, author of *Wuthering Heights*.

152 Editor: General Charles George Gordon (1833–85) was a British army officer and administrator in both China and Sudan. He was regarded in Britain as a sort of martyr for the Empire, having died defending Khartoum. (Charlton Heston played him in the 1966 movie *Khartoum*.)

153 Editor: Dinah Maria Mullock (1826–87) was a novelist and poet.

154 Editor: Fredericka Bremer (1801–65) was a Swedish novelist and campaigner for women's rights.

155 Editor: Ellice Hopkins (1836–1904) was an Anglican social campaigner.

156 Editor: Hesba Stretton was the pen name of Sarah Smith (1832–1911), a very popular evangelical author of children's books.

157 Editor: Florence Nightingale (1820–1910) was a social reformer and a pioneer of reform in the nursing profession, best known for her care of wounded soldiers during the Crimean War. She was highly regarded in Victorian society.

158 Editor: Presumably Karl Wilhelm Friedrich Schlegel (1722–1829), a German philosopher, poet, and linguist. He was a key inspiration for the Romantic movement.

159 Editor: Thomas de Quincey (1785–1859) was an essayist, best known for his *Confessions of an English Opium Eater* (1821), in which he tells of the joys and horrors of his opium addiction.

PART TWO—Universalism Asserted on the Authority of Tradition

Emerson,[160] [Henry] Longfellow,[161] Mrs. Beecher Stowe.[162] A remarkable fact is the consensus of all the leading poets as well in America as in England in favour of the larger hope, a fact noteworthy if true poetic inspiration be a reality.

In theology, not a few names may be added, as adopting, or at least in sympathy with, the larger hope, e.g., the late Bishop Ewing of Argyll,[163] Canon [Charles] Kingsley,[164] F. D. Maurice,[165] Dr. [Samuel] Cox,[166] [James] Baldwin Brown,[167] Bishop Westcott,[168] Dr. [R. F.]

---

160 Editor: Ralph Waldo Emerson (1803–82) was a celebrated American poet, essayist, and lecturer.

161 Editor: Henry Wadsworth Longfellow (1807–82) was one of Boston's literary elite, best known for his poems and his translation of Dante.

162 Editor: Harriet Beecher Stowe (1811–96) was an American author. Her most famous novel is *Uncle Tom's Cabin* (1852). She was an abolitionist and after the Civil War campaigned for married women's rights.

163 Editor: Alexander Ewing (1814–73) was Anglican Bishop of Argyll and the Isles in Scotland. His theology was said to be akin to that of F. D. Maurice and Thomas Erskine.

164 Editor: Charles Kingsley (1819–75) was a professor of history at Cambridge, a novelist, and a priest—a canon of Chester Cathedral and later of Westminster Abbey. He was one of the first to welcome to publication of Darwin's *On the Origin of Species* (London: 1859). His concern for social reform is seen in his most famous novel, *The Water Babies* (London: 1863), a tale about a chimney sweep.

165 Editor: Frederick Denison Maurice (1805–72) was a well-know Anglican theologian and Christian Socialist. He had two professorial chairs at King's College London (in English history and divinity) until the publication of his *Theological Essays* (London: 1853). The principal misunderstood Maurice's subtle and nuanced views on eternal life and eternal punishment and declared the book unsound. So Maurice was dismissed. He was not in fact a universalist, though he was not unsympathetic to such views.

166 Editor: Samuel Cox (1826–93) was a Baptist minister in London then Nottingham. He wrote for and edited some religious periodicals, including *The Expositor*. He penned over thirty books, but is best known for his universalist works: *Salvator Mundi* [Saviour of the World] (London: 1877) and *The Larger Hope* (London: 1883).

167 Editor: James Baldwin Brown (1820–84) was a Congregational minister in Derby then London. He is best known as a theological author.

168 Editor: Brooke Foss Westcott (1825–1901) was a celebrated New Testament scholar at Cambridge University and later Bishop of Durham.

What the Church Teaches

Littledale,[169] the Bishop of Manchester,[170] F. W. Robertson,[171] Sir G. W. Cox,[172] [Andrew] Jukes,[173] Archer Gurney,[174] Phillips Brooks,[175] Professor [J. B.] Mayor,[176] Canon Farrar,[177] Principal Caird,[178] the Bishop of Meath,[179] Dean Church,[180] [August] Neander,[181] [Hans] Martensen,[182] [August]

---

169 Editor: Richard Frederick Littledale (1833-90) was an Anglican clergyman from Ireland who ministered in London.

170 Editor: Rev. James Moorhouse was Bishop of Melbourne from 1877 to 1885 and Bishop of Manchester from 1886-1903.

171 Editor: Frederick William Robertson (1816-53) was an evangelical Anglican priest who published various collections of sermons and various theological and exegetical works.

172 Editor: Rev. Sir. George William Cox (1827-1902) was an Anglican clergyman and a historian, best known for his work on ancient Greek myths.

173 Editor: Andrew Jukes (1815-1901) was an ex-Anglican curate who founded and became a minister of an Independent church in Hull. He was a capable defender of universalism, his best-known work being *The Second Death and the Restitution of All Things* (London: 1869). Later in life he rejoined the Church of England.

174 Editor: Archer Thompson Gurney (1820-87) was an Anglican hymn writer, poet, and priest.

175 Editor: Phillips Brooks (1835-93) was an Episcopal priest in Boston. He wrote the words for the Christmas carol "O Little Town of Bethlehem."

176 Editor: Joseph Bickersteth Mayor (1828-1916) was an Anglican priest and Professor of Classics then Professor of Moral Philosophy at King's College London.

177 Editor: Frederic William Farrar (1831-1903) was a classicist and an Anglican clergyman—canon of Westminster, archdeacon of Westminster Abbey, Dean of Canterbury. He arranged for Charles Darwin to be buried in Westminster Abbey in 1882 and preached at his funeral. His books on "the wider hope"—*Eternal Hope* (London: 1878) and *Mercy and Judgment* (London: 1881)—generated some controversy.

178 Editor: John Caird (1820-98) was a Church of Scotland (Presbyterian) minister and theologian. He became Professor of Divinity at Glasgow University (1862-73) then Principal (1873-78).

179 Editor: Most Rev. Charles Parsons Reichel (1816-94), Bishop of Meath from 1885 to 1894. He had been dead for some time by 1905, when this edition of the book came out, but Allin had not updated the reference. Prior to being a bishop, he was a professor of Latin in Belfast and the first principal of University College in Bangor (North Wales), as well as being Vice Chancellor of the University of Wales.

180 Editor: Dean Church is a tricky bloke to find out about, for obvious reasons.

181 Editor: August Neander (1789-1850) was a German church historian and theologian. He studied under Friedrich Schleiermacher in Halle and was greatly influenced by him. His greatest work was his *General History of the Christian Religion and Church*.

182 Editor: Hans Lassen Martensen (1808-84) was a Danish Lutheran bishop and theologian.

PART TWO—Universalism Asserted on the Authority of Tradition

Tholuck,[183] [Edouard] Reuss,[184] [Friedrich] Schleiermacher,[185] [Johann] Bengel,[186] [Johann] Eberhard,[187] [Johann] Lavater,[188] [John] MacLeod Campbell,[189] the Dean of Wells,[190] Canon Wilberforce,[191] Pastor Oberlin,[192] Bishop Ken,[193] etc.

I do not represent this list as at all exhaustive, yet it is enough to prove that this movement is deep-seated, long continued, and extending itself widely amongst men of the most varied schools of thought. Besides this, we must not forget the very numerous cases in which the traditional

---

183 Editor: August Tholuck (1799–1877) was a German professor of theology in Berlin and later in Halle. He was orthodox, but emphasized the importance of Christian experience in opposition to mere adherence to doctrine.

184 Editor: Edouard Reuss (1804–91) was a liberal Lutheran professor of theology at the Protestant faculty in Strasburg. His was primarily a church historian.

185 Editor: Friedrich Schleiermacher (1768–1834) was a hugely influential German Reformed theologian and the so-called "Father of Modern Liberal Theology." He developed the Calvinist doctrine of election in universalist directions.

186 Editor: Johann Albrecht Bengel (1687–1752) was a German Lutheran priest and pioneering New Testament scholar.

187 Editor: Johann August Eberhard (1739–1809) was a German theologian, a professor at Halle, where he taught Schleiermacher. He critiqued the doctrine of eternal hell and defended a kind of inclusivism in his *Neue Apologie des Socrates*, 2 vols. (1776–78).

188 Editor: Johann Kasper Lavater (1741–1801) was a Swiss Zwinglian pastor. He was a poet, theologian, and philosopher, but was best known for his work in physiognomy, the attempt to assess a person's character from their appearance.

189 Editor: John McLeod Campbell (1800–1872) was one of the great British theologians of the nineteenth century. He was a Scottish Reformed theologian and was accused of heresy for denying the doctrine of limited atonement (a doctrine that Church of Scotland ministers were then expected to affirm). As a result he was dismissed from the ministry. He was not a full-blown universalist, though was friends with those, like Thomas Erskine, who were.

190 Editor: Edward Plumptre (1821–91), F. D. Maurice's brother-in-law, was chaplain at King's College London and became Dean of Wells in 1881. He wrote, *The Spirits in Prison* (London: 1884), a study of the afterlife.

191 Editor: Basil Wilberforce (1841–1916), a parish priest, honorary canon of Winchester, then Canon of Westminster Abbey, then Archdeacon of Westminster. He was a grandson of William Wilberforce. A letter from Wilberforce to Allin is reproduced at the front of this book.

192 Editor: Johann Friedrich Oberlin (1740–1826), a Lutheran pastor from Strasbourg. He worked as a pastor in Waldersbach, where he did a lot to help the local farmers and local industry.

193 Editor: Thomas Ken (1637–1711) was Bishop of Bath and Wells from 1685. He is best known as a hymn writer.

creed has been wholly abandoned for the "conditional immortality" theory[194] and those cases, also very numerous, in which the larger hope is (practically) held in silence. How vast has been the change in men's minds may be seen in this fact, that in the Church Congress of this year (1890) at least two bishops—one of them the president, and the most eminent living Anglican theologian[195]—advocate the larger hope.

I do not write these chapters with a view to magnify patristic authority. My aim is historical. Place, for argument's sake, the Fathers in the lowest rank. They are, at the least, our only possible witnesses to the teaching of Christianity in those ages when the language of the New Testament was a living tongue. It is certainly a most important fact in this controversy to find that in an age so little merciful, and when the inducements to silence were so very strong, the larger hope was so widely held, and based on the authority of Scripture. The higher patristic theology, in its view of death, of penalty, and of the future state is totally unlike our modern views. If *we* do not, our opponents are wise enough to see the importance of all this. They are wise enough to see how grievously impaired thereby is their appeal to Scripture as teaching endless penalty; and how their chance is gone of appealing to that ignorance of history, which calls universalism a modern novelty, or the product of an indifferent and sentimental age.

Here I beg my readers to note that these pages are only a plea for a truly catholic church, for a genuine, and not a nominal, catholicity. I am pleading that Christ's holy catholic church may not be narrowed or dwarfed, but may, with a true catholicity, savingly embrace (sooner or later) every soul for whom its Founder died. I believe this to have been the deepest conviction of many, of very many, of the primitive saints.

It is possible that in spite of all care and labour—now extending over several years—some errors of detail may be found in these chapters; some passages may have been misunderstood. I ask my readers to believe that, if so, I have offended involuntarily. I ask my critics to blame, if they must blame, in a spirit of fairness, not wielding a tomahawk in the service

---

194 Editor: This was the view that human souls were not inherently immortal, but that immortality was a gift granted to them by grace. As such, they could be annihilated. This view experienced a revival in the nineteenth century, especially among some evangelicals, as an alternative to eternal torment.

195 Editor: The 1890 Church Congress was held in Kingston-upon-Hull. The acting president that year was B. F. Wescott, Bishop of Durham.

Part Two—Universalism Asserted on the Authority of Tradition

of the God of Love, nor using scorn and taunt in the service of Jesus Christ. But all the main conclusions are, I believe, absolutely true.

The so-called inconsistency of the Fathers has been frankly faced, and the complete unfairness of the mode of interpretation which is still too common, has been exposed. When *all the facts* are fairly weighed, the evidence for the existence of a great body of universalistic teaching in early times remains clear and wholly unshaken.

Taking a rapid survey of facts, I think we may thus arrange early eschatological teaching. There were at first, probably, three distinct currents. Some held the final annihilation of the wicked; some, especially in North Africa, held their endless punishment; some, perhaps even a majority, taught universalism. By the days of Gregory of Nyssa, the latter view—aided doubtless by the unrivaled learning, genius, and piety of Origen—had prevailed, and had succeeded in leavening, not the East alone, but much of the West. While the doctrine of annihilation had practically disappeared, universalism had established itself, had become the prevailing opinion, even in quarters antagonistic to the school of Alexandria.

The waning fortunes of the dogma of endless penalty soon revived, however, and in their turn gained the ascendency. The church of North Africa, in the person of Augustine, enters the field. The Greek tongue soon becomes unknown in the West and the Greek fathers forgotten. A Latin Christianity, redolent of the soil, develops itself, assuming, in accordance with the Roman bent, a rigid forensic type. On the throne of him whose name is Love, is now seated a stern Judge (a sort of magnified Roman Governor). The sense of sin practically dwarfs all else. The Father is lost in the Magistrate.

In the East, the decay of the earlier belief was, if less rapid, nearly as complete. Strife within and without the church, increasing ignorance and corruptions, bitter controversy (and other factors) combined to form a soil in which the larger hope of earlier days at length dwindled and almost expired. Indeed, who can wonder that this was so, if he will but reflect how cruel was the age, how narrow is the natural heart of man, how slowly, *even now*, it responds to that which is most divine. The true wonder (to me, at least) is this, viz., the appearance in such an age as that of the later Roman empire of the very idea of universalism—a phenomenon which can, I think, be alone accounted for by the fact that the early Fathers found it, as they tell us, in the New Testament.

So I close this sketch of early universalism, under a deep sense of my personal deficiencies, increased as they are, at once, by the difficulties of limited space (e.g., St. Gregory of Nyssa alone would furnish extracts enough to fill this volume); and by the no less real difficulty of inducing my readers to view this evidence from the standpoint of the early centuries.

Let us take the facts as they then were; let us try to picture a state of society in which the sentiment of mercy was practically unknown; in which all things reeked with vices too loathsome even to name; add the fear of cruel persecution, often threatening the repose, if not the very existence of the church; then, under such circumstances, to promise these bloodstained persecutors, these votaries of lust (even though unrepentant in life), a final salvation in the ages to come must have seemed almost treason to the cause of Christ, because only too likely to arrest conversions. When to this we add the undoubted fact that the moral principles then current within the church explicitly sanctioned dissimulation—thus rendering lawful that concealment (or denial) of universalism, which must have seemed so expedient; then it is that we gain some idea of the depth of conviction needed to account for even indirect teaching—for hints even—of the larger hope in the early centuries. And, if so, how much more for a universalism, often, as we have seen, wide enough to assert or imply the final salvation of every fallen spirit. For in two respects the teaching of this book—let us note the fact—*falls short* of a great body of primitive teaching: (a) it states a hope instead of a certainty of restoration, (b) it does not extend this *to all rational and fallen spirits*; a point which lies beyond my immediate province.[196]

---

[196] Editor: Despite Allin's claims to modesty here, it is clear that he warms to the idea of the restoration of all spirits and very clear that he considers the wider hope to be as certain as anything can be in matters of religious faith.

PART THREE

Universalism Asserted on the Authority of Scripture

6

Universalism and Doctrine

> "...ADAM, WHICH WAS THE SON OF GOD"
> LUKE 3:38

Our next step is an important one, to show briefly how universalism, instead of disturbing the due proportion and harmony of Christian doctrine, is precisely the element that affirms and establishes both.

We shall find—and the fact is a striking confirmation of the larger hope—that the great verities of our faith *grow into a living unity* in the light of the great purpose of restoration. Creation, incarnation, resurrection, judgment, etc., thus assume their places as parts of one great whole, the "one thought of the one God."

Creation

The Bible story opens with creation, which the New Testament so closely connects with restoration (Col 1:16–20; Heb 1:2–3). As all created beings issue out of God, so they return unto God [Rom 11:36]. All are emphatically pronounced "good," "very good" (Gen 1:4, 10, 12, 18, 21, 25, 31)—pregnant words. Man is created in God's very image and likeness (Gen 1:26–28). What does this involve? It is (1) God's affirmation of universal Fatherhood; (2) God's assumption of the holiest duties towards every man; (3) God's investing every man with inalienable rights.

Part Three—Universalism Asserted on the Authority of Scripture

I contend that such a tie between God and man can never be broken, that in the origin of mankind Scripture bids us see their destiny, that God must realize finally that ideal which he traced in creation. We are told God is not the Father of all men; *he is only their Creator!*[1] What a total misapprehension these words imply of all that is involved in creating man in the likeness of God, in the image of God. Viewed thus, creation contains the gospel in germ; it involves universal Fatherhood. "Have we not all one Father," asks the Prophet, why? "Has not one God *created* us?" (Mal 2:10). "Lord, you are our Father . . . we are all the work of your hand" (Isa 64:8). "The Protevangelium (the earliest gospel) is Genesis 1:26. 'Let us make man in our image, after our likeness.'"[2]

Indeed, we may perhaps say of creation that it is fatherhood extended, it is paternity and something more. For what do we mean by paternity and the obligations it brings? The idea rests essentially on the communication of life to the child by the parent. Now paternity is for us largely blind and instinctive; but creation is Love acting freely, divinely; knowing all the consequences, assuming all the *responsibility*, involved in the very act of creating a reasonable immortal spirit.

> Dieu, dit on, ne doit rien a ses creatures. Le crois qu'il leur doit tout ce qu'il leur promit, en leur donnant l'etre. Or c'est leur promettre un bien, que de leur en donner l'idee, et de leur en faire sentir le besoin.
> —*Émile*[3]

It seems, then, very strange to seek to escape the consequences of the lesser obligation, by admitting one still greater; to seek, in a word, to evade the results of a divine universal Fatherhood, by pleading that

---

1 Editor: The objection to the notion of God's universal Fatherhood is that in Scripture, God speaks of himself as the Father of his chosen people—of Israel or of the church. So while God is the Creator of all people, he is not the Father of all people. Allin takes a different view.

2 Editor: Brooke Foss Wescott, *The Epistle to the Hebrews: The Greek Text with Notes and Essays* (London: 1889), commenting on Hebrews 1:2. Wescott (1825–1901) was a British New Testament professor in Cambridge, and later Bishop of Durham (1890–1901).

3 Editor: Jean-Jaques Rousseau (1712–78), *Émile*, a treatise on education and on the nature of humanity. Published in French in 1762 and in English in 1763. The quotation says, "God, it is said, owes nothing to his creatures. For my part, I believe he owes them every thing he promised them when he gave them being. Now what is less than to promise them a blessing, if he gives them an idea of it, and has so constituted them as to feel the want of it?"

God is only the Creator of all. Hence a good Creator, freely creating for a doom of endless sin, freely introducing a dualism, is a profound moral contradiction. Can we even imagine [the] Good Being of his own freewill calling into existence creatures to hate him for ever, or certainly creating those who will, *as he knows, hate him for ever, and sin for ever?*[4] Thus, in the awful yet tender light of creation, the traditional creed shrinks and shrivels up—"Seeing then that the spirit comes from God," says St. Jerome, "it is *not just* that they should perish eternally who are sustained by his breath and spirit" (*Comm. Isa.* 57.6).

Incarnation

I pass to consider the incarnation. It is the great fact of Christianity. From it flow, and on it depend, the atonement, the sacraments, the resurrection; they are, as it were, results of the incarnation, and extensions of it. Now there are many aspects of this mystery that I do not touch; content to note that one point is quite clearly admitted, that Jesus Christ became incarnate as the second Adam. Therefore, to justify such a title, the incarnation involves the idea of the unity, absolute and organic, of the race of man. "For what purpose is the history of our race traced to its earliest origin . . . unless its fortunes were regarded *as a whole*, and *it must stand or fall together*"[5] "To that old creation is opposed the regeneration of man's race, through its new creation in the second Adam."[6] But this logically involves the salvation of the race, "which stands or falls together." It is, to borrow a homely phrase, *all or none*. If this were to be stated in the

---

4 "The Church," says [John Henry] Newman, "holds that it were better for the earth to fail and for all the many millions who are upon it to die of starvation in extremist agony, as far as temporal affliction goes, than that one soul, I will not say, should be lost, but should commit *one venial sin*" (*Difficulties of Anglicans*, 190). But, if so, how inconceivable does it become that God should freely create millions of beings whose destiny will, to his certain knowledge, be an endless existence in evil hopeless and aggravated, evil *rotting, festering for ever and ever.*

5 [Editor: Robert Isaac Wilberforce, *The Doctrine of the Incarnation of Our Lord Jesus Christ: In Its Relation to Mankind and to the Church* (London: 1848), 51. Robert Isaac Wilberforce (1802–57) was a son of William Wilberforce, and a clergyman active in the Anglo-Catholic Oxford Movement.] These statements, from the pen of one who teaches that a part of the human race is severed for ever from the second Adam, are remarkable. They illustrate what has been said of the virtual untruth that runs through our traditional theology.

6 Ibid.

Part Three—Universalism Asserted on the Authority of Scripture

language of science, it would stand thus—Adam = x, where x represents all humanity. And so Christ, as the last Adam, sums up all humanity in the spiritual equation.

The traditional creed, in fact, constructs an incarnation of its own, not that of Scripture. Its Incarnate Son may be the Son of God, but is not the Son of Man (of humanity),[7] not the second Adam. And as the Christ of the traditional creed is not the Christ of Scripture, so its human race is not the true humanity, for it teaches that the race is a collection of atoms, separable, inorganic. But Scripture affirms the reverse: it is quite true that every man bears his own burden of sin and suffering; but there is a truth higher still—the solidarity of the race, in the divine idea and plan. Says Wescott, "Our lives are fragments of some larger life."[8] This is the truth, without which the fall and the incarnation are unintelligible. In the highest sense Christ does not deal with the units of humanity, for humanity itself is the divine unit in redemption. Therefore I feel constrained to charge the traditional creed with making void the idea that underlies the incarnation, the organic unity of mankind.

A further point must here be noted: as we think of man's creation in God's image and likeness, and all it involves; of the stupendous glory of the incarnation; of the splendour of the atonement, there comes of itself a conviction that no anticipations we can form are too magnificent of the destiny of humanity as such, i.e., *as* a whole: no ideals are too lofty. The traditional creed stands self-condemned when confronted with these noble facts; it bears the brand of utter meanness; its message of ruin without remedy, of eternal chaos, and darkness is a denial of the whole purpose and essence of creation; it is a denial, no less, of the message of the incarnation to humanity as such, as an organic whole.[9]

---

7 Editor: Allin here appeals to the traditional Christian association of the title Son of Man with Christ's humanity and Son of God with his deity. The New Testament usage of these titles is somewhat more complicated, but that need not nullify the main point that Allin wishes to make.

8 Editor: B. F. Wescott, *The Revelation of the Father: Short Lectures on the Titles of the Lord in the Gospel of St. John* (London: 1884), 98.

9 Editor: Allin's claim, setting aside his strong rhetoric, is not that traditionalists *actually* deny the fall and the incarnation; rather, he is saying that they affirm beliefs that *if consistently thought through* would undermine the doctrines of the fall and the incarnation.

Atonement

I pass to the atonement. It is an atonement made by Christ as the last Adam. Not alone, then, does Christ sooner or later draw to himself all men [John 12:32], but *he cannot draw less than all men* if he be a new and better Adam [Rom 5:12–21]. Therefore, I repeat, the traditional creed, while in words teaching, *in fact* denies the atonement of the Bible. It asserts a universal salvation, but it really means a salvation that does not save universally—one in which Christ tries to save all, and is defeated. What is this but to dishonor the cross in its very essence: to deny that our Lord is truly the last Adam, and to treat him as one who, in the face of assembled creation, in the sight of men and angels, has challenged the powers of evil and has failed?

Long familiarity has blinded us to the significance of the startling provision by which Adam is linked organically with the whole race in the transmission of guilt. This tie is formed universally, and independently of any volition. To call Christ the second (i.e., last) Adam is either to dupe men, or it is to assert a tie equally organic and absolute with the *whole human race*. But it is said that as men can shake off the heritage of Adam, so they may the grace of Christ: I reply: (1) so they may, *if* the grace of Christ be only as strong as the sin of Adam, which St. Paul clearly denies (e.g., Rom 5:15–21, etc.). (2) Before men can shake off a heritage they must have received it. Hence, unless Christ *replaces the race in paradise*, he has not undone the evil of the fall (a fact that is *steadily denied, or ignored*, by the traditional creed), and so is not the second Adam. (3) It is an illogical process to say that because a partial failure took place (foreseen, and permitted for wise ends), therefore a new dispensation expressly designed to remedy that failure will itself fail. (4) In the highest and truest sense, God never fails, never can fail.

And here it is right to point out that two very popular views of the atonement lead, logically, to the larger hope.[10] One theory says that Christ died as the sinner's substitute. If so, and if he, as is certain, died for all, then all have a clear *right* to salvation. If the substitute be accepted all have a *right* to go free. Similarly, if Christ's death be the price paid for mankind's redemption, then the acceptance of that price gives mankind a clear *right* to salvation. The substitute being accepted, and the price fully

---

10 Their truth I do not discuss. [Editor: Despite saying that he will consider two views of the atonement, Allin only actually considers the penal substitution view.]

paid for all, it is wholly unfair to exact the penalty *twice over*, in any one case, in hell. These obvious conclusions are too often ignored.[11]

A few words may be added on a strange view not seldom held. An infinite atonement presupposes, it is said, an infinite guilt, and an infinite penalty. An infinite atonement, it may be replied, presupposes rather an infinite love and an infinite hope; and excludes the chance of failure, possible to a finite Saviour. I have shown the illogical and unscriptural assumption involved in speaking of human guilt as infinite. But, even admitting that the penalty of sin is infinite (for argument's sake), my argument as above is wholly untouched. Be the penalty infinite or no, you cannot equitably exact it twice over.

Sacraments

Let us pass to the sacraments.[12] They are an extension of the incarnation. "The influence of the Incarnation extends itself through that sacramental system, which binds *all* men to the head of the race."[13] "As there is a recapitulation of *all*, in heaven and earth in Christ, so there is a recapitulation of all in Christ in the holy sacrament."[14] In the language of theology, the tie formed in Baptism (renewed in Holy Communion) with Christ is so close that in the famous words of St. Leo,[15] *"Corpus regenerati fit caro Christi"*—"The body of the baptized *becomes the flesh of Jesus Christ."* But if so, it is impossible to believe that the very flesh of Christ can be sent

11 Editor: Though, to be fair, mainstream traditional Calvinism has long conceded this point. Indeed, it is for precisely this reason that the doctrine of *limited* atonement was developed—because the alternative, as Allin argues, would be universalism.

12 Editor: Some of the universalists in the post-Reformation period belonged to radical sects that rejected outward sacraments. Allin, however, stands in the mainstream Christian tradition. As such he holds the sacraments in high regard as a means of divine grace—of union with Christ.

13 Editor: Robert Isaac Wilberforce, *The Doctrine of the Incarnation of Our Lord Jesus Christ*, 14.

14 Editor: Lancelot Andrewes, *Works. Volume One. Sermons of the Nativity and of Repentance and Fasting*. Edited by J. Bliss and J. P. Wilson (Oxford: 1841), 281. This sermon of the Nativity was preached upon Christmas Day, 1622, before King James, at Whitehall. The text Andrewes was preaching on was Ephesians 1:10. Lancelot Andrewes (1555–1626) is a giant within the Anglican tradition, serving in high positions within the church during the reigns of Elizabeth I and James I. He was Bishop of Chichester, Ely, and Winchester, and oversaw the translation of the Authorized Version of the Bible.

15 Editor: St. Leo the Great was Pope from 440 to 461.

into an endless hell. Can Jesus Christ cut off, so to speak, his own flesh and sever it from himself for ever? Or rather, to state the case fully, can Christ assign a portion of himself to the society of devils for ever? Even Keble seems to feel this. When dwelling on these aspects of redemption, the cruel theology to which he clings drops off; and rising to true catholicity, he bids us view "Christ's least and worst with hope to meet above," and says, in suggestive words, "Christ's mark outwears the rankest blot."[16] Need I again point out how these words really involve universalism, for our Lord always teaches that those who have been brought nearest to him and yet disobey, as do impenitent Christians, will fare worse in the final judgment than those who have never heard of him.

Resurrection

Next, let us pursue the incarnation into another field of thought, and contemplate in its light the resurrection. The resurrection is—admitting fully its work for the body—yet *essentially* far more than this. "It is the new birth of humanity."[17] It is the crown of redemption. (1) It is life from Christ permeating the whole man, body and spirit. (2) It is life permeating the whole of humanity, through the last Adam. "As in Adam all die, so in Christ shall he made alive" [1 Cor 15:22]. To a collective death in Adam is here opposed a collective life in Christ; to a fall, a rising again; to a loss, a gain; and that universal and absolute, one dealing with the race. I say, *a gain, necessarily;* and as involved in the very idea of the resurrection. For what is the resurrection? It comes *only* through Christ, who not merely gives, but who *is* the resurrection and the life [John 11:25]. It is thus the closest union with Christ: it is to share the "kingdom of God": to bear "the image of the heavenly" [1 Cor 15:49]: to draw from Christ the gifts of "life," "power," "glory," "incorruption," "immortality," as St. Paul teaches [1 Cor 15:42–44]. And to share all these is, necessarily, to share blessedness; a point I must press. By what imaginable process can death, and blight, and evil be the result of that resurrection which *is* Christ? Again, death is in Scripture a name under which are grouped the results

---

16 Editor: Allin here quotes from John Keble's poem for the second Sunday after Trinity Sunday. Keble was one of the Anglo-Catholic Tractarians involved with the Oxford Movement, and a defender of eternal torment.

17 Editor: B. F. Wescott, *The Gospel of Resurrection: Thoughts on Its Relation to Reason and History* (London: 1866, revised 1879).

Part Three—Universalism Asserted on the Authority of Scripture

of sin. Hence to abolish death, as the resurrection does, is to abolish sin and its results. But by the resurrection death is swept away, is, indeed, "swallowed up" [1 Cor 15:54], and life in all its fulness of meaning, life in Christ, life which is Christ, is communicated.

Meantime, let us notice that this view of the resurrection seems implied in our Lord's words (John 6:39, 40, 54). There the resurrection is contrasted with loss, and is stated as the result of believing (cf. John 11:25–26): here notice our Lord's rejection of the idea of a resurrection deferred to the last day, as elsewhere he says, "Truly, truly, the hour *now is*, in which they that are in the graves shall hear the voice of the Son of Man, and they that hear shall live" (John 5:25).

Here we have to guard against the common error, which destroys the whole force of Christ's words, by severing this present resurrection from that which is to come. To our Lord, no such division occurs: *nay, to deny any such division* seems his very object, and to teach that the true idea of the resurrection is of a force essentially spiritual, ever acting; a leaven that, working here and now, shall one day transform and raise the whole man, body, soul, and spirit. Further, the idea of the resurrection as a gain from its very nature seems in harmony with our Lord's words (Matt 22:30; Mark 12:25; Luke 20:35–36). The same conception underlies St. Paul's teaching. "*If* the Spirit of him, who raised up Jesus from the dead, dwell in you, he that raised up Jesus from the dead, shall also make alive your mortal bodies" (Rom 8:9). Here resurrection is represented as flowing from the indwelling Spirit. Thus, too, St. Paul preaches as good news the resurrection (Acts 17:18) and connects the resurrection and light (Acts 26:23), and significantly hopes for the resurrection of the unjust (Acts 24:15), i.e., hopes that the unjust, shall, with the just, share the benefit of the resurrection.

Doubtless there is (and we are glad to admit it), a resurrection of judgment (John 5:29). For judgment, as we shall see, is itself a part of the great scheme of salvation; and is curative, while, nay rather, *because* it is retributive. To this treatment of the impenitent dead, St. Paul seems to allude in saying, "But *every man in his own order*: Christ the firstfruits; afterward they that are Christ's"; "Then comes *the end*" i.e., after the time necessary for the subjection to him of all opposing creatures "when he shall have put down all rule, and all authority and power" (1 Cor 15:23–24). In other words, *all are to be made alive in Christ*, but in due order and succession (1 Cor 15:22–23). The reign of Christ is to be prolonged until

Universalism and Doctrine

its aim is attained (1 Cor 15:25), i.e., the aim just referred to of universal life (1 Cor 15:22).

Such, broadly speaking, seems to be the view of the resurrection given in Scripture. Taken narrowly, its statements may seem to conflict. Thus, they describe the resurrection as successive (1 Cor 15:23; Rev 20:6), and yet simultaneous (1 Cor 15:51–52); as present (John 5:25), and as future (in many passages). All becomes clear if we keep in mind the central idea of the resurrection as a *spiritual redemptive force* exercised over the whole man—a force present and ever acting (as in the parallel case of judgment); a force that is successive, as it transforms individuals or classes of men; and yet future and simultaneous in some special sense, when the end has come, when the whole of humanity are "risen," when the climax has been by all attained.

I have reserved for the last a more detailed examination of St. Paul's great argument in 1 Corinthians 15. Two points of the greatest moment are there taught: (1) St. Paul is speaking of the resurrection of the dead generally, i.e., *of all humanity*. (2) He asserts in the case of all, the life-giving, healing force of the resurrection; *he knows no other resurrection than this healing restoring process*.

(1) That the apostle is speaking of the resurrection of *all* seems clear from his words, "For as in the Adam *all* die, so in the Christ shall *all* be made alive" (vv. 22–23). Here he plainly describes a process *coextensive with the race, coextensive with sin*: again he proceeds to state clearly this universal reference by explaining that life does not reach all at once, but "every man in his own order." He divides the *all*, taking first "they that are Christ's" (v. 23), who obtain the resurrection life at his parousia. Thence he passes to the mass of humanity, who are to be gradually "subjected" in the interval before "the end" (v. 24). Finally, everything whatsoever and wheresoever is to be subjected to Christ. (On this process, see notes on 1 Cor 15:25–28; Eph 1:10, 22; Col 1:15–20; Phil 3:21—chap. 8.) The final result is summed up in very striking words—"And when all things have been subjected unto him [Christ] then shall the Son himself also be subjected unto him [the Father] that did subject all things unto him [Christ] in order that God may be *all in all*."

Observe the *same* relation subsists *finally* between the whole universe (whatsoever and wheresoever), as that between Christ and the Father—the same original word [*hupotassō*, subjection] is used of both. The language of the Apostle admits of no exception at *the end*; of no death

PART THREE—Universalism Asserted on the Authority of Scripture

whatsoever, first or second, for all are made alive in Christ; of no annihilation, for all are restored; of no blot or stain of evil, moral or physical. Finally, as the grand result—God is *all* and *in all*.

This conception of the resurrection as a spiritual force, conveying blessedness, we find asserted by many early writers. The first traces of this teaching are perhaps in the works of those Fathers who seem to teach the extinction of the wicked and to confine the resurrection to the righteous. (See Clemens (Romanus)[18] quoted p. 99.) They who contradict the gift of God die "in their wrangling," says St. Ignatius.[19] "It would have been better for them to love, so that they might *rise*," i.e., obtain the resurrection (Ign. *Smyrn.* 7; see also Ign. *Trall.* 9). "He who raised Christ from the dead, will raise us up also, if we do his will," says St. Polycarp[20] (Pol. *Phil.* 2). So, too, apparently, "The Teaching of the Apostles."[21] Theophilus of Antioch[22] teaches that those keeping God's commandments "can be saved, and obtaining the resurrection, can inherit incorruption" (*Autol.* 2.27); and Irenaeus[23] very probably takes the same view. Arnobius[24] asks "what man does not see that that which is immortal . . . cannot be subject to any pain; and, on the contrary, that cannot be immortal which does suffer pain?" (*Adv. gen.* 2.14).

Passing on from these Fathers, we find abundant early evidence to support the view, which makes the resurrection a process of restoration

---

18 Editor: Clement of Rome (considered by Catholics to be Pope Clement I) was a significant Christian bishop at the end of the first century. He is the author of 1 *Clement* in the collection known as the *Apostolic Fathers*.

19 Editor: Ignatius was a first-century Christian leader in Antioch who was taught by the apostle John himself. He was martyred in Rome. *En route* to his death he wrote a series of letters to different churches. These are preserved in the *Apostolic Fathers*.

20 Editor: Polycarp (80–167) was a second-century Bishop of Smyrna. His martyrdom is recounted in *The Martyrdom of Polycarp*. *The Letter to the Philippians* is his only surviving work.

21 Editor: Allin is referring to *The Didachē*, a first- or early second-century instruction guide dealing with Christian ethics, rituals, and church organization.

22 Editor: Theophilus (d. 183/185) was Bishop of Antioch. He is the author of the *Apology to Autolycus*.

23 Editor: Irenaeus was a second-century bishop in Gaul (what is now Lyon, France). He is best known for his fierce opposition to Gnosticism and his defence of apostolic Christianity.

24 Editor: Arnobius (d. 330) was a Christian apologist

from its very nature (See earlier on Athenagoras and Methodius). Again, St. Hilary[25] speaks thus:

> When the only begotten Son was about to reconcile to God *all things* in heaven, and on earth, ... when death ... should come to an end, ... by redeeming man from the law of sin— by making God an object of praise to all, and through all the eternities, by the gift and dignity of our immortality. Now *all these things the virtue of the resurrection accomplished.*
> —*Tr. Ps.* 69

St. Gregory of Nyssa[26] abounds with such teaching as the following: "The resurrection is the *restoration* of our nature to its pristine state" (*De an.* 2). "Therefore, like a potter's vase, man is resolved once more into clay, in order that ... he may *be moulded anew into his original form, by the resurrection*" (*Or. cat.* 8).

> Lest sin adhering to us should last for ever, the vessel is, by a kindly providence, dissolved by death for a time, in order that ... mankind should be remoulded; and restored, free from the admixture of sin, to its former life. For that is the resurrection, namely, the replacing of our nature in its former state.
> —*In Pulch.* 2

St. Ambrose[27] teaches that: "The resurrection was given that by death sin should end" (*Bon. mort.* 4). "The resurrection is that by which all the bonds of the enemy are loosed" (*Exp. Ps.* 118 41). So, too, the Ambrosiaster:[28] "On the *abolition* of sin, the resurrection of the dead takes place" (*Comm. in Col.* 2). "The resurrection," says an early author, "is the remoulding of our nature" (*De Sacr.* 2.6). "Not to sin," says Gennadius,[29]

---

25 Editor: Hilary (c.300–c.368) was Bishop of Poitiers, an opponent of Arianism.

26 Editor: Gregory (c.330–c.395), Bishop of Nyssa, was one of the Cappadocian Fathers.

27 Editor: Ambrose (c.340–397) was Bishop of Milan and a fierce opponent of Arianism.

28 Editor: Between 366 and 384 a commentary on Paul's epistles was written. It was attributed for a long time to Ambrose of Milan, but during the Renaissance this attribution was rejected. Ambrosiaster is the name given to the unknown author.

29 Editor: Gennadius I of Constantinople (d. 471) (not to be confused with Gennadius of Massilia) was Abbot of a monastery in Constantinople and became patriarch in 458. Only parts of his commentary on Romans are extant.

"belongs to the immortal and impassible nature" (*Comm. in Rom.* 6.12). In the same tone speaks Clement of Alexandria (see *Paed.* 3.1).³⁰

The school of Antioch strongly insisted on this view of the resurrection. Diodorus has been quoted, and Theodore.³¹ From the latter I add here: "Christ gave the resurrection in order that, placed in an immortal nature, we should live free from all sin" (*Comm. in Rom* 5.18). "The apostle proves at length that those who are mortal serve sin, but those who are become immortal are set free from it" (*Comm. in Rom* 8.3). "The resurrection of the dead [is] the final [greatest] good" (*Comm. in Rom* 11). In the same spirit, Theodoret³² says, "In the future life the body, when made incorruptible and immortal, cannot admit the filth of sin" (*Comm. in Col.* 2.11). "For after the resurrection, when our bodies become incorruptible and immortal, grace shall reign in them, sin having no place left for it. For when sufferings (passions, *pathon*) are put an end to [by the resurrection], *sin will have no place*" (*Comm. in Rom.* 5.21). Viewed thus, surely a clearer light falls on the Saviour's words, "I am the resurrection and the life" [John 11:25], words reechoed in our Creed—"I believe in the resurrection of the dead, and the life everlasting"—the resurrection as bringing to all life everlasting.

Eschatological Death, Judgment, and Fire

Eschatological Death

From the resurrection, let us pass by an easy transition to consider those texts that speak of "death" and "destruction" and "perishing" as the portion of the ungodly. To ascertain the true meaning, let us inquire what is meant by death. There are two answers commonly given. First comes that of the popular creed, which says death in the case of sinners means living for ever in pain and evil. The recoil from such teaching has produced the second view of "death" as meaning "annihilation," now maintained by some. I have already spoken of this view; what follows will show how completely it seems to me to contradict the true scriptural idea of death.

---

30 Editor: Clement (c.150–c.215) taught at the catechetical school in Alexandria. He was a pioneer in the Christian Platonist tradition.

31 Editor: Theodore (c.350–428) was Bishop of Mopsuestia

32 Editor: Theodoret (c.393–c.458/466) was Bishop of Cyrus.

First, I would ask, in the words of Mr. Jukes,

> are any of the varied deaths which Scripture speaks of as incident to man, his nonexistence or annihilation? Take as examples the deaths referred to by St. Paul, in the sixth, seventh, and eighth chapters of the Epistle to he Romans. We read (ch. 6:7), "He that is dead is free from sin." Is this "death," which is freedom from sin, nonexistence or annihilation? Again, when the Apostle says (ch. 7:9), "I was alive without the law once, but when the commandment came, sin revived, and I died." Was this "death," wrought in him by the law, annihilation? Again, when he says (ch. 8:6), "To be carnally minded is death," is this death nonexistence or annihilation? And again, when he says (ch. 8:38), "Neither death, nor life, shall separate us," is the "death" here referred to annihilation? When Adam died on the day he sinned (Gen 2:17), was this annihilation? When his body died, and turned to dust (Gen 5:5), was this annihilation? Is our "death in trespasses and sins" (Eph 2:1–2) annihilation? Is our "death to sin" (Rom 6:11), annihilation? ... Do not these and similar uses of the word prove beyond all question, that whatever else these deaths may be, not one of them is nonexistence or annihilation?[33]

But if death be neither living for ever in pain, nor annihilation, what then is it? Death is, in its narrower aspect, bodily dissolution; it is for man a separation from some given form of life which he has lived in. It is the way out of one state of being into another. Thus understood, how should death shut out hope in any case? Nor is it really opposed to life; in fact it is, when viewed in a truer and higher aspect, a pathway to life; nay, the very condition of life. "Except a corn of wheat fall into the ground and die, it abides alone, but, *if it die,* it brings forth much fruit" (John 12:24).

Is there not here a great truth hinted at, of universal application? Is not the connection a very real and vital one between dying and life? So the apostle says that "he that is *dead* is freed from sin" (Rom 6:7), i.e., is alive to God. Must it not be that this death threatened against the ungodly is, after all, the way, however sharp, to life, even for them? As St. Paul, asks, "what shall the reconciling of them [i.e., Israel] be but *life from the dead?*" (Rom 11:15). On the view generally held, these words, so significant, lose all real force. A tradition, wholly unwarranted, has spread

---

33 Editor: Andrew Jukes, *The Second Death and the Restitution of All Things* (London: 1867). Andrew John Jukes (1815–1901) was an Independent minister in Hull and a significant nineteenth-century defender of universalism.

PART THREE—Universalism Asserted on the Authority of Scripture

almost universally, which regards death as the close of our training; as assigning a limit beyond which Christ himself has no power or no will to save the obstinate sinner.

I reply that in both the letter and the spirit, this view contradicts at once the deductions of reason, the teachings of the early church, and the express language of the New Testament. Indeed, to teach truer views of death seems one of the essential objects of the gospel. Death is, in fact, the crossing from one stage of our journey to another. It is not an end; it is a transit; it is an episode in life, and not its goal. It is not really a terminus, but a starting point. It is "that first breath which our souls draw when we enter Life, which is of all life centre."[34] "Death is the shadow, the dream, and not life, as we hastily judge who measure being by our senses."[35] The day of death was by a true instinct named in the early church the day of birth. To teach that our training ends at death is to say that a child's education ends with the nursery.

Therefore, let me ask, on what authority is the common doctrine taught, unknown to antiquity, unknown to Scripture? Who commissioned any to teach that to die is to pass into a state beyond the reach of Christ's grace? If so, why are we told, so significantly, the story of Christ's evangelizing the spirits in prison? Why are those *especially selected for evangelisation* who had been in life disobedient, and had so died? Why does the apostle [Peter] tell us that *the gospel was preached even to the dead?* (1 Pet 4:6), a fact obscured in the Authorized Version.[36] Why these repeated and exultant questions, "O grave where is your victory?" "O death where is your sting?" [1 Cor 15:55]. Why has the New Testament, with such varied illustrations, pressed on us this fact (as of special moment) that Christ has destroyed death, if death is ever to put a stop to his power to save? How could Christ be the Conqueror of death, if death can in *any case* reduce him to impotence? Can death disarm its Victor? So far from this, St. Paul invokes the analogy of nature, as showing that death is the condition of life. "You fool, that which you sow is not quickened, *except it die*" [1 Cor 15:36]—in fact:

---

34 Editor: The quotation is from a poem by Sir Edwin Arnold (1832–1904), entitled "After Death in Arabia."

35 Westcott, *Revelation of the Father*, 94.

36 Editor: The KJV reads: "For for this cause was the gospel preached also to them that are dead, that they might be judged according to men in the flesh, but live according to God in the spirit."

> There is no gain except by loss,
> There is no life *except by death*[37]

Who shall limit this truth in its operation? It certainly does hold good in the spiritual order—of that we are assured. St. Paul, in a passage already quoted, speaks of death as freeing from sin. Let me quote further. "If we be *dead* with him, we shall live with him" (2 Tim 2:11). "We which live are always delivered unto *death* for Jesus' sake, that the *life* also of Jesus might be manifested in us" (2 Cor 4:11). And so our Lord declares that "he that loses his life shall save it" (a statement more than once repeated in the Gospels. And the apostle adds, "if you put to death the deeds of the body, you shall live" (Rom 8:13). Thus, too, the psalmist[38] strikingly prays, "that the wicked may perish, in order that they may know that God reigns over the earth" (Ps 83:17–18). See, too, the verse, "When he [i.e., God] slew them then they sought him" (Ps 78:34). On these words Origen comments, "He does not say that some sought him after others had been slain, but he says that the destruction of those who were killed was of such a nature that, when put to death, they sought God" (*Princ.* 2:5.3). So, too, Elam is to be first consumed and then restored (Jer 49:37–39). So Canaan is to be destroyed and yet restored (Zeph 2:5–7).[39] So is Ammon to be restored after perpetual desolation (Zeph 2:9; Jer 49:6). So the dead bones are made alive (Ezek 37), and Israel comes up out of her graves (Exek 37:13; cf 1 Sam 2:6).

We thus learn how death becomes the very instrument by which God quickens the sinner, and that in two ways:

(1) By the death of the body, which takes a man out of the present age into a state more fitted to rouse and to save.

(2) By the death of the spirit, i.e., its being searched through and through by God's fiery discipline—by his sharp surgery—till it die to sin and live to righteousness. In all this subject of death, there is an extraordinary narrowness in the views held generally, as though the fact of dying

---

37 Editor: This quotation comes from the last book of an epic poem by Walter Chalmers Smith (1824–1908), called "Olrig Grange" (1872). Walter Chalmers Smith was a minister in the Free Church of Scotland, a hymn writer, and a poet.

38 True, in the Old Testament the threatenings of "death" and "destruction" are mainly temporal. But the same *principle* underlies God's dealings in both dispensations, and renders the quotations of this chapter strictly relevant.

39 Editor: Allin ought to have been a little more careful with this text. It speaks of the removal of local inhabitants from the land of Canaan and then its being filled with "the remnant of the house of Judah."

could change God's unchanging purpose; as though his never-failing love were extinguished because we pass into a new state of existence; as though the power of Christ's cross were exhausted in the brief span of our earthly life. So far from this, has not Christ abolished *death* [2 Tim 1:10]? Is he not Lord of the *dead* [Rom 14:9]? Did he not evangelize the *dead* [1 Pet 4:6]? Has he not the keys of *death* [Rev 1:18]? On the popular view, what depth of meaning can you possibly assign to these words?

It may be said, is there not "the second death?" Yes, assuredly. But though it were not the second merely but the thousandth death, yet it is but death: and death absolutely, in every degree and power, is destroyed, is blotted out, or there is no real meaning in St. Paul's song of triumph (1 Cor 15:55). No true victory has been won by Christ if the second death is too strong for him. Will our opponents explain how "death" can be "*swallowed up*" in victory, and yet survive in its most malignant form, i.e., the second death? As Martensen well puts the case, "When St. Paul teaches that death is the last enemy that shall be conquered, evidently in this death he comprehends the second death, else there would still be an enemy to conquer."[40]

A vast body of early opinion affirms that the sinner's "death" and "destruction" is the Great Artist remoulding[41] his own work; is the Physician healing, not annihilating. To pulverize the sinner, to destroy, to slay, *all mean reformation*. Such is the testimony of a crowd of illustrious names, to most of whom the language of the New Testament was familiar as the language of their everyday life. So Clement asserts that the law in ordering the sinner to be put to death designs his being brought from death to life (*Strom.* book 8). Origen has been already quoted. St. Methodius[42] asserts that the custom of Scripture is to call destruction that which is only a change for the better (*Ex.*); as does Epiphanius[43] (*Pan.* 2:1. § 32). Irenaeus speaks of death as ending sin (*Haer.* 3.23–26). St. Gregory

---

40 Editor: Hans Lassen Martensen, *Christian Dogmatics: Compendium of the Doctrines of Christianity*. Translated from the German by William Urwick (Edinburgh: 1874). Martensen (1808–84) was a minister in the Danish Lutheran Church and a professor in Copenhagen. He was influenced by mystical writers like Jacob Böhme.

41 So, in heathen mythology the same deity, Apollo, is the Healer and the Destroyer.

42 Editor: Methodius (d. 311) was Bishop of Olympos in Lycia then Bishop of Tyre. He was an early opponent of Origen, though like Origen, he was influenced by Plato.

43 Editor: Epiphanius (c.315–403) was born in Palestine, lived as a monk in Egypt, founded a monastery, and was later Bishop of Salamis (c.366–403). He was a fierce defender of orthodoxy against heresy.

of Nyssa is full of similar teaching: "They who live in the flesh ought, by virtuous conversation, to free themselves from fleshly lusts, lest *after death, they should again need another death, to cleanse away* the remains of fleshly glutinous vice that cling to them" (*De an.* 2). This seems to show the healing agency of even the "second death." "When the psalmist prays, let sinners and the unrighteous be destroyed, he is [really] praying that sin and unrighteousness may perish" (*Or. cat.* 1). The passage continues thus: "And if there be found any such prayer elsewhere [in the Scriptures], it has exactly the same meaning, viz., that of expelling the sin, and not of destroying the man." For St. Gregory of Nazianzus and for St. Basil, see earlier. Hilary has been quoted to the same general effect. So have Eusebius and Rufinus, Macarius Magnes, Titus of Bostra, Clement of Alexandria, Chrysostom, and Cyril of Alexandria; to these I may add Maximus and Didymus, and Ambrose. It would be hardly possible to adduce a stronger chain of testimony.

I now turn to St. Jerome.[44] "All God's enemies shall be destroyed, his enemies shall perish and cease to exist, but perish in that wherein they are enemies." St. Jerome even seems to assert the salvation of the "Man of Sin," for the passage proceeds thus: "Just as St. Paul writes to the Thessalonians [of the Man of Sin], whom the Lord shall slay with the breath of his mouth. [So] this slaying signifies *not annihilation*, but the *cessation of the evil life*, in which they formerly used to live" (*Comm. Mich.* 5.8). From the Ambrosiaster I take the following, on the words, "They shall perish." "They perish . . . while they are being changed for the better" (*Comm. in Heb.* 1.11). And so in the Sibylline Books,[45] the wicked first *perish* and afterwards are *saved* (book 2 vv. 211, 250–340).

Judgment

What is true of "death" as threatened against the sinner, is true no less of "judgment," even in its most extreme form. We are not without very

---

44 Editor: Jerome (331–420) was a very learned priest and scholar in the Western church. He translated the Bible into Latin (the Vulgate). He was initially a supporter of Origen, but later became an opponent.

45 Editor: The Sibylline Oracles are a collection of prophetic-style oracles written in the period from the second to the sixth century and ascribed to the Sibyls. (Sibyls were women that the ancient Greeks believed to be possessed by divinity and to speak prophetic words, often in a frenzied state.) Parts of the text were written by Christians, and the whole was valued by many Christians in the early church.

PART THREE—Universalism Asserted on the Authority of Scripture

distinct teaching in Holy Scripture on this point. "Everywhere," says St. Basil,[46] "Scripture connects God's justice [righteousness] with his compassions" (*Hom. in Ps.* 116.5).

Doubtless in a certain sense judgment may be opposed to mercy, and contrasted with it (Jas 2:13), but this is on the surface rather than in essence. As, to take an illustration, death is often contrasted in Scripture with life, and yet is the very pathway to life. Whenever judgment comes, it comes on love's errand, if it comes from God. Here is the spiritual watershed between the two theologies. There is the popular theology that says, God loves his enemies, *till they die*. His love then turns into hate and vengeance. His love is, in fact, a question of chronology, or, if one will, of geography, i.e., bounded to this world. And there is the truer theology that teaches with the Bible that God *is* love [1 John 4:8]—love unchanging and eternal in all his ways.

Judgment in the Old Testament

In the first judgment recorded in Scripture, mercy goes hand in hand. If Adam is to die, mercy follows; the serpent's head is to be bruised [Gen 3:15]. So, too, even the vengeance of eternal fire on Sodom ends in her restoration (Jude 7; Ezek 16:53–55). We thus understand the striking juxtaposition of mercy and judgment in God's revelation of himself to Moses (Exod 34:6–7): the same connection we shall find in Deuteronomy 32:35 and 39 (cf. Rom 12:19–20). Thus, too, Israel's Judges were saviours (Judg 3:9: Obad 21). Few more beautiful illustrations of the view I am urging can be found than that afforded by the story of Achan, stoned by a terrible judgment with all that he had, in the Valley of Achor (Josh 7:24–25); for if we turn to Hosea 2:15 we shall find this promise, "I will give her the Valley of Achor for a door of *hope*"—words pregnant with suggestion.

If now we turn to the Psalter, we may note that the fact of God's coming to judgment is a matter of deep joy (Ps 67:4); nay, the psalmist bids the sea to roar, the floods to clap their hands, the hills to sing for joy, at the prospect of judgment (as being a part of the great scheme

---

46 Basil of Caesarea (329/330–379), his brother Gregory of Nyssa, and his friend Gregory of Nazianzus are known as the Cappadocian Fathers. They were very influential defenders of Nicene Christianity against its various critics. Basil was strongly influenced by the ascetic tradition of monasticism.

of redemption) (Pss 96:11–13; 98:4–9). And so he hopes in God's judgments (Ps 119:43) and comforts himself with them (Ps 119:51–52; cf. Ps 47:8). Of Psalm 2:8–9 I have already spoken. It would be interesting to know how the traditional creed can fairly reconcile Christ's taking the heathen as *his inheritance*, with the terrible judgment inflicted on them, "breaking them in pieces." The more we study the Bible the more clear does the fact become that *salvation is essentially linked with the divine judgments*. And so, conversely, there is an awfulness even in the divine compassion. "There is *mercy* with you, *therefore* you shall be *feared*" (Ps 130:4). And in this spirit we read the suggestive words, "You, Lord, are merciful," says the psalmist, "for you render to every man according to his work" (Ps 62:12). Here is the essence of the question—*retribution is mercy; judgment means salvation*.

"The thought," says Maurice, "of God's ceasing to punish is the real—the unutterable horror. Wrath is not the counteracting force to love, but the attribute of it."[47] So Psalm 67:1–4 presents to us the picture of God as judge, in connection with his saving health reaching all nations. So in Psalm 72:1–17, judgment leads to a reign of universal righteousness. Again, in Psalm 99:8, forgiveness and vengeance go together; so Psalm 101:1 combines mercy and judgment, and Psalm 33:5, judgment and loving-kindness. And so we read, "Your judgments are a great deep, O Lord, you preserve man and beast" (Ps 36:5).

The Prophets are full of similar teaching. Note Isaiah connecting the words of comfort and pardon to Israel with her having received "double for all her sins" (Isa 40:1–2). So it is said, "Zion shall be *redeemed with judgment*" (Isa 1:27). "When your *judgments* are in the earth, the inhabitants of the world learn righteousness" (Isa 26:9). "Princes shall rule in *judgment*, and a man shall be a hiding place from the wind" (Isa 32:1–2). "I will make my *judgment* to rest for a light of the people.... My *salvation* is gone forth" (Isa 51:4–5). "Therefore will he be exalted that he may have mercy ... for the Lord is a God of *judgment*" (Isa 30:18). So again, "He has filled Zion with *judgment* ... and there shall be abundance of *salvation*" (Isa 33:5–6). "The Lord is our *Judge* ... He will *save* us" (Isa 33:22).

---

47 Editor: This is actually a composite of two quotations from F. D. Maurice (1805–72), *Theological Essays* (London: 1853). The first reads: "[T]he thought of His ceasing to punish them, of His letting them alone, of His leaving them to themselves, is the real unutterable horror." The second reads: "For wrath against that which is unlovely is not the counteracting force to love, but the attribute of it. Without it love would be a name, and not a reality."

PART THREE—Universalism Asserted on the Authority of Scripture

We may note how this connection of judgment and salvation runs through the Bible. See Isaiah 45:21–22, where God is described as a just God and a Saviour; and the passage proceeds to invite all the ends of the earth to look and be saved. Compare with this, Zechariah 9:9, "*just* and having *salvation*," and 1 John 1:9, "He is . . . *just* to *forgive* us our sins." So do we read of judgment in connection with the future setting up of God's kingdom of peace and love (Isa 2:2–4).

Nor should we overlook the connection in Christ between God's rule and *salvation* (Isa 40:10–11; 9:7, so Ps 103:19–22). And let us note the juxtaposition of the "helmet of *salvation*," and "garments of *vengeance*" (Isa 59:17). So the "day of *vengeance*" and the acceptable year are linked together (Isa 61:2). And in Isaiah 42:1–12 (applied to Christ in the New Testament) we find him described as setting judgment on the earth (v. 1), but the issue is salvation (v. 7–12). Again, speaking of Christ as the branch, another prophet tells how "He shall execute *judgment* . . . in the land. In those days Judah shall be *saved*" (Jer 33:15). And "I will *betroth you to me* for ever . . . *in judgment*[48] and in mercy" (Hos 2:19). So in Daniel 7:10–14, the universal dominion promised to Christ is closely connected with the judgment day. So in Ezekiel 24:13–14, it is said of Israel, "You shall not he purged of your filthiness any more, *till I have satisfied my fury upon you.*"

The passages just quoted (and those that follow) may be compared with those already cited to illustrate the scriptural meaning of death and destruction. It will also probably help our attaining a true view of judgment if we remember that, in a sense most real, judgment is present and continuous. "Les grandes assises de la vallée de Josaphat commencent pour nous chaque soir."[49] "The world," says Emerson, "is full of judgment days."[50]

---

48 And we may note a remarkable reading in the Septuagint, "I will set judgment unto hope" (Isa 28:17).

49 Editor: The quote is from Anne Sophie Swetchine (1782–1857), known as Madame Swetchine. She was the daughter of the Russian Secretary of State and lived at the Court of Catherine the Great. In 1815 she became a Catholic and moved to live in Paris. There she kept a salon that became famous and gave her a wide range of influential contacts through which she was an influence on French Catholicism. She was known as a mystic. The quotation says, "The great assizes of the valley of Jehosaphat begin for us each evening." The Valley of Jehosaphat was a place for the judgment of the nations (Joel 3:2, 12; 3:14), the point here being that this judgment begins every night.

50 Editor: The quotation is from "Spiritual Laws," an essay by Ralph Waldo

Judgment in the New Testament

Let us now pass to the New Testament: there we shall find ample proof worthy of our closest study, and showing the true meaning of judgment, alike here and hereafter, as *conveying salvation*.

Take, for instance, the context, so often overlooked, of our Lord's famous words in John 12:32—"Now is the *judgment* of this world, now shall the prince of this world be cast out. And I, if I be lifted up, will draw all men unto me," i.e., the judgment of the world is the salvation of the world, is the drawing of all men to Christ. Thus, if it be objected that we are told Christ came not to judge, but to save the world (John 3:17), we can point to the above passage, and to the express statement, *"For judgment came I into this world"* (John 9:39).

But all difficulty ceases when we remember that *primarily* salvation is Christ's object, but in practice this salvation is attained very often through judgment. Thus note Matthew 12:18–21, where the bringing of judgment unto victory is stated as our Lord's object: and again, note the connection of judgment and quickening in John 5:21–22.

Very striking are the words of St. Paul which refer to the last judgment, and seem to show conclusively that that great day brings salvation to all who are judged. Turn to Romans 14:10—"We must all stand before the judgment seat of Christ," must each render his account to God. But that is far from being the only object of that judgment. Its main and essential purpose is salvation. To show this is easy. For note, that to illustrate the purpose of God in judging, St. Paul here quotes from Isaiah 45:23, which runs thus: "Look to Me and be *saved, all you ends of the earth,* for I am God . . . I have sworn by myself that to me every knee shall bow. . . . The word is gone out and shall not return empty"; it *must* be fulfilled, i.e., God's purpose of salvation must reach effectually the entire race. But this prophetic assertion of a universal salvation is here quoted by the apostle, and is *linked with the day of judgment, which, according to him, it describes.* In that judgment, St. Paul sees not the final damnation of any man, but the fulfillment of the prophetic promise—a pledge that salvation shall reach every soul of man. Pause, and realize the full significance of this. Beyond the grave, we have St. Paul looking on to the closing

---

Emerson, in *Essays: First Series* (Boston: 1847). Emerson (1803–82) was an American poet, philosopher, and essayist. The quote in full reads: "The world is full of judgment-days, and into every assembly that a man enters, in every action he attempts, he is gauged and stamped."

scene; to that judgment that winds up the great drama of life, and sin, and redemption. And as the apostle looks he sees in the very judgment[51] a process of salvation, he sees a picture bright with hope for every human soul—a picture that he can only describe in terms of the joyful outburst of the prophet, "Look to me [i.e., the LORD] and *be saved, all you ends of the earth.*"

Bearing all this in mind, a light, clear and distinct, falls on those words of St. Paul (so unintelligible on the ordinary view), where he declares the gospel to be "the power of God unto salvation, ... *for* therein is the wrath of God revealed." Note salvation and wrath linked together; *salvation because the wrath* of God is revealed against all sin (Rom 1:16–18)—a connection obscured by the arrangement of the text in our translations.

Note, too, the teaching of Romans 12:19–21, which surely implies that true divine vengeance is the overcoming of evil by good, by kindness: and Deuteronomy 32, which is there quoted, refers to the healing character of God's vengeance (v. 39).[52]

Consider next what St. Paul says of the case of Hymenaeus and Alexander (1 Tim 1:20). They had sinned. He thereupon hands them *over to Satan.* You can hardly imagine a more desperate state—thrust by apostolic authority out of God's church, and handed over to God's enemy, and that after having made shipwreck of their faith. But what follows? It is that they may *learn* not to blaspheme. As an old Father puts it, "Sinners are handed over to the devil. Wherefore? That they may perish eternally? And where then is the mercy of God? Where is the tender Father? What the apostle says is this, I have handed over sinners to the devil, that, tormented by him, they may be *converted* to me" (Jerome, *Comm. Ps.* 108.9).

Another equally striking instance is furnished by the case of the incestuous Corinthian. "I have judged already . . . to deliver such a one to Satan for the destruction of the flesh, that the spirit may be *saved*" (1 Cor 5:3–5). And so, as it has been well put, this wretched Corinthian was delivered *from* the power of the devil, by being delivered *into* the power of the devil. Few more suggestive passages exist in the New Testament. Here

---

51 So the Creed, "He shall come to judge the living and the dead, whose kingdom shall have no end." Thus judgment leads to the setting up of Christ's universal empire: and so (suggestively) the Judge sits on a white throne (a sign of amity) (Rev 20:11).

52 Editor: "See now that I myself am he! There is no god besides me. I put to death and I bring to life, I have wounded and I will heal, and no one can deliver out of my hand" (Deut 32:39).

is a man delivered by apostolic authority—in the name of Jesus Christ—to Satan, handed over to Satan. But mark the object and the result. It is to end, not in death, but in life—say, rather in life attained by means of God's awful judgment. "O mon ame sois tranquille, et attends en paix le jour des vengeances eternelles, c'est le jour de Christ, et ce sont les vengeances de Christ. C'est donc *un jour de salut, et ce sont des vengeances d'amour.*"[53]

In this connection, as showing how the utmost conceivable severity of the divine judgments is consistent with final salvation, I ask you next to remember how St. Paul tells of Israel that "wrath is come upon them to the uttermost" (1 Thess 2:16). The wrath of God to the *uttermost*, and yet the same apostle tells us that *all Israel shall be saved* [Rom 11:26]. Weigh well these words. It is as though God had exhausted all his vials of anger, and left himself no more that he could do. And even then does all this wrath mean that hope is at an end, that salvation is impossible? It means the very reverse. Salvation to the uttermost—for *all Israel* shall be saved—is the end of wrath to the uttermost.

Quite as striking, perhaps even more significant, are St. Peter's words, as he tells the story of the preaching of Christ to the spirits in prison. The spirits are specially described as those of the *disobedient* dead. And mark what follows: "For this cause," he adds, "was the gospel preached even to the *dead*, that they might be *judged* according to men in the flesh, but *live* according to God in the spirit," i.e., in order that even those who had died *in sin* might have the benefit of judgment, and so live to God. Here we have (1) judgment bringing to the sinner not condemnation, but life (2) salvation by judgment extended beyond this life (3) extended to those who neglected, while living, the greatest light then available; and *died impenitent*. All this involves a precise contradiction to the common view of the future of the impenitent dead. The thoughtful reader will note further that the "times of restitution[54] of all things" come

---

53 Editor: Guillaume Monod, *Le judgment dernier*, 28. The quotation says: "O my soul be calm and wait in peace for the day of eternal vengeance. It is the day of Christ and these are the vengeances of Christ. It is therefore *a day of salvation and these are vengeances of love.*" Monod (d. 1896) was a French universalist who founded a short-lived universalist church. In 1845 he published an article calculating an estimate regarding the number of people who would go to hell according to mainstream Protestant doctrine. He calculated the number at 30 billion!

54 Editor: The Greek word used here is *apokatastasis*, which became the term used by the Fathers to designate the final restoration of all things. Many Fathers took this text to refer to a restoration of all creatures. Arguably, Peter's words in Acts draw more

when Jesus returns (Acts 3:21), but he returns *to judge* the living and the dead. Let us finally quote, "I saw another angel, having the everlasting gospel to proclaim . . . and he said, fear God and give him glory, for the hour of his judgment is come" (Rev 14:6–7). Note the *everlasting gospel* proclaimed—how? By *God's judgments.*

Judgment in the Fathers

This view of judgment is precisely the teaching of ancient catholic Fathers, which I shall here give. Take in proof St. Jerome's striking comment on Zephaniah 3:8–10.[55] There, speaking of the day of judgment and its terrors, he says:

> The nations, even the multitude of the nations, are gathered to the judgment, but the kings, i.e., the leaders of perverted dogmas, are led up for punishment, in order that on them may be poured out *all the wrath of the fury of the Lord.* And this is not done from any cruelty, as the bloodthirsty Jews fancy,[56] but in *pity*, and with a design to *heal.* . . . For the nations being assembled for judgment, and the kings for punishment, in order that wrath may be poured out on them: not in part but in whole, and, both *wrath and fury being united* [in order that] whatever is earthy may be consumed in the whole world.
> —*Comm. Zeph.* 3.8-10

The object aimed at (and gained) being that (as the passage proceeds) every one may lay aside his error, and every knee bend in Jesus' name. Need I point out the extreme significance of these words? They are unhesitating in their frank recognition of, nay, in the emphasis laid on "the wrath of the fury of the Lord," "the whole mass both of wrath and fury." But this is a means of salvation. The great day of wrath that *is to burn like fire*, and to *consume* the adversaries of God, burns up only what is earthy, bringing to every sinner salvation.

---

on Jewish prophetic expectations of the ultimate restoration of Israel and the pilgrimage of the nations, but the gap between this and the universalism imagined by Origen et al. is not an unbridgeable chasm.

55 St. Jerome adds that it is possible to understand this passage of Christ's first coming, but he evidently adopts the view above given.

56 Editor: Regrettably, Jerome's anti-Semitism was typical of the Christianity of his day.

Again, we have St. Jerome commenting on Romans 1:18. "Therein is the wrath of God revealed against all ungodliness," "where wrath is revealed it is *not* inflicted; it does not smite, but it is revealed in order that it may terrify, and may not be inflicted on the terrified" (*Comm. Habac.* 3). Writing on Micah 7:17, he compares the wicked to serpents, who, as they creep over the earth, drag along with them earthly matter. So the wicked, "shall be troubled *so long as the sinful matter clings to them.*" But when (by the judgment) this has been cleared away, they too shall end by fearing God.

Equally forcible and clear is the teaching of St. Gregory of Nyssa. "Therefore the divine judgment does not ... bring penalty upon those who have sinned, but ... *works good alone* by separating from evil, and drawing to a share in blessedness." In other words, the penalty is the cure—the unavoidable pain attending the removal of the intruding element of sin (*De an.* 2). And again:

> If this [sin] be not cured here, its cure is postponed to a future life. As sharp *remedies* for obstinate cases, so God announces his future judgment *for the cure* of the diseases of the soul, and *[note these words]* that judgment is a threat to the frivolous and vain, "in order that, through fear, ... we may be trained to avoiding evil; *but by those who are more intelligent, it* [the judgment] *is believed to be a medicine,*[57] a *cure* from God, who is bringing the creature, which he has formed, back to that state of grace which first existed.
> —*Or. cat.* 8.

It will be interesting to compare with them the following from St. Basil: "Fear edifies the *simpler* sort" (*Deus non est auct. mali*), and from Didymus:[58] "For although the judge at times inflicts tortures and anguish on those who merit them, yet he who *more deeply scans* the reasons of things, perceiving the purpose of his [God's] goodness, who desires to *amend* the sinner, confesses him [God] to be good" (*De Spir. S.* 44). Again, St. Gregory says that the wrath of God, which is to swallow up the sinful, is not wrath at all. "In the case of God, his wrath, though to sinners it seems wrath, and is so called by them, is nothing less than wrath (i.e., *is not wrath at all*), but as though [it were] *wrath* comes to those who,

---

57 St. Gregory does not mean to deny the terror of the judgment day. Hear his words: "All creation trembles, who is without fear? (*In verba fac. hom. Orat.* 2).

58 Editor: Didymus the Blind (c.313–398) led the catechetical school in Alexandria, Egypt. He was a loyal follower of Origen's theology.

PART THREE—Universalism Asserted on the Authority of Scripture

according to God's justice, call it a retribution . . . [but] *God himself is not really seen in wrath*" (*In Ps.* 2.15). Origen goes quite as far:

> When you hear of the wrath of God, believe not that this wrath and indignation are passions of God: they are condescensions of language, designed to convert and improve the child. . . . So God is described as angry, and says that he is indignant, in order that you may convert and be improved, while in fact he is not angry.
> —*Hom. in Ier.* 18.6.

So an old commentator on the Psalms (in St. Jerome) says on Psalm 7 that God "awaits the day of vengeance with a *quasi-wrath*, in order that he may correct [amend] by fear the sinner." To the same general effect write St. Basil, St. Gregory of Nazianzus, and Clement; and St. Hilary, on Psalm 67:3–4, who says that the cause of the nations' *joy* arises from "*the hope of eternal judgment*, and of the nations [Gentiles] directed into the way of life." To bring such teaching home, let us suppose one of our archbishops were to declare that God's judgment may terrify *simple* souls, but that *the intelligent see its real end to be the cure of sin;* or imagine a very eminent bishop asserting that *the eternal fire purifies sinners.*

Divine Fire

Again, how shallow is the common view of "fire" as only or chiefly a penal agent. "Fire, in Scripture, is the element of 'life' (Isa 4:5), of 'purification' (Matt 3:3), of 'atonement' (Lev 16:27), of 'transformation' (2 Pet 3:10), and never of 'preservation alive' for purposes of anguish."[59] And the popular view selects precisely this latter use, never found in Scripture, and represents it as the *sole* end of God's fiery judgments! If we take either the teaching of Scripture or of nature, we see that the dominant conception of fire is of a beneficent agent. Nature tells us that fire is a necessary condition of life; its mission is to sustain life; and to purify, even when it dissolves. Extinguish the stores of fire in the universe, and you extinguish all being; universal death reigns. Most strikingly is this connection of

---

59 Editor: F. W. Farrar, *Mercy and Judgment: A Few Last Words on Christian Eschatology with Reference to Dr. Pusey's "What Is of Faith"* (London: 1881). Frederic William Farrar (1831–1903) was a head teacher and a Church of England cleric (a canon of Westminster, a rector near the Houses of Parliament, archdeacon of Westminster Abbey, Dean of Canterbury). In this book and in *Eternal Hope* (1878) he defended a larger hope.

fire and life shown in the facts of nutrition. For we actually burn in order to live; our food is the fuel; our bodies are furnaces; our nutrition is a process of combustion; we are, in fact, "aflame to the very tips of our fingers."[60] And so it is that round the *fireside* life and work gather: when we think of home we speak of the family hearth.[61]

What nature teaches, Scripture enforces in no doubtful tone. It is significant to find the Great Source of all life constantly associated with fire in the Bible. Fire is the sign, not of God's wrath, but of *his Being*. When God comes to Ezekiel there is a "fire unfolding itself" (Ezek 1:4, 27), and "the appearance of fire" (Ezek 8:2); Christ's eyes are a flame of "fire" (Rev 1:14); and seven lamps of "fire" are the seven Spirits of God (Rev 4:5). So a fiery stream is said "to go before God"; his throne is fiery flame, its wheels are burning fire (Dan 7:9, 10); his eyes are lamps of fire (Dan 7:10, 6); he is a wall of fire (Zech 2:5); at his touch the mountains smoke (Ps 104:32); and God's ministers are a flame of fire (Ps 104:4; Heb 1:7).

It is not meant to deny that the divine fire chastises and destroys. It is meant that purification, not ruin, is the *final* outcome of that fire from above, which consumes—call it, if you please, a paradox—in order that it may save. For if God be love, then by what but by love can his fires be kindled? They are, in fact, the very flame of love; and so we have the key to the words: "Your God is *a consuming fire*" and "Your God is *a merciful God*" (Deut 4:24–31). So God *devours the earth* with fire, in order that finally all may call upon the name of the Lord (Zeph 3:8–9)—words full of significance. So Isaiah tells us of God's *cleansing* the daughters of Zion by . . . the spirit of burning (Isa 4:4)—suggestive words. And, so again, "By *fire* will the Lord plead with *all* flesh" (Ps 66:16). And Christ coming to save, comes to purify by "fire" (Mal 3:2).

Let us note, also, how often "fire" is the sign of a favourable answer from God: when God appears to Moses at the Bush it is in "fire": God answers Gideon by "fire"; and David by "fire" (1 Chr 21:26). Again, when he answers Elijah on Carmel, it is by "fire"; and in "fire" Elijah himself ascends to God. So God sends to Elisha, for aid, chariots and horses of "fire": So when the psalmist calls, God answers by "fire" (Ps 18:6–8). And by the pillar of "fire" the Israelites were guided through the wilderness,

---

60 Editor: I have been unable to source this quotation fragment.

61 Editor: The image of the family gathered around the fireplace at home is one that had sentimental associations in the Victorian era.

Part Three—Universalism Asserted on the Authority of Scripture

and in "fire" God gave his law. And in "fire" the great gift of the Holy Spirit descends at Pentecost.

These words bring us to the New Testament. There we find that "fire," like judgment, so far from being the sinner's portion only, is the portion of *all*. Like God's judgment again, it is not future merely, but present; it is *"already kindled,"* i.e., always kindled: its object is not torment, but cleansing. The proof comes from the lips of our Lord himself. "I am come *to send fire on the earth"* [Luke 12:49], words that in fact convey all I am seeking to teach, for it is certain that he came as a Saviour. Thus, coming to *save*, Christ comes *with fire*, nay, with fire already kindled. He comes to baptize with the Holy Ghost, and *with fire*. Therefore it is that Christ teaches in a solemn passage (usually misunderstood, Mark 9:43) that *every one* shall be salted with fire. And so the "fire is to try *every man's* work." He whose work fails is saved (mark the word *saved*), *not damned* "so as by fire," for God's fire, by consuming what is evil, saves and refines. The ancient tradition that represents Christ as saying, "He that is near me is near fire,"[62] expresses a vital truth.

So Malachi, already quoted, describes Christ as being in his saving work "like a refiner's fire." And so, echoing Deuteronomy 4:24–31, we are told that "our God is a consuming fire," i.e., God in his closest relation to us: God is love: God is spirit: but *"our* God is a consuming fire"—a consuming fire, "by which the *whole material substance of sin* is destroyed."[63] When, then, we read that "coals of fire" go before God (Ps 18:12–13), we think of the deeds of love, which are "coals of fire" to our enemies (Rom 12:20). Thus, we who teach hope for all men do not shrink from, but accept *in their fullest meaning*, these mysterious "fires" of Gehenna, of which Christ speaks (kindled for purification), as in a special sense the sinner's doom in the coming ages. But taught by the clearest statements of Scripture (confirmed as they are by many analogies of nature), we see in these "fires" not a denial of, but a mode of fulfilling, the promise—"Behold, I *make all things new"* [Rev 21:5].

Abundant quotations might be made from the Fathers in support of the above view. St. Ambrose, on Psalm 1, says: the fiery sword at the gate of paradise [Gen 3:24] shows "that he who returns to it comes back by fire." Origen says,

---

62 Editor: *Gospel of Thomas*, saying 82. "Jesus said: He who is near to me is near the fire, and he who is far from me is far from the kingdom."

63 Editor: I have been unable to source this quotation.

> As bodily diseases require some nauseous drug ... or actual cautery, how much more is it to be understood that God, our Physician ... should employ [for healing] penal measures of this kind, and even the punishment of fire. ... The *fury of God's vengeance* is profitable for the purgation of souls. That the punishment, which is said to be applied by fire, is *applied with the object of healing*, is taught by Isaiah 4:4.
> —*Princ.* 2:10.6.

St. Jerome says: "Fire is God's *last medicine* for the ten tribes, and for heretics, and for *all sinners,*" that after God has tried death and destruction, and they have not even then repented, "he may consume them as he did Sodom and Gomorrah; that when consumed, and when the divine fire shall have burned up all that is vilest in them, *they themselves shall be delivered* as a brand snatched from the burning" (*Comm. Am.* 4.11). "Therefore [i.e., to effect a cure] the world which '*lies in the evil one*' is burned with divine fire in the day of judgment, and the bloody city is laid upon coals of fire"[64] (*Comm. Ezech.* 24). "When they perish in fire ... or are destroyed in the fire of their prince the devil, or certainly are burnt in the fire of which the Lord said, 'I am come to send fire on the earth,' and are [thus] *brought back from their former ways and do penance*, the whole earth shall be full of the glory of the Lord" (*Comm. Habac.* 2.12). Indeed, St. Jerome is full of this teaching, see, e.g., his remarks on Malachi 3:2–3; Hosea 4:13; Joel 2:1; Amos 7:4, etc., etc.

> Finally, after tortures and punishments, the *soul brought forth from the outer darkness, and having paid the very last farthing*, says, I shall behold his righteousness. ... Now he who after God's wrath, says that he sees God's righteousness [justification] promises himself the sight of Christ.
> —*Comm. Mich.* 7.8.

So the old commentator (in St. Jerome), speaking of God, says, "He is fire, that he may expel the devil's cold" (*Comm. Ps.* 167.18).

To the same effect much might he quoted from St. Gregory of Nyssa. The evil man after death will not become "a sharer in the divine nature, till the cleansing fire shall have removed the stains mingled with the soul" (*De mort.* 2). And again, "Thus ... the soul which is united to sin must be set in the fire, so that, that which is unnatural and vile ... may be

---

64 See Isaiah 47:14–15, quoted by many Fathers, where the Septuagint has a remarkable reading—"You have coals of fire, sit upon them, they will be to you a help."

Part Three—Universalism Asserted on the Authority of Scripture

removed, consumed by the *eternal fire*" (*De an.* 2). Here the *eternal fire* cleanses.

Election

There remains for our consideration a very important class of passages, supposed, erroneously, to favour the popular creed. These passages are those that speak of the "elect," and their fewness; of the "many" called, but the "few" chosen.[65] That God's election is a doctrine clearly revealed in Scripture, no impartial reader can doubt: although unfortunately, around few subjects has the battle of controversy been so furiously waged. One party has, in affirming God's election—which is true, so affirmed it as to make him into an arbitrary and cruel tyrant—which is false. But the truer and deeper views of God's plan of mercy through Jesus Christ—now in the ascendant I trust—teach us to affirm distinctly the doctrine of the divine election of "the few": and just because we so affirm it, to connect with it purposes of *universal* mercy. For what is the true end and meaning of God's election? The elect, we reply, are chosen, not for themselves only, but for the sake of others. They are "elect," not merely to be blessed, but to be a source of blessing. It is not merely with the paltry object of saving a few, while the vast majority perish, that God elects; it is with a purpose of mercy to all; it is by "the few" to save "the many"; by the elect to save the world.

Dr. Cox says:

> If you go to Scripture, you will find this its constant teaching. Even in those early days when one man, one family, one nation, were successively chosen, to be the depositories of divine truth, when, therefore, if ever we might expect to find the redemptive purpose of God disclosed within narrow and local limitations; when unquestionably it was much fettered and restrained by personal promises, and by national and temporary institutions; the divine purpose is for ever overstepping every limit, every transient localisation and restraint, and claiming as its proper share, all the souls that are and shall be.
> —*Salvator Mundi*

---

65 Editor: It is telling that at this point Allin makes no reference to Friedrich Schleiermacher's important essay "On the Doctrine of Election" (1819), nor his classic work, *The Christian Faith in Outline* (2nd ed., 1830–31), though both would have provided interesting fuel for his reflections on election.

This admits of easy proof. Take a typical case to show what God's election really means. Take the case of Abraham, the father and founder of God's elect people. What was the promise to him? "That in his seed should *all the families of the earth* be blessed" [Gen 12:3]. This was of the essence of God's election. And to this effect St. Paul speaks with perfect clearness. And thoughtful readers will remark that it is precisely the apostle who lays most stress on the divine sovereignty, who most clearly teaches universal reconciliation.

The promise to Abraham was, St. Paul tells us, that he should be the heir of the *world* (Rom 4:13), words most expressive, and yet without meaning on the common view of election. In other words, the Jews, as God's elect, have as their inheritance all lands, all peoples. In the same Epistle, St. Paul points out how close the connection is between Israel and the world. Three times over he asserts their very fall to be the riches of the world, and asks if so, what will not the reconciling of Israel be (to the world) [Rom 11:11–12]. In short, on God's elect people hangs the lot and destiny of mankind (see Gal 3:8, and Acts 3:21–25); the latter passage is very interesting, for St. Peter there asserts the connection between a *universal* restoration, and the promise to Abraham, i.e., his election.

A further admirable illustration of this may be given (furnished by Holy Scripture) from its teaching as to the "firstfruits," and as to the "firstborn." Israel, as God's elect, is the "firstfruits"—Israel the "firstborn." But the "firstfruits" imply and pledge the *whole* harvest; the "firstborn" involve and include, in the divine economy, the *whole* family. Hence, the promise that "all Israel shall be saved" [Rom 11:26] implies the world's salvation. "The firstborn and firstfruits are the 'few' and the 'little flock'; but these, although 'first delivered from the curse,' have *relation to the whole creation*, which shall be saved in the appointed times by the firstborn seed, that is by Christ and his body."[66]

It is thus clear that we, so far from denying the election of the *few*, lay stress on it as *essential* to God's plan of mercy for all. It becomes indeed a cornerstone, so to speak, in the edifice of the world's salvation; for his "elect" are the very means by which our Father designs to bless all his children—designs to work out his plan of universal salvation. "The

---

66 Editor: Andrew Jukes, *The Second Death and the Restitution of All Things* (London: 1869).

sovereignty by which God reigns is eternal love."[67] "The Lord is King, the earth may be glad thereof" (Ps 97:1).

In Conclusion: The Doctrine of God is at Stake

A few closing remarks are needed here to indicate the principle that is really at stake in these questions. For that principle is vital and fundamental. It is no less than the unity of the Godhead; no less than the first article of the Creed, "I believe in *one* God the Father Almighty"—in God who is *one*, not in nature alone, but in purpose and in will—one and unchanging. In place of this God, the popular creed presents us with a Being who fluctuates between tenderness and wrath;[68] One who has ever-changing plans, and a will that is divided, and baffled. For half his creatures his love is in fact momentary, and his vengeance endless. For the other half, his pity is endless, and his wrath transient.

"The God we have preached has not been the God who was manifested in His Son Jesus Christ, but another altogether different Being, in whom we mingle strangely the Siva and the Vishnu."[69] This God is not even Lord in his own house; for the worst and feeblest of his creatures can finally defeat his most cherished plan; can paralyze the cross of Christ. In such a God I cannot see him, who is almighty and unchanging, whose property is *always* to have mercy; whose love, though always punishing sin, never ceases to help the sinner, for "love never fails" [1 Cor 13:8]; *never* to all eternity. Against the popular caricature of God, this chapter is thus a special protest—that caricature, which represents eternal love as turning to hate as soon as the sinner dies; which vainly talks of an Eternal Father, whose judgments mean salvation in one world, and change to

---

67 Editor: Peter Sterry, *The Rise, Race, and Royalty of the Kingdom of God in the Soul of Man opened in several sermons upon Matthew 18.3: as also the loveliness & love of Christ set forth in several other sermons upon Psal. 45. v. 1, 2.: together with an account of the state of a saint's soul and body in death* (London: 1683). Peter Sterry (1613–72) was a theologian associated with Cambridge Platonists. He was a chaplain to Oliver Cromwell and a member of the Westminster Assembly. He was also a universalist.

68 Thoughtful readers may consider how far anger and resentment can be strictly predicated of God, who changes not.

69 Editor: The quotation is from F. D. Maurice, in a letter of Miss Williams Wynn, Eastbourne, May 1858. In F. D. Maurice, *The Life of Frederick Denison Maurice: Chiefly Told in His Own Letters, vol.* 2. (London: 1884). Shiva and Vishnu are Hingu gods: Shiva is the destroyer and Vishnu is the protector.

damnation in the next; of eternal love, whose fire purifies and refines in time, and then beyond the grave turns to mere (purposeless) torture. What wonder if unbelief abounds, when we invite it by such teaching?

Against this mass of contradiction stands the view here given of "death," "judgment," "fire," "election." The old truths remain on a basis firmer than before, in harmony and no more in conflict, because they rest ultimately on the unity of God—unity of essence and unity of purpose. God's essential unity is destroyed when we assign to him conflicting actions, as though his love demanded one course of action, and his justice another; as though God the Saviour were one person, and God the Judge a wholly different one. Or, again, when we blindly teach that, if his judgments now mean salvation, they at the great day mean endless damnation. God, I repeat, in his "judgments," in his "fires," in "death," in "election," God in time and in eternity is *one* and the same God (Heb 13:8), and has, and must have to all eternity, but one unchanging purpose—is and must be for ever God our Saviour.

The divine unity is no merely abstract question: it reveals God's essence and character; it is rooted not in the laws of number, but of spirit and will. When Zechariah says, "The Lord shall be king over all the earth," he adds, "in that day shall the Lord be *one*, and his name *one*" [Zech 14:9]. And St. Paul, in declaring that God "will have all men to be saved," bases this not on God's love but on his unity, "for there is *one God*" (1 Tim 2:3–5), he who is one in all, and all in one, who will finally bring back his entire creation to that unity from which it started. Thus, elsewhere, St. Paul contrasts the unconditional unchanging promises of God in the gospel with the law, by laying emphasis on this divine unity—"For God is *one*" (Gal 3:20).[70] To sever God's action into love and harshness is, says St. Gregory of Nyssa, but madness, nay, *"the madness of babblers!"* At the bare idea that God can be really hard or cruel to his enemies (see note on Luke 6:27, ch. 8), and loving to his friends, he exclaims with a scorn (most rare in his writings)—"Oh, the madness of these babblers! for if God is unmerciful to his foes, he will not be truly kind even to you his friend" (*Or. cat.* 1).

---

70 See Lightfoot, *Saint Paul's Epistle to the Galatians* (London: 1865).

7

What the Old Testament Teaches

> "From the time at which this great and far-reaching promise or gospel was given to Abraham, the universal scope of the divine redemption is insisted on with growing emphasis, even in those Hebrew Scriptures, which we too often assume to be animated only by a local and national spirit."
> —Samuel Cox[1]

> "The whole history of the world is the uninterrupted carrying through of a divine plan of salvation, the primary object of which is His people: in and with them however *also the whole of humanity.*"
> —Franz Delitzsch on Psalm 33:11[2]

From the church I turn next to the Old Testament. There we shall find abundant, perhaps to many readers, unexpected confirmation of the

---

1 Samuel Cox (1826–93), *Salvator Mundi: Or, Is Christ the Saviour of All Men?* (London: 1877).

2 Franz Delitzsche, *A Commentary on the Book of Psalms.* 3 vols. Translated by the Rev. David Eaton and Rev. James Duguid (Edinburgh: 1876–77). Franz Delitzsch (1813–90) was a well-known Lutheran Hebrew Bible scholar, professor at Rostock (1846–50), Erlangen (1850–67), and Leipzig (1867–90). He was active in opposing anti-Semitism and in supporting Christian mission work among Jewish people.

larger hope, though I can merely attempt to give an outline of its teaching. True, in the Old Testament, the promises are, it may be said, mainly temporal; but still we have unmistakable evidence of a plan of mercy revealed in its pages, and destined to embrace all men. Nor need this interpretation of the older volume of God's word rest on mere conjecture: let me call as a witness, no less a person than the apostle St. Peter. The apostle in one of the very earliest of his addresses (Acts 3:21) takes occasion to explain the real purpose of God in Jesus Christ. There is to come, finally, a time of universal restoration, "restitution of *all* things." He adds the significant words that God has promised this "by the mouth of all his holy prophets since the world began"; and, therefore, we who teach this hope are but following in the steps of all God's holy prophets. Thus, St. Peter would have us go to the Old Testament, and weave, as it were, its varied predictions into one concordant whole, till they, with one voice, proclaim the "restitution of all things."

Creation and the Covenant with Abraham

Of the gospel of creation I have already spoken: here it is enough to note that in the divine act that stamps upon man the image and likeness of God, we have the gospel in germ. Thus the opening chapters of Genesis "give to us the largest views of the loving sovereignty of God; and of the divine origin, and destiny of mankind."[3] In this great fact, that mankind comes from God, and returns unto (or into) God (Rom 11:36), and in the divine plan to ensure this return, lies the center of unity of the Bible—the point to which its "many parts" and "many modes" (Heb 1:1) converge.

Thus we see the true meaning of the Jewish economy—"Its work was for humanity, the idea of Judaism is seen not in the covenant from Sinai, but in the covenant with Abraham."[4]

I have not space to consider minutely the promises of blessing to all men contained in the Old Testament, though they can be traced almost everywhere. At the very moment of the fall[5] is given a promise, that the

---

3 B. F. Westcott, *Revelation of the Father: Short Lectures on the Titles of the Lord in the Gospel of John* (London: 1884).

4 Ibid.

5 Here I may note that even those who take extreme views of future punishment seem to agree in the belief that Adam and Eve found mercy. But, if so, it may well be asked—shall they who were the authors of the fall, and all its woe, escape; shall they who, created upright, fall—yet find mercy at the last, while so many involuntary

PART THREE—Universalism Asserted on the Authority of Scripture

serpent's head shall be bruised, intimating a complete overthrow [Gen 3:15]. Two points are very significant here. The promise is not of the serpent's wounding only, but of such a wound as involves his destruction; and next the promise is conveyed in close connection with a terrible judgment; it is part of the sentence, it is embedded, so to speak, in it.

Passing on, we find that with the promise to Abraham was blended an intimation of blessing to the race of man. And this intimation of a worldwide blessing, as has been often pointed out, grows more frequent as the stream of revelation flows on. We find that in the Law, the Psalms, and the Prophets, are traces, clear and distinct, of universal blessing.

The Law

Thus of the teaching of the Law a fundamental part rested on the institution of the "firstfruits" and the "firstborn." Elsewhere in this volume has been pointed out the extreme significance of this as bearing on the larger hope, and as fulfilled in Jesus Christ (chapter 6). As the "firstfruits" pledge the whole harvest, and the "firstborn" the whole family, so are the elect people, i.e., God's "firstborn" ("Israel is my son, my firstborn"), a pledge that all are God's, that all are destined to share his blessing (to this the whole story of the Jewish race, when rightly viewed, bears witness; as "first-fruits" they are the channels of blessing to all mankind). Hence it is that we have the repeated promises to Abraham, that "in his seed should all the families of the earth be blessed." Thus, the Jewish patriarch becomes, in the apostle's striking phrase, "heir of the world" [Rom 4:13], and no less.

This principle, by which the elect become a means of blessing to all the rest, is strikingly affirmed in the Jewish Law. A sheaf of the "firstfruits" was to be presented to the Lord as pledging and consecrating the whole harvest (Lev 23:10–11). All the "firstborn" of the herds and flocks were the Lord's (Deut 15:19), as a pledge that all were his. So were the "firstborn" of their sons (Exod 22:29). If now we turn to the New Testament, we learn the essential bearing of all this on Christ's kingdom. First the apostle assures us that if the "firstfruits" be holy, *the lump is also holy* (Rom 11:16). Next he asserts that not Israel only, but in a higher sense Christ is the "firstfruits" (1 Cor 15:23). And the context implies that Christ conveys, actually imparts, life to *all*, as did Adam death to *all*.

inheritors of a fallen nature are doomed?

And as Israel was the "firstborn" son (Exod 4:22), so in a sense far higher is Christ the "firstborn" of *every* creature (Col 1:15–20), the Head of *every man* (1 Cor 11:3). Here, too, the context involves the reconciliation through the "firstborn," Christ, of *every creature* to God. We have thus a double "firstfruits," i.e., Christ, the true "firstfruits," and his people, "a kind of firstfruits" (Jas 1:18). Christ the "firstborn" (Col 1:18), and again his people (his elect), the "church of the firstborn" (Heb 12:23). Now it is very striking to find all this exactly prefigured in the Law; for it speaks of a *double firstfruits;* one which was offered at the Passover, and *on the very day on which Christ rose*, on "the morrow after the Sabbath" (Lev 23:10, 11); the other also distinctly called "firstfruits" (though distinguished by a separate name), which was offered fifty days later at Pentecost[6] (Lev 23:17). Thus does even the Law contain intimations of universal blessing to accrue to all men.

Psalms

Let us pass on to the Psalter and there also trace this promise of the restitution of all things; for the psalmists, too, are God's prophets, and are full of the largest forecasts.

> When they speak of the coming Messiah, they are at the farthest from claiming the blessings of His reign exclusively for themselves; on the contrary, they say, "His name shall endure for ever: his name shall be continued as long as the sun; and men shall be blessed in him; all nations shall call him blessed." ... They constantly breathe forth the invitation, O praise the Lord all you nations; praise Him all you people.
> —Samuel Cox[7]

Other examples of the same address to all nations—to all peoples—bidding them join in God's praise, and surely anticipating that they would one day do so, are frequent in the Psalms. Take, for example, those our Prayer Book[8] has made familiar, e.g., *Cantate Domino* (Ps 98). In it all lands are bidden to show themselves joyful unto the Lord. To the same effect is the familiar clause of the *Jubilate* (Ps 100), "O be joyful in the

---

6 See for fuller details, Andrew Jukes, *The Second Death and the Restitution of All Things* (London: 1867), 35–37.
7 Samuel Cox, *Salvator Mundi* (1877).
8 Editor: The Book of Common Prayer (1662).

Part Three—Universalism Asserted on the Authority of Scripture

Lord all you lands." To show how deeply this idea is embedded in the Psalter, let me add a few passages here. "Praise the Lord *all* you nations" (Ps 117:1). "Unto you shall *all* flesh come" (Ps 65:2). "You shall inherit *all* the nations" (Ps 82:8). *"All* nations shall come and worship you" (Ps 86:9). *"All* the earth shall worship you" (Ps 66:4). "Sing unto the Lord *all* the whole earth" (Ps 96:1). And so we read, *"All* nations shall do him service; ... *all* the heathen shall praise him; *all* the earth shall be filled with his majesty" (Ps 72:11–19). "Let *all flesh* give thanks unto his holy name, for ever and ever" (Ps 145:21). So again, "Praise the Lord you kings of the earth and *all people*" (Ps 148:11). "Bless the Lord *all* you his works" (Ps 103:22). "Let *all* the people praise you" (Ps 67:3–5). *"All* the ends of the world shall fear him" (Ps 67:7).

"All the ends of the world shall remember and turn unto the Lord, and *all* the kindreds of the nations shall worship before you" (Ps 22:27). This text has a special significance on account of the close connection of this psalm with the atonement; as a result of which all the ends of the world shall turn, as it predicts, to the Lord. Surely all this constitutes a remarkable array of evidence for the complete universality of Christ's kingdom. Can any fair mind accept the traditional creed as a satisfactory explanation of these passages. Here, as ever, men have delighted to narrow the breadth of the divine purpose, and dwarf its proportions. But would these promises, worldwide in their range, be fairly met, by saying that out of all the countless generations of man, only those, yet unborn, shall indeed fully learn to know God? It is impossible so to think; impossible not to see here a foreshadowing of those times of "restitution of *all things"*—which must come if the Bible speaks truly. In this universal hope is to be found the true spirit of the Psalms, in these invitations addressed, not to Israel, but to all nations—nay, to whatsoever exists. Note how, as the Psalter draws to its end, the tone of triumph rises, expands, broadens into the very widest anticipations of universal blessedness (Pss 148–50). In this spirit it closes, *"Let everything that has breath,* praise the Lord" (Ps 150:6).

Prophets

Of the greater prophets the same is true; though I need not speak in detail of them. From amid their varied contents, at times break forth promises of the widest, amplest hope; anticipations of a time of universal bliss and joy; of a world in which all pain and sorrow shall have passed away. But these passages are in the main familiar to you, and I need hardly quote them. They have found their way to the heart of Christendom, and have stamped themselves on its literature.

> Take, however, only this one sentence from the evangelical prophet, and take it mainly because St. Paul echoes it back, and interprets it as he echoes it. It is Jehovah who speaks these words by the mouth of Isaiah: "Look unto Me and be you saved, all you ends of the earth: for I am God and there is none other: I have sworn by Myself and the word is gone out of My mouth in righteousness and shall not return, that unto Me every knee shall bow and every tongue confess" [Isa 45:22–23]. Could any words more emphatically declare it to be the divine purpose that the whole earth, to the very end of it, shall be saved; that every knee shall bend in homage before God, and every tongue take the oath of fealty to Him? Are we not expressly told that this declaration, since it has come from the righteous mouth of God, cannot return unto Him void, but must accomplish its object; that object being the salvation of the human race? St. Paul echoes this great word (in Rom 14:11) and again in the epistle to the Philippians, and though on his lips it gains definiteness and precision, assuredly it loses no jot or tittle of its breadth: he affirms, Phil 2:9–11, "that God has highly exalted Him, and given Him a name which is above every name, in order that at the name of Jesus every knee shall bow"; not only every knee of man—for now the promise grows incalculably wider—but every knee in heaven and on earth, and under the earth: "and that every tongue shall confess that Jesus Christ is Lord, to the glory of God the Father." It is hard to understand Isaiah as proclaiming less than an universal redemption, but if St. Paul did not mean to proclaim a redemption as wide as the universe, what use or force is there in words?
> —Samuel Cox[9]

On one passage I must briefly dwell. "He shall see of the travail of his soul, and be *satisfied*" (Isa 53:2). By what ingenuity can hopeless, endless evil be reconciled with these words? How can I accept a creed that asks me to believe that Christ is satisfied, while his own children are given over to endless ruin. Who believes this of Jesus Christ? Who can believe

---

9 Samuel Cox, *Salvator Mundi* (1877).

Part Three—Universalism Asserted on the Authority of Scripture

him "satisfied" with the final and utter ruin of any one soul for whom he died?—"satisfied" that his cross should fail?—"satisfied" with the victory of evil, in so much as a solitary case?

Remember how full are the Prophets, and the Psalms no less, of pictures of the vastness of the divine mercy, of his tenderness that never fails. Even from amid the sadness of the Lamentations, we hear a voice assuring us that "the Lord *will not cast off for ever*, but though he cause grief, yet will he have compassion according to the multitude of his mercies" (Lam 3:31).

Or take these words, "I will not contend for ever, neither will I be *always angry*, for the spirit should fail before me, and the souls which I have made" (Isa 57:16). This idea is a favourite one; the contrast between the short duration of God's anger, and the enduring *endless character of his love*. "So in a *little* wrath I hid my face from you for a moment; but with *everlasting kindness* will I have mercy on you, says the Lord your Redeemer" (Isa 54:8).

Let us pause here for a moment to dwell on the significance of this fact of the limited duration of the divine anger, so clearly taught in the Old Testament. Take a few instances, "I am merciful, says the Lord, *I will not keep anger for ever*" (Jer 3:12). "His anger endures *but a moment*" (Ps 30:5), "while his mercy endures for ever" (Ps 136)—a statement repeated no less than twenty-six times in this one psalm. "He will not always chide, neither keeps he his anger for ever" (Ps 103:9). "He retains not his anger for ever, because he delights in mercy" (Mic 7:18).

But if this be true, *what becomes of the popular creed?* If God's anger is temporary, how can it be endless? If it endure but a moment, how can it last for ever in even a solitary instance? I would invite our opponents fairly to face these plain and reiterated assertions: and to explain why they feel justified in teaching that God's anger will in many cases last for ever, and that his mercy will not endure for ever.

I may in passing ask attention to two passages in the book of Daniel. In one, a dominion absolutely *universal* is promised to the Son of Man (Dan 7:14), words which may be compared with the numerous passages to the same effect noted in the next chapter. In the other, a promise is made of a decree to finish transgression, and to *make an end of sins* (Dan 9:24).

We have spoken of the pictures of universal blessedness that are to be found in the greater prophets, "perhaps," says the author already quoted, "some of you may not be equally familiar with the fact that these same pictures are also to be found in the minor prophets"; (a fact very suggestive) that "every one of these brief poems, or collections of poems, has its tiny Apocalypse. And mark this point well, while each of the minor prophets sees the vision of a whole world redeemed to the love and service of righteousness, this vision of redemption is invariably accompanied by a *vision of judgment*."[10]

At least, if not all, yet very many of the minor prophets do predict the coming of a time of universal redemption. So Hosea 13:14, exclaims, "O death, I will be your plagues. O grave, I will be your destruction" (see 1 Cor 15:55). So Joel 2:28, tells of the Spirit as being poured upon all flesh. Habakkuk can look beyond the terrors of judgment and see the *"earth* filled with the knowledge of the glory of the Lord, as the *waters cover the sea"* (Hab 2:14). Is not this wonderful? Can you not enter into St. Peter's words as he stood forth, while yet Christianity was scarcely born, to proclaim as its glorious aim and scope, the universal restoration—the paradise of God regained for mankind—all things made new (Acts 3:21).

I resume. In Zephaniah we read the same glorious prospect, the same universal hope. He speaks of God's judgments as being terrible to the nations, in order that "men may worship him, *every one* from his place, even *all the isles of the heathen"* (Zeph 2:11). And again, in the same prophet, we are told how God is to send his fiery judgments to purify men, "that they may all call upon the name of the Lord to serve him with one consent" (Zeph 3:8–9). So Malachi closes the prophetic line with an intimation indeed of judgment—of a refining fire—but together with this is the prospect unfolded that from the *"rising of the sun to the going down of the same* God's name shall be great among the nations, and in every place incense and pure offerings shall be offered to him" (Mal 1:11). The words that introduce this prospect "from the rising up of the sun to the going down of the same," may well recall the beautiful and suggestive phrase of Zechariah 14:7, "At evening time it shall be light."

---

10 Editor: Samuel Cox (1826–93), *Salvator Mundi* (1877).

PART THREE—Universalism Asserted on the Authority of Scripture

Conclusion

Brief as the above survey has been, it has, I trust, served to indicate how, even through all the Old Testament, the thread of *universal* hope runs: how the Law, Prophets, and Psalms of Israel did foreshadow a coming age, when sin should be no more, and sorrow and sighing should flee away for ever. To the New Testament I propose to devote an examination more in detail, as its great importance demands, in the next chapter.

8

What the New Testament Teaches

Universal Salvation

> "And here I may briefly say, that to my own mind, the language of the New Testament appears *unequivocally to affirm the redemption of all men*; their actual redemption from this evil and diseased state in which we now are; the actual raising up of all to a perfect life. To my mind this universality seems to be clearly expressed in Scripture."
> —James Hinton[1]

Preliminary Comments

We now turn to an examination of the very many passages in the New Testament that clearly declare, or imply, the salvation of all men—how numerous these are we shall see. The time has fully come for appealing with all boldness on behalf of the larger hope, alike to the letter and the spirit of the New Testament. One thing only I ask, which

---

[1] James Hinton, *The Mystery of Pain: A Book of the Sorrowful* (London: 1866). James Hinton (1822–75), son of a Baptist minister, was an aural surgeon at Guy's Hospital in London.

Part Three—Universalism Asserted on the Authority of Scripture

common fairness and honesty require, that our Lord and his evangelists and apostles may be understood to *mean what they say*.

Thus, we shall look at a *few* instances out of *many*. When they speak of all men, I assume them to mean *all* men, and not some men. When they speak of all things, I assume them to mean *all* things. When they speak of life and salvation as given to the world, I assume them to mean *given*, and not merely offered. When they speak of the destruction of death, of the devil, and of the works of the devil, I assume them to mean that these shall be *destroyed* and not preserved for ever in hell. When they tell us that the whole of creation suffers, but that it shall be delivered, I assume that they mean an *actual* deliverance of all created things. When they tell us that redemption is wider, broader, and stronger than the fall, I assume that they mean to tell us at least this, that *all* the evil caused by the fall shall be swept away. When they describe Christ's empire as extending over all things and all creatures, and tell us that every tongue must join in homage to him, I assume them to mean what these words convey in their ordinary sense. If I did not, should I not be making God a liar?

What does the traditional creed require? It practically requires a *mutilated Bible*. More than this, it bids us to expunge precisely that which is noblest and divinest in Holy Scripture. I have no desire to ignore "the terrors of the Lord" (see next chapter). They deserve and shall have full recognition. I do insist, however, that those teachers misread Holy Scripture who forgets that its essential purpose is to unfold his name, who is "our Father," and to proclaim his full victory in the extinction of all evil, and not in its perpetuation in hell. I protest against teaching that "all" means in scriptural phrase absolutely "all" when some evil is foretold, but that "all" means only "some" when spoken of final salvation. So rooted is this most inequitable mode of interpretation, that it has become involuntary. The restitution of all things means, we are told, that only some beings are to be restored, while some are tortured for ever, or annihilated. That God shall be finally "all in all" means that he will shut up many for ever in endless evil, to blaspheme and hate him eternally, and only save the rest. That his tender mercies are over all his works means, in the ordinary creed, that his tender mercies expire at the gates of hell. Solemn as is the question, there is something almost ludicrous, when we find those who so teach, then turning around to charge us with evading the words of Scripture.

What the New Testament Teaches

I submit that the entire history of exegesis contains no stranger fact than this persistent ignoring of so large a part of the New Testament. To bring this out clearly, I append the following chain of passages from a long series. They, clearly and closely linked, claim for Christ a saving empire coextensive with the race, or (perhaps) rather with the whole universe. This connection is clearly marked, for each passage suggests or contains the same central idea, and thus forms a link in a continuous chain.

This chain begins at creation, when *all* things were created by Christ, who therefore, as St. Paul implies, reconciles (re-creates) *all* things unto God (Col 1:16–20). Hence, his work is the restitution of *all* things (Acts 3:21). He is Heir of *all* things (Heb 1:2). The Father has given him authority over *all* flesh, to give to *whosoever* was given to him eternal life (John 17:2, see original). So *all* flesh shall see the salvation of God (Luke 3:6). For God—whose counsel is immutable (Heb 6:17,18), whose attitude towards his enemies is love unchanging (Luke 6:27–35)—will have *all* men to be saved (1 Tim 2:4) and *all* to come to repentance (2 Pet 3:9). He has shut *all* up unto unbelief, so that he may show mercy upon *all* (Rom 11:32). For (out) of him, as Source, and unto (or into) him, as End, are *all* things whatsoever (Rom 11:36). He has, therefore, put *all* things in subjection under Christ's feet (Eph 1:22). So we are assured that God wills to gather into one *all* things in Christ (Eph 1:10). His grace comes upon *all* men unto justification of life (Rom 5:18). So Jesus, knowing that the Father had given *all* things into his hands (John 13:3), promises by his cross to draw *all* men unto himself (John 12:32). For having, as stated, received *all* things from the Father (John 3:35), *all* that was given comes to him, and he loses none (John 6:37–39), but if any stray, goes after that which is lost *till he finds it* (Luke 15:4), and so makes *all* things new (Rev 21:5).

Thus, he comes in order that *all* men may believe (John 1:7); that the *world* through him may be saved (John 3:17). His grace brings salvation to *all* men (Titus 2:11). He takes away the sin of the *world* (John 1:29). He gives his flesh for its life (John 6:51). Because the gifts and calling of God are irrevocable (Rom 11:29), he *gives* life to the *world* (John 6:33). He is the light of the *world* (John 8:12). He is the propitiation for the sins of the *whole world* (1 John 2:2). He is the Saviour of *all men* (1 Tim 4:10). He *destroys* the works of the devil, not some of them only (1 John 3:8), and the devil himself (Heb 2:14). He *abolishes* death (2 Tim 1:10). He is manifested to put away sin (Heb 9:26), and thus subdues *all* things unto

PART THREE—Universalism Asserted on the Authority of Scripture

himself (Phil 3:21—the context clearly shows this subjugation to be *conformity* to himself). He does not forget the *dead*, but takes the gospel to Hades (1 Pet 3:19), of which he holds the keys (Rev 1:18). He is the *same* (Saviour) for ever (Heb 13:8). Thus, even the dead are evangelized (1 Pet 4:6), and death and Hades destroyed (Rev 20:14). *All* are therefore made alive in him (1 Cor 15:22). Christ finishes, completes his work (John 17:4), restores *all* things (Acts 3:21), and there is no more curse (Rev 22:2, 3). *Every knee* of things in heaven and earth, and under the earth, bends to him (Phil 2:10). The *creation* is delivered from the bondage of corruption (Rom 8:21), and *every creature* joins in the song of praise (Rev 5:13). So comes the *end*, when he delivers up the kingdom to God, who is then *all in all* (1 Cor 15:24–28).

These passages are, I repeat, not taken at random and piled up any way. They are the expression of that purpose that runs though the Bible. It is a purpose first stated in man's creation *in God's image;* a purpose to be traced in the Law, the Psalms, and [the] Prophets; and most clearly in the New Testament. From it we learn that (1) Christ came, claiming as his own the entire human race, to the end that he might save and restore the *whole*, and not any fraction of it, however large. (2) He came with full power "over all flesh," having received power in heaven and on earth— over all hearts, all evil, all wills. (3) He lived and died, and rose again, victorious in the fullest sense, "having *finished* his work" as he expressly claims.

Thus, to deny the absolute universality of Christ's redeeming sway, as destined to embrace *all souls and all things whatsoever*, seems no less than to withdraw from the New Testament an *essential* and *vital* part of its teaching. For here we are not dealing with some few passages, in which it might be possible to say that *"all"* was used in a lax sense. We have a connected series in which link follows link, a series in which the actual, not the potential, universality of Christ's kingdom is the center and essential thought.

Universalist Texts

Let us now consider a little more in detail the passages themselves, taking them in their natural and fair meaning, not obscured by traditional gloss.

Matthean, Lukan, and Johannine Texts

Matthew

> For the Son of Man is come to save that which was lost.
> (Matt 18:11)

Here the question is simply this, will Jesus Christ do what he has come to do, or will he *fail*—as the traditional creed, in spite of all denials, indubitably teaches? Will he save *that which was lost* and not *some of the lost merely*, a totally different thing? How can "that which was lost" be saved, if any soul be finally lost?

> And Jesus said unto them, "Truly I say unto you, that you which have followed me, in the regeneration (*palingenesia*) when the Son of Man shall sit in the throne of his glory, you also shall sit upon twelve thrones, judging the twelve tribes of Israel . . . ."
> (Matt 19:28)

This passage, too often passed over, seems certainly to promise that new creation of all things, in which Christ, who first made, is one day to remake all things (cf. Col 1:15–20; Heb 1:2). The thoughtful will notice (see context) the connection of restoration and judgment.

Luke

> All flesh shall see the salvation of God.
> (Luke 3:6)

Quoted from Isaiah 40:5,[2] "The seeing is twofold, as appears from the sequel (see Isa 40). It is (I) the natural sight of Jehovah's glorious deeds on behalf of his people; and (II) the spiritual recognition of Jehovah as the Lord."[3] Surely, then, these words point in the direction of a salvation

---

[2] Editor: Luke's text concerns the ministry of John the Baptist. He quotes Isa 40:5, "and the glory of the LORD shall be revealed, and all flesh shall see it together: for the mouth of the LORD hath spoken it" (KJV).

[3] Editor: T. K. Cheyne, *The Prophesies of Isaiah: A New Translation with Commentary and Appendices*. 2 vols (London: 1880). Thomas Kelly Cheyne (1841–1915) was a biblical scholar at Oxford University trained in German higher critical methods of interpretation.

Part Three—Universalism Asserted on the Authority of Scripture

that shall be quite universal, "for without holiness no man shall see the Lord" (Heb 12:14). "The pure in heart shall see God" (Matt 5:8).

> But I say to you, love your enemies, do good to them who hate you . . . and you shall be the children of the Highest.
> (Luke 6:27–35)

"But I say, *'love your enemies.'*" Will the advocates of endless penalty frankly tell us how that can be reconciled with the letter, or the spirit, of this text? Will they explain why God commands us to love our enemies, when he consigns his own enemies to an endless hell; and why he bids us to do good to those who hate us, when he means for ever to punish and do evil to those who hate him?

> But when a stronger than he shall come upon him and overcome him, he takes from him all his armour, in which he trusted, and divides his spoils.
> (Luke 11:22; Matt 12:29)

Here it is asserted (a) that Christ is stronger than Satan, (b) that Christ will overcome Satan, (c) will take from him all his armour, (d) will divide (i.e., take away) his spoils. Each of these statements contradicts the popular creed, for that teaches (a) that evil is stronger than good, (b) that it overcomes good in numberless cases, (c) that Satan's power for evil is not taken away, but lasts for ever, (d) that his spoils—the souls he has captured—are not divided (i.e., taken from him). And observe our Lord's victory over the powers of evil does not consist in shutting up any of their captives in hell, but in liberating all.

> What man of you having a hundred sheep . . . if he loses one of them, does not leave the ninety-nine . . . and go after that which is lost until he find it?
> (Luke 15:4)

Ancient commentators follow two main lines, the hundred sheep are either (1) all men, or (2) all spiritual creatures: in the former case the wicked are the strayed sheep: in the latter, mankind itself, which by the fall has strayed from the heavenly fold. Both views seem to involve universalism. For in the one all the wicked, in the other all humanity, are sought till they are found. Any narrowing of the "sheep" to the elect is quite alien from the whole spirit of this parable, which was *specially* addressed to the publican and the sinner. See how broadly Christ bases his argument, "what man of you," he asks, "would not do this?" Observe the immense significance of Christ's teaching. It expressly sanctions the right to argue from those feelings of humanity, shared even by the outcast and sinful, to the divine feelings. Note, too, the ground taken—*the divine loss*. It is not the man who loses his soul, *it is God who loses the man*—a fact ignored (with much else) in popular teaching.

> Or what woman, having ten silver coins, if she loses one coin, does not light a lamp and sweep the house and seek diligently until she finds it?
> (Luke 15:8)

Here is precisely the same broad human basis, and the same broad hopeful teaching. Keep steadily in view these facts taught here: (1) Our own feelings of love and pity are a safe guide to God's feelings; on these very feelings Christ expressly builds, asking, "what man of you?" (2) Every lost soul is *God's loss*, who, therefore, seeks its recovery; and (3) will seek *till he find it*. (4) The whole of the loss is repaired. (5) If God feel the loss of man, he will *always* feel it. Hence, if sin be endless, the divine passion must surely be endless too.

> For the Son of Man came to seek and to save the lost.
> (Luke 19:10)

If so, I gather from his own parables, and his essential nature, that so long as *anything is lost*, Jesus Christ will go on seeking and saving; for is he not always the same? (Heb 13:8). "The lost" are his charge, and not some of the lost, a very different thing. Or are we to read this verse thus: "He came indeed to save 'the lost'—but those in the fullest sense 'lost' he will never save"?

Johannine Texts

> He [John the Baptist] came as a witness, to bear witness about the light, that all men might believe through him [Christ].
> (John 1:7)

Yes, that all men might believe, that is indeed the divine purpose—the purpose of him who sent the Baptist. But dare we say that what God purposes, he will fail to do? I read distinctly of the *immutability* of his counsel (Heb 6:17). Am I to believe that the immutable purpose of the almighty and unchanging God shall finally come to nothing?

PART THREE—Universalism Asserted on the Authority of Scripture

> [John] saw Jesus coming toward him, and said, "Behold, the Lamb of God, who takes away the sin of the world!"
> (John 1:29)

Here is the extent of the work of Christ set forth. It is the world's sin, and not less, that he takes away. But, if it is *taken away*, how can there be an endless hell for its punishment? Is all this playing with words? Are we, then, to assert of Christ, "Behold the Lamb of God who tries to take away the sin of the world, but fails"?

> For God did not send his Son into the world to condemn the world, but in order that the world might be saved through him.
> (John 3:17)

Our opponents say that God's purpose will fail. He, on the contrary, assures us by his prophet, that his word shall not return unto him void, but shall accomplish his pleasure [Isa 55:11].

> The Father loves the Son and has given all things into his hand.
> (John 3:35)

The relevance of this is obvious, for *"all* that which the Father gives me," says Christ, "shall come unto me" (6:37). This is one of the large group of passages showing the absolute universality of Christ's kingdom; compare John 13:3, and see the connection of the gift of *all things* to Christ and his atoning death. Also see Matthew 11:27, where, just before the well-known appeal, "come unto me," Jesus has been saying that *all things* were delivered unto him by his Father; a connection surely suggestive. Read, too, Matthew 28:18, and note the connection between all power given to Christ, and his claim over all nations. So, too, in Hebrews 2:8–9, the connection is significant between the gift of *all things* to Jesus Christ, and his tasting death for every man. As he creates *all* things (actually) so he redeems and restores all things (actually, not potentially); God has given to him all things; and all things given to him shall come to him.

> They [the Samaritans] said to the woman, "It is no longer because of what you said that we believe, for we have heard for ourselves, and we know that this is indeed the Saviour of the world."
> (John 4:42)

Christ is here called the Saviour of the *world*. The larger hope simply pleads, that Christ will, in fact, save the world.

> For the bread of God is he who comes down from heaven
> and gives life to the world.
> (John 6:33)

The world (*kosmos*) is in Scripture the ungodly mass. It is contrasted with the inner circle of the faithful, the elect. But this world is over and over again claimed by Christ. He gives life to it, and his gifts are "irrevocable."

> All that the Father gives me will come to me. . . . And this is the will of him who sent me, that I should lose nothing of all that he has given me, but raise it up on the last day.
> (John 6:37–39)

We have seen that God the Father has given to Christ, not some things, but *all* things; and here we have the promise of Jesus Christ, that all that has been given to him shall come to him, and that nothing shall be lost (John 6:12).

> And the bread that I will give for the life of the world is my flesh.
> (John 6:51)

Again, it is the *world* for whose life Christ is to give his flesh. Can he give in vain? His gifts are "irrevocable," i.e., must be *finally* effective, though they may be resisted.

> Again Jesus spoke to them, saying, "I am the light of the world."
> (John 8:12)

Here, too, the *world* is that of which Christ is the light as well as the life.

> And I, when I am lifted up from the earth [on the cross],
> will draw all men to myself.
> (John 12:32)

The plainest comment is the best. A partial drawing, i.e., a partial salvation, makes his words *untrue*. What our Lord does say—in the consciousness of power, and using the term applied to the Father's constraining grace (6:44)—is, I will (actually) draw all men. He does not say, or imply, I will try to draw, and fail. One reads the comments of good men on this passage, with a feeling akin to despair, as they attempt to make Jesus Christ say that which he did not say, and not say that which he did say. What he does say is exactly given in the following lines:

PART THREE—Universalism Asserted on the Authority of Scripture

> So shall I lift up in My pierced hands ...
> Beyond the reach of grief and guilt ...
> *The whole creation.*
>   —E. Barrett Browning[4]

> I did not come to judge the world but to save the world.
> (John 12:47)

This is as distinct a statement of Christ's purpose as is possible; its force can only be evaded by asserting that Christ would fail to accomplish that very thing which he came to do: and this assertion must be made in the teeth of those explicit passages, which declare the completeness of his triumph.

> Jesus, knowing that the Father had given all things into his hands, ...
> (John 13:3)

These words carry us to the very eve of the Passion. "Knowing that his hour was come" (v. 1), Jesus knows, too, that all things have been given into his hands (See 3:35; 17:2; Matt 28:18; 11:27; Eph 1:22). Such knowledge at such an hour is deeply significant. As the cross draws near, there comes to cheer him the knowledge that to him have been given all things, i.e., an assurance of absolute victory.

> ... even as thou [the Father] gavest him [the Son] authority over all flesh, that whatsoever thou hast given him, to them he should give eternal life.
> (John 17:2, RV)

Even the Revised Version fails to bring out with clearness the central fact, that eternal life has been given to all flesh by Christ. Literally the original runs: "You gave to him authority over *all* flesh, in order that (as to) *all* which You have given to him, to them [i.e., to all], he should

---

4 Editor: Elizabeth Barrett Browning, "A Drama of Exile" (1844). Browning (1806–61) was a well-known Victorian poet who moved in circles with the likes of Wordsworth, Coleridge, Tennyson, and Thomas Carlysle. The quote without the cuts reads:
> As I shall be uplifted on a cross
> In darkness of eclipse and anguished dread,
> So shall I lift up in my piercèd hands,
> Not into dark, but light—not unto death,
> But life,—beyond the reach of guilt and grief,
> The whole creation.

give eternal life." The Greek is clear; but our versions fail, in not repeating the emphatic *all* (repeated in the original), which involves the gift (not the offer) of eternal life to *all* by Christ—thus obscuring the meaning. It is necessary to remark, if we would understand St. John's teaching, the emphasis laid on the divine *sovereignty*[5] in redemption, a sovereignty that is love. (Our recoil from Calvinism has blinded most readers to this truth which pervades all Holy Scripture.) Thus, the Father disposes all things, and gives all things to Christ (13:3; 3:35; 17:2; Matt 28:18). At the very hour appointed (17:1; 2:4; 12:1, 23); each part of the great work is accomplished.

> It is finished!
> (John 19:30; cf. 17:4)

What is finished? The pain—the cross? It is inconceivable that such a speaker, at such an hour, should mean less than this, viz.; *all* is finished in all its extent. The great end and goal is now attained—attained in all its length and breadth and height. In no respect can that purpose of salvation fail, which embraces all humanity; for—though the very opposite may seem true—*it is finished*.

> He [Christ] is the propitiation for our sins, and not for ours only but also for the sins of the whole world.
> (1 John 2:2)

Notice here the world contrasted with the true disciples; and yet the propitiation is not to be confined to the few, it is for all. St. John's anxiety is to *assert this for all*. Here, as so often, the narrower and wider purposes of salvation are both mentioned: the narrower not excluding, as in the popular view, but *including* and *implying* the wider; a truth of the deepest importance.

> You know that he appeared in order to take away sins . . . .
> (1 John 3:5)

This should he compared with John 1:29. There Christ takes away the *sin*—regarded as one vast whole—of all humanity: here the *sins*, i.e., the individual sins of men.

---

5 It is well to remember this, when we are gravely told that "Omnipotence itself cannot save obstinate sinners." Now, in the matter of salvation we have an express assertion that even the camel can go through the needle's eye; for with God "*all things are possible*" [Matt 19:26].

PART THREE—Universalism Asserted on the Authority of Scripture

> The reason the Son of God appeared was to destroy the works of the devil.
> (1 John 3:8)

The very purpose of the manifestation of God's Son is here stated to be the sweeping away of Satan's works. How then can this *possibly be true*, while pain and sin endure for ever? No ideas can be more exactly opposed than the permanence of evil, and yet the destruction of the works of the devil. Is sin, and all that sin involves, the work of the devil? Yes, or No? You cannot answer in the negative, if you accept the standpoint of Scripture. But, if the affirmative be true, then all hell and sin and sorrow are to be swept away.

> And we have seen and testify that the Father has sent his Son to be the Saviour of the world.
> (1 John 4:14)

Does it not savor of mockery to say that the Father sent the Son to destroy evil, and to save the world, and that the Son is victorious; and yet that neither shall evil be destroyed or the world saved?

REVELATION

> Fear not. ... Behold I am alive forevermore, and I have the keys of death and Hades.
> (Rev 1:18)

Significant words; doubly significant when we remember that Christ had just *used these keys to open the prison doors*, in his descent into Hades. How, if so, can death (the second, or any death) sever from Jesus Christ (*who holds the keys*)—from his power to save?

> And I heard every creature in heaven and on earth and under the earth and in the sea, and all that is in them, saying, "To him who sits on the throne and to the Lamb be blessing and honor and glory and might forever and ever!"
> (Rev 5:13)

These words embrace every created thing—on the earth, and under the earth, and in the sea. All are represented as swelling the chorus of praise to God, and to the Lamb. Yes, to such an end we trust and hope that all creation is indeed coming, because we believe God's distinct promise, that all things shall be made new. How else could *all things* join in this glorious chorus? Compare notes on Ephesians 1:10 and Philippians 2:11.

> Then death and Hades were thrown into the lake of fire. This is the second death, the lake of fire.
> (Rev 20:14)

"The sense of the whole seems to be that at the final consummation of all things, all evil, physical and moral, will be abolished."[6]

> And he who was seated on the throne said, "Behold, I am making all things new."
> (Rev 21:5)

This is the same glorious hope, not for some, but for all; no less than *all things* are to be made new.

> I am the Alpha and the Omega, the beginning and the end.
> (Rev 21:6; cf. 1:8; 22:13)

A thoughtful reader will note that this claims for God a position, which negatives a final dualism: as he was the Source, so he is the Goal of all things. God is the *Terminus* of creation; the stream shall return to its source. The unconscious dualism of current theology is a barrier to any true apprehension of the thought of the apostle,[7] which seems to be the same as that St. Paul expresses in Romans 11:36.

> On either side of the river, [was] the tree of life .... The leaves of the tree were for the healing of the nations. No longer will there be anything accursed ....
> (Rev 22:2–3)

Here is a striking hint as to a future restoration; a hint that the nations are one day, in a future age, to be healed, for all this is subsequent to the passing away of the present earth, heaven (Rev 21:1). And as a result of this healing, there shall be no more curse—no pain; no tears—but *all things* made new.

---

6 Editor: The quotation is from William Warburton (1698–1779), Bishop of Gloucester (1759–79). Warburton was a capable theologian and literary critic and not adverse to entering into controversy. I have been unable to establish which of his works the quotation is from.

7 Editor: Allin refers to the apostle John, who tradition associates with the John who wrote Revelation.

PART THREE—Universalism Asserted on the Authority of Scripture

ACTS

> [Christ,] whom heaven must receive until the time for restoring all the things about which God spoke by the mouth of his holy prophets long ago.
> (Acts 3:21)

All things are to be restored (*apokatastasis*, i.e., complete restoration), and this is said to be the meaning of the work of Christ, the meaning of the promise to Abraham, of the Jewish covenant (v. 25). This God has spoken by all "the prophets since the world began," and this is what the larger hope teaches.

> ... having a hope in God ... that there will be a resurrection of both the just and the unjust.
> (Acts 24:15)

Note these words. Could St. Paul have hoped for a resurrection of the *unjust* if that meant hopeless punishment to them? "Who is *so great a fool*," asks a famous Father, "as to think so great a boon as the resurrection can be, to those that rise, an occasion of endless torment?"[8]

GOD'S EXPANDING FAMILY

I may take this opportunity of asking attention to the fact that there runs through Scripture a definite law of *expansion*. First one family is chosen, then this family expands into a nation, then the nation is declared to be the source of blessing to all nations. Side by side with this numerical expansion there is visible a spiritual expansion. The prescribed sacrifices, the elaborate ritual, are pushed aside in favour of a spiritual creed, even in the Old Testament. Passing to the New Testament the law is the same, but more active still. By what to a hasty judgment seems strange, Christ devotes half his time to the bodies of men, but we see the meaning to be that he cares for the whole man, and this care expands into the noble promise of the resurrection. Next comes a most significant expansion. All barriers fall before the march of redemption. The dead, the *unrepentant* dead, are evangelized; the cross penetrates Hades (1 Pet 3:18–20; 4:6). Nor is this all, there are hints plain enough of a greater expansion still. "All things in heaven," "the principalities and powers" (Eph 1:10; 3:10,

---

8 Editor: I am uncertain which "famous Father" Allin had in mind.

etc.; Col 1:15–20), are drawn within the range of the atonement. Can any hope be broader than that here directly suggested by the Bible itself? The question seems rather this: are our broadest hopes *broad enough*? Shall there be a corner or nook or abyss in all the universe of God finally unlighted by the cross? Shall there be a sin or sorrow or pain unhealed? Is the very universe, is creation in all its extent, a field wide enough for the Son of God?

Paul, Peter, and Hebrews

We have seen how numerous are the passages which the writings of St. Matthew, St. Luke, and St. John contain, teaching directly or indirectly, the salvation of all men. Let us now consider the epistles of St. Paul, St. Peter, and that to the Hebrews. We shall find in these books the stream of promise still widening—the universality of redemption indicated with a precision of language and a variety of illustration, which it seems not possible to reconcile with endless evil. *I do not mean* that every passage quoted is in itself conclusive. I do mean that all are relevant, as *links* in that great chain of promise, which enshrines the doctrine of universal restoration. And here an important question arises. How—on the hypothesis of endless evil—can we account for such passages, as naturally and obviously point to the larger hope? That the Bible holds out a hope of universal reconciliation, etc., etc., cannot be denied. And, if this universal restoration is never to take place, *how came this promise to be made?* How came the Bible to raise expectations never destined (as we are told) to be fulfilled, in a matter so unspeakably important? Inspired writers, aware that all things (in the natural sense of the words) will never be restored, and yet asserting positively that they will be restored, present us with a fact, which our opponents may well be invited to account for and explain.

PAULINE TEXTS

St. Paul's writings naturally claim special notice here. He is, so to speak, the statesman-apostle, whose mind ranges over the whole field of the divine purpose and of human destiny. Two points I must note. (1) Not merely does St. Paul assert the divine sovereignty, but it lies at the center of his teaching. He sees everywhere a purpose slowly but surely fulfilling itself, a purpose which may be resisted, but must finally prevail. (2) In this apostle the resurrection is set in striking prominence, as from its

PART THREE—Universalism Asserted on the Authority of Scripture

essential nature, a spiritual, redemptive force, as indeed the climax of Christ's work for man.

> "For the promise to Abraham and his offspring that he would be heir of the world...."
> (Rom 4:13)

Here remark that the election by God of the Jews really involves *the world's* salvation; for Abraham *is* "heir of the world" (see on election in chapter 6), i.e., receives as his inheritance the *whole* world.

> For the judgment following one trespass brought condemnation, but the free gift following many trespasses brought justification. ... Therefore, as one trespass led to condemnation for all men, so one act of righteousness leads to justification and life for all men.
> (Rom 5:16–18)

I earnestly commend a study of the whole drift and argument of this passage. It is, I think, *absolutely irreconcilable* with a partial salvation. It contains a statement, as explicit as words can convey it, of this great truth—God's remedy is *coextensive with, and is stronger than, sin*. Wherever, upon whomsoever sin has lighted, there shall God's grace, through Jesus Christ, come to heal. In the very same sense as "the many" (all people) were made sinners, so "the many" shall have righteousness—not merely offered them—but be made righteous. And here I take my stand on these plain words of Scripture, and maintain that no state of final sin, for any soul, is compatible with them. Will our opponents explain how the grace of God (v. 15) can be *mightier* in fact, than sin, if there be a hell without end? Will they explain how grace can *much more* abound than the offense—if there be a place of endless evil? Note the great underlying principle, viz., that grace is stronger than sin, always and everywhere stronger (finally).

> The creation itself will be set free from its bondage to corruption and obtain the freedom of the glory of the children of God. For we know that the whole creation has been groaning together in the pains of childbirth until now. And not only the creation, but we ourselves, who have the firstfruits of the Spirit, groan inwardly as we wait eagerly for adoption as sons, the redemption of our bodies.
> (Rom 8:21–23)

As to the details of St. Paul's meaning, men may fairly differ; but his central thought seems clear. All created things have been subjected to vanity—to pain and suffering, no account taken of their will (*ouk hekousa*). Yet these are but the travail pains of a new birth; all that suffers shall be delivered from the bondage of corruption. Note how here (alone in the New Testament) are the sufferings of the whole creation alluded to, and how emphatic is the assertion that *every created thing* (*pasa hē ktisis*) is awaiting redemption; and this reaches them by the manifestation of the sons of God, "the firstfruits," or the elect.

> For if their [Israel's] rejection means the reconciliation of the world, what will their acceptance mean but life from the dead? If the dough offered as firstfruits is holy, so is the whole lump, and if the root is holy, so are the branches.
> (Rom 11:15-16)

The calling of the Jews is linked in God's plan with the world's salvation (v. 12). They are his people, in the truly divine sense, that by them the world's salvation may be worked out. They, as "firstfruits," represent and pledge the whole world.

> And so all Israel shall be saved.
> (Rom 11:26)

Here the apostle's whole argument and the tenor of the context—see particularly verse 7 (and 10:21)—very clearly distinguish "Israel" from the "election" (taken out of Israel), and show that by Israel *the whole nation* is meant. (Nor does this "election" conflict with the truth that in a wider sense, Israel itself (all Israel) forms the "firstfruits," i.e., the elect people; in fact, as already noticed, there is a double "firstfruits," both in the law and the gospel.) To sum up—(a) God's rejection of Israel is apparent only, for his calling is indefeasible, and therefore (b) *all* Israel shall be saved—without exception. (c) Israel, i.e., the elect, is so closely linked with the world, that their very rejection means the world's salvation—in God's mysterious plan. (d) So close is this tie between the elect and the world, that a further promise follows, that Israel's restoration shall be to the world "life *from the dead*" (v. 15)—a very suggestive phrase (chapter 6 on death). (e) This final salvation of Israel is coextensive with the whole nation for this further reason, because God's gifts are irrevocable, and were made to all.

> For the gifts and the calling of God are irrevocable.
> (Rom 11:29)

That is, what God gives, he gives effectually. His gifts and his call are *irrevocable*; this meaning our versions fail to convey (cf. Isa 40:11).[9] His word cannot fail of its purpose *finally*. When he calls, men *must hear*—a fact of the deepest significance. Let me ask the advocates of the popular creed, how, if God's call *must be obeyed* (for the whole context seems to show this to be clearly the apostle's meaning), sooner or later, there is any room for endless disobedience in hell?

> For God has consigned all to disobedience, that he may have mercy on all.
> (Rom 11:32)

The original is the widest possible; it is the whole mass of men to whom St. Paul refers. *The whole* is shut up unto unbelief in order that *the whole* may find mercy; and as the unbelief is actual and absolute, so, if there be a parallelism, must the mercy be equally actual and absolute.

> For from [out of] him and through him and to [into] him are all things.
> (Rom 11:36)

If so, God is the *End* of all things, i.e., unto (or perhaps into) him all things shall return. The original imports that God is at once *Source* and *Goal*; *Author* and *End* of all creation. No outlook can be more magnificent; no hope more divine, or broader, than this. Naturally, and characteristically, popular teaching practically ignores such a passage. (How different would have been its reception had it contained an anathema.)

> For it is written, "As I live, says the Lord, every knee shall bow to me, and every tongue shall confess to God." So then each of us will give an account of himself to God.
> (Rom 14:11–12)

St. Paul here quotes the great passage—Isaiah 45:22–23—in which salvation is promised to the entire human race, and which the apostle connects *with the judgment*. From the whole context it seems that Christ's

---

9 Editor: The Authorised Version and the Revised Version read: "For the gifts and the calling of God are without repentance"

empire over all is absolute; extends to the dead; implies salvation; and this salvation is linked with his (future) judgment. The word translated "confess" is properly to "offer praise" or "thanksgiving." Thus, St. Paul's view of the true meaning of the judgment day and its issues, seems in direct conflict with endless ruin.

> For as in Adam all die,
> so also in Christ shall all be made alive.
> (1 Cor 15:22)

As Adam actually brought death, spiritually, to all, so the last Adam actually gives life, spiritually, to all. No mere offer of life can satisfy the plain language of the text. Nothing less than life really—spiritually imparted to all by the last Adam—can fairly express St. Paul's meaning. But it is objected that as death in Adam is not final in some cases, so life in Christ is not final in some cases. (1) It would perhaps be enough to answer that the objection misses the mark, for the apostle's thoughts are set simply on one point—on asserting that a universal life succeeds, and *absorbs*, a universal death. But I will reply further, that (2) the plain words of the text require an *actual communication of life to all* through Christ, else the comparison between Adam and Christ is *not true;* for it is certain that the link of evil between Adam and the race is absolute, actual, and universal. And to call Christ the last Adam, while denying a tie of grace and life equally actual, absolute, and universal, is to dupe men. (3) The context involves the permanence of this life through Christ, for it claims for Christ a full victory; and requires us to believe that God will be all in all, at the end. (4) Life in Christ is thus not alone universal, it is final (vv. 24–28).

> For he must reign until he has put all his enemies under his feet. The last enemy to be destroyed is death. . . . When all things are subjected to him, then the Son himself will also be subjected to him who put all things in subjection under him, that God may be all in all.
> (1 Cor 15:25–28)

There is here, at *the end*, no place for sin—no trace of evil—no hell—for is not God *all and in all?* His empire is to be unbroken, universal, absolute. And the subjection of all to Christ is the same subjection by which he is to be subject to the Father, i.e., harmony and love, and peace; so the context requires. For note that in summing up the final results of Christ's work, the *same word* [*hupotassō*] is used (in the original) of Christ's own subjection to the Father, and of the subjection of Christ's own enemies to him. But, obviously, Christ's own subjection can only be love and harmony—hence *the subjection of Christ's enemies cannot mean their endless incarceration in evil and pain*. Such a conception is no less excluded by the assertion that finally God shall be all in all.

> O death, where is your victory? O death, where is your sting?
> (1 Cor 15:55)

I ask my readers quietly to think over the whole drift of this chapter and to mark the apostle's increasing rapture, as his argument expands, and as the prospect opens before him of a universe yet to be, from which every form of death and sin are banished. St. Paul's words are indeed explicit; and yet is there not more than this? There is surely in St. Paul a conviction, underlying all beside; a conviction (to which his warmest words give but imperfect expression) of the absolute triumph of Christ, of the flood of glory that is to sweep over all creation, in its widest sense.

> In Christ God was reconciling the world to himself, not counting their trespasses against them.
> (2 Cor 5:19)

Is God in earnest in telling us that he reconciles the *world*? *Does he mean what he says*, or does he only mean that he will try to reconcile it, but will be baffled? This question often rises unbidden, as we read these statements of the Bible, and compare them with the popular creed, which turns "all" into "some," when salvation is promised to "all," and turns the "world," when that is said to be saved, into a larger or smaller fraction of men.

> And the Scripture, foreseeing that God would justify the Gentiles by faith, preached the gospel beforehand to Abraham, saying, "In you shall all the nations be blessed."
> (Gal 3:8)

The relevance of texts like this lies in the fact that they show the true meaning of God's election, and are links in that great chain of promise of universal restoration—which St. Peter assures us God spoke by the mouth of all his holy prophets, and which he declares to mean the restitution of all things.

> ... as a plan for the fullness of time, to unite all things (*ta panta*) in him, things in heaven and things on earth.
> (Eph 1:10)

The universe in all its extent—the sum total of all existence—is to be brought back to Christ as Head, in unity. Such seems the view of the apostle. It is the same process as the reconciliation of all things (Col 1:15–20) and the subjection of all things to Christ (1 Cor. 15:27–28)—the homage and praise of all things rendered to Christ (Phil 2:10–11). But if the universe and its contents are summed up in Christ, where is any possibility of an endless hell, or of a creation permanently divided? The word translated "gather together in one" is found only here, and in Romans 13:9, as the law is summed up in one commandment, so is the universe to be summed up in Christ one day.

> And [God] put all things under his [Christ's] feet and gave him as Head over all things to the church.
> (Eph 1:22)

The original verb here is the same as that used of the subjection of Christ to the Father (1 Cor 15:28 and Phil 3:21; see note there).

> This mystery is that the Gentiles are fellow heirs, members of the same body, and partakers of the promise in Christ Jesus through the gospel.
> (Eph 3:6)

That is, fellow heirs with the Jews. But the promise to the Jews was that *all* Israel should be saved (see note on Rom 11:26.), and because Jew and Gentile are made one (Eph 2:14)—therefore all Gentiles seem to be included in the promise to all Israel (Rom 11:26).

> He who descended [i.e., Christ] is the one who also ascended far above all the heavens, that he might fill all things.
> (Eph 4:10)

But if Christ is to fill all things—the universe—how can evil subsist eternally? This cannot be eluded by asking whether Christ, as God, has not always filled all things; for, to the apostle, there is some further and

Part Three—Universalism Asserted on the Authority of Scripture

special sense in which Christ is to fill all things (by the expulsion of evil), as a consequence of his completed work.

> He is the image of the invisible God, the firstborn of all creation. For by him all things were created, in heaven and on earth, visible and invisible, whether thrones or dominions or rulers or authorities—all things were created through him and for him. ... [God was pleased] through him to reconcile to himself all things, whether on earth or in heaven, making peace by the blood of his cross.
> (Col 1:15–20)

I gladly substitute for my own comments Lightfoot's note on verse 16:

> All things must find their meeting point, their reconciliation at length in Him from whom they took their rise; in the Word as the mediatorial agent, and through the Word in the Father as the primary source. The Word is the final cause[10] as well as the creative agent in the universe. This ultimate goal of the present dispensation in time is similarly stated in several passages. Sometimes it is represented as the birth throe and deliverance of all creation through Christ, as Rom 8:19.... Sometimes it is the absolute and final subjection of universal nature to him as 1 Cor 15:28.... Sometimes it is the reconciliation of all things through him as below, v. 20. Sometimes it is the recapitulation, the gathering up in one head of the universe in him, as Eph 1:10 ... all alike enunciate the same truth in different terms. The Eternal Word is the Goal of the universe, as he was its starting point. It must end in unity, as it proceeded from unity, and the center of this unity is Christ.[11]

If I venture to add anything it is to protest against explaining away these words. *Whatsoever* has issued from the Eternal Word, returns to him as its goal, reconciled, purified, and restored; no other meaning can be fairly extracted from the words quoted.

> That at the name of Jesus every knee should bow, in heaven and on earth and under the earth, and every tongue confess that

---

10 Editor: In Aristotelian metaphysics, a "final cause" is the *telos*, the end, the goal, the purpose of a thing—that at which it aims.

11 Editor: J. B. Lightfoot, *Saint Paul's Epistle to the Colossians and Philemon* (London: 1875). Joseph Barber Lightfoot (1828–89) was a highly respected New Testament scholar and Bishop of Durham (1879–89).

> Jesus Christ is Lord, to the glory of God the Father.
> (Phil 2:10–11)

This is St. Paul's statement of the great vision (Rev 5:13), in which every created thing in heaven and on earth and under the earth unites to sing blessing, etc., to God Most High. Could a picture more universal be painted—*every* knee, in heaven, on earth, under the earth bending, and every tongue proclaiming God's praise. Such is the force of the original. All things, says Lightfoot, "whatsoever and wheresoever they be. The whole universe, whether animate or inanimate, bends the knee in homage and raises its voice *in praise*."[12]

> [Christ] who will transform our lowly body to be like his glorious body, by the power that enables him even to subject all things to himself.
> (Phil 3:21)

In what sense this subjugation of all things to Christ is to be understood, is clear from the context, "who shall fashion anew the body of our humiliation, that it may be *conformed* to the body of his glory, according to the working whereby he is able even to subdue all things unto himself." Note the significance of this. No one can doubt that Christ is destined to subdue all things, but this passage shows *decisively* that Christ's subduing all things (in the scriptural sense) is *making them like unto himself*. (See note on 1 Cor 15:25.)

> This is good, and it is pleasing in the sight of God our Saviour, who desires all people to be saved and to come to the knowledge of the truth. For there is one God, and there is one mediator between God and men, the man Christ Jesus.
> (1 Tim 2:3–5)

"None can hinder his doing as he wills . . . Now his will is that *all* should be saved" (Jerome, *Comm. Eph.* 1.11). St. Paul here directs thanksgiving and prayer to be offered for all men on the express ground that God wills the salvation of all. And this divine will St. Paul grounds on the divine unity—a fact which marks this passage noteworthy: for the One God can have but one eternal (irresistible) purpose. "God is One, the One that is All, that binds up all in one, and one in all, and makes all one."[13] This divine oneness is no merely arithmetical proposition. It states

---

12 Editor: J. B. Lightfoot, *Saint Paul's Epistle to the Philippians* (London: 1868).

13 Editor: Jeremiah White, *The Restoration of All Things: Or, A Vindication of the*

PART THREE—Universalism Asserted on the Authority of Scripture

a deep spiritual fact, viz., that *oneness* is of the essence of the divine plan. A Creator who is *one*, and a creation perpetually *two* (i.e., perpetually divided into two classes), is to St. Paul a thing inconceivable. (See chapter 6 towards the end.)

> We have our hope set on the living God, who is the Saviour of all people, especially of those who believe.
> (1 Tim 4:10)

Any obscurity in this passage becomes clear the moment we reflect on God's plan by which the elect—those who believe—are first saved, and then become the means, here or in the ages yet to come, of saving all men.

> . . . our Savior Christ Jesus, who abolished death and brought life and immortality to light through the gospel.
> (2 Tim 1:10)

Death is *abolished*, and with death that which it in Scripture implies, sin and evil. For death *abolished*, and yet death in its worst form, the second death, maintained for ever, are plain contradictions. Will those who maintain the doctrine of conditional immortality explain how death can be abolished, and yet swallow up finally all sinners in a sentence of annihilation?

> For the grace of God has appeared, bringing salvation to all men.
> (Titus 2:11)

Yes, "bringing salvation to all men": this is precisely the larger hope. But how is "salvation brought to all men" consistent with the damnation of myriads of men—nay, of any man—if, as we are distinctly told, God's gifts are without repentance (i.e., effective and irrevocable)?

Petrine Texts

> He also went and preached to the spirits in prison.
> (1 Pet 3:19)

Goodness and Grace of God, to be Manifested at Last in the Recovery of His Whole Creation out of Their Fall (London: 1712). Jeremiah White (1629–1707) was a nonconformist minister and a chaplain to Oliver Cromwell. His defence of universalism was published posthumously.

These words amount to a complete overthrow of the popular view of the state of the sinful dead; for plainly they assert a process of redemption as *going on after death*. Remark, carefully, who they were to whom Christ took the gospel, and whom, as the following passage shows, he saved. They were those who had sinned against the greatest light known in their day, and *died in their sins*.

> For this is why the gospel was preached even to those who are dead, that though judged in the flesh the way people are, they might live in the spirit the way God does.
> (1 Pet 4:6)

Notice again here *the connection between judgment and salvation*. Even the (impenitent) dead were evangelized, *in order* that they should have the benefit of judgment, and thus live to God. (See on judgment, chapter 6.) Such a text literally cuts up the traditional creed root and branch.

> The Lord is not slow to fulfill his promise as some count slowness, but is patient toward you, not wishing that any should perish, but that all should reach repentance.
> (2 Pet 3:9)

If then any do perish finally, God's will and design must have been finally overthrown: it is obvious that a temporary resistance, permitted for wise ends, differs wholly from a final defiance of God's will.

Hebrews

> His Son, whom he appointed the heir of all things, through whom also he created the world.
> (Heb 1:2)

It is enough to say that these words express the larger hope, if fairly and fully understood. They teach the absolute universality of Christ's reign, which the repeated testimony of Scripture shows to be love and peace.

> You have put all things in subjection under his feet (etc.)
> (Heb 2:8–10)

Here is an addition to that very large class of passages which speak of Christ's kingdom as destined to extend over all things (e.g., Eph 4:10;

Part Three—Universalism Asserted on the Authority of Scripture

1:10; Phil 3:9–11; Rev 5:13, etc.). I have already shown that subjection to Christ means perfect harmony and peace, in the usage of the New Testament, see notes on Philippians 3:21, and 1 Corinthians 15:25. This remarkable passage proceeds to lay stress on Christ's death as embracing "every man" (v. 9)—the writer has already strongly asserted the dignity of man, and his vast inheritance, simply *as man* (vv. 6–7). This dignity, impaired by the fall, has been recovered by Christ, the Son of Man. And it was right that Christ should suffer in fulfilling the will of him [God], for whom are all things, and through whom are all things" (v. 10)—*all things whatsoever*; words that authorize the widest hope, for God is the goal of all creation (See Rom 11:36).

> Since therefore the children share in flesh and blood, he himself likewise partook of the same things, that through death he might destroy the one who has the power of death, that is, the devil.
> (Heb 2:14)

But the destruction of the devil, as holding the power of death, is quite inconsistent with the continuance of death and evil eternally.

> So when God desired to show . . . the unchangeable character of his purpose . . . .
> (Heb 6:17)

We admit that a seeming failure there may be of God's purpose: but no real failure is possible. What God's immutable counsel is, we see in 2 Peter 3:9, where the original word translated "willing" is the same as "counsel" here.

> He has appeared once for all at the end of the ages to put away sin by the sacrifice of himself.
> (Heb 9:26)

Sin has intruded and caused an appearance of failure in God's plan. Christ comes to *sweep sin away*. When will our opponents meet fairly the dilemma, viz., Christ fails, or succeeds in his purpose. If he fails, you contradict Scripture. If he succeeds, you contradict your dogma.

> Jesus Christ is the same yesterday and today and forever.
> (Heb. 13:8)

The same throughout "the ages"; words little heeded I fear; and yet which virtually contain the essence of the gospel—the sum and substance of our hope. For what is it these words teach? Not the superficial view that Christ is now a Saviour, and will in future be merely a Judge to condemn; but that, what he was on earth that he is now, and that he will be, through "the ages" (judging ever, but only a Judge that he may by it be a Saviour). They bid us look to a series of ages yet to come, and there see Jesus Christ still working to save; doubtless by penalty, by fiery discipline, in the case of hardened sinners; but still the same Jesus, i.e., Saviour, and destined to continue his work of salvation till the last wanderer shall have been found.

Conclusion

So far from producing every possible passage that teaches the larger hope, I might have easily cited other texts that teach, or imply, the same. Take but two clauses of the Lord's prayer: "Our Father," these two words really involve the whole question—they form a tie, never to be broken, between man and God. "Your will be done on earth as it is in heaven." But how is his will done in heaven? It is *universally* done. Shall it not then be *universally* done on earth too? Does Christ put into our mouths a petition that he does not design to fulfill, in even larger measure than we can hope? I might have also quoted "God is love." To this point all his attributes converge. Love is that character that united they form (love infinite and unchanging). Can this love consign to endless agony its own children? Can infinite love ever cease to love?—let the apostle [Paul] reply: "love *never fails,*" it is inextinguishable.[14]

I would sum up by repeating the three propositions already stated: (1) Christ's purpose of salvation was deliberately formed to include the whole of our race, and no less. (2) He received for this end *all power*, i.e., power over all wills, all evil, all obstacles, whatsoever and wheresoever. (3) The Bible claims; the prophets claim; the evangelists claim; the apostles claim; Christ claims absolute success in this task (Isa 45:22–23;

---

14 In the above brief notes I have not attempted an exhaustive comment. It has been my aim to point out the plain natural meaning of the passages cited, in their bearing on the future destiny of man, and to present this meaning in the most simple and straightforward way. Specially have I urged the imperative necessity of truthfulness, of assuming that what the sacred writers say, that they mean, in the ordinary acceptation of their words—that in saying, e.g., "I make all things new," Christ really meant all things and not some things; that in saying, "God is the Saviour of all men," the apostle meant that God really does save all men.

PART THREE—Universalism Asserted on the Authority of Scripture

55:11; 53:11; John 12:32; 17:4; 1 Cor 15:22, 27–2; Rom 5:15–21; 11:29–32; 2 Tim 1:10, etc).

A few words of earnest caution must be added here. I trust it has been made plain in these pages that in teaching universal salvation I have not for a moment made light of sin, or advocated the salvation of sinners while they continue such. I earnestly assert the certain punishment of sin (awful it may well be, in its duration and its nature for the hardened offender), but in all cases directed by love and justice to the final extirpation of evil. Nay, I have opposed the popular creed on this very ground, that it in fact teaches men to make light of sin, and that in two ways: first, because it sets forth a scheme of retribution so unjust as to make men secretly believe its penalties will never be inflicted; and second, because it in fact asserts that God either will not, or cannot, overcome and destroy evil and sin, but will bear with them for ever and ever.

I repeat that not one word has been written in these pages tending to represent God as a merely good-natured Being, who regards as a light matter the violation of his holy law. Such shallow theology, God forbid that I should teach. Infinite Love is one thing; Infinite Good-nature a totally unlike thing. Love is never feeble, it is (while most tender) most inexorable. In the light of Calvary it is that we are bound to see the guilt of sin. But let us beware, lest, as we stand in thought by the cross, we virtually dishonour the atonement by limiting its power to save—by teaching men that Christ is after all vanquished; lest, while in words professing to honour Christ, we, in fact, make *him a liar*, for he has never said, "if I be lifted up, I will draw some men," or even "most men," but *"I will draw all men to me."*

9

What the New Testament Teaches

Eschatological Punishment

"The word 'hell' the sacred writers *never* use in the sense which is generally given to it."
—Dr. Ernest Petavel[1]

"Nous sommes peutêtre engages dans quelque erreur enorme, dont le Christianisme un jour nous fera rougir, comme il nous a fait rougir de la torture, de l'esclavage, de la contrainte en matiere de religion."
—Alexandre Vinet[2]

---

1 Editor: Emmanuel Pétavel-Olliff, *The Struggle for Eternal Life; Or, The Immortality of the Just, and the Gradual Extinction of the Wicked.* 2 vols. (London: 1875). Emmaunel Pétavel-Olliff (1836–1910) was a Swiss pastor and biblical scholar. The book in question was a translation of *La fin du Mal*, his defence of conditional immortality.

2 Editor: Alexandre Rodolphe Vinet (1797–1847) was a Swiss Protestant theologian and pastor. He defended freedom of conscience in religious matters. The text says, "We are perhaps engaged in an enormous mistake of which Christianity will make us roar, as it made us roar about torture, slavery, and coercion in matters of religion."

Part Three—Universalism Asserted on the Authority of Scripture

Orientation

Affirming the Whole Bible

WE are often met with the objection, "You look only *at one side of the Bible.*" I am determined that, in these pages, no room shall be given for the objection. Most true then it is, that there runs through Holy Scripture a current seeming (to an English reader) to teach the final destruction of the impenitent, and in some few passages their endless punishment. Most fully do I admit all this. I say, *seeming* to teach, advisedly. For the Bible was not written, as vast numbers appear to think, in English, by some Englishman in the nineteenth century, for his fellow Englishmen. It comes to us from very distant ages; in very many parts; the work of very many minds, but one and all writing from an oriental standpoint, saturated with oriental habits of thought, and in oriental phrase and style. Therefore, all depends *on the sense* in which the terms in question are used. Let us go to the Bible itself to decide. Those who turn to the paragraph which follows the note on St. Matthew 3:12 (in this chapter) will see how far from indicating hopeless ruin are the very strongest phrases employed. In the usage of Scripture itself "death" and "destruction" are indeed very often the path to life (see chapter 6).

Admitting then these two currents, we at once feel that they are not equal in *quality;* we feel instinctively the divineness of the one; it is deeper, diviner, broader, stronger. We feel its kindred with all that is noblest in our nature—I do not mean with what we like best, but with what we recognize as best and most divine, alike in God and in man.

"But the current of terror is louder." No, I do not think so. It may seem so from habit, or because sinners do not readily rise to what is broad and divine. To them vengeance is more credible than love. Yet even were it the louder current, I may point out that God is ever found "in the still small voice" [1 Kgs 19:11–13]. Nor is that which lies on the surface always, or even often, the true meaning of Scripture. Thus, in the predictions of the Messiah, the surface current, which wholly misled the Jews, spoke of a Conqueror, and of splendid earthly triumph. But the true meaning lay underneath the surface, in those fewer, less prominent, but diviner predictions of a suffering Saviour, of his life of toil.[3]

3 See Samuel Cox, *Salvator Mundi* (London: 1877).

Feeling this, I would face in all frankness all the facts, and entreat an honest and thorough examination. I hope to show, that while undoubtedly the penalties threatened against sinners are terrible, still they are not endless. I believe that *not one passage* can be found anywhere in the Bible that so teaches, when fairly translated and understood.

Preliminary Considerations

I must ask you, before examining these passages, carefully to bear in mind the following considerations:

(1) When the horrors of endless sin and pain are so stoutly defended on the (supposed) authority of the Bible, it is well to remember that slavery was *unanimously* defended for more than fifteen hundred years on exactly similar grounds; so was the infliction of most cruel tortures; so was religious persecution with its indescribable horrors; so was the existence of witches, and the duty of burning them alive. Nay, every theologian in Europe was for centuries persuaded of the truth of actual sexual intercourse between evil spirits and men and women.[4] "Holy men," you say, "everywhere defend endless pain and evil on the authority of Scripture." Holy men, I reply, have with *absolute unanimity* defended, on the authority of Scripture, tenets and practices so abominable that one shudders in attempting to recall them.

(2) A fact of the *deepest significance* is this: that although certain phrases existed, by which the idea of unendingness might have been conveyed, yet none of these is applied by our Lord amid his apostles to the future punishment of the impenitent. Those interested are invited carefully to weigh this very striking fact.

(3) Thus, *aidios* [eternal] or *ateleutetos* [endless] are never used of future punishment in the New Testament. Nor is it anywhere said to be *aneu telous* "without end," nor do we read that it shall go on *pantote*, or *eis to diēnekes* " for ever."

(4) Is it, I ask, conceivable that a sentence so awful as to be absolutely beyond all human thought, should be pronounced against myriads upon myriads of hapless creatures, in language ambiguous, and *admittedly*

---

4 Editor: Genesis 6:1–4, in which the sons of God (i.e., members of the divine council) interbred with the daughters of men, was the biblical basis for such beliefs. In folklore, the incubus was a demon that took on a male form to impregnate a woman and a succubus was a demon that took on female form to seduce a man.

Part Three—Universalism Asserted on the Authority of Scripture

capable of a very different meaning, and *habitually so used in the New Testament*, and in the Greek version of the Old Testament, from which our Lord and the apostles quote?

(5) It is certainly a strong confirmation of the view that asserts that no unlimited penalty is taught in the New Testament to find so great a body of primitive opinion (and that specially of the Greek speaking Fathers), teaching universalism *on the authority of the New Testament* (See chapters 4–5). All such teaching obviously contains an implied assertion that the texts, usually relied on, do not teach endless penalty.

(6) Again, while the texts quoted in favour of the salvation of all men use language clear and explicit, and are a fair rendering of the original in all cases, it is not so in the case of the passages usually alleged to prove endless torment. In those cases where they seem to the English reader so to teach, they are either mistranslated or misinterpreted, or both. Hence, we see how inaccurate is the assumption, all but universally made, that these terms that seem to teach endless pain and evil *are in the Bible*. They are merely in a certain human and fallible translation of the Bible, a totally different thing.

(7) It is also to be noted that not a few of the passages usually quoted in support of the traditional creed do not, even if the accuracy of the translation be admitted, contain any assertion of endless pain, though they may seem to teach final destruction (to an ordinary reader).

(8) Finally, in addition to all the above, a great difficulty remains in the way of the advocates of the traditional creed. They *dare not carry out their own principles*. Their principle of interpreting the Bible would compel them to believe what they do not believe, and to teach what no reasonable person could presume to teach. (a) First, it would compel them to believe in the endless torment of the vast majority, at least of all adults. (b) Next it would compel them to believe that this torment goes on for ever and ever *in the sight of the Lamb and the holy angels* (for their satisfaction?) (Rev 14:10) and indeed probably in the sight of all the Blessed (Isa 66:24; Luke 16:23). But these two things they disbelieve. Nor do they believe the statement that God creates evil (Isa 45). Nor have they any ground, so far as I know, for their disbelief, except that these statements, taken literally, are unworthy of God, i.e., are immoral. Thus, in fact, they stand self-condemned. Nor do they really believe that Israel is to fall and rise no more (Amos 5:2); nor do, or can they, take literally the

many threats of the same kind which Scripture contains (see paragraph after note on Matthew 3:12, in this chapter).

Translating "Hell"

(9) As instances of wholly incorrect rendering, take the words translated "hell," "damnation," "everlasting," "eternal," "for ever and ever." "Hell" is, in the New Testament, the rendering of three widely differing Greek words, viz., "Gehenna," "Hades," and "Tartarus," such is the *accuracy* of our translation!

"*Gehenna*" occurs eleven times in the New Testament as used by our Lord, and once by St. James. In the original Greek it is taken almost unchanged from the Hebrew (*Ge-hinnom*, i.e., valley of Hinnom), an example which our translators ought to have followed, and rendered *Gehenna*, as it is, by *Gehenna*. By retaining the term hell, with its inevitable associations, they in fact are prejudging the question, and are assuming the part not of translators but of commentators. This valley lay outside Jerusalem: once a pleasant vale, and later a scene of Moloch worship, it had sunk into a common cesspit at last. Into it were flung offal, the carcasses of animals, and it would seem, of criminals, and in it were kept fires ever burning (for *purification* be it remembered), while the worms were for ever preying on the decaying matter. The so-called undying worm and flame, of which so much has been made (a) were—at least in their literal and primary use—temporal and finite, (b) preyed only on the dead body, (c) and were for purification; three particulars essential to the due understanding of the passages on which the dogma of endless torments has been so unfairly based.

Hades is a term denoting the state or place of spirits, good and bad alike, after death. Our revisers[5] have, by a tardy justice, struck "hell" as its translation out of their version. It occurs in the Gospels and Epistles five times, twice in the Acts, and four times in Revelation. It denotes that intermediate state or place that succeeds death; a state which, in our recoil from Romansh error,[6] we have almost ceased to recognize at all.

---

5 Editor: Allin refers to the translators of the Revised Version (1885), a revision of the King James Version, commissioned by the Church of England.

6 Editor: Allin refers to the Catholic teaching on purgatory, rejected by most Protestants.

PART THREE—Universalism Asserted on the Authority of Scripture

Tartarus occurs once only (in the verbal form) in the New Testament, in 2 Peter 2:4. It also is a classical term, used there most often, although not always, for the place of future punishment of the wicked. Here St. Peter applies it not to human beings, but to the lost angels;[7] and in their case it denotes *no final place of torment*, but a prison in which they are kept *awaiting* their final judgment; hence, to render it by the term "hell" is simply preposterous.

"Damnation," "damned"—both of these terms represent merely two Greek words (and their derivatives), *krinō* and *katakrinō*, i.e., to judge and to condemn. Our revisers have felt how unwarrantable the former translation was, for which there is indeed this excuse, that probably, when the Authorized Version was made [1611], the meaning of the word "damn" was far milder than it has since become (as was certainly the case with the term "hell"). To import into these words the idea of endless torment is to err against all fairness, for they simply mean[8] to "judge," and at most, to "condemn."

Most significant is it that in the original of the New Testament, the horrors of unending agony, which these terms conjure up for so many, vanish when we come to know that by "damnation" is simply meant "judgment," or at most "condemnation," as our revisers now fully admit in their version; and by "hell" is only meant, either the place of disembodied souls, *Hades*, (as our revisers now render it) or the Jewish *Gehenna* (see Revised Version), a place of temporary punishment in its literal sense, where the worms fed continually, it is true, and the fire for ever burned; but in both cases purifying, and causing no pain (for the bodies were those of the dead); and where both "undying" worm and "unquenchable" fire have long since, in their literal sense, passed away.

True it is that Gehenna was by the Jews used, symbolically, of the place of future punishment—a fact to be fully admitted. But the evidence adduced by Farrar,[9] by Cox,[10] and by an Article in the *XIX Century*, August, 1890, seems to make it clear that, *normally*, at least, Gehenna

---

7 Editor: In this Petrine text, the "lost angels" in question are the members of the divine council (the "sons of God") who came down and interbred with the daughters of men in Genesis 6:1–4. The biblical text is drawing on the story told in *1 Enoch*.

8 In one passage (2 Pet 2:3), the word "damnation" represents a different Greek word, *"apōleia,"* and is rightly rendered by our revisers as "destruction" in that place.

9 F. W. Farrar, *Mercy and Judgement: Last Words on Christian Eschatology with Reference to Dr. Pusey's "What Is of Faith?"* 2nd ed. (London: 1882), 180–215.

10 Samuel Cox, *Salvator Mundi*, 70–75.

was not believed to involve endless punishment.[11] It was *certainly* a place from which deliverance was possible, and probably one from which deliverance was the rule.[12] Jewish opinion was by no means fixed, but fluctuated much as to the details and the duration of future punishment. Some Rabbis seem to have held (as did certain of the Fathers) the final annihilation of the wicked.

True it is, most true, that while no unending torment is threatened by our Lord, yet his words do convey most solemn warning to the sinner—warning that gains in real weight when its true import is discerned, because the conscience recognizes its justice. I accept, then, heartily—as their true natural sense, every warning, however terrible, and every penalty threatened against sinners in Scripture; but that true natural sense is not, as I hope to show, in any case that of endless evil and torment. My quarrel with the advocates of the popular view (as far as the Scripture is concerned) is that, while assigning to one class of texts a meaning, which they cannot fairly bear, they at the same time wholly put out of view, blot out from the Bible in fact, a very large and weighty class of passages, furnished by the New Testament, in favour of universal salvation. Thus, as so often happens, when men persist in seeing only one side, they fail to apprehend the true meaning, even of that one side, which they present to us as though it were the whole.

Aiōn and Aiōnios

Let us next consider the true meaning of the words *aiōn* and *aiōnios*.[13] These are the originals of the terms rendered by our translators "ever-

---

11 Editor: *The Nineteenth Century* was a monthly magazine founded in 1877 as a forum for debate between leading intellectuals of the day.

12 Editor: This final clause is going too far. The notion of Gehenna as an afterlife punishment was an undeveloped and somewhat fluid image, used by some early Jewish writers to speak of annihilation, by others of eternal torment, and by others of a punishment from which there would be deliverance for many (though not for all). Some authors used it in more than one of these ways. It was *not a fixed concept* that Jesus could take "off the peg" and use. Indeed, Jesus is the *first* person for whom we have evidence using Gehenna to speak of judgment. *All* other examples of its use come from several decades later, after the fall of Jerusalem in AD 70, and may well reflect later developments. So we need to allow Jesus' own usage to determine what he may have meant by it.

13 "The word by itself, whether adjective or substantive, never means endless" (Canon F. W. Farrar [*The Wider Hope*, London: 1890]). "The conception of eternity,

PART THREE—Universalism Asserted on the Authority of Scripture

lasting," "for ever and ever": and on this translation, so misleading, a vast portion of the popular dogma of endless torment is built up. I say, without hesitation, misleading and incorrect; for *aiōn* means "an age," a limited period, whether long or short, though often of indefinite length; and the adjective *aiōnios* means "of the age," "age-long," "aeonian," and never "everlasting" (of its own proper force). It is true that it may be applied as an epithet to things that are endless, but the idea of endlessness in all such cases comes not from the epithet, but only because it is inherent in the object to which the epithet is applied, as in the case of God.[14] Much has been written on the import of the aeonian (eternal) life. Altogether to exclude, with F. D. Maurice,[15] the notion of time seems impracticable, and opposed to the general usage of the New Testament (and of the Septuagint). But while this is so, we may fully recognize that the phrase "eternal life" (aeonian life) does at times pass into a region above time, a region wholly moral and spiritual. Thus, in St. John, the aeonian life (eternal life) of which he speaks is a life not measured by duration, but a life in the unseen, life in God. Thus, e.g., God's commandment is life eternal (John 12:50); to know him is life eternal (John 17:3); and Christ is the eternal life (1 John 1:2; 5:20).

Admitting, then, the usual reference of *aiōnios* to time, we note in the word a tendency to rise above this idea, to denote quality, rather than quantity, to indicate the true, the spiritual, in opposition to the unreal,

in the Semitic languages, is that of a long duration and series of ages" (Rev. J. St. Blunt, *Dictionary of [Doctrinal and Historical] Theology* [2nd ed. London: 1872]). "'Tis notoriously known," says Bishop [George] Rust [d. 1670], "that the Jews, whether writing in Hebrew or Greek, do by *ōlām* (the Hebrew word corresponding to *aiōn*) and *aiōn* mean any remarkable period and duration, whether it be of life, or dispensation, or polity" [*A Letter of Resolution concerning Origen and the Chief of His Opinions*. London: 1661]. "The word *aiōn* is never used in Scripture, or anywhere else, in the sense of endlessness (vulgarly called eternity, it always meant, both in Scripture and out, a period of time; else how could it have a plural—how could you talk of the aeons and aeons of aeons as the Scripture does?" (Charles Kingsley ["Endless Torments Unscriptural," 1857]). So the secular games, celebrated every century were called "eternal" by the Greeks (See Huet, *Origeniana* 2:162).

14 Editor: A book-length defence of this very point has now been made by Ramelli and Konstan in *Terms for Eternity: Aiônios and Aidios in Classical and Christian Texts*.

15 Editor: F. D. Maurice had argued that "eternal" referred, not to time, but to God. As such, it designated a timeless quality and not to a temporal duration at all. Eternal life was sharing in God's nature; eternal death was being excluded from God. He strongly opposed any notion of everlastingness. It was his view that eternal punishment did not mean endless punishment that famously cost him his chair at King's College in London.

or the earthly. In this sense, the eternal is *now* and *here*. Thus, "eternal" punishment is one thing, and "everlasting" punishment a very different thing, and so it is that our revisers[16] have substituted for "everlasting" the word "eternal" in every passage in the New Testament where *aiōnios* is the original word. Further, if we take the term strictly, eternal punishment is impossible, for the "eternal," strictly speaking, has no beginning.

Again, a point of great importance is this, that it would have been impossible for the Jews, as it is impossible for us, to accept Christ, except by assigning a limited—nay, a *very limited* duration—to those Mosaic ordinances that were said in the Old Testament to be "for ever," to be "everlasting" (aeonian). *Every line of the New Testament, nay, the very existence of Christianity is thus in fact a proof of the limited sense of* aiōnios *in Scripture.* Our Baptism in the name of Jesus Christ, our Holy Communion, every prayer uttered in a Christian church, or in our homes, in the name of the Lord Jesus: our hopes of being "for ever with the Lord"—these contain one and all an affirmation most real, though tacit, of the temporary sense of *aiōnios*.

As a further illustration of the meaning of *aiōn* and *aiōnios*, let me point out that in the Greek version of the Old Testament (the Septuagint)—in common use among the Jews in our Lord's time, from which he and the apostles usually quoted, and whose authority, therefore, should be decisive on this point—these terms are *repeatedly* applied to things that have long ceased to exist.

Thus, the Aaronic priesthood is said to be "everlasting" (Num 25:13). The land of Canaan is given as an "everlasting" possession, and "forever" (Gen 17:8, and 13:15). In Deuteronomy 23:3, "for ever" is distinctly made an equivalent to "even to the tenth generation." In Lamentations 5:19, "for ever and ever" is the equivalent of from "generation to generation." The inhabitants of Palestine are to be bondsmen "for ever" (Lev 25:46). In Numbers 18:19, the heave offerings of the holy things are a covenant "for ever." Caleb obtains his inheritance "for ever" (Josh 14:9). And David's seed is to endure "for ever," his throne "for ever," his house "for ever"; nay, the Passover is to endure "for ever"; and in Isaiah 32:14, the forts and towers shall be "dens *for ever, until* the spirit be poured upon us." So in Jude 7, Sodom and Gomorrah are said to be suffering the vengeance of eternal (aeonian) fire, i.e., their temporal overthrow by fire, for they have a definite promise of final restoration (Ezek 16:55).

---

16 Editor: The translators of the Revised Version (1885).

Part Three—Universalism Asserted on the Authority of Scripture

Christ's kingdom is to last "for ever," yet we are distinctly told that this very kingdom is to end (1 Cor 15:24). Indeed, quotation might be added to quotation, both from the Bible and from early authors,[17] to prove this limited meaning of *aiōn* and its derivatives; but enough has probably been said to prove that it is wholly impossible, and indeed absurd, to contend that any idea of endless duration is *necessarily* or *commonly* implied by either *aiōn* or *aiōnios*.

Further; if this translation of *aiōnios* as "eternal," in the sense of endless, be correct, *aiōn* must mean eternity, i.e., endless duration. But so to render it would reduce Scripture to an absurdity. In the first place, you would have over and over again to talk of the "eternities." We can comprehend what "eternity" is, but what are the "eternities"? You cannot have more than one eternity.[18]

The doxology would run thus: "Yours is the kingdom, the power, and the glory, 'unto the eternities.'" In the case of the sin against the Holy Ghost, the translation would then be, "it shall not be forgiven him, neither in this eternity nor in that to come." Our Lord's words in Matthew 13:39, would then run, "the harvest is the end of [the] eternity," i.e., the end of the endless, which is to make our Lord talk nonsense. Again, in St. Mark 4:19, the translation should be, "the cares," not of "this world," but "the cares of this eternity choke the word." In St. Luke 16:8, "The children of this world," should be "the children of this eternity." Romans 12:2 should run thus; "Be not conformed to this eternity." In 1 Corinthians 10:11, the words, "upon whom the ends of the ages are come," should be: "the ends of the eternities." Take next, Galatians 1:4: "That he might deliver us from this present evil age," should run thus: "from this present evil eternity." In 2 Timothy 4:10, the translation should be: "Demas has forsaken me, having loved this present eternity." And "Now once at the end of the ages has he been manifested," should read, on the popular view, "at the end of the eternities."

---

17 Thus Josephus calls "aeonian," the temple of Herod, which was actually destroyed when he wrote. Philo never uses *aiōnios* of endless duration. [Editor: Ramelli and Konstan, in *Terms for Eternity*, survey all instances of *aiōnios* in Classical Greek sources, Second Temple Jewish sources, and patristic sources, and argue that the word almost never meant everlasting or eternal, except when applied to God.]

18 Editor: This is not necessarily the case. One can certainly have many infinite sets (e.g., the set of all whole numbers, the set of all even numbers, the set of all prime numbers). However, if one is speaking of endless periods of time that are *sequential*, one following the other, then one does have a problem. Obviously, the first *aiōn* would never cease, so none of the subsequent *aiōns* would ever start. This is Allin's point.

What the New Testament Teaches

Let me state the dilemma clearly. *Aiōn* either means endless duration as its necessary, or at least its ordinary significance, or it does not. If it does, the following difficulties at once arise: (1) How, if it mean an endless period, can *aiōn* have a plural? (2) How came such phrases to be used as those repeatedly occurring in Scripture, where *aiōn* is added to *aiōn*, if *aiōn* is of itself infinite? (3) How come such phrases as "for the *aiōn*" or "*aiōns* and *beyond*"? (*ton aiōna kai ep aiōna kai eti: eis tous aiōnas kai eti.*—See LXX Exod 15:18; Dan 12:3; Mic 4:5). (4) How is it that we repeatedly read of the *end* of the *aiōn*? (Matt 13:39–40, 49; 24:3; 28:20; 1 Cor 10:11; Heb 9:26). (5) Finally, if *aiōn* be infinite, why is it applied over and over to what is strictly finite? (E.g., Mark 4:19; Acts 3:21; Rom 12:2; 1 Cor 1:20; 2:6; 3:18; 10:11, etc., etc.) But if an *aiōn* be not infinite, what right have we to render the adjective *aiōnios* (which depends for its meaning on *aiōn*) by the terms "eternal" (when used as the equivalent of "endless") and "everlasting"?

Indeed our translators have really done further hurt to those who can only read their English Bible. They have wholly obscured a very important doctrine, that of "the ages." This, when fully understood, throws a flood of light on the plan of redemption, and the method of the divine working.

Take a few instances which show the force and clearness gained, by restoring the true rendering of the words *aiōn* and *aiōnios*. Turn to St. Matthew 24:3. There our version represents the disciples as asking "what should be the sign of the end of the world" [Authorized Version]. It should be "the end of the *age*"; the close of the Jewish age marked by the fall of Jerusalem.[19] In St. Matthew 13:39–40, 49, the true rendering is not the end of the "world," but of the "age," an important change. So St. John 17:3, "this is life eternal," should be "the life of the ages," i.e., peculiar to those ages, in which the scheme of salvation is being worked out.

Or take Hebrews 5:9; 9:12; 13:20, "eternal salvation" should be "aeonian" or of the ages; "eternal redemption" is the redemption "of the ages"; the eternal covenant is the "covenant of the ages," the covenant peculiar to the ages of redemption. In Ephesians 3:11, "the eternal purpose" is really the purpose of "the ages," i.e., worked out in "the ages." In Ephesians 3:21, there occurs a suggestive phrase altogether obscured (as usual, where this word is in question) by our version, "until all the generations of the age of

---

19 Editor: The residual supersessionism in Allin's theology is typical of much Christian theology and is to be regretted. However, Allin is correct that Jesus is speaking of the end of the age, not the end of the world.

the ages." Thus it runs in the original, and it is altogether unfair to conceal this elaborate statement by merely rendering "throughout all ages." In 1 Corinthians 10:11, "the ends of the world" are the "ends of the ages." In chapter 2:6–8, the word *aiōn* is four times translated "world," but it should be "age" or "ages" in all cases.

Here it is impossible to avoid asking how—assuming that *aiōn* does mean "world"[20] in these cases—how it can yield, as an adjective, such a term as "everlasting"? If it mean "world," then the adjective should be "worldly," "of the world." And great force and freshness would be gained in our version by always adhering to the one rendering "age."

Again, in Hebrew 11:3, "the worlds were framed," should be "the ages." In Hebrews 9:26, "now once in the end of the world" should be, "in the end of the ages." Take, again; the closing words of St. Jude, which run literally, "To the only God, be glory . . . before every age, and now and unto all the ages," i.e., before the ages began, and now, and throughout all the ages yet to come. So Revelation 1:6, "glory" is ascribed to Christ, "unto the ages of the ages," in the original. In 1 Timothy 1:17, "the King eternal" should be "the King of ages"; in 6:17, "charge them that are rich in this world" should be "in this age." 2 Peter 2:17, "the mist of darkness is reserved for ever" should be "for the age," for a period finite, but indefinite. A striking phrase closes this epistle, chapter 3:18, obscured in our translation—which renders "to him be glory both now and for ever," instead of, as the original requires, "unto the day of [the] age," see verse 5, which explains the reference.

I might easily go on, but enough has been said to show that Scripture designs teach us the "doctrine of the ages." In these repeated instances there must he some definite purpose in the use of these peculiar terms; and we must deeply regret the unfairness and inconsistency which in the case of *aiōn* mars and renders unfair our versions. Thus, it would be interesting to ask on what principle our revisers[21] have in one brief epistle employed *five* different words (or phrases) to translate this one word, *aiōn* (e.g., Eph 1:21; 2:2, 7; 3:11, 21, e.g., "world," "course," "age," "eternal," "for ever"). Such are the devious ways of our teachers, and our translators.[22]

---

20 Editor: The so-called King James Version (1611), standard in English churches of Allin's time, translated *aiōn* as both "eternal" and as "world." The latter translation is now rarely employed by Bible translators.

21 Editor: The translators of the Revised Version (1888).

22 Editor: Allin needs to be careful here. Every translator knows that to insist that

Let me state briefly the doctrine of "the ages."

> It will, I think, be found, that the adjective—*aeonian*—whether applied to "life," "punishment," "covenant," "times," or even God Himself, is always connected with remedial labour, and with the idea of ages or periods, in which God is working to meet and correct some awful fall.
> —Andrew Jukes[23]

There is present in the word in fact a certain spiritual force, and a reference to "the ages" in which a redeeming process is going on. It is the more needful to insist on this, because in our recoil from the Roman Catholic teaching about Purgatory, etc., we have gone too far; we have been trained to limit all God's possible dealings with us to the narrow span of our earthly existence. But this is to shut our eyes to the truer and higher teaching of the gospel. What does God mean by the repeated reference to these "ages," when he speaks in the New Testament of his redeeming plan? On the popular view these passages go for nothing. Is this fair or reasonable? But by accepting what they plainly teach, we are enabled to harmonize God's threatenings with his clearly expressed purpose to save all men finally. Indeed, in these "ages" is indicated the true scope of redemption, as a vast plan, extending over many periods or ages, of which our present life forms but one, and it may be, a very brief part.[24] Through these "ages" it is clearly taught that Christ's work is to go on, for "Christ is *the same* today, and yesterday, and unto 'the ages'" (Heb 13:8); and he assures us that he is alive "unto the ages," and has the "keys of death and of Hades" (Rev 1:18), words significant in this connection. This then, we, taught by Scripture, believe to be the "purpose of the ages" (Eph 3:11). Nay, we are permitted in Holy Scripture a momentary glance beyond that limit, in these glorious words: "Then"—at the expiry, it would

---

a single word in one language must translate as a single word in another language, irrespective of context, is a recipe for disaster. The context must determine which word best renders the meaning. That said, in this case, Allin has a point.

23 Andrew Jukes, *The Second Death and the Restitution of All Things*.

24 Editor: Samuel Cox's *Salvator Mundi*, on which Allin draws at various points, contains a key chapter on "The Christian Doctrine of the Aeons." It was a theme that was strong in the patristic universalist tradition developed by Origen, but it plays little if any role in mainstream theology today. In the Origenian tradition, the final *apokatastasis* was "beyond" the ages to come and would dawn when they ceased. This notion had some unexpected resonances with the growing nineteenth-century appreciation of the vast age of the earth and its other-things-being-equal long future duration.

seem, of these ages—"comes the *end*," when every enemy vanquished and every wanderer found, "Christ shall have delivered up the kingdom unto God, and God shall be all in all" (1 Cor 15:28).

Examining Some "Hell" Texts

Matthew's Gospel

MATTHEW 3:12

> He shall burn up the chaff with unquenchable fire.
> (Matt 3:12; Luke 3:17).

Any good lexicon will show us how little the term translated "unquenchable" [*asbestos*] really conveys that idea. Homer often applies it to "glory," "laughter," "shouting," to the brief fire that consumed the Grecian fleet. Eusebius twice says that martyrs were consumed in "unquenchable" fire (*Hist. eccl.* 6.41). Cyril calls the fire that consumed the burnt offering, unquenchable (*De ador.* book 10).

It is terrible to think of the agony caused to loving hearts by misleading translations; perhaps most of all by that disgraceful rendering that "never shall be quenched" (Mark 9:43–45)—now removed[25] *after* it has worked such evil.

Further, if the context be examined, it points to a *present*, and impending judgment, and not a future punishment. The whole figure implies not the endless torture of the wicked in a future life, but the destruction by Christ's fiery baptism, already working, of that chaff which surrounds every grain. Nor can any figure express more completely than does burning *chaff* the idea of evanescence.

And here I earnestly beg my readers to pause and seriously consider, not traditional prejudices, but plain facts. The usage of Scripture shows

---

25 Editor: The KJV's "the fire that never shall be quenched" was modified to "where the fire is not quenched" in the RV (1885). The point of the biblical image is that no one can stop the fire doing its work—it is unquenchable. Allin is objecting to the Authorized Version implicitly importing the notion of a fire that burns *for ever*. The Greek text itself, he says, does not make such claims.

What the New Testament Teaches

decisively that to press words like "unquenchable," etc., to a narrow literal meaning makes perfect nonsense. Take some typical instances. A fire is kindled against Israel which is to burn for ever (Jer 17:4), and yet *all* Israel is to be saved (Rom 11:26), so is "the whole house of Israel" (Ezek 39:25). And again, Israel's hurt is "incurable"; her pain is "incurable" (Jer 30:12, 15), but in a moment it is added, "I will heal you" of the (incurable) wound (v. 17). So, too, Hosea more than once declares the rejection of Israel by God, and that no more mercy remains for her: and yet in the same breath asserts her final pardon and reconciliation (Hos 1:6–10; 2:4, 10, 14, 15, 19, 23; 9:15; 13:14; 14:4); passages well worth our pondering over.

In Amos the same striking teaching occurs. Israel, it is said, shall no more rise (Amos 5:2). Yet God will raise her up (Amos 9:11). All fair readers can see the extreme significance of all this; and how very far the principle of interpretation, so plainly involved, really goes. Again, though, as we have seen, an express promise of the restoration of all Israel is given, and repeated in the New Testament (Rom 11:26), yet an "unquenchable" fire is to burn them up (Jer 7:20); "everlasting" reproach and "perpetual" shame is to come on them (Jer 23:40); "perpetual" hissing (Jer 18:16); and "perpetual" desolations (Jer 25:9); "perpetual" backsliding (Jer 8:5).

Surely some righteous indignation is called for against those who construct a sentence of endless damnation against countless millions of God's children (very largely) on the strength of phrases like the above, whose meaning is so completely misapprehended.

Let us examine further. Not alone is the sin of Israel "incurable," but so is the wound of Samaria (Mic 1:9). And yet this "incurable" wound is to be cured, for the captivity of Samaria is to be turned again (Ezek 16:53). Nor is this all. Sodom and Gomorrha suffer the vengeance of "eternal fire" (Jude 7), and are to be a "perpetual" desolation (Zeph 2:9), and yet the "perpetual" desolation is to end in restoration (Ezek 16:53); and this temporary meaning is constantly that of "perpetual" in Scripture (e.g., Lev 3:17; 24:9, 25:34; Jer 33:40). So, too, Ammon is to be a "perpetual" desolation (Zeph 2:9); is to fall and rise no more (Jer 25:21, 27); and yet it is to be restored (Jer 49:6). And so Elam is to fall and rise no more (Jer 25:27), yet in the latter days it is to be restored (Jer 49:39). The same is true of Egypt (compare Jer 25:19, 27, with Ezek 29:13, etc.). And Moab is to be destroyed, and yet restored (Jer 48:4, 47).

Part Three—Universalism Asserted on the Authority of Scripture

Now why is all this? Why in the prophets do threats most awful and hopes most radiant jostle one against another? Why do mercy and terror, despair and joy, alternate, as the portion of the *same* persons? Why this seeming chaos? Not because God has conflicting purposes, but precisely because he has no conflicting purposes: threats and hopes are blended because threats and hopes serve the same end. Nay, were the threats of Scripture still more awful than any recorded, were they as clear as they are so often figurative and obscure; and were we stripped of most (or all) of the *direct* promises of universal salvation, still we might have hope, knowing that "God is love," and that with God "all things are possible."

Matthew 5:22

> I say to you, that whosoever is angry with his brother without a cause shall be in danger of the judgment: and whosoever shall say to his brother, Raca, shall be in danger of the council: but whosoever shall say, You fool, shall be in danger of hell fire.
> (Matt 5:22)

The popular interpretation reduces these words to an absurdity.

> It is incredible that to call a man a fool should be so much a worse crime than to call him Raca, that, whereas for the one offense men are to be brought before a court of justice, for the other they are to be damned to an everlasting torment.
> —Samuel Cox, *Salvator Mundi*

The hellfire of this passage is the fire of *"Gehenna."*

Matthew 10:28

> Fear him who is able to destroy both body and soul in hell.
> (Matt 10:28)

These words point to God's power, rather than to his intention. They say God is able to destroy soul and body; they do not say that God will do so. And if they do point to an intention, those who read what has been said above on "death," "destruction" (chapter 6), will readily perceive how accordant with the usage of Scripture it is to make destruction and death a path to life.

MATTHEW 16:26

> For what is a man profited, if he shall gain the whole world, and lose his own soul [life]?
> (Matt 16:26)

This certainly shows that a man by persisting in sin may lose his soul, a loss greater than that of the whole world. But (1) how does this loss teach endless torment, or endless sin? (To be shut out of God's presence for an age would far overbalance the enjoyment of the whole world for a lifetime.) Or how (2) does it prove anything against a final restitution, against Christ's seeking and finding the lost soul?

MATTHEW 23:33

> You serpents, you generation of vipers, how can you escape the damnation of hell?
> (Matt 23:33)

No comment is needed here, but to reinstate the true rendering—"the judgment of *Gehenna*."

MATTHEW 5:29–30; 18:8–9

> And if your right eye offends you, pluck it out, and cast it from you: for it is profitable for you that one of your members should perish, and not that thy whole body should be cast into hell. And if your right hand offends you, cut it off, and cast it from you: for it is profitable for you that one of your members should perish, and not that your whole body should be cast into hell.
> (Matt 5:29–30, cf. 18:8–9)

These passages are so similar that they may be considered together, and may be compared with Mark 9:43–50, where a full comment is given. The "hell" of the text is "Gehenna," and in chapter 18:8–9, "hellfire" is the fire of Gehenna, and everlasting fire is aeonian fire.

Part Three—Universalism Asserted on the Authority of Scripture

Matthew 25:46

> And these [the goats] shall go away into everlasting punishment: but the righteous [the sheep] into life eternal.
> (Matt 25:46)

This text, if fairly translated, seems to require an interpretation quite distinct from that of the popular theology, and opposed to it. (a) "Everlasting" and "eternal" represent *aiōnios*, and mean "of, or belonging to, an age"—aeonian. (b) If a punishment absolutely endless were intended it seems unaccountable that a word should be used which *habitually* does not mean endless, but the opposite. (c) The word translated punishment [*kolasis*] means *pruning*, i.e., corrective punishment, and should be so rendered.[26]

So that which is threatened seems the *opposite* of our popular hell; it is a corrective process, "proper to the age"—or "ages." And of this beneficent purpose there is a hint, often unnoticed, in the term applied to those on the left hand; it is properly "kids" or "kidlings" [*epiphos*], a diminutive, implying a certain affection. And so for the paschal offering a kid was eligible (Exod 11:5) equally with a lamb; and in the catacombs [in Rome] the Good Shepherd is at times depicted as bearing home on his shoulders *a kid*, not a lamb, i.e., a *goat*, not a sheep. Nor must we forget that in Revelation 20:11, the throne of judgment is *white*—the sign of peace and amity.

But it is said that the same word [*aiōnios*] is applied to the happiness of the saved and to the punishment of the lost; and that, if it does not mean endless in the latter case, the bliss of the redeemed is rendered uncertain. I reply (1) even were it so, we are not at liberty to mistranslate, but (2) in fact it is certainly not so. True, the text does assign an aeonian penalty and an aeonian reward, but this *leaves perfectly open* the whole question of the precise duration of either.[27] For the term aeonian is quite indefinite, it does not touch the question of the limit of time; it simply teaches that

---

26 Editor: See p. 52, fn. 46 for some caution about this claim.

27 It must be noted that the endlessness of the happiness of the redeemed depends, not on any meaning we assign to *aiōnios*, but on its own intrinsic nature, as resulting from union with him, who is endless life; and on texts easily to be found elsewhere, e.g., "he that does the will of God abides for ever" (1 John 2:17); "because I live you shall live also" (John 14:19); "if a man keep my saying he shall never taste of death" (John 8:51; cf. Ps 102:28).

both reward and penalty go on to a future age or ages. The question what will happen *after* this age or ages is not raised in this passage.

I have in these comments made two assumptions, both very doubtful, and both favourable to the traditional creed. (1) I have assumed the reference of *aiōnios* to time, which is not capable of proof; for with perfect fairness it may have here that spiritual, ethical meaning it unquestionably at times has in the New Testament; and the meaning then would be, that just and unjust pass into aeonian (i.e., spiritual) states of punishment and bliss respectively.

(2) I have assumed the primary reference of this passage to the final judgment, but that is most improbable; for these words close a continuous discourse extending over chapters 24–25, which our division into chapters obscures. There is no break throughout. And the question of the disciples in chapter 24 is not about the end of the "world," but of the "age."

Thus, if we divest ourselves of traditional impressions, and take Scripture itself as our guide, we see that it is not fair to refer to a distant future that judgment of which Christ himself says distinctly that *all the things* he is speaking of should be fulfilled before the passing away of the then generation (24:34); and which finds a perfectly natural fulfillment in the terrible calamities, consequent on the fall of Jerusalem, and the end of the (Jewish) age (as these events would be described in Eastern metaphor). And indeed our Lord's words, "all the nations" (v. 32) seem to refer to national judgments, and to indicate, in dramatic form, the principle on which judgment falls on nations; certainly increasing reflection makes this reference seem increasingly probable.[28]

---

28 Editor: Allin's tentative proposal that the judgment of the sheep and the goats refers to the fall of Jerusalem in 70 AD, rather than to final judgment, is not unlike some recent proposals within the guild of New Testament scholarship. The problem of linking it with the fall of Jerusalem, however, is that the judgment in question is of the *nations*, not of Israel—in biblical language "the nations" does not include Israel. The nations are judged according to the way in which they treated God's covenant people. But Allin is right to draw attention to the possibility that the judgment in question is not final judgment, but a historical judgment: the context and the fact that the judgment in question is primarily concerned with "nations" are indeed suggestive. The language of *aiōnois* punishment and life does not rule out such interpretations.

Part Three—Universalism Asserted on the Authority of Scripture

Mark's Gospel

Mark 9:43–50

> 43 And if thy hand cause thee to stumble, cut it off: it is good for thee to enter into life maimed, rather than having thy two hands to go into hell, into the unquenchable fire. 45 And if thy foot cause thee to stumble, cut it off: it is good for thee to enter into life halt, rather than having thy two feet to be cast into hell. 47 And if thine eye cause thee to stumble, cast it out: it is good for thee to enter into the kingdom of God with one eye, rather than having two eyes to be cast into hell; 48 where their worm dieth not, and the fire is not quenched. 49 For every one shall be salted with fire. 50 Salt is good: but if the salt have lost its saltness, wherewith will ye season it? Have salt in yourselves, and be at peace one with another.
> (Mark 9:43–50, Revised Version)

(a) Note, first, that the revised text omits verses 44 and 46 [both of which say, "Where their worm dieth not, and the fire is not quenched," KJV], which lend so much weight to the threats here uttered.²⁹

(b) The whole passage depends on the statement of verse 49—a fact generally overlooked—*"For every one* shall be salted with fire." These words assign the reason for the preceding clauses, and seem to show that the true reference in this passage is to some sacrificial or purifying process, which every one must undergo; as in 1 Corinthians 3:13, "The fire shall test every man's work." If the sacrifice be not made voluntarily, if the eye or the foot be not sacrificed, a sharper sacrifice and a severer penalty will be demanded.

(c) The word translated hell is *Gehenna*.

(d) The phrase, "the fire is not quenched," is quoted from the Old Testament, where it, or a similar phrase, occurs in the Septuagint twelve times (Lev 6:13; 2 Kgs 22:17; 2 Chr 34:25; Isa 1:31, 34:10; Jer 7:20; 17:27; Ezek 20:47–48; Amos 5:6; Jer 21:12). In *all* these passages the flame is *temporary*. Isaiah 66:24 is the text specially quoted here; and the natural and primary reference is to the worm and to the fire that preyed on the

---

29 Editor: A wide range of ancient Greek manuscripts of Mark omit verses 44, and 46. The general scholarly consensus is that the original text of Mark omitted these verses. It was such a judgment that lies behind the RV removing the verses.

dead bodies of malefactors, cast out into Gehenna. In Eastern metaphor these worms and this fire are said not to die, and not to be quenched; because the fires were kept always burning to drive away pollution, and the worm was always preying on the corpses and offal.

(e) In nature both fire and worm purify.

(f) The (indefensible) translation, "the fire that never shall be quenched" (v. 45) disappears in the Revised Version.[30] The original word is the same occurring in Matthew 3:12, and in the note on that text, proved to have been frequently applied to fire, (and to many things,) even of the briefest duration.

MARK 3:29

> But he that shall blaspheme against the Holy Spirit shall never have forgiveness, but is in danger of eternal damnation.
> (Mark 3:29; Matt 12:32)

On a question involving the interpretation of a phrase, drawn from a language still living in their day, it is most important to note the attitude of most Fathers towards this sin. "The notion," says Bingham, "that most of the ancients had of the sin against the Holy Ghost, was not that it was absolutely unpardonable, but that men were to be punished for it both in this world and in the next, unless they truly repented of it."[31] So Athanasius[32] says of this sin, "If they repent they may *obtain pardon*, for there is no sin unpardonable with God to them who truly repent" (*Comm. essent.*). So St. Chrysostom,[33] "We know that this sin *was forgiven to some*

---

30 Editor: The KJV adds these words to the end of v. 45. Thus, "it is better for thee to enter halt into life, than having two feet to be cast into hell, *into the fire that never shall be quenched.*" As mentioned previously (see on Matt 3:12), the evangelist's point is that the fires cannot be stopped from doing their work, not that they will burn *for ever*.

31 Editor: Joseph Bingham, *Origines ecclesiasticae, or The Antiquities of the Christian Church*. 10 vols. (London: 1708–22), 2:921. Rev. Joseph Bingham (1668–1723) was a tutor at Oxford University, but was compelled to leave after giving a controversial sermon. He moved to the country, near Winchester, and began work on his magnum opus, intended to organize the mass of data on the early Christian writings into topics, so that readers could see the range of views presented on the topic in question.

32 Editor: Athanasius (c.297–373) was Bishop of Alexandria, best known for his fierce opposition to the Arian heresy.

33 Editor: John Chrysostom (c.349–407) was Archbishop of Constantinople, famed for his preaching.

Part Three—Universalism Asserted on the Authority of Scripture

that repented of it." What is then the than meaning of it? That it is a sin less capable of forgiveness than all others (*Hom.* 42; *In Matt.* 12). So Victor of Antioch[34] (*Cat. Marc.* 3), St. Ambrose (*De penit.* 2.4, etc.). And so Dionysius (Syrus),[35] as late as the tenth century,[36] says: *"Many, who did blaspheme against the Holy Ghost, afterwards repented, and obtained pardon"*[37] Two points are *very noteworthy*: (1) that these Fathers did not believe any sin to be in itself unpardonable, (2) that they did not believe the phrases *eis ton aiōna* or *aiōnios* to mean literally "never" or "everlasting," as our version renders them. And so nobody will press the similar phrase as to the iniquity of Eli's house not being purged *for ever* (1 Sam 3:14) to mean that it was literally unpardonable.

I may add that if we retain the authorized text in St. Mark, the word rendered "damnation" is merely "judgment." But the true reading is probably *hamartēmatos* = sin, i.e., is guilty of a sin, whose results last into a future age or ages.[38] The phrase translated "never," is so far from meaning this literally, that it is elsewhere in Scripture followed by *"and beyond,"* i.e., and *after* (e.g., Exod 15:18; Dan 12:3, etc.). In St. Matthew, the parallel passage is differently worded. "It shall not be forgiven in this world (i.e., *age*) nor in that which is to come." These words imply that there is forgiveness for sin after this life in very many cases—an awkward fact for the traditional creed—and therefore repentance *after* death is quite possible. Next, there is no assertion whatever that *after* this age, and that to come, there may not be forgiveness, even for the sin against the Holy Ghost.

A few words may be added. This terrible sin is the sin of the Scribes and Pharisees, i.e., of the hard, narrow religionist, and not of the ungodly. The sin itself is very clearly defined, "because they said, he has an unclean spirit" (v. 30). Its essence lies in confounding the works of the good [Spirit] and evil spirits, as, e.g., assigning to God any kind of evil

---

34 Editor: All we know of Victor of Antioch is that he was "a presbyter of Antioch" in the fifth century. The only work attributed to him is his commentary on Mark.

35 Editor: Dionysius Syrius is Dionysius bar Salibi (d. 1171), Bishop of Mar'ash then Metropolitan of Amid. He was a very learned Syrian Orthodox scholar and writer, composing a commentary on the whole Bible.

36 Dionysius lived in the twelfth century, not the tenth.

37 Translated from a Syriac MSS. (Dublin 1762). [Editor: I do not know which Syriac manuscript Allin translated here, though it is presumably held at Trinity College, Dublin.]

38 Editor: The Greek *hamartēmatos* is not the usual word for sin (*hamartia*), but is clearly related to it.

act. Must it not be a near approximation to this awful sin to assign to God deeds that, like endless torture, our conscience tells us are evil and cruel?

Mark 14:21

> The Son of Man indeed goes, as it is written of him: but woe to that man [Judas] by whom the Son of man is betrayed! Good were it for that man if he had never been born.
> (Mark 14:21; Matt 26:24)

Note *carefully* that our revisers admit that the original requires a different rendering, viz., "Good were it for *Him* [Christ], if that man had not been born." This obviously alters the meaning completely: it gives an intelligible sense to say that, if there were no Judas, it would have been better for the Master, whom he betrayed. The common rendering *certainly violates* the ordinary rules of Greek syntax. Our opponents must be reminded of this, and also that even if taken in their extremist sense, the words of Judas' doom wholly fail to prove that he was condemned to endless suffering; for they would be satisfied to the utmost if Judas were annihilated at the last day: nay, had he at the moment of betrayal died, "and never suffered one pang more, they would be to the fullest extent true."[39]

The difficulty of pressing these words literally, even taking the ordinary rendering, is very great. For Judas did in some sort repent (Matt 27:3).

> Four signs of true repentance are present: (1) his rejection of the wages of iniquity; (2) his open confession of his guilt; (3) his public testimony to the innocence of the man whom he had betrayed, and (4) his profound consciousness that the just wage of such a sin was death.
> —Samuel Cox[40]

Judas, as one of the twelve, had a special promise of sitting to judge the twelve tribes of Israel [Matt 19:28]. But this was, you will say, *conditional*. Yes, I reply, just so. And may not a threat be as conditional as a promise? And if not, then will any one explain, *why not?* The rich are

---

39 Editor: I do not know which source this brief quotation is taken from. It could be from a work by an annihilationist.

40 Editor: Samuel Cox, *Expository Essays and Discourses*. 8 vols. (London: 1877) 1:356. Samuel Cox (1826–93) was a Baptist minister and a defender of universal salvation.

expressly shut out of the kingdom of heaven. Do our opponents take that literally?

Luke's Gospel

LUKE 16:19–31

There was a certain rich man who was clothed in purple and fine linen and fared sumptuously every day. But there was a certain beggar named Lazarus, full of sores, who was laid at his gate, desiring to be fed with the crumbs which fell from the rich man's table. Moreover the dogs came and licked his sores. So it was that the beggar died, and was carried by the angels to Abraham's bosom. The rich man also died and was buried. And being in torments in Hades, he lifted up his eyes and saw Abraham afar off, and Lazarus in his bosom.

Then he cried and said, "Father Abraham, have mercy on me, and send Lazarus that he may dip the tip of his finger in water and cool my tongue; for I am tormented in this flame."

But Abraham said, "Son, remember that in your lifetime you received your good things, and likewise Lazarus evil things; but now he is comforted and you are tormented. And besides all this, between us and you there is a great gulf fixed, so that those who want to pass from here to you cannot, nor can those from there pass to us."

Then he said, "I beg you therefore, father, that you would send him to my father's house, for I have five brothers, that he may testify to them, lest they also come to this place of torment.'"

Abraham said to him, "They have Moses and the prophets; let them hear them."

And he said, "No, father Abraham; but if one goes to them from the dead, they will repent."

But he said to him, "If they do not hear Moses and the prophets, neither will they be persuaded though one rise from the dead."
(Luke 16:19–26, NKJV)

(a) Dives, like Judas, is a son of Abraham, who so addresses him, "and *all* Israel shall be saved." (b) Dives was not in hell, but in Hades (see Revised Version), i.e., in the intermediate state before the day of judgment, for his brethren are alive. (c) Dives is distinctly improved by his chastisement: he has learned to think for others. Can God by his fiery discipline *produce this amendment merely to crush it out in a future state of hopeless pain?* Is this credible? (d) It is not said that the gulf shall continue impassible; what is said is that it is so (was then so). The case is as if a man were imprisoned for a fixed time, and his friends are sternly told "between him and you is a barrier placed which cannot be passed." This would be exactly true, though the barrier were to be removed, when the fixed period of punishment ceased. (e) And in any case why may not this gulf be passed by Christ, by him who has the *"keys of death and Hades"*? (f) Those inclined to doubt what I have just said may be well referred to St. Ambrose, who, commenting on Psalm 119, says thus: "So then that Dives in the Gospel, although a sinner, is pressed with penal agonies that he may *escape the sooner" (Exp. in Ps.),* thus asserting clearly his belief in Dives' final salvation. And St. Jerome expressly asserts twice over that Christ liberated those souls *who were in this very place (Comm. Zach.* 9.11; *Comm. Isa.* 14.7); thus asserting his belief that the great gulf may be crossed. (g) Those taking this parable as a literal description of hell and heaven must be reminded of a very serious difficulty which they ignore.[41] The blessed *look on at the torments of the lost.* Is, then, this vision of a ghastly hell and its lost and suffering ones to be really for ever before the eyes of the blessed? (Rev 14:10, 11, to enhance their joy?)

John's Gospel

John 3:36

> He that believes on the Son has everlasting life: and he that believes not the Son shall not see life; but the wrath of God

---

41 Editor: Since Allin wrote, New Testament scholars have drawn attention to various 'parallels' to the parable in ancient Egyptian, Hellenistic, and Second Temple Jewish sources. This has led to a growing caution on the part of scholars regarding attempts to deduce from the parable anything about Jesus' beliefs about postmortem existence. The suggestion of some is that Jesus was simply taking motifs from widely known folk tales and adopting and adapting them to make a point about wealth and poverty. He was not necessarily thereby affirming a literal understanding of the picture painted.

> abides on him.
> (John 3:36)

The meaning is clear—the unbeliever, *continuing such*, shall not see life, but if he repent he may obtain peace. If it were not so, all would be lost.

JOHN 5:29

> And shall come forth; they that have done good, unto the resurrection of life; and they that have done evil, unto the resurrection of damnation.
> (John 5:29)

Here it is enough to point to the revised translation, "the resurrection of *judgment*" [*krinō*], not even condemnation.

Miscellaneous Texts

Of the parables of judgment, let me say that to build awful doctrines on these sacred stories, and their metaphors, is quite unfair. Take perhaps the most stern of all—those in St. Matthew 13, and even in these there is no question of the end of "the world," which is a total mistranslation—it should be "the age" merely; and no hint is given that the "fire" spoken of should go on for ever. Admitting to the fullest the warning they convey, and the stern side of Christ's teaching, yet their true meaning is obscured by adjourning to some remote future the facts asserted; forgetting that the judgment throne is now standing, and that we are now standing before it; and that Christ's "unquenched" fire is now burning; *unquenchable*, thank God, till (as the whole usage of the word in the original imports) it has fully done its work.

Here I add a few notes on certain passages that escaped notice in former editions. It is said that Esau "found no place of repentance" (Heb 12:17). But Esau, though he lost irrevocably the birthright, was blessed. "By faith Isaac blessed Jacob and Esau" (Heb 11:20).

St. Paul speaks of aeonian destruction as awaiting sinners (2 Thess 1:9); and of destruction as their end (Phil 3:19). I must refer my readers to what has been sufficiently said already on the word "aeonian," and on the scriptural use of such terms as "destruction" and "death."

Some argue from the words "Behold now is the day of salvation" (2 Cor 6:2) that salvation is confined to this life only. I might reply in the words of an old Father,[42] "with God *it is always now*"; and might ask whether the more reasonable adherents of the traditional creed are prepared in all cases to limit salvation to this present life? But a reference to the original shows here, too, mistranslation and misinterpretation. St. Paul is quoting Isaiah 49:8, which speaks *of Christ*: "In *a* day [not the day] of salvation have I helped you." It is Christ (*not the sinner*) who is helped, i.e., made strong for the task of saving. In fact, St. Paul is warning the Corinthians not to receive in vain the gospel, and he supports this plea by a quotation, which reminds them of the grace given to Christ to save in this dispensation. Don't reject, he would urge, an offer accompanied by so much grace. As to a limit of time set, beyond which Christ cannot finally save those who now reject the gospel, that is not in St. Paul's mind here or in Isaiah's.

I take next Hebrews 6:4–6. (a) Almost all the Ancients explained this of Baptism, i.e., the writer, in their view, simply forbids a repetition of Baptism. Certainly (b) few, if any, teachers of today would understand this text to deny the power of repentance to any sinner in this life; but why, if so, *so far as this text is concerned*, should the power of repentance be denied after this life? (c) The impossibility here spoken of is not *qua God*, i.e., these words do not bar his grace. (d) Thus, Christ saves those whose salvation he seems to pronounce impossible, e.g., the rich Zacchaeus [Matt 19:24–26; Luke 19:1–10].

Hebrews 10:26–31 presents us with a passage parallel to the above, which asserts that for willful sin fearful judgment is reserved, and that there is no more sacrifice available. Many Fathers understand this passage merely to teach the impossibility of a second Baptism. The true meaning seems to be that for those continuing in willful and aggravated sin, only the certain prospect of terrible judgment remains: they need cleansing by fire (see, chapter 6 on fire and judgment). The writer is here quoting Deuteronomy 32, where the divine judgment is viewed rather on its hopeful side, "I kill *and I make alive*, I have wounded *and I heal*" (v. 39). I am perfectly aware that this cleansing by fire and judgment will seem strange to some. Why? Because a narrow tradition shuts out from their creed a vital doctrine of Scripture.

---

42 Editor: I do not know which of the Fathers Allin had in mind. The view expressed is that of the majority.

PART THREE—Universalism Asserted on the Authority of Scripture

A few words I may add on that saying of our Lord's, "If the salt has lost his savor wherewith shall it be salted?" (Luke 14:34; stated more strongly in Matt 5:13; cf. Mark 9:50). It is enough to say, though to human power the salt be wholly lost, yet he, who makes the camel to pass through the needle's eye, can assuredly restore the salt. (Scientifically speaking, I believe salt never does lose its savour.)

Revelation

We have now considered all the passages of any weight in the New Testament, and supposed to teach the popular creed, except those of the book of Revelation. To this let us turn, first protesting against the unfairness of building a definite theory of hell on the imagery of a book of mysterious visions, and full of highly-toned metaphors. Its visions speak the language not of prose, but of poetry, the poetry of an Eastern race, far more imaginative and highly wrought than that of the West. To judge these metaphors as though they spoke the language of scientific theology is worse than unfair, it is even absurd.

REVELATION 14:9–11

> And the third angel followed them, saying with a loud voice, If any man worship the beast and his image, and receive his mark in his forehead, or in his hand, the same shall drink of the wine of the wrath of God, which is poured out without mixture into the cup of his indignation; and he shall be tormented with fire and brimstone in the presence of the holy angels, and in the presence of the Lamb: and the smoke of their torment ascends up for ever and ever: and they have no rest day nor night, who worship the beast and his image, and whosoever receives the mark of his name.
> (Rev 14:9–11)

Take, then, the passages most often quoted to support endless evil and pain (e.g., Rev 14:9–11). Terrible as it seems at first sight, it is, I believe, really concerned with the times of Nero—who is the Beast. The worshippers of the Beast who are to be tormented are his followers; and the reference in the torment is to the terrible earthly calamities actually happening to Rome at that epoch.[43] Who, of whatever school of thought, is there who does not feel a weight rolled away, when he perceives that the true meaning of the worshippers of the Beast being tormented night and day for ever and ever, *in the presence of the Lamb and the holy angels*, may be fully found in the terrible earthly sufferings which befell Rome, "while the Lamb and the holy Angels are, in human language, represented as cognizant of this punishment"?[44] Even Mr. Elliott, in his *Horae Apocalyptica*, explains this passage of merely temporary judgment.[45]

I should like our opponents to be frank and to say whether they really believe that the smoke of the torment of the lost goes up *for ever and ever in the sight of the Lamb and of the holy angels*? If they do not—as I believe to be the case—will they with equal fairness explain why *on their own principle* they require us elsewhere to take literally similar sayings and similar figures? But—to resume—whether Nero be or be not the Beast, it remains certain that language equally strong is used elsewhere of *merely transient* and *temporal* judgments. In proof of this, turn to Isaiah 34:9–10, and read the deeply impassioned language in which it describes the temporal calamities of the land of Idumea—its streams are "to be turned into pitch—*its dust into brimstone—its land into burning pitch—it shall not be quenched night nor day—its smoke is to go up for ever.*"

Now when we know that these metaphors—sounding so awful—do yet refer to judgments of a momentary duration, so to speak, we shall the better be able to assign its true meaning to all the figurative and poetical language of this book. Nor do I speak of this book only. The whole Bible is Oriental. Every line breathes the spirit of the East, with its hyperboles and metaphors, and what to us seem utter exaggerations. If such language be taken literally, its whole meaning is lost. When the sacred writers want to describe the dusky redness of a lunar eclipse, they say the moon is "turned into blood." He who perverts Scripture is not the

---

43 Editor: This preterist reading of the fiery punishment of Revelation 14 (i.e., one that sees the fulfillment in past historical events) has defenders in the modern New Testament guild. A recent overview of Revelation that takes such a historical approach and which defends a universalist reading is Nik Ansell, "Birthpangs of the New Creation," in Nik Ansell, *The Annihilation of Hell*, 391–423.

44 Editor: I have been unable to locate the source of this short quotation.

45 Edward Bishop Elliott, *Horae Apocalypticae; Or, A Commentary on the Apocalypse, Critical and Historical* (London: 1844). This was a massive commentary on Revelation that became something of a standard work. It went through five edition (1844, 1846, 1847, 1851, and 1862). Edward Elliott (1793–1875) was an evangelical Anglican priest with a premillennialist eschatology.

PART THREE—Universalism Asserted on the Authority of Scripture

man who reduces this sacred poetry to its true meaning. Nay, that man perverts the Bible who hardens into dogmas the glowing metaphors of Eastern poetry—such conduct Lange, in his preface to the Apocalypse, calls "a moral scandal."[46] So with our Lord's words, if I take them literally I very often pervert their sense. Am I in very deed to *hate* my father and mother because Christ says it is necessary so to do [Luke 14:26]; or to pluck out my right eye literally [Matt 5:29]? Or take a case, well put by Canon [F. W.] Farrar, Egypt is more than once said, in the Bible, to have been an *iron furnace* to the Jews [e.g., Deut 4:20]; and yet their condition there was so far removed from being one of torment that they actually said, "it was well with us there," and positively sighed for its enjoyments. Therefore I maintain that no doctrine of endless pain and evil can be based on Eastern imagery, on metaphors mistranslated very often, and always misinterpreted. Having, then, considered the well-known passage in chapter 14, I close this chapter by discussing another often quoted passage.

REVELATION 21:8

> But the fearful, and unbelieving, and the abominable, and murderers, and whoremongers, and sorcerers, and idolaters, and all liars, shall have their part in the lake which burns with fire and brimstone: which is the second death.
> (Rev 21:8)

(a) It will be necessary to consider the entire context of this verse, if we desire to understand its purport. It opens with the vision of the great white throne (20:14), and we find that after the judgment of that great day, so far from death and hell (Hades) continuing, they are "cast into the lake of fire"—very unlike, nay, contradicting the popular view.

(b) Then comes a declaration that God is to dwell with men—not with the saints—but with men as such, and that as a consequence, they shall be *his people, and God shall be with them and be their God.*

(c) It is distinctly said, there shall be *no more death, neither sorrow, nor crying, nor any more pain.* Is this not a denial of an endless hell rather than an affirmation of it—nay, an emphatic denial of such a doctrine?

---

46 J. P. Lange, *The Revelation of John*. Translated by Evalina Moore (New York: 1874). John Peter Lange (1802–84) was a German Calvinist, Professor of Theology at Bonn, and a preterist in his interpretation of Revelation.

(d) Then comes a voice from the throne with a glorious promise, *"Behold I make all things new,"* not some things. Note, too, this promise is remarkably emphasized, it opens with the word *"Behold,"* to draw attention to it: it closes with the command to write it, "for these words are true and faithful." Was there no reason for this? Is there not thus attention drawn to this as the central point of the whole vision, i.e., *all things made new?* But this again is a denial of the popular creed.

(e) In close connection with such promises come the highly figurative threats of the lake of fire. It is perhaps possible to argue that this may imply (although I do not think so) the destruction of those cast into it; but it is *wholly impossible to understand it as teaching endless torment* in the face of what has just been promised—no more crying nor pain (v. 4).

Therefore, I conclude, looking at the repeated promises (see "c" and "d") of this very passage, which contrast in their *perfect clearness* with the highly figurative language of its threats,[47] looking at the true meaning of God's judgments and at the whole spirit of Holy Scripture—nay, its express declaration of universal restoration—that what is here taught is a fire that purifies while it punishes, a fire that is, in God's mysterious way, an agent in making all things new. (On the second death, see chapter 6.)

Conclusion

We thus see that the Apocalyptic visions lend no support to the dogma of endless torment. That doctrine is not, I believe, to be found in a single passage of Scripture if translated accurately and fairly interpreted. And here I would ask those who honestly believe that with this dogma of hell-fire is bound up the sole force able to deter men from sin, to remember that to assert this is to contradict the weight of human experience. For in every age experience has shown decisively that it is not the magnitude of the penalty that deters men from sin or crime, it is its reasonableness and the certainty of its infliction. On the contrary, few doctrines have done so much to shake the belief in any real punishment of sin hereafter as has

---

47 "How little can we build dogmas on such metaphors as the devil being cast with the Beasts (Nero and the Roman world powers) and the false Prophet (ch. 20:10–14) into the lake of fire and brimstone ... into which also are to be cast two such abstract entities as 'Death' and 'Hades.' At any rate this lake of fire is on the earth; and immediately afterwards we read of that earth being destroyed, and of a new heaven and a new earth, in which there is to be no more death or curse" [Editor: F. W. Farrar, *Mercy and Judgment*, chapter 15].

Part Three—Universalism Asserted on the Authority of Scripture

that of an endless hell. For nobody can be found who, *by his acts*, shows that he in fact believes it.

Hence, so long as it is taught, the whole subject of future punishment becomes, for the mass of mankind, doubtful and unreal. Thus, a tone of secret incredulity is fostered, an incredulity that, beginning at this particular dogma, assuredly does not end there, but affects the whole of revealed religion. It is not merely that those who still teach the popular creed thus furnish the sceptic with the choicest of his weapons by enlisting the moral forces of our nature on the side of unbelief. They do more than this. They thus, unconsciously I admit, but most effectively, teach men to profess a creed with the lips, to which the spirit and the life render no vital allegiance. By this means the whole gospel of Jesus Christ is lowered and discredited, for if men see a doctrine of this kind maintained in words, but in fact denied (because in practice found to be wholly incredible), they will assuredly apply the lesson, so learned, of professed belief and real scepticism, to the whole system of Christian truth.

I have, I trust, not shrunk from the appeal to Scripture; that appeal, I repeat, we court in the interests of the larger hope. But should some doubt still linger, some objections seem to be not wholly answered, then I would remind the wavering that to ask for mathematical certainty on these points is to ask for that which they never can obtain. No reasonable person expects mathematical proof of the existence of God. No great theological question exists that is not open to some questionings, more or less plausible, on scriptural grounds. To ask for a demonstration of the larger hope that shall leave no room for any plausible objection is to ask for that which no reasonable man asks in any similar case.

Before closing, I would dwell on a significant fact that often escapes notice. Even assuming, for argument sake, the accuracy of the interpretation placed by the traditional creed on the passages just discussed, even that wholly fails to prove endless punishment: that might be a reasonable ground for saying, "there are in Scripture two seemingly contradictory sets of passages. I must wait and pray till all becomes clear; and meantime I can formulate no conclusion." But it would furnish no fair ground for saying, "I must expunge from the Bible those passages that teach universal restoration." This is often forgotten, but it is not to be denied. And even this way of putting the case strains many points in favour of the traditional creed: (1) Because, since all admit God to be love, and nobody admits that God is cruel, the presumption is wholly in favour of the milder view, turning out the true one. (2) Because this view is in harmony with the declared will of God to save all men. (3) Because it is a maxim with theologians, uncontested and incontestable, that passages of Scripture which teach things unworthy of God are not to be understood literally: on this ground they refuse to believe literally the assertions of Scripture that God hardens the heart, and creates evil. If so, why are we bound to accept literally passages that, on the common interpretation, assign to God acts of terrible cruelty? (4) Because the popular view is not only cruel, but is dualistic: while the opposing view rests on this great principle, that good is always, finally, stronger than evil. (5) Because a promise binds in a sense that a threat does not, for nobody is aggrieved, though a threat remains unfulfilled: take, e.g., the case of Nineveh, where the threat was most precise and distinct.

And so I am unable to see, *even on the ground taken by advocates of the traditional creed*, that their conclusions are warranted. How much less are they warranted, when the interpretations of Scripture on which they rest, are shown to be untenable?

PART FOUR

*Conclusion:
Universalism Asserted*

10

Summary and Conclusions

"The little Pilgrim listened with an intent face, clasping her hands, and said, 'But it never could be that our Father should be overcome by evil. Is that not known in all the worlds?'"
—*A Little Pilgrim*[1]

"This word is strange and often terrible; but be not afraid, all will come right at last. Rest will conquer Restlessness; Faith will conquer Fear; Order will conquer Disorder; Health will conquer Sickness; Joy will conquer Sorrow; Pleasure will conquer Pain; Life will conquer Death; Right will conquer Wrong. *All will be well at last.*"
—Charles Kingsley[2]

---

1 Editor: Margaret Oliphant, *A Little Pilgrim in the Unseen* (London: 1882). Margaret Oliphant (1828–97) was a Scottish historical writer and novelist.

2 Editor: Charles Kingsley, *Madam How and Lady Why; Or. First Lessons in Earth Lore for Children* (London: 1869). The book was written to introduce children to the revolutionary new geology of the nineteenth century.

PART FOUR—Universalism Asserted

The Choice: God the Victor or God the Failure?

THE question of universalism is usually argued on a basis altogether misleading, i.e., as though the point involved was chiefly, or wholly, man's endless suffering. Odious and repulsive to every moral instinct, as is that dogma, it is not the turning point of this controversy. The vital question is this, that the popular creed, by teaching the perpetuity of evil, points to a victorious devil and to sin as finally triumphant over God. It makes the corrupt, nay, the bestial in our fallen nature to be eternal. It represents what is foulest and most loathsome in man, i.e., the most obstinate sin as being enduring as God himself. It confers the dignity of immortal life on what is morally abominable. It teaches perpetual anarchy, and a final chaos. It enthrones pandemonium as an eternal fact side by side with paradise; and, gazing over its fetid and obscene abysses, is not afraid to call this the triumph of Jesus Christ, this the realization of the promise that God shall be *"all in all."*

A homely illustration may make my meaning more clear. What should we say of a householder who, prizing purity before all things, and with ample power to gratify his tastes, should sweep into some corner every variety of abomination, there to rot on for ever under his sight? Nor is this all, for it is precisely the least rotten and offensive of the mass of moral filth that he removes and cleanses, while permitting the foulest of all (i.e., the most obstinate and the very worst sinners) to rot and putrefy for ever. Indeed, according to the current theology, it is exactly because the moral foulness of this mass is so great that it must endure for ever.

I have spoken very plainly, for our opponents do not realize what it is that they have been teaching, and still teach. I have spoken very plainly because of the moral scandal involved in lowering God below the level of humanity; because such teaching justly makes God odious to thousands; because of the manifold and painful evasions of the great moral issues involved; because of scepticism justified and increased.

How instructive is the evident perplexity our opponents feel in reconciling with the triumph of Christ the perpetual duration of that evil, which he expressly came to destroy (1 John 3:8). Thus some (able) men now plead that the resistance of the lost to God will be "passive" only, and their evil "inactive."[3] But passive resistance, if it be not a contradiction

---

3 Editor: He is possibly referring to the view of T. R. Birks, in *The Victory of Divine Goodness* (London: 1867). On which, see the Introduction.

in terms, is some form of resistance, and inactive evil is some form of evil, and in both cases Christ's very purpose is defeated. And obviously the worst forms of obstinate sin, for which hell is reserved, are the most active, are essentially active. Therefore, to say that they become inactive is to say that hell exercises a *remedial* influence. And if hell be remedial how near are our opponents to the larger hope?

Further, I wish they would frankly tell us how this perpetuity of evil is possible. De Quincey says:

> Having anchorage in God, innumerable entities may possibly be admitted to a participation in the divine *aiōn*. But what interest in the favour of God can belong to falsehood, to impurity, to malignity? . . . Evil would not be evil, if it had that power of self-subsistence which is imparted to it in supposing its aeonian life to be co-eternal with that which crowns and glorifies the good.
> — *Theological Essays*[4]

And as already noticed, how can a process of degradation be endless?

With all earnestness, I repeat that our choice lies between accepting the victory of Christ or of evil, and *between these alternatives only*. Escape from this dilemma there is none. It avails nothing to diminish, as many now teach, the number of the lost; or to assert that they will be finally annihilated. All such modifications leave quite *untouched* the central difficulty of the popular creed—the triumph of evil. Sin for ever present with its taint, even in a *single* instance, is sin triumphant. Sin that God has been unable to remove (and has had no resource but to annihilate the sinner) is sin triumphant and death victorious.

How strange, too, is the delusion, often advocated, viz., that all real objections to the traditional creed are met if the grosser forms of teaching it are abandoned. This means, I presume, "let us still punish for ever, though all chance of amendment is over. But do not shock the mass of men, do not mention a literal fire: that is to go too far; retain the agony, but be careful to apply the suffering to the highest part—to the spiritual nature. Rack the spirit with endless woe, and remorse; hand over to the devil for ever one formed in God's image, one for whom the Son of God

---

4 Editor: Thomas De Quincey, *Theological Essays and Other Papers*. 2 vols. (London: 1854). Thomas De Quincey (1785–1859) was an essayist and journalist made famous by his book *Confessions of an English Opium-Eater* (1821), in which he talked about his experiences as an opium addict—both the pleasures and the pains. Note the Platonic view here of evil's lack of substance—evil is not a "thing," but a lack in a things. Such lack, such brokenness, has no place in new creation.

died; consign man's spirit to endless evil, it lasts only *for ever and ever!* Who can be so *unreasonable* as to murmur?"

Men's minds must be deeply drugged by prejudice, and the power of reasoning partly paralyzed, when such pleas are advanced; or when they fancy that by diminishing the area of damnation they elude all objections to endless evil. As though you could solve moral questions by process of arithmetic, or annul the devil's victory by diminishing the number of his victims. So long as one soul for whom Christ died remains in the devil's grip for ever, so long and so far, is the devil victor. Nothing can by a hair's breadth alter that fact.

Recasting God as Governor and Taskmaster

A further vital point there is; how far Bishop Butler[5] designed to teach that "probation" is an adequate description of our moral relationship to God may be uncertain. Yet it is certain that practically his great name is (largely) the authority with those who teach in fact, if not in words, that God is primarily the Judge, or the Moral Governor of his creatures. Against this idea, which is working untold mischief, I earnestly protest. It is the fatal legacy, the *damnosa hereditas*, which the stern and narrowly legal mind of Rome, with a natural bent to cruelty, bequeathed to the gospel.[6] The God who is love is thus in practice changed into an almighty Proconsul, while the Saviour of men is disguised in the garb of a Roman Governor. Not the mercy-seat, but the seat of judgment is presented to the eye. An inflexible code and an unbending Judge rule all; on every side is diffused a sense of terror. Love is subordinate, sin becomes the central

---

5 Editor: Joseph Butler (1692–1752) was Bishop of Bristol and briefly of Durham. He is best known as an apologist for the reasonableness of orthodox Christianity in the face of challenges raised by the Enlightenment. His best-known work was *The Analogy of Religion, Natural and Revealed* (1736). He argued for "the general analogy between the principles of divine government, as set forth by the biblical revelation, and those observable in the course of nature, [an analogy which] leads us to the warrantable conclusion that there is one Author of both" (*Encyclopedia Britannica*, 1911 ed.). Perhaps in response to challenges from Deism, with its focus on God as Moral Governor, he too felt drawn to think of God as Divine Governor of his creation.

6 Editor: In Roman law, the *damnosa hereditas* (harmful inheritance) was the inheritance from a person who died and left their debts for the heirs to pay off. Allin sees the notion of damnation itself as an unwanted legacy from Roman culture that was taken on by the church to its own harm. He develops this idea in *Race and Religion: Hellenistic Theology: Its Place in Christian Thought* (1899).

Summary and Conclusions

fact; guilt, not grace, comes first. "Our Father," to all practical purposes, disappears, while the great Taskmaster, or the Moral Governor, or the Accountant-General takes his place. It is not that in so many words the love of God and the divine Fatherhood are denied, but that they are so often recognized in words only. Shrunken, atrophied, palsied, the doctrine remains, as in some country where the rightful monarch has not been formally dethroned, but has dwindled into a puppet.

Such a system may call itself the gospel, may point to the support of the greatest names, and be taught in thousands of pulpits (often softened, but the same essentially), yet it is a counterfeit and no true gospel.

Where has the bright and joyous Christianity vanished which covered the dark recesses of the [Roman] catacomb; with every symbol that could attest joy and triumph, but gave no place to any dark and painful image, *not even to the cross?* Why was this? Because to these men the victory of Jesus Christ was a thing really believed in, a fact actually realized, and dominating all else. Because they believed that death, and its sting, was really, truly, universally *swallowed up in victory.* And so they loved to paint Christ radiant with youth and strength, true and absolute Conqueror of death and hell. Perpetual death, moral rottenness for ever festering, what place—such were their thoughts—have such things in a restored creation? Why is the Christ of religious art now so sad, with anguished features and drooping head—is it because he mourns his approaching defeat? Why have we so very generally banished from our churches the figure of the risen and triumphant Lord—is it because in our heart of hearts we feel in how many cases he fails to triumph? Whither has gone the vision so noble, so tender, and yet so strong, of the victorious Christ as he descends into Hades, and opening the prison doors brings the disobedient dead back to life?

Yes, "they have taken our Lord away and we know not where they have laid him." They have taken "our Father," too, "the All Father," and we know not where to find him. For bread they give us a stony creed; judgment without mercy; hell without hope; evil without end; heaven without pity for the lost and the suffering; and a world here, in which to live is truly misery to the thoughtful, as being but the portal and antechamber to endless woe, for so many of their brothers and sisters in Christ, whom they are commanded to love as they love themselves.

Catholics (?) indeed we call ourselves, while not one pulpit in a thousand in all England ventures so much as to hint at these glad tidings

PART FOUR—Universalism Asserted

of the release of the dead from Hades, which catholic antiquity universally taught.[7] Whither, too, has vanished that happier and higher view of death, as a *cure*, as the remoulding by the Great Artist of his own likeness and image, a view so significant and taught by so many and so famous names? By what right have we virtually added to the ancient creeds the fatal clause, "I believe in an eternity of evil"? Why do we never hear the nobler view of the resurrection as from its very nature a process of restoration? Why has the important fact been steadily ignored, or even denied, of the wide diffusion of universalism in the primitive church? Why has the church delighted to accept a cruel and uncatholic Africanism from the Bishop of Hippo, while refusing the nobler and more catholic teaching which the Bishop of Nyssa, and so many saints freely taught in the church's greatest age?[8]

I do not mean that there has been a formal acceptance or rejection. I mean that Augustinianism has in fact leavened all Latin Christianity, banishing the nobler teachings of true catholicity. Thus, if God is to damn man eternally, there is a step certain to be taken (to justify, if possible, such a sentence), viz., the degrading and slandering that nature which man has received from God, and which the Son of God assumed and wears for ever. Thus, too, the incarnation loses its proper place; the true lesson of creation is ignored; the fact of the divine image and likeness in every man is displaced and forgotten. "Can anything be so precious as is the image of God?" asks St. Ambrose. The very elect are *"lepers covered*

---

7 Editor: The doctrine of the descent of Christ into Hades had been a prominent belief in the church historically, but by the nineteenth century in English Protestantism it was all but ignored. Allin sees this as a challenge to (presumably) Anglican claims to be truly catholic.

8 Editor: Allin sees Gregory of Nyssa as more "catholic" than Augustine of Hippo, presumably because on the question of hell Gregory was in clear continuity with earlier tradition, while Augustine, in certain respects at least, was more of a theological innovator. That said, Allin is not being fair to Augustine here. The Bishop of Hippo was *very* concerned to be true to the catholic tradition and his innovations were intended as innovations *within* that tradition. Even his views on original sin, election, and hell were not *de novo* creations, but drew on elements contained within the tradition itself.

Allin's accusation of non-catholicity against Augustine's theology of hell is also of an indirect kind. He argues that Augustine's theology of hell is *incompatible* with some of the central elements of Christian orthodoxy and thereby serves to undermine them. It is not that Augustine or his heirs actually deny God's love or God's sovereignty—on the contrary, they strongly affirm them—but their belief in hell strikes at the very heart of such beliefs. Thus, from Allin's perspective, their orthodoxy or catholicity is only saved by their inability to see the inconsistency in their beliefs.

with dung and mire, ulcers putrefied in their father's loins."[9] If even Hooker, the judicious, can so write, how deeply must the fatal leaven have penetrated—indeed, its traces are most legible to this day.

To resume, I believe that no doctrine has ever gained so wide a currency, with so little support in Scripture, as has probation; (and so little support in all the higher patristic theology). It fact, it is not the product of Scripture, it comes from the philosophers, not from the prophets, or the apostles. And anyone can notice how it is assumed, and not proved from Scripture, in the books that are current. Doubtless there is an element of probation in education, but, if God is our Father, the fact that dominates all else in our moral relationship to him is the education of humanity as his children. Certainly no education can go on without trial, but we are

> tried that we may be educated, and *not educated that we may be tried*. . . . The essential characteristic of a Father's love is that it is *inextinguishable*. . . . If I am here simply on trial, if I regard God as one who is keeping a debtor and creditor account with me, I may in word call Him Father, and in word ascribe love to Him, but I cannot really regard Him as Father.
> —Thomas Erskine[10]

Be it remembered that no reasonable man doubts that God is truly our Governor[11] and our Judge. But we deny such a Governor and such a Judge, as the traditional creed depicts; we deny that the Father is ever (practically) lost in the Judge. We are forced to ask: have these our teachers learned aright the alphabet of the gospel? If they had, could they talk as they do? For to say that God is "loving" is in fact to make love an attribute merely, like justice or wrath. God is not loving, for *God is love*,

---

9 Editor: Richard Hooker, *Mr Hooker's Answer to the Supplication that Mr Travers Made to the Council*, § 22. Richard Hooker (1554–1600) was an Anglican priest and theologian and is one of the giants of the Anglican tradition. He is associated with the theological method combining the claims of Scripture, tradition, and reason—the very method Allin himself seeks to follow. He is also associated with the view that presents Anglicanism as a *via media* between Catholicism and Protestantism.

10 Editor: Thomas Erskine, *The Spiritual Order and Other Papers Selected from the Manuscripts of the Late Thomas Erskine of Linlathen* (Edinburgh: 1871), "The Purpose of God." Thomas Erskine (1788–1870) was an influential and highly regarded Scottish Anglican lay theologian. He sought to modify the strict Scottish Calvinism of his day and took it in the direction of universalism.

11 In fact, we admit this divine rule far more truly than our opponents. To them God's rule is, in fact, baffled finally and hopelessly by evil, which he never succeeds in extinguishing.

a distinction which is vital; which affects the whole Christian scheme in its essence. Nor is this error all. Our opponents seem not to understand what love really is; else they could not accuse us of making light of retribution, because we insist that God is love.

For the very essence of love is misconceived when it is confounded with mere good nature; forgetting the awful, inexorable, side of true (divine) love; forgetting, too, that this love is essentially inextinguishable. With a gospel based on errors so cardinal as to substitute for the Father, the almighty Inspector; for his training, the idea of probation merely—with the central fact wrong, what wonder if all the rest is out of gear? Who could expect astronomy to flourish if men were taught that this earth is the center, and not the sun? So with the moral universe. If I place sin at the center, and not love—I paralyze every motion, and wholly invert the divine order.

It is a sad fact that Christian teachers should only admit that God is love provided no due practical conclusions are drawn from it. It is a sad fact, perhaps the saddest of all facts to those who try to see fairly, that in so very few out of the vast number of Christian pulpits is there preached a God who is even as good as an average human parent. Those who so preach would themselves loathe the very touch of a human father or mother who should act as they say God will act towards many (or any, what do numbers matter here?) of his creatures; or as God has in fact acted, when he forced on these unhappy ones the fatal gift of life, and thus in the phrase of the poet, "cursed them into birth."[12]

Divine Sovereignty and Victory

How seldom, again, is this question treated as it should be from the divine standpoint. Truly we need the profound lesson conveyed by the divine Spirit to an old prophet, "The battle is not ours, *but God's*" (2 Chr 20:15). This weary, age-long battle with sin is, in its final issue, not ours, but God's. It is "the salvation of the Lord," emphatically (2 Chr 20:17). Nowadays it is deemed the profoundest theology to forget all this: it is deemed the highest wisdom to hang the final issue of this awful conflict on the sin-stained, frail, ignorant will of a being like man. Instead of a

---

12 Editor: The phrase is a slight misquote from Edward Young (1683–1765), "The Last Day: A poem in three books" (1713). The line is from Book III and is part of a poetic paraphrase of the book of Job. The poem actually says "cursed me into birth."

Summary and Conclusions

theology they give us an anthropology; instead of a science of God, a science of man. We hear little of God's will, because as it may be conjectured that will points so emphatically to universal salvation.

The question remains, and will remain till it receives due answer. Is God really Master? or is sin to oust him from any part of his own house for ever? To reject Calvinism is easy enough, but to reject the divine sovereignty is to reject Holy Scripture, and may I not add, to reject the verdict of reason too?

Again, I entreat my readers to pay no heed to the delusive plea that claims victory for Christ if he shuts up his enemies in hell, as though the sole victory possible to a divine Being were not the conversion of his enemies; as though the perpetuation of evil in hell were not his defeat. But, in truth, the traditional creed is essentially, if not formally, dualistic. There is a deity (nominally) supreme, and a rival demigod, Satan. There are two confronting empires, destined to exactly the same duration. In the Middle Ages we find actually represented in painting a rival Trinity, a Trinity of Evil.[13] How profound is the revelation thus made of the beliefs ruling the minds of men, still ruling in those who believe that the devil is all but omnipotent, and practically omnipresent.

Let us go to the Bible. Those who have reason to shrink from this appeal are not universalists, but are the advocates of endless sin; of a baffled Saviour; of a victorious devil. It is they who shut their eyes to the teaching of the Bible. It is they who make light of its repeated promises of a restitution of all things. It is they who make Scripture of none effect by their traditions. To the Bible they come drugged by early prejudice; saturated with cruel traditions, to whose horror long familiarity has deadened the mind. And so it is that many really cannot see the true force of Scripture, when it plainly asserts the restitution of all things. Hence the painful evasions; the halting logic that honestly (for I gladly admit this) but blindly turns the Bible upside down, i.e., teaching that all men drawn to Christ, means half mankind drawn to the devil; all things reconciled through Christ, means the final perdition of half the universe. The notion of the popular creed, i.e., that God is in the Bible detailing the story of his own defeat, how sin has proved too strong for him, this notion seems wholly unfounded. Assuredly the Bible is not the story of sin, deepening

---

13 Editor: Adolphe Napoléon Didron, *Iconographie Chrétienne: Historie de Dieu* (Paris: 1843) 2.23. Adolphe Didron (1806–67) was a French iconographer, archaeologist, and preserver of artifacts. The book Allin refers to was a major study of mediaeval iconography.

PART FOUR—Universalism Asserted

into eternal ruin, of God's Son, worsted in his utmost effort; it is from the opening to the close the story of grace stronger than sin—of life victorious over every form of death—of God triumphing over evil.

Once more I repeat that the larger hope *emphatically and fully accepts* the doctrine of retribution. Those who picture universalism as some easygoing system, which refuses to face the stern facts of sin and misery and retribution, are hopelessly wrong. *We press on all the impenitent the awful certainty of a wrath to come,* and this with far more chance of acceptance, because taught in a form that does not wound the conscience; because we dare not teach that finite sin shall receive an infinite penalty. Few things have so hindered the spread of the larger hope as the wholly and absolutely groundless notion that it implies an inadequate sense of sin, and pictures God as a weakly indulgent Being, careless of holiness, provided the happiness of his creatures is secured. In fact, it is those who teach the popular creed, and not we, who make light of sin. To teach unending sin in hell, even in a solitary instance, and under any conceivable modification, is to teach the victory of evil. To us this seems at once a libel on God and an untruth—a libel because it imputes to God a final acquiescence in sin; an untruth, because it teaches that his omnipotence breaks down at the very moment it is most needed, and that his love and purity can rest with absolute complacency, while pain and evil riot and rot for ever.

The Mystery of Sin and Evil

Here we may ask, can any light, however small, be thrown on this awful mystery of sin? For all practical purposes, I reply, there are but two possible views of moral evil. It is endless as God himself, which is in fact dualism;[14] or it is temporary, and in God's mysterious plan, permitted only to serve a higher end. Indeed, this view of moral evil seems to be substantially that of St. Thomas Aquinas: "he makes the elevation of the creature above the original capabilities of his nature to depend on the introduction of sin."[15] Thus, it is a stage in the development of the

---

14 May it not be said a peculiarly evil form of dualism, for in it the Good Spirit freely permits the entrance of evil, which he knows will endure for ever?

15 Editor: Augustus Neander, *General History of the Christian Religion and Church*. Translated by Joseph Torrey. 2nd ed. 4 vols. (London: 1853), 8:216. Johann Augustus Wilhelm Neander (1789–1850) was a German church historian, a student of Friedrich Schleiermacher in Halle, and a professor of theology in Berlin.

Summary and Conclusions

creature, and of this there seems a *hint* conveyed in the story of the first sin. By it man is said to have *"become as one of us,"* as though the very fall implied a rise.[16] Certainly Scripture asserts that "God has shut up all men unto disobedience, in order that he might have mercy upon all!" Note here the stress boldly laid (1) on God's agency, and not on man's will. (2) The universality alike of sin and of salvation, both are equally absolute and universal. (3) But sin is permitted only as leading up to, as involving, salvation. And thus we see not an arrangement by which man starts innocent, free to choose sin or not, but a (virtual) provision for the hereditary transmission of evil; by which innocence *becomes impossible* to all; by which every child of Adam is, in the divine plan, *"shut up unto [sin] disobedience,"* an arrangement inconceivable on the part of a good and loving Father, except with a settled purpose of mercy to every one. I am not presumptuous enough to fancy that I have a novel solution to offer of this profound mystery, but if the Bible be truly from God, then no solution is possible which refuses (as do almost all interpreters) to treat seriously the following striking passages, on the ground probably that reverence for the Bible is reverence for those parts of the Bible that suit our own views. These passages have been, in fact, completely ostracized.

"I am the Lord; I make peace and *create evil; I the LORD do all these things*" (Isa 45:7). Note the emphatic repetition, for true reverence, true honesty, demands a frank recognition of these words. Nor do they stand alone in their general teaching. Take, e.g., the memorable scene when Satan appears before God, and receives from him power over Job, and those passages in which we read of an evil spirit *from the Lord* (1 Sam 16:14; 18:10; 19:9). Again, God is represented as saying to the lying spirit, "Go forth and do so"; and the Lord is said to have *"put a lying spirit"* in the mouth of the prophets (1 Kgs 22:23). So in Judges 9:23, God sends an evil spirit. I advance no theory, but quote Scripture, and protest against explaining it away under the plea of reverence. In addition to all this, we have repeated statements that "God hardens" the human heart, "shuts the eyes lest they should see; and the ears lest they should hear." (See Exod 4:21; 7:3; 9:12; 10:1; Deut 2:30; Josh 9:20; Isa 6:10; 19:14; 29:10; 63:17; Jer 13:13; 20:7; Ezek 14:9; 20:25; Amos 3:6; Ps 105:25, etc.)

Thus is text heaped upon text, line upon line. It is most strange to find all these brushed away, by the very men who contend for a literal

---

16 Does Clement of Alexandria mean this when he speaks of Adam as "made a man by disobedience" (*Adm. ad gent.*)?

meaning elsewhere? They say, "It is wrong to press these, *because they are unworthy of God.*" Be it so. But, if so, pray remember that you cannot play fast and loose with a principle. If you brush away a mass of plain texts, because they are unworthy of God, will you explain why I may not brush away texts (quoted to prove endless pain) that are far from plain, crowded with metaphor, ambiguous, and in their cruelty, *as generally interpreted,* unworthy, I will not say of God, but of any decent human being. Observe, that I do not desire to brush them away, but to interpret them rightly; yet it is well to show once more that our opponents do not carry out consistently their own principles. Nor is this all. When they brush away texts because unworthy of God, they are again inconsistent, for they thereby affirm the capacity of our moral sense to judge of religious truth and the ways of God, which the traditional creed nearly always in effect, and very often in words, denies.

Nor can we say that in the Old Testament God is represented as doing that which he permits to be done; for the New Testament is emphatic on this point. "Whom he will he *hardens*"[17] (Rom 9:18). "*He has shut* up all men unto unbelief" (Rom 11:32). "*God gave* them a spirit of stupor, eyes that they should not see" (v. 8). "*God shall send* them strong delusion, that they should believe a lie" (2 Thess 2:11). Such is St. Paul's emphatic testimony. St. John, too, echoes and reaffirms (John 12:39–40) Isaiah's saying that the Jews *could not* believe, *because God had blinded their eyes* and *hardened their hearts.* And so our Lord declares that God had "hid certain things from the wise" (Matt 11:25) and that he spoke in parables in order that seeing his hearers might not perceive (Mark 4:12; Luke 8:10; cf. 1 Pet 2:8). The uncompromising, fearless tone of Scripture is remarkable: everywhere it sees the divine hand, and in everything traces a divine purpose and will. It seems a false reference for the Bible to explain away all this. Indeed, to a thoughtful mind light comes from calmly facing these hard sayings. And so St. Paul adds: the law was given *in order* that the "offense might abound" (Rom 5:20). The law "reveals (Rom 3:20), provokes (Rom 7:7–13), multiplies (Rom 5:20) sin or transgression."[18] This, Lightfoot adds, is St. Paul's leading conception of the function of the law.

---

17 We are not entitled to evade this, because it is sometimes said in Scripture that men harden their own hearts—which is, of course, most true.

18 Editor: Joseph Barber Lightfoot, *St. Paul's Epistle to the Galatians* (London: 1865), commenting on Gal 3:19.

Summary and Conclusions

Here let me sum up briefly and with due reverence: (1) the facts that the law was given "in order that the offense might abound," and that the law was our "tutor" (Gal 3:24), suggest the *educational* aspect of evil: we seem to understand better the statements of Genesis 3:5, 22. Fresh light falls on the significant words, *"God has shut up* all men unto disobedience," and on these, the creation "was made subject unto vanity," *not willingly,* but by reason of him who has subjected the same in hope.

(2) God's sovereignty is everywhere to be traced: the error lies in failing to see that this sovereignty is that of love.

(3) Again it has been well said that there is no such thing as "pure evil"; "so unrestrained is the inundation of the principle of good into . . . selfishness and sin itself."[19] "There is a soul of goodness in things evil," says the greatest of Englishmen.[20]

(4) We have hints in Scripture that by evil permitted *and overcome*, something is gained which, perhaps, could not have been otherwise had, e.g., there is *"more joy* over one repenting sinner, than over ninety-nine just persons who need no repentance" [Luke 15:7]. And if there is more joy in heaven, there is more love on earth from the same source, "for to whom little is forgiven the same loves little" [Luke 7:47].

(5) Sin is very often the result of ignorance; how far this consideration goes I do not decide, but may there not be an element of ignorance in all sin?[21]

(6) Nor should we forget that in sinning, if I may say so, the raw material is very often the same as in the practice of virtue, but turned the wrong way—"there is," says Emerson, "no moral deformity but is a good

---

19 Editor: Ralph Waldo Emerson, "Circles" (1841). This is a philosophical essay in which Emerson reflects on many circles found in nature. Here is the paragraph from which Allin quotes/paraphrases: "I am not careful to justify myself. I own I am gladdened by seeing the predominance of the saccharine principle throughout vegetable nature, and not less by beholding in morals that *unrestrained inundation of the principle of good* into every chink and hole that selfishness has left open, yea *into selfishness and sin itself;* so that *no evil is pure,* nor hell itself without its extreme satisfactions. But lest I should mislead any when I have my own head and obey my whims, let me remind the reader that I am only an experimenter."

20 Editor: Shakespeare, *Henry V*, Act 4, Scene 1.

21 Nor would it be true, in my judgment, to call this ignorance willful in all cases, so vast is the network of illusions surrounding us (see 1 Cor 2:8). "Most sins," says St. Gregory of Nyssa "are committed from a confusion of judgment as to what is truly good" (*De mort.* 2).

passion out of place."²² I have steadily enforced in these pages the guilt of sin, but it remains true that to sin greatly often demands the same qualities that rightly used would have been great virtues.

(7) Whatever the value of the above considerations, the larger hope has nothing to fear from any theory of sin that can be maintained. Take a lenient view of human guilt, and you thereby shut out endless penalty. Take the very sternest view, and the perpetuation of this awful hostility to God becomes inconceivable.

A further consideration remains. As creation is for the Deity to enter into finite relations, and to subject his plans to definite limits, so, perhaps, evil, physical and moral, is in a sense inevitable. And it may be that, by the training and collision, thus involved, a higher type of character is formed than would be otherwise possible, e.g., self sacrifice, self restraint, sympathy, mercy, etc., seem to require a background of evil for their existence; although I believe that certain results of this have not always been thought out by its advocates.²³ A creation thus advancing to perfection by a certain, if slow, victory over evil, may possibly be a nobler thing than a creation so safeguarded as to have never fallen. In St. Bernard's words, *"ordinatissimum est, minus interdum ordinate fieri aliquid"*²⁴ (*Ep.* 276, *ad. Eug.* 3). I shall neither affirm, nor deny, these propositions. But morality and reason require one thing, viz., that creation shall be in fact so advancing; that the victory over evil shall be a victory indeed, and not a compromise—i.e., they require not partialism *in any form*,²⁵ but universalism.

Evil in process of extinction, nay, in the divine plan already extinguished—is tolerable. Evil permitted for a time, in order that it may be more completely vanquished, and men thereby trained—that we can understand. But when evil, moral or physical, becomes perpetual; when it ceases to be a means and becomes an end; when it is no merely passing stain, but is wrought into the very tissue of the universe—enduring as

---

22 Ralph Waldo Emerson, "Considerations by the Way," in *The Conduct of Life* (Boston: 1860, rev. 1876).

23 Thus, if so, what of heaven? Must evil be present there to elicit virtue? Again, if the highest type of character be the result of conflict with evil, must the seraphim and cherubim, etc., have known evil? and so on, up to the very throne of God.

24 Editor: the Latin means: "It belongs to the great order that there should be some small disorder." St. Bernard of Clairvaux (1090–1153) was a significant French Cistercian abbot.

25 For annihilation is no victory: it is death triumphant over life.

Summary and Conclusions

God himself: when God is taught as freely and deliberately permitting the entrance of evil, destined, as he knows, to be an eternal horror in his creation; then we are compelled to refuse assent, compelled by our very reverence for God, by the supreme voice within, which if God anywhere speaks with man, is indeed his voice.

This prepares us for a very interesting question, viz., whether the evil effects of long continued willful sin ever wholly pass away. It may be replied, perhaps never in some cases. Some men, if I may for the moment so apply our Lord's striking words, may, in some sense, enter into life halt and maimed. Obstinate persistency in sin may leave on the spirit a wound whose evil effects are permanent. There may be, for I will not attempt to decide, a permanent weakness, though the disease of sin be cured.

Two results of this deserve notice. (1) It furnishes us with a fresh answer to the plausible taunt cast at the larger hope as leading the careless to say, "if this be true I will have my fling, for all will come 'right at last.'" On any view, your fling I reply, will bring on you "the wrath to come"—a retribution terrible[26] in proportion to the willfulness of your sin. But, further, your fling *may* involve you in a penalty strictly everlasting. You may, though pardoned, for ever suffer from the numbness and spiritual weakness that your sin leaves behind. (2) May not this furnish a meeting place for reasonable men on both sides? For final and universal restoration is not opposed to perpetual penalty in a certain sense; because the willful sinner, though saved, may yet suffer a perpetual loss, a *paena damni*[27] loss of the highest spiritual blessedness hereafter.

The Traditional Hell is Selfish

Further, every form of partial salvation is rooted in selfishness. This selfishness is largely unconscious, but not the less real. Most people will have noticed a shocking unwillingness, on the part of the so-called religious world, even to entertain the idea of universalism. The unspoken feeling is often this—if hell is gone, perhaps my heaven is gone too. And

---

26 An evil result of the traditional creed has been that it, by exaggerated threats, deadens men to any true sense of future penalty. Men grown familiar with endless punishment practically think very lightly of any less penalty, however awful. Thus a critic of this book maintains that the "tragic" element in religion is lost except we retain endless penalty! Is, then 10,000 years (or 100,000) of pain and banishment from God a comic thing, and not tragic?

27 Editor: a negative future punishment, a punishment of loss.

then comes the deduction—what, if so, is to become of *me?* We have thus a heaven actually, in some true sense, built on hell; buttressed on endless misery and sin. And this is received as the true gospel of Jesus Christ.

A degrading selfishness is popularized, nay, is sanctified; religion is tainted. Salvation becomes a sort of stampede for life, a universal *sauve qui peut*,[28] a chase, in which the powers of evil are always catching the hindmost. And most strange of all, this grotesque and tragic scene is gravely asserted to be the victory of Jesus Christ. I do not know whether all this is more strange, or more shocking. For what can be more shocking than that any of the blessed should be for a moment happy in a heaven literally built over the anguish and blasphemies of the lost—nay, so long as a solitary mourner sits for ever in hopeless despair? Heaven is likeness to Jesus Christ; and likeness to Jesus Christ is undying sympathy with the lost; is love unquenchable towards his worst enemies. But the heaven which the traditional creed (and every modification of it) offers to us is a thing so hardened, so awful that merely to think of it fills the mind with horror. Deadened sympathies; palsied love; selfishness incarnate; pity for ever withered; such is the heaven too many of the masters of our Israel teach. "It is a mystery," they reply. It is hell, I answer, disguised as heaven. Do they then imagine that we have not wit enough to see that so to answer, where the gravest moral questions are concerned, is a confession that no answer is possible?

The Theological and Pastoral Chaos of Traditional Hell

"Will you *speak wickedly for God?*" [Job 13:7] asks the indignant patriarch. "Woe unto them that call evil good and good evil" [Isa 5:20]. Here is the peculiar horror of the traditional creed. In the very holy of holies, it places that which revolts and degrades. The God it worships bids us love our enemies, while he consigns to endless perdition his own enemies. Hating sin with an eternal hatred, he provides for it an endless duration, an abiding home. Because it is so very evil, therefore it must go on for ever, for this is the meaning of saying that for the very worst sinners there is after death no hope. Their guilt is so vast, therefore it must endure for ever; it is so very foul, therefore it must defile for ever God's redeemed universe. The blessed are content to gaze placidly over the abyss of hell, their satisfaction unbroken; their joys undimmed, if not

---

28 Editor: meaning, "every man for himself."

Summary and Conclusions

actually heightened, by the torments of the lost. And when, finally, the curtain falls on a universe darkened by endless sin, they actually call this the triumph of the cross; and are content to retire into a heaven of ineffable selfishness, where love is paralyzed, and the Spirit of Christ dead; not caring though the wail of the lost for ever rise; the husband grown for ever deaf to the appeal of the wife; the mother unheeding the eternal agony of her child.

Dante inscribed over the gate of the medieval hell, "Abandon hope, you who enter here."[29] Our teachers bid us inscribe over the gate of heaven, words, if possible, more awful, "Abandon love and sympathy: abandon the spirit of Jesus Christ, you who enter here." They bid us sing:

> O saints of God, for ever blest,
> In that dear home how sweet your rest.

How *sweet your rest*, O wives whose husbands for ever burn; O mothers, how sweet your rest, while your children for ever agonize. *In that dear home, how sweet your rest!*

You are shocked at reading that the blessed rejoice over the agonies of hell. But have you any reason, nay, any shadow of reason, to be shocked, on your principles? Are you afraid to face the inevitable result of your teaching? *Must* not the blessed acquiesce in, nay be *pleased* with the divine judgments, whatever they be? Pray consider this. These judgments, whether healing and finite as we think, or vindictive and endless as you think, are certainly the outcome of the divine will. They claim your approval as of right. The Bible tells you "The righteous shall *rejoice when he sees the vengeance*" (Ps 58:9). Can you escape the conclusion that the shocking passages are justified substantially if your dogma be true?

To resume, these horrors are taught when, as now, agnosticism is so threatening; when science looks on the gospel with hardly disguised scorn.[30] And too often, an ignorant, if well meaning, clergy are content to cry, "Have faith"; as though God were not the author of reason; as though loyalty to conscience were not the supreme duty of every rational

---

29 Dante, *Inferno*, Canto III. Dante is led by Virgil to the gateway of hell, and these infamous words are inscribed above the door.

30 Editor: By the late Victorian period many Christians were starting to feel the challenges presented by the developing fields of geology (Charles Lyell) and biology (Charles Darwin), both of which challenged a literal reading of parts of Scripture, and the growing influence of so-called "higher criticism" in biblical studies. There was a growing crisis of faith for many educated people. Allin feels that the traditional doctrine of hell made the faith even more unbelievable to such people.

being; and a recognition of its supremacy the very condition by which alone any religion is possible. I am content at the bidding of faith to accept a mystery that transcends my reason; but to prostitute conscience, to dethrone the moral sense, is treason to God; it is *"propter, vitam vivendi perdere causam."*[31]

I do not mean willful untruth, but I do mean that virtual falsehood stains almost the whole body of our religious literature.[32] Falsehood is to say one thing, while meaning another. Hence, to assert that the world is saved, while meaning that in fact half the world will be damned; that mankind is rescued, while meaning in fact that many (or few, it matters not which) go to the devil for ever: to do this in a thousand forms, in hymns, in sermons, tracts, treatises, is falsehood; and with such untruth our religious literature is, I repeat, *honeycombed through and through.*

> It is a terrible business to have a falsehood domiciled with truth, and for its possessor, when he is only half convinced or not all convinced of its truth, to take the greatest pains to dress it up like a truth. For the falsehood gets no good from the truth, but the truth gets all maimed by the falsehood. They talk of the love of God, and His mercy, and His pity, and His justice, and His righteousness ... while all the time they are speaking, this hideous companion in their own soul is laughing at all these things. Love of God—what of eternal torture? Righteousness of God—what of eternal evil? Good news, salvation—oh, have done with it all.
> —Stopford Brooke[33]

But so long as the popular creed and the Bible are held together, so long must this system of untruth continue. We pray to "our Father," to whom in the next breath we assign acts towards his own children more

---

31 Editor: "to destroy the reasons for living for the sake of life." A comment on the folly of those who throw away what makes life worth living in order to stay alive. The result being that you live, but your life is no longer worthwhile. Juvenal, *Satyricon* VIII, verses 83–84.

32 "There appears to me in all the English divines a want of believing, or disbelieving, anything because it is true or false. It is a question which does not seem to occur to them" (Arthur Stanley, *Life of Arnold*, Letter 152).

33 Editor: Stopford Brooke, *The Unity of God and Man: and Other Sermons Preached at Bedford Chapel, Blomsbury* (Boston: 1886). Stopford Brooke (1832–1916) was an Irish Anglican cleric, educated, like Allin, at Trinity College, Dublin. He was for a while chaplain to the Empress Frederick in Berlin and to Queen Victoria, but in 1880 he left the Church of England and became a Unitarian minister, linked to Bedford Chapel in Bloomsbury, London.

cruel than any to which the worst earthly parent would stoop. We thus degrade the Godhead below, *far below, the level of humanity*. What is left for us to worship if the truth be a lie—if love essential be cruelty itself—if God be that which I dare not write?

Nor is this all. Having thus assigned to God acts of infinite cruelty, the popular creed goes on to assure us of his tenderness that *never* wearies—his love that *never* fails. What falsehood, what cruel mockery is this, coming from those who really mean that this unfailing, eternal love watches to all eternity, callous and unsympathising, the undying evil, the endless agony of its own children.

A merchant who has two contradictory measures is dishonest; but what of the theologian of whom the same is true, is he less dishonest? It is cruel to torment a cat or a dog for five minutes, but to be callous to all eternity about the endless misery of a wife or a child is quite right and good. The transient wrongs of a chimney-sweep excite the sincerest pity;[34] but the eternal anguish of the lost human spirit awakes not even a passing gleam of pity in the blessed. Let a criminal be tortured for an hour by human law, and all the civilized world is roused; but let the same criminal pass to torture without end, and these endless pangs do not disturb for a moment the raptures of the inhabitants of heaven. Vivisection is odious on this earth, but is most just in hell. Is it, then, odious when temporary, and most righteous when endless? E.g., is it most righteous for Eternal Love to vivisect for ever, or at least permit to be vivisected, his own children, in the sight of the Lamb, and the holy angels (Rev 14:10) (for the true meaning of this passage see pp. 296–98).

That philanthropists (whom we honour) should be unable to bear the sight of the momentary suffering of the outcast here, while they are prepared to accept heaven's joy unmoved by the endless agony of the outcast hereafter, fills the mind with thoughts, for which amazement is too feeble a term.

The apologies offered for the traditional creed are truly worthy of it. Thus, many shelter themselves under the phrase, "God will do his best for every man." I can only suppose such an apology meant, not as

---

34 Editor: Houses in Victorian Britain were heated by coal fires. The chimney sweeps were children who would climb the chimney's to clean them out. It was a grim and dangerous job with numerous health hazards (spinal deformity, stunted growth, deformity of arms and legs, blindness, burns, cancer) and a real risk of death. Numerous laws were passed through the nineteenth century (1834, 1840, 1864, 1875) to deal with the problem.

an argument, but as an ill-timed piece of pleasantry. For what are the admitted facts? An almighty Being, who is, on any possible hypothesis, perfectly free to create or not, yet *forces on* myriads of hapless children of his own the fatal gift of existence, knowing that in fact this life of theirs will ripen into endless misery and woe. To call this doing his *best* for them is an abuse of language—could he do worse for them?

Some actually try to defend endless evil by asking, "would the lost be happy if put into heaven?" As if the larger hope did not expressly teach the conversion of the lost in the first place.

Another plea for endless evil is made. This I shall state and answer in Mr. Foster's words.

> It is usually alleged that there will be an endless continuance of sinning, with probably an endless aggravation, and therefore the punishment must be endless. Is not this like an admission of disproportion between the punishment and the original cause of its infliction? But suppose the case to be so—that is to say, that the punishment is not a retribution *simply* for the guilt of the momentary existence on earth, but a continued punishment of the continued, ever aggravated, guilt in the eternal state: the allegation is of no avail in vindication of the doctrine, because the first consignment to the dreadful state *necessitates a continuance of the criminality*, the doctrine teaching, that it is of the essence, and is an awful aggravation, of the original consignment, that it dooms the condemned to maintain the criminal spirit unchanged for ever. The doom to *sin* as well as to suffer, and, according to the argument, to sin *in order to suffer*, is inflicted as the punishment of the sin committed in the mortal state Virtually, therefore the eternal punishment is the punishment of the sins of time.
>
> —*Life and Correspondence*, vol. 1[35]

If, indeed, the sentence on the ungodly involve a virtual necessity to sin for ever, then the excuse offered is the deepest accusation possible of the traditional creed. Further, there is a duplicity in this plea when urged by those who quote texts, e.g., Matthew 25, which state the future punishment to be inflicted for sins already past.

---

35 Editor: John Foster, *The Life and Correspondence of John Foster* (London: 1846). John Foster (1770–1843) was a Baptist minister and essayist.

Summary and Conclusions

The Perplexing Resilience of Traditional Hell

Few things are more wonderful in this whole question than the reluctance so many feel to follow out these unhesitating convictions to their *only possible* legitimate conclusion—the rejection of that dogma, which flatly contradicts them. I do not assert that these convictions are an infallible guide; for indeed of what can it be said that its directions reach us in an infallible form? Can that be said of the Bible itself? Are those who translate it, or who comment on it, infallible? Are those who read it free from error, from prejudice? But no Christian, therefore, doubts its divine authority, or fails to see in it a guide practically sufficient, and binding. So in the case of that other and *primary revelation* of God to man. We do not claim infallibility for it, yet we do claim that the deliberate verdict of our moral sense represents to us the voice of God speaking for our guidance in daily life, and on which we are absolutely bound to act.

Our opponents will not remember that the moral sense is God's revelation to us; that it is *his Word* speaking to us, quite as truly as from the pages of any book. It is pure sophistry to say, "you must yield your ideas to God's revealed will," as though our true moral feelings were not God's revealed will to us.

Let us consider how false it is to say, "We must yield our ideas." Must we? What! Our ideas of truth, are they to be yielded? May God say that which we call false, and, if so, does it become truth? But if I must not yield up my idea of truth, as applied to God, why am I to yield my ideas of mercy, and right, and love? Does God perhaps hate in fact, while professing to love, the righteous? This question is vital. It is bad and terrible to use a cruel plea: it is far worse to use it when you do not, just because you dare not, use it honestly all round. If our human ideas of right and wrong are not to be trusted when applied to God, then anything may happen; anything may be right, anything may be wrong; anything may be true, anything may be false. All is medley, chaos, anarchy: hell and heaven may change places. And so, for all we know, may good and evil. We are in fact agnostics, for we know nothing really. We may call ourselves anything we please, but (moral) agnostics we are, and we remain.

This volume has strongly urged the moral degradation due, directly and indirectly, to the doctrine of endless penalty. Here I may state a final instance in an unexpected quarter. It has helped in large measure to promote that immoral casuistry against which at length the human conscience rose in open revolt. This it has effected because that system had its origin in the distinction between mortal and venial sin.[36] Now, as the results of mortal sin were supposed to be so unspeakably awful, if in any way unrepented of, a direct incitement was furnished to narrow, as far as possible, the range of these sins. And thus a perverted ingenuity was set to work in *breaking down* great moral distinctions, and in attenuating systematically the guilt of the graver crimes, in order to stamp them as merely venial offenses.[37]

Summary of Chapters 4–9

Tradition (Chapters 4–5)

I have shown further by abundant evidence, the wide currency, in the early ages, of the broadest universalism, a fact too little known and ignorantly denied. May I again point out that this universalism was essentially based on Scripture, and that it has been reechoed in later years by the most saintly souls. You may search in vain in all the annals of English religion for a name more saintly than William Law, the universalist.[38] Men talk of the "laxity" of universalism. Was it this "laxity" that recommended it to the glowing devotion of Law, to the sainted Macrina[39] (whose deathbed is the most impressive in all primitive annals), to Origen, whose life was one continuous prayer;[40] to a crowd of men like-minded in the early church? Was the devout Erskine of Linlathen drawn by this "laxity" to

---

36 Editor: Catholic theology distinguishes mortal sins from venial sins. The former lead to eternal damnation, unless forgiven; the latter do not.

37 Editor: Henry James Sumner Maine, *Ancient Law: Its Connection with the Early History of Society and Its Relation to Modern Ideas*, (London: 1861), 352. Henry Maine (1822–88) was a jurist and historian, best known for the book Allin references here.

38 Editor: William Law (1686–1761) was a Church of England priest who had to step down because he refused to make the oath of allegiance to George I. He was a mystical theologian and his *A Serious Call to a Devout and Holy Life* (London: 1728) was a significant influence on early evangelicalism. Law believed in universal salvation.

39 Editor: Macrina the Younger (c.330–379) was a nun, and the sister of the Cappadocian's Gregory of Nyssa and Basil of Caesarea. She had a profound influence on her brothers. Gregory's *Dialogue on the Soul and Resurrection* is presented as a description of a conversation he had with Macrina on her deathbed.

40 Editor: Origen (182–254) was highly regarded for his deep piety.

universalism,[41] or Charles George Gordon,[42] or Florence Nightingale?[43] Was the holy Ken[44] attracted to a wider hope than that current in his day by this "laxity?" Or was it not that these, like so many of the early saints, had caught more truly the Spirit of him, the All-Father, who loving, loves to the end, who seeks the lost, till he finds them?

Systematic Theological Coherence (Chapter 6)

Next we have seen (chapter 6) how close is the connection between universalism and creation, incarnation, atonement, and resurrection; and have inquired carefully into the meaning of "election," "death," "judgment," "fire." I have attempted to show that the true teaching of Holy Scripture and of Antiquity on these points is in absolute harmony with the larger hope, that to insist on one and all is to bring into clearer relief the doctrine of universal salvation.

To attempt to introduce fresh ideas, especially in things religious, into minds saturated with doctrines taught in childhood, and hallowed by so many ties, has been well compared to trying to write on paper already scribbled over. Hence the many compromises, excuses, modifications,

---

41 Editor: Thomas Erskine (1788–1870) was a highly respected nineteenth-century Anglican lay theologian from Scotland.

42 Editor: Charles George Gordon (1833–85) was an esteemed British army officer who served in the Empire in China and Africa.

43 Editor: Florence Nightingale (1820–1910) is best known for her work tending wounded soldiers during the Crimean War (1853–56). She transformed the status of nursing and revolutionized the nursing profession. She had this to say regarding God and hell: "I can't love because I am ordered. Least of all can I love One who seems only to make me miserable here to torture me hereafter. Show me that He is good, that He is loveable, and I shall love Him without being told.

But does any preacher show this? He may say that God is good, but he shows Him to be very bad; he may say that God is 'Love', but he shows him to be hate, worse than any hate of man. As the Persian poet says; 'If God punishes me for doing evil by doing me evil, how is he better than I?' And it is hard to answer, for certainly the worst man would hardly torture his enemy, if he could, for ever. And unless God has a scheme that every man is to saved for ever, it is hard to say in what He is not worse than man; for all good men would save others if they could . . . .

It is of no use saying that God is just, unless we define what justice is. In all Christian times people have said that 'God is just' and have credited him with an injustice such as transcends all human injustice that it is possible to conceive." From, "A 'Note' of Interrogation," *Fraser's Magazine*, new series, 7.41 (May 1873) 567–77.

44 Editor: Presumably Thomas Ken (1637–1711), Bishop of Bath and Wells from 1685. He is best known as a hymn writer.

PART FOUR—Universalism Asserted

now current, on the part of those half convinced that the traditional creed is false. The first shelter that offers is accepted, thus many snatch at conditional immortality, not pausing to inquire (even writing volumes without inquiring) whether it so much as fulfills the great primary point of teaching the victory of Jesus Christ.

I have steadily sought in these pages, even when necessarily most outspoken, to recognize the perfect sincerity of my opponents; my quarrel, when most earnest, is not with individuals, but with a system. Here I would make a final appeal and ask, if some who read will not try to rise to higher levels, and to see in the larger hope the only view worthy of the All-Father, and of his justice, which is the handmaid of his love. Alone this hope explains the wonders of our creation in God's image; alone it satisfies the majesty of love and its unquenchable thirst to raise the fallen, and most of all to save finally the most hopeless, the most unrepentant. Alone it really teaches that with God "all things are possible" [Matt 19:26]: alone it sweetens every sorrow, and wipes away every tear. By its light alone are we able to gaze at the very saddest depths of sin, and in its worst discords to hear an undertone of hope. It alone enables us to believe truly in the eternal goodness, and its final victory: by it alone do we gain a full and adequate idea of the divine unity—one will, one love, one law, one Lord, and "one far-off divine event to which the whole creation moves."[45]

Scripture (Chapters 7–9)

We have carefully considered the all-important question of the teaching of Holy Scripture. We have noted even in the Old Testament, intimations from the very first of a future blessing, designed to embrace all the race of man. These become more distinct as the plan of God is more fully disclosed; and both psalmists and prophets unite in their promises of an age yet to come, when the knowledge of the Lord shall cover the earth as the waters cover the sea.

---

45 Editor: The line is from Lord Alfred Tennyson, *In Memoriam* (1849). This poem, a requiem for Tennyson's friend, Arthur Hallam, was perhaps the most influential Victorian poem on death. The verse reads:
>That God, which ever lives and loves,
>One God, one law, one element,
>And one far-off divine event,
>To which the whole creation moves.

Summary and Conclusions

Nor have we forgotten the argument for the larger hope from the tendencies of the Bible and from the great principles that pervade its teaching. I have also tried to show how completely the traditional creed misapprehends the language and usage of Scripture in its threatenings, a subject well worth careful study.

The New Testament received the attention, due to its supreme importance. The passages supposed to teach the popular creed, have been carefully considered, and we have seen reason to conclude that they, one and all, while emphatically warning sinners of the wrath to come, teach nowhere an *endless* punishment.

Lastly, a chapter has been devoted to pointing out how full the New Testament is of passages too often explained away, and yet teaching, or implying, the final salvation of all. So important is this evidence, that I here append a brief summary. We have seen how to Christ is assigned a kingdom absolutely without bound or limit, how *all* flesh shall see the salvation he gives. You have read how the Good Shepherd seeks on, till each sheep he has lost is found, and how the Son of Man came to seek and to save, not some of the lost, but simply "that which was lost." This might also be rendered, "the destroyed," so little does "destruction" involve final loss. His mission is exactly described as having for its object the salvation of the world, and he is said *to take away* the sin of the whole world. Do these terms represent a partial salvation? Are they honestly consistent with it?

Again, it is said *all things* have been given to the Son, and that all that is so given shall come to him. He is repeatedly described as the "Saviour of the world," which yet he does not save on the popular view. He is called the "Light the world." He is said not to offer, but to *give* life to the world, a totally different thing. He says (no words can be more absolute), speaking of his cross, that he will draw *all* men to himself. He adds, that he came not to judge, but to save the world. Can you, on any fair theory of the meaning of human language, reconcile all this with the horrors of endless evil? If the sin of the *whole world be taken away*, how shall there be a hell for its endless punishment. If *all* things without exception (the original is the widest possible) are given to Christ, and all so given to him shall come to him, can you reconcile this with unending misery?

Let us go on, however. We find language employed by the Evangelists quite as decisive against the popular creed as that just quoted. When, for instance, we read in St. John how God's Son was manifested for the

Part Four—Universalism Asserted

very purpose of *destroying the works of the devil*, we are forced to inquire if that is consistent by any possibility with preserving these works in hell for ever? Is there no significance in Christ's telling us that he is "alive unto the ages," and has the *keys* of hell and death? Then again, what do the promises to make all things new, and that there shall be no more curse or pain mean? If these be not promises of universal restoration, what are they? Lastly, ponder over the vision of the Apocalypse, where *every creature* in heaven, on earth, and under the earth (the dead), joins in the song of praise to God. Can you truly say that anything less than a universal salvation can satisfy the plain sense of these words!

To (virtually) evade such words is bad enough, but having done so, to charge universalists with fearing to appeal to Scripture is surely not fair. Take next, a very large body of fresh passages teaching the larger hope, from the Epistles of St. Paul, St. Peter, and Hebrews. St. Paul, especially, is full of glowing anticipation of the assured triumph of Christ's kingdom over all evil. Thus, Abraham is to receive the world and no less as his portion (i.e., in the elect, all are to be saved). Whatever sin has done to injure man is to be more than repaired by the grace of Christ. But is it possible *to undo, in fact, all that sin has done, if a single soul[46] be left in endless evil?* Would not St. Paul be speaking *untruly* in such a case? Surely a fair answer is due to this inquiry (even though a fair answer seems to lead to universalism). Further, the apostle says that *the whole creation* shall be delivered into the glorious liberty of God's children. Again, *all Israel is to be saved* (and being the firstfruits, their salvation involves that of the entire world). The apostle affirms that God's gifts and calling are irrevocable. This is very significant, for what is the popular creed but an assertion that God's gifts can be set at naught finally. Further, what St. Paul asserts is echoed in the Epistle to the Hebrews, which assures us of the immutability of God's counsel. Again, if God has shut up *all* in

---

46 "If but one soul were to remain in the power of the devil, death, or hell, to all endless eternity, then the devil, death, and hell would have something to boast of against God. Thus death would not be entirely swallowed up in victory, but always keep something of his sting, and hell would ever more be able to make a scorn of those who would say, 'O hell, where is, your victory?'" Paul Seigvolck, *The Everlasting Gospel* (1753). [Editor: the book Allin quotes here was originally published in German by a radical pietist, most likely George Klein-Nicolai writing under a pseudonym, in 1700. It was first published in English by a radical pietist group in Philadelphia in 1753 and then published in London by Elhanan Winchester in 1792. Interestingly, Allin seems to reference the American edition.]

unbelief, it is, as St. Paul says, that he may have mercy upon *all*. Does *"all"* mean *"some"* in the latter clause, and not in the former?!

Again, he assures us that if the first Adam brought death universally, then the last Adam brings universal life, and that if sin abounds, *much more* shall grace abound. However, in saying that the last Adam has failed in myriads of cases to undo the evil caused by the fall, you are giving these words a flat contradiction. Then, as to Christ's empire, we are told that to him every knee shall bow (i.e., "all creation, all things, *whatsoever* and *wheresoever* may be"[47]) and every tongue confess—the original term means thanksgiving, indeed, is *the very term used of our Lord's giving his Father thanks* (Matt 11:25). Finally, we are told that one day—at the end—God shall be *all in all*. It is the Father's good pleasure to sum up all things in Christ, to reconcile *all* things unto himself through Christ. Are we indeed to believe that anything can be reconciled to God by being consigned to hopeless evil? For it is a virtual, if unconscious, evasion to say that all things are reconciled to God, if, after countless generations have sent their contingents to the devil, some one generation and those succeeding it, shall be fully saved. Further, the apostle assures us that the living God is the Saviour of *all*, that Jesus Christ has *abolished death*, and that the grace of God brings salvation to *all* men. Are these statements fairly consistent with a partial salvation?[48] Why also, do our opponents never allude to the noble and most inspiring hope, suggested by such a passage as Romans 11:36?

St. Peter, too, speaks to the same effect. He tells of Christ's preaching the gospel *to the dead*, who had been disobedient and died—a story whose significance is the greatest possible, as indicating how behind the veil Christ works on to heal and to save even those who died in sin. He adds, that the Lord is not willing that *any* should perish. Is God's deliberate counsel—such is the original word—to come to nothing?

Then, in the Epistle to the Hebrews, we have this same remarkable testimony, e.g., the assertion that all things are to be put under Christ. It is stated that his object in dying was to destroy the devil—that once, at the conclusion of the ages, he has appeared to put away (i.e., *abolish*) sin by

---

47 Editor: Joseph Barber Lightfoot, *Saint Paul's Epistle to the Philippians* (London: 1888), on Phil 2:10

48 Further, it is impossible for any thoughtful reader to escape noting how, at times, this apostle seems on fire, as it were, as he catches sight of a vision of surpassing glory, of a future kingdom to be won by Christ; boundless, limitless, embracing every created thing whatsoever and wheresoever.

his sacrifice of himself. Can anyone explain how the abolition of sin can be consistent with maintaining evil in hell for ever? Thus, the traditional creed seems to stand hopelessly opposed to the teaching of Scripture. Does it not almost deny God himself, because if we are to believe in God at all, there is no room for a *defeated* God. Therefore, either God really wills to save all men, and if so, he will assuredly accomplish this, or he does not so will. The first proposition involves the larger hope; the second is mere Calvinism. I can see no rational alternative.

Such is a brief outline of the teaching of the New Testament, for I have not quoted all its promises of universal salvation. It is no case of building upon Eastern metaphors, of dogma resting upon mistranslations or misconceptions of the original, as in the case of the traditional creed. It is evidence, clear and unambiguous, and repeated. We have without doubt line upon line, promise upon promise, assertions reiterated, accumulated, yet amid all their variety, closely linked and pointing to one central thought. This thought is none less than the completeness of the triumph of Jesus Christ! It includes the boundless nature of his saving empire over all, to the assurance of a victory won by his incarnation, his death, and his resurrection over all the powers of evil. "The Father willed through Christ to reconcile the universe once more unto Himself, . . . and so to restore all things *whatsoever* and *wheresoever* they be."[49]

A Final Challenge

This being so, let me next ask, have you, who maintain the traditional creed, ever quietly thought over the terrible slight you unconsciously offer to the whole work of Christ, to his incarnation and his passion, by asserting the final loss of countless myriads of our race, or even of any soul for whom he died? He has come, we know, to save the *world*, he, very God of very God,[50] but you proclaim in all your writings, in all your pulpits, that which is, in fact, his defeat. His apostles announce, in language strong and clear, in words that still throb with life, his victory over death. You announce death's victory over him, for hell filled to all eternity with its wailing millions is his defeat, nay, his utter defeat. Could you more effectually make light of his atonement?

---

49 Editor: Joseph Barber Lightfoot, *Saint Paul's Epistle to the Colossians and Philemon* (London: 1875), on Col 1:19–20.

50 Editor: This is, of course, a quote from the Nicene Creed.

I read in the Bible that in his death all (actually) died (so vital is the union between him and all the race of man). Are they, then, to go down to endless evil and woe, those lost ones, *who died with Jesus* (2 Cor 5:14, RV)—these souls of his creating, still wet, so to speak, with his most precious blood, still pursued by his love (for love is unfailing); are these souls to spend an eternity in sin and pain? Is our Lord's passion to be for these, endless, fruitless, hopeless? Am I to proclaim this as the victory of Jesus Christ, this as the glad tidings of great joy? I do not impugn, I fully recognize, the honesty of my opponents; but it is something more than strange to see thoughtful men teaching that Christ "sees of the travail of his soul and is *satisfied*," while he surveys to all eternity even one immortal spirit for whom he died—one child of his love in the grip of endless evil, or annihilated.

Permit me further—for I want again to protest against the dishonour done to Scripture by the popular creed—permit me to ask what the meaning is, on the popular view, of the oft-repeated promises of the New Testament assigning to Christ a universal empire? Is *it true* that it is the Father's pleasure that in Christ *all things* (Eph 1:10—the original words are the widest possible) are to be summed up? Is it true that Christ has actually abolished death; nay, that he has been manifested for this very end, that he might destroy *all* the works of the devil? Or is it a mere dream of the Evangelist, when he tells us that God has given to him all things, and that all things that the Father has given to him shall come to him? But if all this is actually written in Scripture, how can it be truly taught that sin and hell are *endless?* Can sin be everlasting, and yet the sin of the world be truly taken away by the Lamb of God? Can hell for ever prey on the lost and yet the whole creation be delivered into the glorious liberty of the children of God? Once again, let me say, that a fair answer is due to these questions, and not an answer that is, however honestly meant, in fact an evasion.

Reflect what it is the popular creed is, in fact, teaching—see its inconsistencies, the contradictions of Scripture [it generates], to which long usage has deadened its supporters. Christ "holding the keys of hell" and never opening; Christ "making all things new," and yet things and persons innumerable not renewed; the Good Shepherd "seeking till he finds," and yet never finding those precisely who need him most; "no more pain," and yet pain for evermore; "no more curse," and yet hell echoing for ever with the curses of the lost; "tears wiped from every eye," and yet the lost for ever weeping; every creature which is in "heaven, and on the earth, and under the earth, and such as are on the sea, and all that are in them, saying, 'Blessing and glory and honour to God," and yet a number of creatures shut up for ever and ever in misery; "all made alive in Christ," and yet many sunk in hopeless, endless death.

I plead for the acceptance of the larger hope, as taught by so many in primitive days (a fact fully proved); a hope, that it has ever been the purpose of "our Father" to save all his human children. To believe or to hope for less than this would be, not alone to contradict Scripture, as I have tried to show, but to mistake its whole scope and purpose. For the Bible is the story of a restoration, wide; deep; mightier than the fall, and therefore bringing to every child of Adam salvation. It is not, as the popular creed teaches, the self-contradictory story of one almighty to save, and yet not, in fact, saving those for whom he died. It is the story of infinite love seeking "till it find"; a love that never fails, *never*, though heaven and earth pass away: a love that is, from its very nature, *inextinguishable*—being the love of a divine Father. It is the story of the unchanging purpose of the unchanging Lord God Omnipotent.

Further, by this larger hope, and by it alone, can we accept and harmonize every line and letter of Holy Scripture, its solemn threatenings to the sinner, no less than its repeated promises of life to all. These threatenings I accept implicitly. They are, as we have seen, fully reconciled with the promises of universal salvation the moment we have learned to realize the true meaning of God's judgments and penalties, and have been led by his word to see in "the ages" yet to come his purposes being steadily worked out. Yes, I believe, because the New Testament so teaches, and all reason confirms it, that to this brief life there succeed many ages, and that "through these ages an increasing purpose runs." In these "ages" and during their progress it is that God's threatenings find their complete fulfillment for the ungodly; and the many successive scenes of the drama of redemption are slowly unfolded, and carried to completion. For God's purpose to save all men once declared must stand firm for ever from his very nature; and to this end it is that his very penalties are inflicted, that in Jesus Christ, one day, all created things may be summed up. And this being so, we who hold the larger hope are prepared fully to believe that there await the sinner in "the ages" yet to come, God's fiery judgments; that aeonian discipline protracted till the will of man yield to the will of

Summary and Conclusions

"our Father," and till, as in the silent prophecy of the familiar words, "that will be done on earth as it is in heaven."

For this I plead, for a *hope*, wide as that which swelled the Saviour's heart, when looking steadily at the cross he said, "I, if I be lifted up, will draw all men to me." I plead for the simple truthfulness of the explicit promise made by all God's holy prophets, "that there shall be a restitution of all things" (Acts 3:21). The issue may be simply stated, *is this promise true* in its fair and natural meaning, *or is it untrue?* The dilemma cannot be avoided—*yes or no?*

For my part, in this promise I believe—in the sole true catholicity of the church of Christ, as destined to embrace all mankind; in the power of his redemption, as something that no will can resist, to which all things must yield one day in perfect submission, love, and harmony. I plead for the acceptance of this central truth as the great hope of the gospel, that the victory of Jesus Christ must be final and complete, i.e., that nothing can impair the power of his cross and passion to save the entire human race. I believe that he shall see of the travail of his soul, and be satisfied. And I feel assured that less than a world saved, a universe restored, could not satisfy the heart of Jesus Christ, or the love of our Father. I ask all fair and reasonable minds to reject as immoral, and incredible the picture of a heavenly Parent, who, being absolutely free and absolute in power and goodness, creates any children of his own, whom he knows to be, in fact, certain to go to endless sin and ruin. Therefore, in these pages I have pleaded for the larger hope. Therefore, I believe in the vision, glorious, beyond all power of human thought fully to realize, of a "paradise regained,"[51] of an universe from which every stain of sin shall have been swept away, in which every heart shall be full of blessedness in which "God shall be all and in all."

Amen.

---

51 Editor: *Paradise Regained* (1671) is an epic poem by John Milton (1608–74). It deals for the most part with the temptation of Jesus as recounted in Luke's Gospel.

Bibiography

Non-Patristic Sources Quoted by Thomas Allin

Periodicals

The Contemporary Review
The Church Reformer
The Church Times
Fraser's Magazine
The Record

Hymns

Alford, Henry. "Ten Thousand Times Ten Thousand."
Baker, Henry W., and John Chandler. "Now, My Soul, Thy Voice Upraising."
Neale, J. M. "Creator of the Starry Height."
Neal, John Mason. "Sing, My Tongue, the Glorious Battle."
Pantycelyn, William Williams. "Guide Me, O Thou Great Jehovah," English translation by Peter Williams.

Poems, Plays, and Novels

Arnold, Edwin. "After Death in Arabia," 1893.
Barrett Browning, Elizabeth. "A Drama of Exile," 1844.
Milton, John. *Paradise Lost*. 2nd ed. London: 1674.
———. *Paradise Regained*. London: 1671.
———. Sonnet VII.
Oliphant, Margaret. *A Little Pilgrim in the Unseen*. London: Macmillan, 1882.
Shakespeare, William. *Hamlet*.
———. *Henry V*.
———. Sonnet 116.

Bibiography

Smith, Walter Chalmers. "Olrig Grange," 1872.
Tennyson, Lord Alfred. *In Memoriam,* 1849.
Whittier, John Greenleaf. "The Grave by the Lake," 1865.
Young, Edward, "The Last Day: A Poem in Three Books," 1713.

Books

Andrewes, Lancelot. *Works. Volume One. Sermons of the Nativity and of Repentance and Fasting.* Edited by J. Bliss and J. P. Wilson. Oxford: John Henry Parker, 1841.
Aquinas, Thomas. *The Summa Theologica III.*
Assemani, Giuseppe Simone. *Bibliotheca Orientalis Clementino-Vaticana.* 4 vols. Rome: 1719–28.
Barlow, James William. *Eternal Punishment and Eternal Death: An Essay.* London: Longman, 1865.
Berrow, Capel. *Theological Dissertations.* London: J. Dodsley, 1772.
Bingham, Joseph. *Origines ecclesiasticae, or The Antiquities of the Christian Church.* 10 vols. London: Robert Knaplock, 1708–22.
Bonnet, Charles. *La Palingénésie philosophique.* Geneva: Philibert and Chirol, 1769.
Brooke, Stopford. *The Unity of God and Man: and Other Sermons Preached at Bedford Chapel, Blomsbury.* Boston: G. H. Ellis, 1886.
Browne, John. *An Essay on Universal Redemption: Tending to Prove that the General Sense of Scripture Favours the Opinion of the Final Salvation of All Mankind.* London: printed for Messrs. Cadell and Davies; and Mr. Deighton, Cambridge, 1798.
Burnet, Thomas. *De Statue Mortuorum et Resurgentium.* 2 vols. London: printed for E. Curll, 1720.
Butler, Joseph. *The Analogy of Religion, Natural and Revealed, to the Constitution and Course of Nature.* London: James, John, and Paul Knapton, 1736.
Casaubon, Isaac. *Exercitationes contra Baronium.* London: 1614.
Chauncy, Charles. *The Mystery Hid from Ages and Generations, Made Manifest by the Gospel Revelation.* London: C. Dilly, 1784.
Cheyne, George. *An Essay on Regimen: Together with Five Discourses, Medical, Moral, and Philosophical: Serving to Illustrate the Principles and Theory of Philosophical Medicine.* London: 1740.[1]
Cheyne, T. K. *The Prophesies of Isaiah: A New Translation with Commentary and Appendices.* 2 vols. London: C. Kegan Paul, 1880.
Clarke, Richard. *A Voice of Glad Tidings to Jews and Gentiles: From the Mysteries of the First-born, and First-fruits Under the Law of Moses, the Servant of Shadows, Explained by the Gospel of Jesus Christ, the Lord in the Spirit and Truth: Wherein the Physical Ground of Regeneration is Shewn, and the Salvation of All Men is Proved from the Oracles of God in Both Covenants.* London: J. Townsend, 1763.
Cooke, J. [unknown book]. London, 1752.
Coppin, Richard. *The Exaltation of All Things in Christ, and of Christ in All Things.* London: 1649.

---

1 Editor: Allin lists this as Cheyne, *Discourses,* 1707. The entry above is my best guess at the book he had in mind.

Corbett, Rowland William. *Letters from a Mystic of the Present Day*. London: Elliot Stock, 1883.
Cox, Samuel. *Expository Essays and Discourses*. 8 vols. London: 1877.
———. *Salvator Mundi: Or, Is Christ the Saviour of All Men?* London: Kegan Paul, 1877.
Dallaeus, Johannes. *De usu Patrum*. 1646. Geneva: 1686.
Delitzsche, Franz. *A Commentary on the Book of Psalms*. Translated by the Rev. David Eaton and Rev. James Duguid. 3 vols. Edinburgh: T. & T. Clark, 1876–77.
De Quincey, Thomas. *Theological Essays and Other Papers*. 2 vols. London: 1854.
Didron, Adolphe Napoléon. *Iconographie Chrétienne: Historie de Dieu*. Paris: Imprimerie Royale, 1843.
Dietelmeier, J. A. [Uncertain which text is quoted. Allin calls it *Comm fanat. de res. omn. αποκατ. hist*]
Dodwell, Henry. "De paucitate martyrum." In *Dissertationes Cyprianicae*. Oxford: Sheldon, 1684.
Doederlein, D. Johann Christoph. *Institutio theologi christiani in capitibus religionis theoreticis, nostris temporibus accomodata*. Nuremberg: In officina Libraria Schuipfeliana, 1780.
Dorner, Isaac August. *History of the Development of the Doctrine of the Person of Christ*. Translated by Rev. D. W. Simon. 5 vols. Edinburgh: T. & T. Clark, 1861–63; first German edition, 1835–39; second, expanded German edition, 1845–56.
Doucin, Louis. *Historie de l'Origénisme*. Paris: Douchin, 1700.
Dudgeon, William. *The Philosophical Works of Mr. William Dudgeon*. no loc: n.p., 1765.
Edwards, Jonathan. "The Eternity of Hell Torments," April 1739. In *The Works of Jonathan Edwards*, . . . , 2 vols., edited by Edward Hickman, 2:83–89. London: William Ball, 1839.
Elliott, Edward Bishop. *Horae Apocalypticae; Or, A Commentary on the Apocalypse, Critical and Historical*. London: Seely, Jackson, and Halliday, 1844.
Emerson, Ralph Waldo. "Circles," 1841
———. *The Conduct of Life*. Boston: Ticknor & Fields, 1860, rev. 1876.
———. *Essays: First Series*. Boston: James Munroe, 1847.
Erskine, Thomas. *The Spiritual Order and Other Papers Selected from the Manuscripts of the Late Thomas Erskine of Linlathen*. Edinburgh: Thomas and Archibald Constable, 1871.
Fabricius, J. A. *Bibliotheca Graeca seu notitia scriptorum veterum Graecorum*. 14 vols. Hamburg: 1705–28. A new, but unfinished edition of Fabricius was published in 12 vols. Hamburg: G. Chr. Harles, 1790–1809.
Farrar, Frederic W. *Eternal Hope: Five Sermons Preached in Westminster Abbey, November and December 1877*. London: Macmillan, 1878.
———. *Mercy and Judgement: Last Words on Christian Eschatology with Reference to Dr. Pusey's "What Is of Faith?"* 2nd ed. London: Macmillan, 1882.
Foster, John. *Letter of the Celebrated John Foster to a Young Minister on the Duration of Future Punishment*. 1841.
———. *The Life and Correspondence of John Foster*. London: Jackson and Walford, 1846.
Furniss, John *The Sight of Hell*. Books for Children and Young Persons 10. Dublin: James Dufft, 1870.

Bibiography

Gieseler, J. C. I. *Text-Book of Ecclesiastical History*. 3 vols. Translated from the third German edition by Francis Cunningham. 3 vols. Philadelphia: Carey, Lea, and Blanchard, 1836.

Gordon, Charles George. *Colonel Gordon in Central Africa, 1874–1879*. Edited by George Birkbeck Hill. London: Thos. de la Rue, 1881.

Greg, William Rathbone. *The Creed of Christendom: Its Foundations and Superstructure*. London: John Chapman, 1851.

Grotius, Hugo. *De Jure Belli ac Pacis*. Paris: 1625.

Guericke, H. E. F. *De schola quae Alexandriae floruit Catechetica*. Halle: 1824.

Haeckel, Ernst. [Uncertain which text is quoted.]

Hallsted, ? [?]

Harvey, Alexander. *Good the Final Goal of All, Or The Better Life: Four Letters to the Ven, Archdeacon Farrar, D.D*. London: Macmillan, 1883.

Hinton, James. *The Mystery of Pain: A Book of the Sorrowful* London: Smith, Elder, and co., 1866.

Holmes, Oliver Wendell, Sr. *The Poet at the Breakfast Table*. Boston: James R. Osgood, 1872.

Hooker, Richard. "Mr Hooker's Answer to the Supplication that Mr Travers Made to the Council." In *The Works of Mr Richard Hooker . . .* , 2:477–99. Oxford: J. Vincent, 1839.

Hopkins, Samuel. *An Inquiry concerning the Future State of Those Who Die in Their Sins*. Rhode Island: Solomon Southwick, 1783.

Huet, Pierre Daniel *Origeniana*. 2 vols. Rouen, 1668; 3 vols. Cologne, 1685.

Jukes, Andrew. *Catholic Eschatology Examined: A Reply to the Rev. H. N. Oxenham's Recent Papers in The Contemporary Review*. London: Longman, Green, and co., 1876.

———. *The Second Death and the Restitution of All Things*. London: Longman, Green, and co., 1867.

Keble, John. *The Christian Year*. London: George Routledge and sons, 1827.

Kingsley, Charles. "Endless Torments Unscriptural." May 9, 1857.

———. *Madam How and Lady Why; Or. First Lessons in Earth Lore for Children*. London: Macmillan, 1869

———. *The Water of Life and Other Sermons*. London: Macmillan, 1867.

Lange, J. P. *The Revelation of John*. Translated by Evalina Moore. New York: Schribner's sons, Armstrong, 1874.

Leade, Jane. *The Enochian Walks with God: Found out by a Spiritual Traveller, Whose Face towards Mount-Sion above was Set; with an Experimental Account of What was Known, Seen and Met withal There. A Revelation of the Immense and Infinite Latitude of God's Love, to the Restoring of his Whole Creation, and How, and after what Way and Manner we are to Look, and wait for this Last Appearance, and Coming of our Mighty God, and Saviour Christ Jesus*. London: 1694.

———. *A Revelation of the Everlasting Gospel Message: Which Shall Never Cease to Be Preach'd Till the Hour of Christ's Eternal Judgment Shall Come; Whereby will be Proclaim'd the Last-Love Jubilee, in order to the Restitution of the Whole Lapsed Creation, Whether Human or Angelical. When by the Blood of the Everlasting Covenant, all Prisoners shall be set free*. London: 1697.

Lecky, W. E. H. *History of the Rise and Influence of the Spirit of Rationalism in Europe*, vol. 1. London: Longmans, Green, 1865.

Bibiography

Leicester, Francis. *Christ Glorified in the Salvation and Final Restoration of Mankind: or the Old and New-Testament Evidence of the Doctrine of Universal Salvation: Set Forth in Two Sermons, on I Tim. IV.9, 10, 11: to which is prefixed an introductory preface.* London: W. Nicoll, 1786.

Lightfoot, Joseph Barber. *Saint Paul's Epistle to the Colossians and Philemon.* London: Macmillan, 1875.

———. *Saint Paul's Epistle to the Galatians.* London: Macmillan, 1865.

———. *Saint Paul's Epistle to the Philippians.* London: Macmillan, 1868.

Lombard, Peter. *Libri Quatuor Sententiarum* (Four Books of Sentences).

Maine, Henry James Sumner. *Ancient Law: Its Connection with the Early History of Society and Its Relation to Modern Ideas.* London: John Murray, 1861.

Martensen, Hans Lassen. *Christian Dogmatics: Compendium of the Doctrines of Christianity.* Translated from the German by William Urwick. Edinburgh: T. & T. Clark, 1874.

Maurice, F. D. *The Life of Frederick Denison Maurice: Chiefly Told in His Own Letters,* vol. 2. London: Macmillan, 1884.

———. *Theological Essays.* London: Macmillan, 1853.

Mill, John Stuart. *Three Essays on Religion.* London: Longmans, Green, Reader & Dyer, 1874

Milman, Henry Hart. *History of Christianity to the Abolition of Paganism in the Roman Empire.* 3 vols. London: John Murray, 1840.

Monod, Guillaume. *Le judgment dernier.* [Unable to find further information.]

Law, William. *Three Letters to the Bishop of Bangor.* London: 1717.

———. *Letters to a Lady Inclined to Enter the Church of Rome.* Written in 1731–32, published in 1779.

———. *The Way to Divine Knowledge.* London: 1752.

Mosheim, Johann Lorenz von. *An Ecclesiastical History: From the Birth of Christ to the Beginning of the Eighteenth Century . . .* 2 vols. Translated by Archibald Maclaine. London: William Tyler, 1842.

Münter, Friedrich. [Uncertain which text is quoted.]

Neander, Augustus. *General History of the Christian Religion and Church.* Translated by Joseph Torrey. 2nd ed. 4 vols. London: Henry Bohn, 1853; German original, 1843; the first German edition was published in four volumes from 1825–42.

Newman, John Henry. *Certain Difficulties Felt by Anglicans in Catholic Teaching Considered: In a Letter Addressed to the Rev. E. B. Pusey, D.D., on Occasion of His Eirenicon of 1864 . . .* 2 vols. London: Burns and Oates, 1879.

Newton, Thomas. "The Final State of Man." 1750.

———. *The Posthumous Works of the Right Reverend Thomas Newton, D.D.* 8 vols. London: Rivington, 1787.

Pétavel-Olliff, Emmanuel. *The Struggle for Eternal Life; Or, The Immortality of the Just, and the Gradual Extinction of the Wicked.* 2 vols. London: Kellaway, 1875.

Petravius, O. *De Ang.*

Pfaf, Christoph Matthaeus. [Unknown which text is quoted.]

Plato. *The Republic.*

Plumptre, Edward Hayes. *The Spirits in Prison and Other Studies on the Life After Death.* London: Isbister, 1884.

Pusey, Edward Bouverie. Sermon on Matthew 25:46.

Bibiography

———. *What Is of Faith as to Everlasting Punishment? In Reply to Dr. Farrar's Challenge in His "Eternal Hope,"* 1879. London: James Parker, 1880.

Quarry, John. *Religious Belief: Its Difficulties in Ancient and Modern Times Compared and Considered. Being the Donnellan Lecture in the University of Dublin for the Year 1877–8.* London: Hodges, Foster & Figgis, 1880.

Relly, James. *Union; or a Treatise of the Consanguinity between Christ and His Church* London: n.p., 1759.

Reuss, Édouard. *Historie de la Théologie Chrétienne au Siècle Apostolique.* 2 vols. Strasbourg: Treuttel & Wurtz, 1852.

Richardson, Samuel. *Of the Torments of Hell: The Foundation and Pillars Thereof Discovered, Searched, Shaken, and Removed.* London: n.p., 1658.

Ridot, Th. *Heredity: A Psychological Study of Its Phenomena, Its Laws, Its Causes, and Its Consequences.* Translated from the French. London: Henry St. King, 1875.

Rousseau, Jean-Jaques. *Émile ou De l'éducation.* 1762.

M. J. Routh, ed., *Reliquiae Sacrae.* 5 vols. Oxford: Oxford University Press, 1815.

Rust, George. *A Discourse on Truth.* London: James Collins and Samuel Lowndes, 1677.

———. *Letter of Resolution concerning Origen and the Chief of His Opinions.* London: Rust, 1661.

Sadler, John. *Olbia: The New Island Lately Discovered. With Its Religion and Rites of Worship; Laws, Customs, and Government; Characters and Language; with Education of their Children in their Sciences, Arts and Manufactures . . . By a Christian Pilgrim, Driven by Tempest from Civita Vecchia, or some other Parts about Rome; through the Straits, into the Atlantick Ocean.* London: 1660.

Schlüter, Christoph Bernhard. Preface to John Scotus Eriugena, *De divisione naturae,* translated by C. B. Schlüter. Münster, 1838. Reprinted in J. P. Migne's *PL*, vol. 122 Paris: Migne, 1853, 101–26.

Seigvolck, Paul. *The Everlasting Gospel, Commanded and Preached by Jesus Christ, Judge of the Living and the Dead, unto All Creatures, Mark xvi.15, concerning the Eternal Redemption Found out by Him whereby Devil, Sin, Hell, and Death, Shall at Last Be Abolished and the Whole Creation Restored to Its Primitive Purity: Being a Testimony against the Present Anti-Christian World.* Philadelphia: Christopher Sower, 1753.

Spurgeon, Charles Haddon. Sermon 66, on the resurrection of the dead, delivered on Sunday 17 February, 1856

St. Blunt, J. *Dictionary of Doctrinal and Historical Theology.* 2nd ed. London: Rivingtons, 1872.

Stafford, R. *Some Thoughts of the Life to Come.* London: 1693.

Stanley, Arthur P. *The Life and Correspondence of Thomas Arnold.* London: Fellowes, 1844.

Sterry, Peter. *A Discourse on the Freedom of the Will.* London: Starkey, 1675.

———. *The Rise, Race, and Royalty of the Kingdom of God in the Soul of Man Opened in Several Sermons upon Matthew 18.3: as also the Loveliness & Love of Christ Set Forth in Several Other Sermons upon Psal. 45. v. 1, 2.: Together with an Account of the State of a Saint's Soul and Body in Death.* London: Thomas Cockerill, 1683.

———. *That State of the Wicked Men after This Life Is Mixt of Evil & Good Things.* Unpublished. MS 291, Emmanuel College Library, Cambridge.

Stonehouse, George. *Universal Restitution, A Scripture Doctrine. This Proved in Several Letters Wrote on the Nature and Extent of Christ's Kingdom, wherein the Scripture Passages Falsly Alleged in Proof of the Eternity of Hell Torments Are Truly Translated and Explained.* London: R. Dodsley, 1761.

———. *Universal Restitution, Further Defended.* Brisol: W. Pine, 1768.

Swete, Henry Barclay. *Theodori episcopi Mopsuesteni: in epistolas B. Pauli comentarii: the Latin Version with the Greek Fragments, with an Introduction, Notes and Indices.* 2 vols. Cambridge: Cambridge University Press, 1880.

Temple, Frederick William. *The Relations between Religion and Science.* London: Macmillan, 1884.

Thayer, Thomas Baldwin. *Theology of Universalism: Being an Exposition of Its Doctrines and Teachings, in Their Logical and Moral Relations.* Boston: Tomkins and co., 1862.

Various authors, lay and clerical. *The Wider Hope: Essays and Strictures on the Doctrine and Literature of Furutre Punishment.* London: T. Fisher Unwin, 1890.

Vinet, Alexandre Rodolphe. [Unknown which text is quoted.]

Wace, Henry, and William Smith, eds. *A Dictionary of Christian Biography, Literature, Sects and Doctrines.* 4 vols. London: John Murray, 1877–87.

Weaver, James. *Free Thoughts on the Universal Restoration of All Lapsed Intelligences from the Ruins of the Fall.* London: R. Hawes, 1792.

Wescott, Brooke Foss. *The Epistle to the Hebrews: The Greek Text with Notes and Essays.* London: Macmillan, 1889.

———. *The Gospel of the Resurrection: Thoughts on Its Relation to Reason and History.* London: Macmillan, 1866.

———. *The Historic Faith: Short Lectures on the Apostles Creed.* London: Macmillan, 1883.

———. *The Revelation of the Father: Short Lectures on the Titles of the Lord in the Gospel of St. John.* London: Macmillan, 1884.

Whiston, William. *Sermons and Essays upon Several Subjects.* London: 1707.

White, Jeremiah. *The Restoration of All Things: Or, A Vindication of the Goodness and Grace of God, to be Manifested at Last in the Recovery of His Whole Creation out of Their Fall.* London: John Denis & son, 1712.

Wilberforce, Robert Isaac. *The Doctrine of the Incarnation of Our Lord Jesus Christ: In Its Relation to Mankind and to the Church.* London: John Murray, 1848.

Wilkins, N. G. *Errors and Terrors of Blind Guides: The Popular Doctrine of Everlasting Pain, Refuted.* London: Elliot Stock, 1880.

Winchester, Elhanan. *The Universal Restoration: Exhibited in a Series of Dialogues between a Minister and His Friend: Comprehending the Substance of Several Conversations that the Author Hath Had with Various Persons, Both in America and Europe, on that Interesting Subject, wherein the Most Formidable Objections are Stated and Fully Answered.* London: Gillet, 1788.

Windet, J. *ΣΤΡΩΜΑΤΕΣ ΕΠΙΣΤΟΛΙΚΟΣ de Vita Functorum Statu, ex Hebraeorum et Graecorum comparatis Sententiis concinnatus.* London: 1763.

Winstanley, Gerald. *The mysterie of God concerning the whole creation, mankinde to be made known to every man and woman after seaven dispensations and seasons of time are passed over, according to the councell of God, revealed to his servants.* London: Giles Calvert, 1649.

Bibiography

Sources Referenced by Robin A. Parry

Adams, Marilyn McCord. "Hell and the God of Justice." *Religious Studies* 11 (1974) 433–47.

———. "The Problem of Hell: A Problem of Evil for Christians." In *A Reasoned Faith*, edited by Eleanor Stump, 301–27. Ithaca, NY: Cornell University Press, 1993.

Allin, Thomas. *The Augustinian Revolution in Theology: Illustrated by a Comparison with the Teaching of the Antiochene Divines of the Fourth and Fifth Centuries.* Edited by J. J. Lias. London: James Clark, 1911.

———. *The Flowering Plants and Ferns of County Cork, with coloured map and introduction.* Weston-super-Mare, UK: J. Marche, 1883.

———. *Race and Religion: Hellenistic Theology: Its Place in Christian Thought.* London: James Clarke, 1899.

Ansell, Nik. *The Annihilation of Hell: Universal Salvation and the Redemption of Time in the Eschatology of Jürgen Moltmann.* Eugene, OR: Cascade, 2013.

Birks, Thomas Rawson. *The Victory of Divine Goodness.* London: Rivingtons, 1867.

Bressler, Ann Lee, *The Universalist Movement in America, 1770–1880.* New York: Oxford University Press, 2001.

Coleman, James. "A County Cork Botanical Author, Rev. Thomas Allin." *Journal of the Cork Historical and Archaeological Society*, series 2 XXII (1916).

Eddy, Richard. *Universalism in America: A History.* 3rd ed. 2 vols. Boston: Universalist, 1891.

Farrar, Frederic W. *Eternal Hope: Five Sermons Preached in Westminster Abbey, November and December 1877.* London: Macmillan, 1878.

———. *Mercy and Judgement: Last Words on Christian Eschatology with Reference to Dr. Pusey's "What Is of Faith?"* 2nd ed. London: Macmillan, 1882.

Green, Paul. *Flora of County Waterford.* Online: http://www.botanicgardens.ie/herb/floras/waterford/waterfd01.pdf.

Gregorovius, Ferdinand. *Wanderings in Corsica: Its History and Its Heroes.* Edinburgh: Thomas Constable, 1855.

Hanson, J. W. *Universalism: The Prevailing Doctrine of the Church during Its First Five Hundred Years.* Boston: Universalist Publishing House, 1899.

Harmon, Steven R. *Every Knee Should Bow: Biblical Rationales for Universal Salvation in Early Christian Thought.* Lanham, MD: Rowman & Littlefield, 2003.

Holyoake, Austin. *Heaven and Hell: Where Situated? A Search after the Objects of Man's Fervent Hope & Abiding Terror.* 1873.

Kronen, John, and Eric Reitan. *God's Final Victory: A Comparative Philosophical Case for Universalism.* New York: Bloomsbury, 2011.

Laufer, Catherine Ella. *Hell's Destruction: An Exploration of Christ's Descent to the Dead.* Farnham, UK: Ashgate, 2013.

Ludlow, Morwenna. *Universal Salvation: Eschatology in the Thought of Gregory of Nyssa and Karl Rahner.* Oxford: Oxford University Press, 2000.

MacDonald, Gregory, ed. *"All Shall Be Well": Explorations in Universal Salvation from Origen to Moltmann.* Eugene, OR: Cascade, 2011.

Maurice, F. D. *Theological Essays.* London: Macmillan, 1853.

Parker, John William, ed. *Essays and Reviews.* London: John W. Parker & Son, 1860.

Pusey, Edward Bouverie. *What Is of Faith as to Everlasting Punishment? In Reply to Dr. Farrar's Challenge in His "Eternal Hope," 1879.* London: James Parker, 1880.

Ramelli, Ilaria. *Christian Doctrine of Apokatastasis*. Supplements to Vigiliae Christianae 120. Leiden: Brill, 2013.

———. "Origen's Anti-Subordinationism and Its Heritage in the Nicene and Cappadocian Line." *Vigiliae Christianae* 64 (2010) 1–29

Ramelli, Ilaria, and David Konstan. *Terms for Eternity: Aiônios and Aidios in Classical and Christian Texts*. Piscataway, NJ: Gorgias, 2013.

Rowell. Geoffrey. *Hell and the Victorians: A Study of Nineteenth-Century Theological Controversies concerning Eternal Punishment and the Future Life*. Oxford: Clarendon, 1974.

Sweetman, Robert. "Sin Has Its Place, But All Shall Be Well: The Universalism of Hope in Julian of Norwich." In *"All Shall Be Well": Explorations in Universal Salvation from Origen to Moltmann*, edited by Gregory MacDonald, 66–92. Eugene, OR: Cascade, 2011

Talbott, Thomas. *The Inescapable Love of God*. 2nd ed. Eugene, OR: Cascade, 2014.

Wheeler, Michael. *Heaven, Hell, & the Victorians*. Cambridge: Cambridge University Press, 1994.

Young, Frances M. *Construing the Cross: Type, Sign, Symbol, Word, Action*. Didsbury Lectures Series. Eugene, OR: Cascade, 2015.

www.ingramcontent.com/pod-product-compliance
Lightning Source LLC
Chambersburg PA
CBHW071230290426
44108CB00013B/1358